The Social Enterprise Zoo

To Greg Dees, Estelle James, Howard Tuckman, and Woods Bowman, all pioneers in developing our understanding of social enterprise, recently lost to us in life, but whose legacies will never be forgotten.

The Social Enterprise Zoo

A Guide for Perplexed Scholars, Entrepreneurs, Philanthropists, Leaders, Investors, and Policymakers

Edited by

Dennis R. Young

Executive in Residence, Cleveland State University and Professor Emeritus, Georgia State University, USA

Elizabeth A.M. Searing

Assistant Professor, University at Albany, State University of New York, USA

Cassady V. Brewer

Associate Professor, College of Law, Georgia State University, USA

Edward Elgar
PUBLISHING

Cheltenham, UK • Northampton, MA, USA

Published by
Edward Elgar Publishing Limited
The Lypiatts
15 Lansdown Road
Cheltenham
Glos GL50 2JA
UK

Edward Elgar Publishing, Inc.
William Pratt House
9 Dewey Court
Northampton
Massachusetts 01060
USA

A catalogue record for this book
is available from the British Library

Library of Congress Control Number: 2016942168

This book is available electronically in the **Elgar**online
Business subject collection
DOI 10.4337/9781784716066

ISBN 978 1 78471 605 9 (cased)
ISBN 978 1 78471 606 6 (eBook)

Typeset by Servis Filmsetting Ltd, Stockport, Cheshire
Printed and bound in Great Britain by TJ International Ltd, Padstow

Contents

About the editors and contributors

EDITORS

Dennis R. Young is Executive in Residence in the Maxine Goodman Levin College of Urban Affairs of Cleveland State University and Professor Emeritus, Georgia State University. His research interests include nonprofit economics and finance, social enterprise and entrepreneurship, and management and governance of nonprofit organizations. He is the founding editor of *Nonprofit Policy Forum*, a journal devoted to the interface between nonprofit organizations and public policy.

Elizabeth A.M. Searing is an Assistant Professor of Public Administration and Policy at the Rockefeller College of Public Affairs and Policy, University at Albany, State University of New York. Dr. Searing's primary research focus is in nonprofit and social enterprise ecology, but she also conducts work in financial management, evidence-based policy, the role of social and psychological factors in economic development and policy effectiveness, and applied ethics for the social sciences.

Cassady V. ("Cass") Brewer is an Associate Professor at Georgia State University College of Law in Atlanta, Georgia. Professor Brewer teaches courses in basic federal income taxation, corporate taxation, partnership taxation, the law of nonprofit organizations, and the law of social enterprise. He researches and writes extensively on the legal and tax aspects of nonprofit organizations, business organizations, and social enterprise organizations. He also is a frequent speaker at conferences and workshops concerning tax, nonprofit, and social enterprise topics.

CONTRIBUTORS

Fredrik O. Andersson is an Assistant Professor of Nonprofit Administration with the Helen Bader Institute for Nonprofit Management at the University of Wisconsin-Milwaukee. His primary research focus is in nonprofit entrepreneurship, but his research interests also include nonprofit governance, nonprofit start-up finance, and voucher schools.

Francesca Calò joined the Yunus Centre for Social Business and Health at Glasgow Caledonian University in October 2013. She is currently undertaking a PhD aiming at understanding the contribution of community-based social enterprises to publicly funded healthcare systems. Her primary research focus is on exploring the role of social enterprise as a public health intervention but she also conducts work in evidence-based policy, non-profit management research, and policy analysis.

Janelle A. Kerlin is an Associate Professor of Public Management and Policy in the Andrew Young School of Policy Studies at Georgia State University in Atlanta, Georgia, USA. Her research interests include the comparative study of social enterprise across countries, social enterprise incubators, nonprofit commercial revenue, and international NGOs. She is an associate editor of the *Social Enterprise Journal*.

Jesse D. Lecy is an Assistant Professor in Public Administration at the Maxwell School of Syracuse University. He teaches classes on public and nonprofit management, urban policy, program evaluation, and data science. His research examines competition and performance of nongovernmental organizations in the social sector.

Wesley Longhofer is an Assistant Professor of Organization and Management in the Goizueta Business School at Emory University, USA, where he teaches courses in corporate social responsibility and social entrepreneurship. His research examines the role of global institutions in policy adoption and organizational diffusion in a number of domains, including environmental protection and human rights.

Thema Monroe-White is the Director of Research and Evaluation at VentureWell. She publishes in the fields of social enterprise and social innovation, science policy and STEM education. Thema holds a Ph.D. in Science, Technology and Innovation Policy from the Georgia Institute of Technology, and an M.S. in Developmental Neuropsychology from Howard University.

Dana Brakman Reiser is Professor of Law and former Vice Dean at Brooklyn Law School in New York City. She teaches courses in nonprofit law, social enterprise, corporations, property, and trusts and estates. Her recent scholarship focuses on law and finance for businesses that pursue a social mission, as well as nonprofit accountability and governance.

Jung-In Soh is a doctoral candidate in Public Policy at Georgia State University. Concentrating on nonprofit management, she is interested in nonprofit financial management, financial health, and effectiveness.

Simon Teasdale is Professor of Public Policy and Organisations at Glasgow Caledonian University. His research focuses on the intersection between public policy and organizational behavior, with a particular focus on how social enterprises negotiate policy discourses.

John E. Tyler III is the General Counsel, Secretary, and Chief Ethics Officer for the Ewing Marion Kauffman Foundation. In addition, he actively bridges scholar and practitioner experiences in social enterprise as a researcher and author, policy advocate, speaker, and advisor.

Sandy Zook is a doctoral candidate in the Department of Public Management and Policy at the Andrew Young School of Policy Studies, Georgia State University. She conducts research on social entrepreneurship, civil society, and cross-sector collaboration from both domestic and international perspectives.

Foreword

My contributions to the social enterprise literature focus on the legal mechanisms that impact the formation of social enterprises formed as businesses, especially the forces that affect their ability to attract capital, grow, change, and ultimately dissolve. I have been extremely critical of new US legal forms intended to house social enterprises more comfortably than traditional nonprofit or for-profit organizations. My critiques center around these forms' lack of clear prioritization mandates requiring elevation of social mission over profit and their failure to erect an effective enforcement structure. The latter change – creating strong enforcement – is especially unlikely in the American legal and political context. But without these components, organizational forms standing alone cannot generate the trust required between social entrepreneurs and impact investors to scale up capital access for social enterprises. In my view, it is much more promising to focus on tools other than specialized legal forms to help social entrepreneurs and investors signal to each other their commitment to pursuing social good. My current work focuses on developing financing and other more practical and surgical solutions for overcoming the trust deficit faced by these two vital parties to social enterprise development.

So, perhaps like you are now, I was skeptical when Dennis Young first shared with me the concept for *The Social Enterprise Zoo*. I had grown weary of the many attempts to theorize, to chart, to taxonomize the large and unwieldy group of organizations attempting to pursue both profit and social goals. Of course, I understand the appeal of a universal theory. A coordinating framework that defines terms precisely and designates phenomena as either within or outside the social enterprise category allows scholars to engage in effective data collection and comparative analysis. From my perch in the legal academe, however, I believed we might as well choose one or another "good enough" conceptual framework, and move on to generating more empirical data, rigorous analysis of that data, and practical and policy initiatives to help social enterprises thrive.

As I learned more about the central thread of *The Social Enterprise Zoo*, however, I realized it offered a potential way out of the theory/practice dichotomy. After all, the universal theory that *The Social Enterprise Zoo* espouses is highly unconventional – defying the very universality it claims.

The "zoo" metaphor posits the social enterprise category as a collection defined by its diversity, responsive to changes in habitat, and curated by humans. I will use this central insight as I continue to push the legal debate to expand beyond its recent focus on developing an ideal legal form. Instead of pursuing their own brand of universality, legal scholars should design and advocate a range of more narrowly tailored legal technologies to suit segments of the social enterprise sector – or animals in the zoo.

The authors of *The Social Enterprise Zoo* also offer insights far beyond taxonomy, addressing the ways in which the broader environment influences whether and how social enterprises form and grow. This question of "habitat" is one my own work on legislation and legal practice addresses directly, and this legal discussion is pushed forward here. The contributors also extend this analysis much more broadly. For example, cross-country studies reveal how the state of a nation's economic development and its type of government interact in varying and complex ways to encourage or discourage social enterprises, and the characteristics they embrace.

The Social Enterprise Zoo also reminds readers that social enterprises and the social enterprise sector are not static. They grow and evolve over time. A number of contributions make the point that as social enterprises mature individually, and as a category, the challenges they face will change. For example, new social enterprises and a nascent sector focus on seeking legitimacy. As they become more established, they must begin to grapple with competition for resources to achieve scale, and to survive in an increasingly crowded niche. Legal scholars and advocates seeking to buoy the sector must respond to these patterns of growth, designing legal tools and policies to support the differing needs of social enterprises and the sector at various points in this life cycle.

Finally, *The Social Enterprise Zoo* draws our attention to the people at the heart of each social enterprise, as it is their choices (once aggregated) that determine the contours of the sector. Many of these individuals will be change agents, disruptors, and true innovators. For the field to grow and achieve scale, however, the contributors here observe that it must also attract more ordinary social entrepreneurs. These "plain vanilla" entrepreneurs will be absorbed in creating their own new enterprises. They neither intend nor are likely capable of creating massive change or impact. The rhetoric surrounding the social enterprise field must take this insight on board. Scholars across disciplines and advocates of all stripes will need to tone down the sometimes florid rhetoric employed to describe the population of social entrepreneurs and their expectations for them.

The ultimate test for social enterprise, of course, will be how it influences our broader society. Generalizations about social enterprises' unique capacity to innovate, the particular robustness they offer, or their ability to create and magnify impact have become all too common. *The Social Enterprise Zoo* replaces these platitudes with rigorous theory, creating and applying the conceptual lenses of entrepreneurship and resiliency theory to various social enterprise species. It also helpfully focuses attention on how social enterprise impacts the larger business and nonprofit communities, through continuing consciousness raising and cross-pollination.

As can be seen from even this brief description, another benefit of the zoo metaphor is the ease with which it allows the chapter contributors to vary the relevant unit of analysis without losing the coherence of the book overall. Some chapters focus on the animals: the social enterprises that are contained within the zoo. Other contributions instead take a step back and consider the institution of the zoo itself. Still others address the zoo's keepers; entrepreneurs' efforts determine which entities will constitute the sector, and the market functions to thin the herd. Legal advocates and scholars developing the tools and frameworks to enable social enterprise's organizational autonomy and access to capital also participate in this important constitutive work. Our work will be strengthened by engaging with *The Social Enterprise Zoo*, and I am grateful to have been involved in the project.

Dana Brakman Reiser
Professor of Law, Brooklyn Law School

Preface

The roots of the formal study of social enterprise trace back at least to the early 1980s; 1983 was a watershed year. Ed Skloot wrote an article for the *Harvard Business Review* on whether nonprofits should go into business, Estelle James wrote her seminal paper on how nonprofits generate surpluses on some products and services in order to cross-subsidize other preferred but loss-making services, and the Rockefeller Brothers Fund supported the publication of a monograph by James Crimmins and Mary Keil that documented the widespread commercial practices of nonprofit organizations in the United States. Since then the subject has become more complex as various other manifestations of so-called social enterprise emerged. In the 1990s, Greg Dees argued that the social enterprise phenomenon was really a spectrum of ventures reflecting some combination of profitmaking and social mission. In this same period, Cyril Chang and Howard Tuckman ferreted out the reasons that nonprofit organizations seek to generate and retain financial surpluses. And in Europe, towards the end of the twentieth century and into the current millennium, researchers such as Carlo Borzaga and Jacques Defourny began to study social enterprise as a strategy for governments to privatize their social welfare efforts by establishing so-called WISEs (Work Integration Social Enterprises), which allowed governments to employ marginalized and challenged populations of workers who could not otherwise succeed in the private labor market. The latter organizations generally took the form of cooperatives as well as nonprofits. Meanwhile, back in the United States, the social enterprise notion was expanding to include so-called socially responsible and sustainable for-profit businesses, with new legal forms such as L3Cs (low-profit limited liability companies) and benefit corporations, as well as the establishment of conventional corporations such as Newman's Own and Ben and Jerry's, which were totally or largely devoted to achieving profits and allocating them to social purposes. Policymakers in the United Kingdom were similarly inventive with new forms, especially CICs (community interest companies), which offered a unique combination of nonprofit and for-profit characteristics in order to attract investors but ensure primary attention to social mission. Legal scholars such as Cassady "Cass" Brewer and Dana Brakman Reiser hopped aboard these developments to document and track this flowering of social enterprise forms (Brewer et al., 2015).

By the early 2000s, social enterprise was a popular topic of discussion and research among scholars across the world. Many models began to emerge, most portraying social enterprise as a relatively homogeneous phenomenon adhering to certain common principles of limited profit, social purpose, and democratic governance. Some scholars, however (including authors in this book), were frustrated by this conception; at first, we threw up our hands at the complexity and diversity of social enterprise, exclaiming "It's just a zoo!" This did not endear us to many of our fellow scholars looking for a starker delineation of what a social enterprise is or should be. But as we began to mull over this expression of frustration, we realized its value as a metaphor for what was really going on under the rubric of social enterprise. It was not just one thing, but took many different forms with the common theme that some mix of social purpose and market success was sought. Within that broad theme there could be many different types of social enterprise, all legitimate in some way, one not necessarily better than another, and differentially adapted to different circumstances – nicely captured by the idea of a zoo with different animals and habitats. That is the genesis of this book. Having explored the idea with papers at scholarly conferences including EMES International Research Network, ISTR (the International Society for Third-Sector Research) and ARNOVA (the Association for Research on Nonprofit Organizations and Voluntary Action), we decided it was time for us to write this book, to put the zoo paradigm on the table and to invite researchers, policymakers, and students to exploit it to good purpose in their own work.

We are indebted to several parties for their encouragement and support along the way. To Edward Elgar Publishing and editor Alan Sturmer for having the confidence in our proposal; to the Ewing Marion Kauffman Foundation for a grant that supported two authors' meetings; and to the Interuniversity Attraction Pole on Social Enterprise (IAP-SOCENT) funded by the Belgian State-Federal Science Policy Office, which allowed the Centre d'Economie Sociale HEC-Management School, University of Liège to partner with the Nonprofit Studies Program of the Andrew Young School of Policy Studies at Georgia State University and help finance summer stipends and travel to conferences where we could present and discuss our research.

Finally, on behalf of all of our authors, we would like to express our gratitude to several close colleagues who took the time to participate in our authors' conferences and provided us with invaluable advice and feedback. These include Gordon Shockley, Peter Frank, Paul Light, and Bruce Seaman.

Dennis R. Young
Elizabeth A. M. Searing
Cassady V. Brewer
January 2016

REFERENCES

Borzaga, C. and J. Defourny (eds) (2001), *The Emergence of Social Enterprise*, London: Routledge.

Brewer, C.V., E.S. Minnigh, and R.A. Wexler (2015), *Social Enterprise by Non-Profits and Hybrid Organizations, Tax Management Portfolio*, No. 489-1st.

Chang, C.F. and H. Tuckman (1990), "Why do nonprofit managers accumulate surpluses and how much do they accumulate?," *Nonprofit Management and Leadership*, 1 (2), 117–35.

Crimmins, J.C. and M. Keil (1983), *Enterprise in the Nonprofit Sector*, Washington, DC: Partners for Liveable Places.

Dees, J.G. (1998), "Enterprising nonprofits," *Harvard Business Review*, 76 (1), 55–68.

James, E. (1983), "How nonprofits grow: a model," *Journal of Public Policy Analysis and Management*, 2 (3), 350–66.

Skloot, E. (1983), "Should not-for-profits go into business?," *Harvard Business Review*, 61 (1), 20–27.

PART I

Concepts and content

1. Introduction

Dennis R. Young and Cassady V. Brewer

BACKGROUND

The modern economy has never been as simple or as tidy as portrayed by economic scholars. For example, classic texts from the mid-twentieth century such as Samuelson's *Economics* (1964) and Musgrave's (1959) *The Theory of Public Finance* essentially reduce the market-based economies of industrialized countries into two parts – business and government. The informal subsectors of family, cooperatives, not-for-profits and associations were below the radar. Not until Weisbrod (1975) and Hansmann (1980) wrote their seminal papers did economists recognize the importance of a third (nonprofit) sector as a key component of market economies in producing critical public and private services that government or business could not efficiently provide in a democratic society. Since that time, the three-sector model of the economy has been widely accepted, albeit with variations on the nature of the third sector itself (McCarthy et al., 1992; Salamon and Anheier, 1997). Still, reality seems to outpace scholarship. Recent texts recognize the increasing complexity and diversity of the "social economy," which now includes many variants and combinations of nonprofit, cooperative, business and governmental organizations, networks, and partnerships (Mook et al., 2015). However, scholars have not yet tied up the social economy, broadly conceived, into a nice neat package with a bow on top. Indeed, the complexity and diversity seems to grow almost by the day. That is one motivation for this book, and the reason we will employ the metaphor of the "social enterprise zoo" to capture, or at least glimpse, this diverse and dynamic and increasingly important part of the economic universe in which we now live.

Certainly there is growing recognition that the paradigm of three sectors – public, private, and not-for-profit – as a system for marshaling the world's resources and satisfying humanity's needs is not perfect, although few would argue that the three-sector approach has been a failure. Quite the contrary: government, business, and nonprofits have dominated the economic landscape for some time and will likely continue to do so. Indeed, historically, these three sectors have combined to create tremendous economic opportunity and prosperity (albeit uneven) around the globe. On the other hand, economic disparity has reached alarming proportions. Soon, 1 percent of the world's population will hold over 50 percent of the world's wealth. Historical economic analysis suggests that gross imbalances in wealth and welfare are unfortunately common but ultimately unsustainable (Pikkety, 2013).

Over the last two centuries, we have relied heavily upon the public and voluntary sectors to redistribute wealth and redirect prosperity to provide for the less fortunate. We also rely upon government and nonprofits to meet many other essential human needs such as healthcare, education, arts, religion, and culture, where for-profit institutions may be absent or insufficient. In some circumstances, however, government and nonprofits either fail to solve social problems or do so in a manner that is inefficient. This is perhaps self-evident or even ironic to economic theorists who conceptualize and analyze government and nonprofits as responses to market failures (Steinberg, 2006). Here we contend, however, that it is entirely reasonable to conceive of social enterprise as a response to failures (or more precisely "inefficiencies") in all three of the conventional sectors – traditional business, government, and nonprofit/voluntary institutions. An expansion of "market failure" theory may thus help to explain the emergence of "social enterprise" in its various and sundry forms.

MARKET FAILURE AND SOCIAL ENTERPRISE

Market failure theory has evolved over the past 40 years to encompass the understanding of inefficiencies not only in the business sector, but also by extension in the government and nonprofit sectors. Very briefly, the arguments go as follows. Achieving economic efficiency through markets depends upon a number of requirements or assumptions of the perfectly competitive model stemming from the ideas of Adam Smith (Young and Steinberg, 1995). Markets must indeed be highly competitive, otherwise monopolists or oligopolists have market power to restrict output and raise prices to inefficient levels, and monopsonists can suppress the price of inputs and restrict their efficient use. Further, efficient markets must exist in a context of transparency where consumers and producers have full information about the quality and prices of alternative products and services. Otherwise, consumers may not receive the value they think they are paying for, with the consequence that they will limit their consumption below efficient levels (forgo anticipated net benefits) or be cheated. And, markets cannot efficiently allocate resource in the presence of "externalities" or "public goods." In the case of externalities, either producers or consumers fail to account for the full social costs or benefits of their actions. For example, industrial polluters make production decisions without factoring in the external environmental or health costs; alternatively, parents of school-age children may neglect to have their children vaccinated, failing to account for the positive external benefits (lower risks of contagion) for other children. In the case of public goods or services such as public safety or environmental conservation, markets suffer from what economists term *nonexcludability* and *nonrivalry*. Without excludability, suppliers cannot bar consumers from using their services without paying for them. Without rivalry, suppliers cannot determine appropriate prices and output levels that would equate consumers' benefits at the margin, with the marginal costs of production. Hence, markets fail to allocate resources efficiently in these circumstances.

Given these limitations of unfettered private markets, economists have theorized on the roles of government and nonprofit organizations to improve the allocation of societal resources. In particular, government can encourage competition through anti-trust policy or it can directly regulate monopolies, monopsonies, or oligopolies. Moreover, government can correct for externalities by imposing taxes or providing subsidies to *internalize* the costs or benefits of externalities facing suppliers or consumers. Government can also raise tax revenues and allocate them to the provision of public goods, either directly or through contracts with private entities. Finally, government can require transparency in the form of product labeling or other means to overcome *information asymmetry*.

Why then is the combination of private business and government action not sufficient to achieve an efficient allocation of societal resources? Following the work of Burton Weisbrod (1975), economists note that government too has its economic failures or inefficiencies. In particular, a democratic government will allocate resources according to the preferences of the median voter. This leaves unsatisfied demand for public goods by segments of the citizenry as well as some citizens who would prefer less service and lower taxes – both sources of inefficiency. Moreover, government agencies, lacking the profit motive and subject to political forces, may not administer its agencies with maximum internal efficiency (cost-effectiveness or x-efficiency) or, having to follow uniform policies and procedures or provide for all of its citizens on a nondiscriminatory basis (equal protection) may not be sufficiently sensitive or responsive to local variations of citizens' preferences and demands.

The forgoing theories of market and government failure lead in turn to consideration of the role of nonprofit organizations in a democratic market society. Nonprofit and voluntary institutions can address a number of the remaining inefficiencies. Following Hansmann (1980) they can address information asymmetry by earning the trust of consumers, based on their requirement that they do not distribute surpluses (profits) for private gain. They can respond to unsatisfied consumers of public goods by organizing and funding supplementary public goods on a voluntary basis. And they can serve as contractors to government for the provision of local public services in a manner that is more efficient and responsive than government can be. Finally, they can bring the public's attention to both government and business shortcomings (such advocacy being a voluntarily supported public good in itself) in efforts to nudge those institutions to become more efficient.

Can this market failure logic now be extended to social enterprise? Certainly the three-sector world of business, government, and traditional nonprofits does not resolve all-important inefficiencies. What is left for social enterprise to address? Interestingly, the answer to this question offers some insight into the utility of the zoo metaphor for social enterprise because the ways in which social enterprise can potentially address societal inefficiencies are manifold.

To begin, consider the limitations of the nonprofit form itself in addressing inefficiencies of business and government (see Salamon, 1987). Nonprofits' principal limitation is their capacity to raise sufficient resources. Essentially, nonprofits can be viewed as private providers of public goods, or goods and services with some element of publicness, including support of vulnerable populations, provision of services plagued by information problems, policy advocacy addressed to government service provision, and more conventional public goods such as environmental protection or social justice. Since nonprofits are limited in the degree to which they can charge for their services, they are substantially dependent on voluntary contributions of money, labor or in-kind resources. The raising of voluntary resources is itself limited by the *free rider problem* – the fact that not all citizens who benefit from or otherwise value the provision of a good or service are compelled to pay for it (because of rivalry and excludability issues). This limitation is particularly acute for capital expenses; since nonprofits cannot have shareholders who profit from the ownership and sale of stock, they cannot directly raise capital in equity markets. A related limitation of nonprofit provision is that nonprofits cannot fully mobilize the entrepreneurial drive associated with wealth accumulation and income maximization. While it is true that entrepreneurs are driven by a variety of motivations (Young and Lecy, 2014; also see Chapter 7), profit-seeking is a key dimension that is explicitly discouraged in the nonprofit environment.

Finally, nonprofits are limited in the kinds of services they can offer. Usually nonprofits are tax exempt, in exchange for which they normally promise to confine their attention to traditional domains of charitable activity such as education, social services, healthcare, environment or the arts, although this varies by national context. However, one can argue that social good can be achieved in many other domains such as the development of new medical techniques and pharmaceuticals, the establishment of small businesses to help communities overcome poverty, better agricultural techniques, or the development of new technologies that make life easier or help people overcome handicaps. Many of the latter will, of course, be explored by conventional businesses, but only if there is sufficient potential profit to be made down the road. Government can assist with subsidies, tax breaks or its own projects (such as space exploration). Still, there is likely to be much left outside the nonprofit domain and beyond business and government interests or capacities that promises substantial social benefit. Indeed, Depedri (2010) nicely summarizes four areas where social enterprises of various types can be more efficient than conventional forms of public or private enterprises. First, they can improve internal efficiency by reducing costs through additional access to free resources (such as volunteers or privately donated space). Second, they can reduce transactions costs by sharing internal control, cultivating relationships with community stakeholders, and by using participatory arrangements for service provision. Third, they can lower costs of controlling manager and worker performance through selection of workers with shared values, internalizing social norms, and using less coercive means of control and reward. And fourth, they can substitute intrinsic for monetary incentives to motivate their employees. Thus, as Borzaga and Tortia (2010) argue, social enterprises may enjoy a number of "supply-side" advantages, based on a broader reading of behavioral determinants of economic enterprise than conventional market failure theory is able to take into account.

In particular, social enterprises (of various sorts) have characteristics that can potentially address some of the limitations of conventional nonprofits identified by market failure theory. For example, nonprofits themselves can undertake profitmaking activities under properly controlled circumstances (Cordes and Steuerle, 2009). Indeed, earned income is the fastest-growing component of nonprofit income (Kerlin and Pollak, 2011; Salamon, 2012) and the dominant source in many countries (Anheier and Salamon, 2006). Given that commercial activity by nonprofit organizations is, by some lights, one manifestation of social enterprise, this is one way in which social enterprise can accommodate remaining market failures of the three-sector model. Another way is that businesses that explicitly accommodate social objectives in some way may be able to harness the profit motive to address the free rider problem, while still contributing to the public good. Such businesses, as discussed through this book, are another form often characterized as social enterprise. Indeed, social business can be broadly conceived not only to include new forms such as low-profit limited liability companies (L3Cs) or benefit corporations, but also conventional small businesses or larger corporations that have decided to follow a strategy and philosophy of economic, social, and environmental sustainability (Gidron, 2010). Finally, the three-sector market failure model fails to accommodate concepts from the social economy as practiced in places like France, Italy, Scandinavia, and Quebec that encourage cooperative forms of enterprise where workers or consumers themselves govern organizations that in turn provide them with direct benefits in the form of (usually limited) financial or material benefits and ownership shares. So-called social cooperatives also incorporate broader social benefits into their missions, such as improving the welfare of challenged populations through training and employment (Osborne, 2008; Depedri, 2010). Accordingly, cooperatives are yet another animal in the social enterprise zoo, which can potentially address inefficiencies of the three-sector economy by helping to overcome free rider effects and incorporating some of the benefits of self-interest (profit) motivation. Finally, cooperatives are less restricted than nonprofits in what they can do to increase social welfare; indeed, industrial production typical of the business sector is well within their purview.

SOCIAL ENTERPRISE: COMPETING INTELLECTUAL FRAMEWORKS

Still, the reader may ask, "But what is the *real evidence* of the emergence of this social and economic movement that we have labeled social enterprise?" First, over the past few decades, the private sector has increasingly demonstrated remarkable sensitivity to issues of social responsibility, environmental impact, and fairness in the marketplace, and has incorporated new thinking about shared values and long-term strategic success (Mook et al., 2012; Jäger and Sathe, 2014). Second, there is growing reliance on earned income by nonbusiness manifestations of social enterprise such as nonprofits and cooperatives. Third, jurisdictions across the globe are creating new and distinct legal forms specifically designed for social enterprise organizations (see Chapter 3). These developments suggest the need for a coherent, comprehensive, and convincing framework for understanding and advancing social enterprise as a whole.

There are currently several alternative intellectual frameworks for understanding social enterprise. These include the cross-subsidy model that views social enterprises as commercial arms of nonprofit organizations (James, 1983; Weisbrod, 1998), the spectrum school that sees social enterprise as a segment of a continuum between pure profitmaking and pure social purpose organizations (Dees, 1998; Borzaga and Tortia, 2010), the innovation school that characterizes social enterprise as a manifestation of the work of Schumpeterian social entrepreneurs (Shockley and Frank, 2011; Nicolls and Murdoch, 2012; also see Chapter 7), and the EMES International Research Network framework that postulates social enterprise as a type of organization guided by certain parameters of governance, social purpose and limited profit distribution (Borzaga and Defourny, 2001; Galera and Borzaga, 2009; Defourny and Nyssens, 2012). Other strands of social enterprise theory emphasize the historical/institutional context in which different forms of social enterprise develop (Kerlin, 2013), the hybridity literature that views social enterprises as combinations of various types of social and business entities (Evers, 2008; Billis, 2010), and the behavioral and evolutionary economics literature that sees social enterprise as a response by entrepreneurs and organizations to changing social needs, policy reforms and entrepreneurial motivations over time (Borzaga and Tortia, 2010).

The multifaceted literature on social enterprise and the increasing variety of enacted and proposed social enterprise forms indicate the desirability of a new, more comprehensive and flexible framework for understanding this phenomenon – one that draws on the disparate conceptualizations and empirical studies extant in the literature and that knits them together into an all-inclusive, yet practical, whole. The problem is that social enterprise is an emerging field and thus far is "chaordic"[1] in its development.

THE "CHAORDIC" NATURE OF SOCIAL ENTERPRISE

The authors submit that it is very difficult to draw meaningful boundary lines differentiating among so-called social enterprises and more familiar, conventional ways of organizing human endeavors through profitmaking corporations, small businesses, nonprofit organizations, and cooperatives. If one clings to the most basic idea of a social enterprise as an organization or venture that contributes a balance of economic, social, and environmental value to society, it is clear that none of the foregoing manifestations of enterprise can be summarily excluded, or for that matter, completely included. Indeed, applying the newly formulated notion of the "sustainability frontier" to enterprises of all kinds, one can easily appreciate that every type of economic enterprise produces some combination of economic, social, and environmental benefits and costs (Young, 2014; also see Chapter 2). So the issue becomes the following: where in the

three-dimensional space of economic, social, and environmental value –
within a frontier defined by limited resources and existing technologies –
do we decide to apply the label of social enterprise and study the forms that
occupy this subspace?

In this book we offer the idea of the social enterprise zoo to address this
challenge. The zoo serves as a metaphor to signal that designation of social
enterprise is an intentional construct, reflecting the limits within which we
are willing to call something a social enterprise versus a conventional business, nonprofit, cooperative, association, or governmental entity. It is not
our purpose in this book to draw those boundaries, but rather to enable
discovery of such boundaries, however elusive they may be, and to bring
attention to the efficacy of the zoo framework for expanding and joining
together alternative scholarly and practical views of the social enterprise
phenomenon.

Accordingly, the book considers several key dimensions and features
of the social enterprise zoo, and the research, practice, and policy questions raised by the zoo framework. As noted in the chapters that follow,
these include the variety of animals in the zoo, the alternative habitats in
which they live, and the interactions of different animals within particular
habitats. The zoo metaphor is particularly well suited for appreciating the
complexity and diversity of social enterprise and the likelihood that no one
simple model will suffice to understand social enterprise as a phenomenon
or to advance it as a social strategy. The zoo framework also makes clear
that social enterprise is a humanly devised and designed notion, constructed by drawing out from the broader "wilderness" of economic enterprises those initiatives that scholars and practitioners of social enterprise
now believe to be especially fertile for solving social and environmental
problems through market-based solutions.

One further word about perspective before we offer an overview of the
contents of the book: a basic requirement of rigorous research is to be clear
about one's "unit of analysis." That is, what is the fundamental variable
around which our theorizing and data analysis are based? In the present
context, is it the individual organization or venture (i.e., the animals in the
zoo); the zoo as a whole as it exists in different forms in different national
(and international) contexts; the populations of different types of social
enterprise animals (such social businesses vs social cooperatives); or the
habitats of social enterprise that give rise to alternative ecological systems
within which social enterprise animals live? Given the multifaceted nature
of our inquiry in this book, we can give no single answer to this question. Rather, we have tried to be explicit in each chapter about what unit
of analysis is employed, so that the reader can be clear as to what we are
learning at different levels of analysis. Roughly speaking, Chapters 1, 2, 12,

and 13 focus on the social enterprise zoo as a whole; Chapters 4, 5, and 9 employ habitat as the unit of analysis; and Chapters 3, 6, 7, 8, 10, and 11 consider individual types of social enterprises as their units of analysis. We believe that this multi-level approach has allowed us to learn about social enterprise in a more comprehensive and insightful manner.

We organize this book in the following way. Part I, including this chapter, sketches the landscape of social enterprise and establishes the conceptual framework through which we view it throughout the rest of the book. In Chapter 2, by Dennis Young and Wesley Longhofer, we elaborate on the use of metaphor in understanding social enterprise, why we find the zoo metaphor compelling, and the particular design, operational, management and governance, and performance questions raised by the zoo metaphor. In Chapter 3 by Cassady Brewer, we describe the richness of the zoo in terms of the variety of forms of social enterprise (flora and fauna) it embraces and the legal structures that accomodate these forms.

Part II of the book examines how the zoo actually works. In Chapter 4 Janelle A. Kerlin, Thema Monroe-White, and Sandy Zook describe the alternative habitats found within the social enterprise zoo, roughly corresponding to the different sorts of national contexts within which social enterprise develops – noting that habitat is highly influential in attracting and nurturing different social enterprise animals. In Chapter 5 Elizabeth Searing, Jesse Lecy, and Fredrik Andersson then examine the ecosystems within these alternative habitats, and the processes through which different species of social enterprise interact, compete, cooperate, differentiate themselves from one another, and ultimately thrive or decline, as well as how the ecosystems themselves evolve over time. Then in Chapter 6, Jesse Lecy and Elizabeth Searing examine the social enterprise animals over the course of their life cycles, addressing issues of infancy, adolescence, growth and maturity – especially the resources and other conditions required for success at each stage.

With the understandings developed in Parts I and II, Part III considers how the social enterprise zoo is managed and governed. In Chapter 7, Dennis Young and Jesse Lecy focus on the role of social entrepreneurs as zoo curators, selecting the animals that populate the zoo, reflecting entrepreneurial styles, preferences, and ideas about social purpose and market success. The underlying proposition in this chapter is that social enterprises are a product of social entrepreneurship, albeit within the constraints of alternative political environments or habitats. Accordingly, these entrepreneurs/curators must have access to the resources required to support their social enterprise animals. Chapter 8 by Elizabeth Searing and Dennis Young makes this connection explicit, relying on empirical evidence and benefits theory to describe the correspondence between forms of social enterprise and forms of economic nourishment that they require. Then in Chapter 9, Francesca Calò and Simon Teasdale consider the role of the zookeepers in governing the social enterprise zoo as a whole. In their view, social enterprise zoos are governed at the national level by alternative governmental policies and regulatory mechanisms and the public officials that administer these instruments. Their analyses of the United States, United Kingdom, and Italy make this clear.

Part IV addresses the all-important question – so what? On the basis of our analysis of social enterprise in terms of the zoo metaphor, what can we actually say about the *impact* or *performance* of social enterprise as a way of organizing economic activity for the public good? We break up this question into three parts. In Chapter 10, Thema Monroe-White and Jesse Lecy focus on social innovation – often a key argument for promoting social entrepreneurship and social enterprise in order to bring about social change and human betterment. In Chapter 11, Jung-In Soh, Elizabeth Searing, and Dennis Young consider the issue of sustainability of social enterprise, employing concepts drawn from resiliency theory as originally applied to environmental systems. In view of the fact the social enterprises must continually balance social impact with economic support, what are the risks and prospects for long-term sustenance of different sorts of social enterprise animals and of the social enterprise zoo as a whole? Then in Chapter 12, John Tyler considers the question of overall social impact – what are the benefits and costs of relying on the social enterprise zoo to address the myriad economic and social challenges facing society? What have we learned about this impact by employing the zoo metaphor? These turn out to be daunting and complex questions but ones worth asking. While incremental knowledge has been gained about the impact of various social enterprise animals in diverse habitats we are some distance from a broader understanding of the impact of the zoo itself, the broader clusters of species, habitats, and ecologies within it, and how it should be shaped through public policy and regulation. Nonetheless, the zoo metaphor appears to have elevated our thinking about the nature of social and economic success, highlighting criteria of social purpose, economic sustainability, flexibility, and adaptability to evaluate alternative approaches to social problem solving.

Finally, in Part V, Chapter 13, we synthesize our learnings from studying social enterprise through the lens of the zoo metaphor and project forward into next steps for social enterprise research, development of public policy, and the arts associated with social enterprise practice. With this convergence, we hope to engage academics, policymakers, and social enterprise leaders in fertile future discussions, collaborations and initiatives, using the common but diverse and accommodating metaphor of the social enterprise zoo.

NOTE

1. Adjective: (of a system, organization, or natural process) governed by or combining elements of both chaos and order (Collins English Dictionary – Complete & Unabridged 2012 Digital Edition).

REFERENCES

Anheier, H. and L.M. Salamon (2006), "The nonprofit sector in comparative perspective," in W.W. Powell and R. Steinberg (eds), *The Nonprofit Sector: A Research Handbook*, 2nd edition, New Haven, CT: Yale University Press, pp. 89–114.

Billis, D. (ed.) (2010), *Hybrid Organizations and the Third Sector: Challenges for Practice, Theory and Policy*, Basingstoke, UK: Palgrave Macmillan.

Borzaga, C. and J. Defourny (2001), *The Emergence of Social Enterprise*, London and New York: Routledge.

Borzaga, C. and E. Tortia (2010), "The economics of social enterprises: an interpretative framework," in L. Becchetti and C. Borzaga (eds), *The Economics of Social Responsibility*, New York: Routledge, pp. 15–33.

Cordes, J.J. and C.E. Steuerle (eds) (2009), *Nonprofits & Business*, Washington, DC: The Urban Institute Press.

Dees, G. (1998), "Enterprising nonprofits," *Harvard Business Review*, 76 (1), 54–69.

Defourny, J. and M. Nyssens (2012), "Conceptions of social enterprise in Europe: a comparative perspective with the United States," in B. Gidron and Y. Hasenfeld (eds), *Social Enterprise: An Organizational Perspective*, New York: Palgrave MacMillan, pp. 71–90.

Depedri, S. (2010), "The competitive advantages of social enterprises," in L. Becchetti and C. Borzaga (eds), *The Economics of Social Responsibility*, New York: Routledge, pp. 34–54.

Evers, A. (2008), "Hybrid organisations," in S.P. Osborne (ed.), *The Third Sector in Europe: Prospects and Challenges*, London and New York: Routledge, pp. 279–92.

Galera, G. and C. Borzaga (2009), "Social enterprise: an international overview of its conceptual evolution and legal implementation," *Social Enterprise Journal*, 5 (3), 210–28.

Gidron, B. (2010), "Policy challenges in light of the emerging phenomenon of social businesses," *Nonprofit Policy Forum*, 1 (1), accessed 13 June 2016 at http://www.degruyter.com/view/j/npf.2010.1.1/issue-files/npf.2010.1.issue-1.xml.

Hansmann, H.B. (1980), "The role of nonprofit enterprise," *Yale Law Journal*, 89 (5), 835–901.

Jäger, U.P. and V. Sathe (eds) (2014), *Strategy and Competitiveness in Latin American Markets: The Sustainability Frontier*, Cheltenham, UK and Northampton, MA, USA: Edward Elgar Publishing.

James, E. (1983), "How nonprofits grow: a model," *Journal of Policy Analysis and Management*, 2 (3), 350–65.

Kerlin, J.A. (2013), "Defining social enterprise across different contexts: a conceptual framework based on institutional factors," *Nonprofit and Voluntary Sector Quarterly*, 42 (1), 84–108.

Kerlin, J.A. and T.H. Pollak (2011), "Nonprofit commercial revenue: a replacement for declining government grants and private contributions?," *The American Review of Public Administration*, **41** (6), 686–704.

McCarthy, K.D., V.A. Hodgkinson, R.D. Sumariwalla, and Associates (1992), *The Nonprofit Sector in the Global Community*, San Francisco, CA: Jossey-Bass.

Mook, L., J. Quarter, and S. Ryan (eds) (2012), *Businesses with a Difference*, Toronto: University of Toronto Press.

Mook, L., J.R. Whitman, J. Quarter, and A. Armstrong (2015), *Understanding the Social Economy of the United States*, Toronto: University of Toronto Press.

Musgrave, R. (1959), *The Theory of Public Finance: A Study in Public Economy*, New York: McGraw-Hill.

Nicolls, A. and A. Murdoch (2012), *Social Innovation: Blurring Boundaries to Reconfigure Markets*, Basingstoke, UK: Palgrave MacMillan.

Osborne, S.P. (ed.) (2008), *The Third Sector in Europe: Prospects and Challenges*, London and New York: Routledge.

Pikkety, T. (2013), *Capital in the Twenty-First Century*, Cambridge, MA: Harvard University Press.

Salamon, L.M. (1987), "Partners in public service: the scope and theory of nonprofit–government relations," in W.W. Powell (ed.), *The Nonprofit Sector: A Research Handbook*, New Haven, CT: Yale University Press, pp. 99–117.

Salamon, L.M. (2012), *America's Nonprofit Sector: A Primer*, 3rd edition, New York: The Foundation Center.

Salamon, L.M. and H.K. Anheier (eds) (1997), *Defining the Nonprofit Sector: A Cross-National Analysis*, Manchester, UK: Manchester University Press.

Samuelson, P.A. (1964), *Economics*, 6th edition, New York: McGraw-Hill.

Shockley, G.E. and P.M. Frank (2011), "Schumpeter, Kirzner and the field of social entrepreneurship," *Journal of Social Entrepreneurship*, **2** (1), 6–26.

Steinberg, R. (2006), "Economic theories of nonprofit organizations," in W.W. Powell and R. Steinberg (eds), *The Nonprofit Sector: A Research Handbook*, 2nd edition, New Haven, CT: Yale University Press, pp. 117–39.

Weisbrod, B.A. (1975), "Toward a theory of the voluntary non-profit sector in a three-sector economy," in E. Phelps (ed.), *Altruism, Morality, and Economic Theory*, New York: Russell Sage, pp. 171–95.

Weisbrod, B.A. (ed.) (1998), *To Profit or Not to Profit: The Commercial Transformation of the Nonprofit Sector*, Cambridge, UK: Cambridge University Press.

Young, D.R. (2014), "The sustainability frontier," in U.P. Jäger and V. Sathe (eds), *Strategy and Competitiveness in Latin American Markets: The Sustainability Frontier*, Cheltenham, UK and Northampton, MA, USA: Edward Elgar Publishing, pp. 18–43.

Young, D.R. and J.D. Lecy (2014), "Defining the universe of social enterprise: competing metaphors," *Voluntas*, **25** (5), 1307–32.

Young, D.R. and R. Steinberg (1995), *Economics for Nonprofit Managers*, New York: The Foundation Center.

2. Designing the zoo

Dennis R. Young and Wesley Longhofer

INTRODUCTION

Modern zoos abound with contradiction and tension (Hanson, 2002). One can simply point to pink flamingos in the Minnesota Zoo or polar bears in San Diego as examples. Zoos are designed to organize the natural world in decidedly unnatural settings in order to educate and entertain patrons fascinated by the exotic, as well as conserve rapidly diminishing biodiversity around the world. The pathways from the entrance through the African savannahs and reptile houses guide the visitor through meticulously manicured landscapes and curated exhibits, giving the illusion that seemingly disparate species can coexist mere yards from one another so long as appropriate cages and barriers are put into place. Zoos can also be misguided and mismanaged, no matter the intentions. The recent euthanization of Watoto the elephant at the Woodland Park Zoo in Seattle due to chronic arthritis follows a continued decline in elephants throughout American zoos as concern over the long-term confinement of pachyderms grows (Berens, 2014).

Such tensions also manifest themselves in our metaphor of the zoo. To us, the metaphor captures the blossoming variety of organizational forms that seemed to beg for a framework that acknowledges that diversity is an intrinsic characteristic of the social enterprise space. The fauna of the social enterprise zoo are not just variations around a single model but rather wholly different varieties of organizations and activities united only by the common notion of seeking social good in the market context. Whereas some scholars place social enterprises along a spectrum of "hybrid organizations" (see Battilana and Lee, 2014), we wanted to acknowledge their unique origins and structural differences through a more taxonomic classification.

Still, our metaphor raised many eyebrows when pitched to scholars. In exploratory conversations prior to organizing this book, some thought the metaphor suggested something more chaotic (like a jungle), others thought we weren't serious (like a circus), and still more thought we were referencing something much more sinister (like the bad practice of exploiting or abusing animals). (Certainly, there are examples to this day of bad zoos that violate professional norms in this field; and there are social critics who feel that zoos should be entirely done away with!) Thus, while the zoo metaphor no doubt embraces variety, it remains incumbent on us, the authors of this book, to be clear about what we mean by a zoo and how we think this metaphor is helpful.

No metaphor is perfect and indeed we do not claim that the world of social enterprise is entirely like a zoo in every respect. For example, animals do not choose to be in a traditional zoo though such selection effects are evident in social entrepreneurship. Like the fiercest tigers and orcas, social entrepreneurs through their offspring enterprises can also be voracious, competitive, or even predatory (recall the controversy surrounding Compartamos Banco, the once small Mexican microfinance firm that raised \$467 million in a public stock sale in 2007; see MacFarquhar, 2010). But before exploring the limits of the zoo metaphor it is important to distinguish it from other related constructs. The zoo in our perspective is not entirely chaotic, unpredictable or uncontrollable, as a jungle or even a protected wilderness area might be. Social enterprises are human constructions and public policies shape the boundaries, contents, and conditions in the zoo. A zoo is designed by teams of architects, landscape artists, and zoologists, yet intended to accommodate within broad bounds the natural conditions under which its inhabitants live. Nor is the zoo entirely a mechanism for entertainment. It is not intendedly a circus; while its exhibits do entertain and educate human visitors, it has a higher purpose associated with conservation of biodiversity and support for policies that protect endangered species and bring attention to natural environments that are under threat worldwide. Certainly we wish to disassociate our metaphor from those actual zoos that abuse animals and fail to adhere to good practices of animal husbandry. Indeed, it is along these lines that the zoo metaphor is most useful to us. In particular, throughout the chapters of this book we inquire about those policies and practices within the social enterprise zoo that work best to promote the effective provision of social goods.

LITERATURE REVIEW: A BRIEF HISTORY OF ZOO DESIGN

A cursory glance at the history of zoos reveals how their design has changed over time. Early Victorian zoos, such as the London Zoo, organized animals taxonomically and displayed them in barred cages amidst ornate gardens (Hyson, 2000). The first American zoos appeared in the late nineteenth century – beginning with the Philadelphia Zoo in 1874 – and espoused missions of education, scientific advancement, and occasionally environmental conservation (Hanson, 2002). By the 1890s, zoos began designing more naturalistic enclosures and developed captive breeding programs for indigenous species, such as bison and beavers. Zoos such as those in San Diego and St. Louis later introduced barless enclosures and moated exhibits, offering panoramic views of exotic species in their supposedly natural habitats. These naturalistic exhibits then gave way to mid-century modernist architecture with a specific focus on sanitary zoo conditions, such as tiled rooms and cement walls (Hyson, 2000).

More recently, zoos have adopted "landscape immersion" as the industry standard, which began in 1978 with David Hancock's famous gorilla exhibit at Seattle's Woodland Park Zoo. Anthropologist Elizabeth Hanson (2002) captures this shift from sterilized modernism to landscape immersion through the story of Willie B., the famous gorilla at Atlanta Zoo who in 1988 was removed from his concrete cage where he had remained detached and listless and introduced to a new naturalistic habitat. According to Hanson (2002, p. 1), Willie B. had "journeyed from being an object of voyeurism in a sterile cage to a muscular silverback, foraging for raisins and behaving like a gorilla." Most zoos today have adopted immersion exhibits as the standard, organizing animals by landscapes – for example, San Diego Zoo's Northern Frontier and Cleveland Metroparks Zoo's African Plains – and designing enclosures devoid of barriers, bars, and other unnatural accoutrements.

This brief history is important for understanding the tension in zoo design that helps frame our own metaphor. Zoos have to balance their goals to preserve biodiversity, provide the best physical, mental, and emotional welfare for animals, and meet the demands of zoo visitors looking to be entertained. They also need to organize distinct and diverse fauna in a way that makes sense to both patrons of the zoo and its staff of curators, zoologists, veterinarians, grounds crew, and other employees. There is a reason why pink flamingos greet zoo visitors as they enter and make their way to the popular lions and monkeys. Elephant exhibits are under constant risk of closing as we learn more about the health consequences of captivity and begin moving the mammals to larger sanctuaries. Just as social categories and valuations depend on the reactivity of an audience, and thus products that span multiple categories underperform in the marketplace (Hsu et al., 2009), so too must zoos be organized in a way that is sensible to its visitors. Such organization is guided by a series of questions, to which we now turn.

METHODOLOGY: QUESTIONS BY ANALOGY

The strength of a metaphor is that it raises questions by analogy – questions whose answers are crucial to understanding the subject at hand. How then can the zoo metaphor help identify and sort out the key questions relevant to social enterprise policy and practice? We can break this down into a number of key questions: What belongs in the zoo? How does the zoo function as a system? How is the zoo managed and governed? How do we measure success or failure of the zoo?

What Animals Belong in the Zoo?

Definitions of social entrepreneurship and social enterprise abound with little consensus and much confusion (Mair and Marti, 2006; Zahra et al., 2009; Santos, 2012; and others). This has obvious implications for our zoo metaphor, particularly in regard to scope – what belongs in the zoo and what does not? This is perhaps the biggest riddle for social enterprise – what distinguishes a social enterprise from various forms of business enterprise on the one hand, and other nonprofit and public sector forms on the other? Is a zoo highly inclusive or more restrictive and exclusive? The zoo metaphor forces us to address this question. In this chapter and later in the book, we provide some preliminary answers to this question, though not necessarily the only possible answers. To begin, it is clear that there are a number of new concepts advanced within the last decade or so, including a variety of organizational forms and other manifestations, each of which might be considered a social enterprise to some scholars, policymakers and practitioners, but not others. These include:

- *Social businesses.* Muhammad Yunus (2010, p. 1) defines a social business as "a non-loss, non-dividend company devoted to solving a social problem and owned by investors who reinvest all profits in expanding and improving the business." Yunus cites the example of Grameen Danone, which provides affordable, fortified yogurt to poor Bangladeshis.
- *Social cooperatives.* According to the United Nations Social Development Network, a cooperative is "an autonomous association of persons united voluntarily to meet their common economic, social, and cultural needs and aspirations through a jointly-owned and democratically-controlled enterprise" (United Nations, 2012). The International Labour Organization estimates that cooperatives are responsible for more than 60 percent of Kenyan livelihoods (International Labour Organization, 2009). Social cooperatives,

such as those now popular in Italy, are a recent variant of the cooperative form that specifically incorporates broader social objectives (Depedri, 2010). Public service cooperatives in Canada offer another example (Quarter et al., 2012).

- *Social innovations.* The Stanford Graduate School of Business defines a social innovation as "a novel solution to a social problem that is more effective, efficient, sustainable, or just than present solutions. The value created accrues primarily to society as a whole rather than private individuals." Sometimes these innovations take the form of new organizations, but they can also be changes in policies or practices. Stanford cites charter schools, emissions trading, and fair trade as examples.[1]
- *Responsible enterprises (or socially responsible corporations).* According to Waddock and Rasche (2012, p. 5), responsible enterprises "live up to clear constructive visions and core values consistent with those of the broader societies within which they operate, respect the natural environment, and treat well the entire range of stakeholders who risk capital in, have an interest in, or are linked to the firm through primary and secondary impacts." Among their examples is Costco and its respectable employment practices.
- *Benefit corporations.* According to the Benefit Corporation Information Center (2015), benefit corporations "are a new class of corporations that are required to create a material positive impact on society and the environment and to meet higher standards of accountability and transparency." Examples of benefit corporations certified by the nonprofit B Lab include Method, Patagonia, and Bull City Burger and Brewery in Durham, North Carolina. (See also Chapter 3 in this volume.)
- *Sustainable businesses.* This is perhaps the hardest animal to define due to its various (and often dubious) meanings. Young (2014, p. 18) defines sustainable businesses as those that "seek to increase their profitability and long-term success by following responsible, social and economic strategies designed to build on synergies between corporate productivity and societal welfare." According to John Ehrenfeld (2008, p. 49), sustainability refers to "the possibility that humans and other life will flourish on Earth forever," though he is critical of corporate sustainability initiatives as they rarely take such a systemic view.

To these relatively new conceptions we can of course add other important old and as well as new variants (which seem to proliferate by the week), including commercial nonprofit organizations that depend at some level on earned income, public sector social enterprises that are private nonprofits or businesses primarily funded and controlled by government, community interest companies as found in the UK, various new legal forms of for-profit socially focused business and an array of public–private partnership arrangements. A full taxonomy and genealogical chart is beyond the scope of this chapter (but see Chapter 3 and below). The more important thing here is that the question of what comprises the organization field (DiMaggio and Powell, 1983) of social enterprise be raised and constantly reassessed, something the zoo metaphor requires. Do TOMS shoe company (commonly viewed as a social venture), online transport company Uber (a social innovation, to be sure), and Allergan (a healthcare company rated as one of the greenest companies in the USA by *Newsweek*, 2015) all belong in the same social enterprise zoo? Perhaps it makes sense to turn to legal definitions for leverage. But, as Brewer notes in Chapter 3, only a handful of jurisdictions define "social enterprise," making classification even more elusive. Fortunately, Brewer is able to provide a summary of the various legal forms adopted by social enterprises, as well as a useful schematic for making a taxonomic classification more reachable. Below we will offer a rough schema for the purpose of providing some uniformity of discussion throughout the chapters of this book.

How Does the Zoo Function?

One can imagine a zoo organized in various ways: alphabetically, taxonomically, synergistically, or even evolutionarily. Indeed, in 2009, researchers at the University of California-Santa Cruz launched the Genome 10K Project, a genomic "zoo" of 10 000 vertebrate species (Wagman, 2009). How a zoo is laid out physically determines whether animals can thrive and be maintained effectively. For example, does one sort out the animals by their natural habitats or are there particular combinations of animals that should be grouped in order to effectively maintain a supportive ecology within the zoo? This is a tricky question in several respects. Zoos differ from the wild by generally trying to keep predators and prey apart. (Placing the antelope in the lion's den might seem natural but doesn't make for the most pleasant or effective zoo experience.) So, too, social enterprises of different kinds may be synergistic or they may compete for scarce resources. The zoo metaphor asks us to consider what the most reasonable combinations are and in which kinds of natural habitats (i.e., national or local contexts) they can thrive. For example, why does New York have less than 50 benefit corporations when Nevada has nearly 400 (Cooney et al., 2014)?

To understand how a zoo *ought* to function, we have to understand how the ecologies and species likely to reside in it work. In Chapter 4, Kerlin,

Monroe-White, and Zook compare the institutional environments in which social enterprises reside through a cross-country comparison, finding that a country's civil society, welfare state, culture, and government all shape the ecologies of social enterprise within them. Searing, Lecy, and Andersson also look to ecologies in Chapter 5, focusing specifically on organizational ecologies within habitats. Just as with any natural habitat, social enterprises compete over scarce resources; some, like the London Underground mosquito (which, you guessed it, evolved to survive in the London Tube) specialize while others are more generalist; and all social enterprises interact in some way with other animals in their habitats. Relatedly, in Chapter 6, Lecy and Searing turn to the life cycle of social enterprises, including their birth, infancy, growth, maturation, and, in many cases, demise.

How to Govern and Manage?

The third key question is one of governance, practice, and management. Zoos have zookeepers and curators. Social enterprises are governed as a group through government policy and they evolve through the initiatives of social entrepreneurs who bring their organizational constructs into the zoo, and let go of their failures over time. For example, since 2011, the Chilean Economic Development Agency has provided equity-free financing to hundreds of entrepreneurs from around the world as part of its unique accelerator program. On a smaller scale, the Social Innovation Park in Bilbao, Spain, brings together entrepreneurs, charities, nongovernmental organizations (NGOs), and other organizations to foster new social (and entrepreneurial) activity. Are these zoos in the making?

The zoo metaphor requires that we answer the questions – who are the zookeepers and curators and how do their policies and practices affect the shape and content of the social enterprise zoo? What should each of the animals be fed and how can stability be maintained among species within the local ecologies in the zoo? How does one deal with destabilizing factors such as weather events? How should animals be managed over their life cycles? Which animals are going to be the most popular and should thus be placed near the front of the zoo? All of these questions have direct analogs in the world of social enterprise. Introducing new forms of social enterprise affects the entire local ecology of social enterprises. Sharp changes in the economy can destabilize certain forms of enterprise. Social enterprises, often stereotyped in the early entrepreneurial stages, also grow, become more mature, and perhaps more bureaucratic and even less effective as organizations over time. How should their care and feeding, and perhaps discipline and regulation, change accordingly over time?

Young and Lecy identify two potential groups of curators in Chapter 7 among the latent entrepreneurial population – conventional versus more innovative Schumpeterian entrepreneurs. The latter break new ground by introducing new animals while the former imitate these pioneers and build on their successes and failures – cultivating and developing the inhabitants of the zoo over time. Both types of curator/entrepreneur shape the population of the zoo by matching their motivations and styles with existing or new organizational forms, thereby populating the zoo with a collection of nonprofits, social businesses, or other animals.

In Chapter 8, Searing and Young turn to perhaps one of the biggest management questions in the zoo: what should we feed the animals? Here, for example, the authors provide a useful summary of available financing to US social enterprises, from traditional grants and earned income to newer crowdfunds and social impact bonds.

Finally, as Chapters 3 and 4 illustrate, the answers to management and governance questions will vary by national or, for example in the case of benefit corporations, subnational context, although the social enterprise zoo worldwide is something like a grand experiment in which one country's zookeepers and curators can learn from the experiences of others. Accordingly, in Chapter 9, Teasdale and Calò discuss the role of government as zookeeper and the impact of social welfare policies in fostering, shaping or restricting the social enterprise zoo. For example, Italy nurtured social cooperatives through government subsidies and thus its zoo is fairly monospecific; in contrast, the UK created regional support agencies that cultivated a more diverse zoo. (Perhaps not surprisingly, the latter zookeepers describe the US zoo more like a safari park where animals roam free.)

How to Measure Zoo Success (and Failure)?

The ultimate key question is how to determine if the zoo is succeeding or failing. For a social enterprise, this is fundamentally a question of impact. Some social enterprises receive the lion's share of adulation and acclaim through social media or popular press, though whether they are more effective social enterprises is another question altogether. For some social enterprises, simply surviving in an environment characterized by scarce resources, intense competition, and high standards on the social ledger is success enough. Other social enterprises are better able to adapt and innovate. In Chapter 10, Monroe-White and Lecy outline how social enterprises are best able to adapt to changing landscapes. In this case, the well-manicured and intentional landscapes of the modern zoo do not apply to the rapidly changing social enterprise space unless the zookeepers tolerate a certain level of "wildness." Similarly, in Chapter 11, Soh, Searing, and Young draw from resiliency theory to explain how social enterprises adapt to changing environments by examining the case of Atlanta housing non-profits following the 2013 federal budget sequester. And more generally, Chapter 12 by Tyler addresses the complex, multifaceted challenge of assessing the social impacts of the zoo as a whole, an issue once on the edges of and now central to social policy decisions.

ANALYSIS: THE SOCIAL EFFICIENCY FRONTIER AND ZOO DESIGN

In order to ensure consistency throughout the book, it is necessary to suggest a common way of thinking about the scope of the social enterprise zoo, although the specifics will clearly vary from one national or subnational context to another. Moreover, subsequent chapters will re-examine the issue of scope as the zookeeper and curatorial functions are analyzed in depth. However, it is desirable to begin on a common page.

Clearly, the variations of social enterprise are potentially enormous – including not only commercial nonprofits, new forms of social business, social cooperatives, and public–private partnerships but also sustainable and responsible businesses that claim to pursue a double bottom line of financial and social impact. Even more broadly one could argue that traditional business forms with innovative solutions to social problems (e.g., better pharmaceuticals, commercial producers of mosquito nets, organic food producers, urban bicycle rental programs, etc.) create social good through the marketplace via their conventional pursuit of profits. So how can we delineate the boundaries of the social enterprise zoo? We argue here that it is sensible to be liberal in the interpretation of these boundaries. Why not encourage traditional businesses and conventional nonprofits or cooperatives to take account of their social impacts in making their decisions? Indeed, why not include corporate social responsibility programs of public corporations within the zoo as well as private organizations commissioned by and contracted to government? At some point, of course, the distinctions would become meaningless if we were to admit any market-based enterprise with a positive social intent into the social enterprise zoo. It would beg the question of what special policies and practices apply to social enterprise versus other forms.

Instead we propose a framework introduced elsewhere to analyze sustainable business (Young, 2014) – namely the social efficiency frontier (Figure 2.1). The idea of the frontier is that all enterprises achieve some combination of profit (horizontal axis) and social impact (vertical axis) (see also Santos, 2012 for a similar distinction between value creation and value capture). An enterprise operates efficiently on the frontier where an

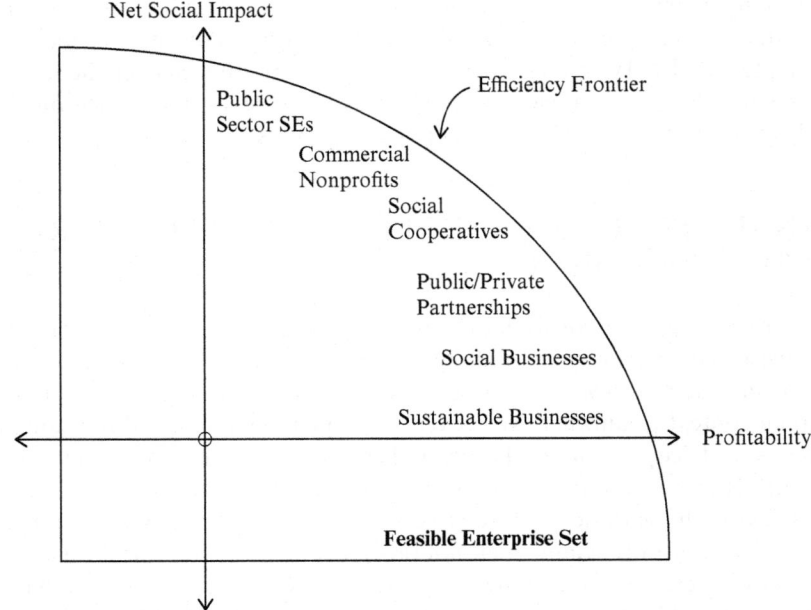

Source: Adapted from Young (2014).

Figure 2.1   The social efficiency frontier

increase in profitability comes as a trade-off with social impact or vice versa. This diagram helps us to differentiate social enterprises from others by taking account of the overall performance of an organization, not just one or two of its programs. Thus, it is not sufficient to operate a corporate social responsibility program if the overall social impact of a corporation is negative (e.g., a beverage company that imposes social costs in the form of obesity or depletion of water resources). However, a sustainable corporation that operates above the horizontal axis (positive social impact) could certainly be considered a social enterprise and might indeed be the organizational vehicle of choice by social entrepreneurs in some situations.

Thus, we may wish to make our definition mildly restrictive. Since social enterprises are expected to be financially sustainable they should also operate to the right of the vertical axis, in the northeast quadrant of the diagram where both profitability and social impact are positive. This poses no problem so long as we allow income to include funding from government or charitable sources as well as direct market-based income. Confining social enterprise to those organizations that operate completely within the private market would be entirely too confining and would eliminate many important examples, including nonprofit organizations, social cooperatives, community interest companies (CICs) in the UK, public sector social enterprises (SEs), and indeed so-called social businesses that get started with government or philanthropic assistance. It would be as if a zoo only displayed animals in local abundance and not those that are rarer or in greater need of zoo protection.

By using the efficiency frontier construct, we are focusing not only on the intent or motivation of a social enterprise but also on its performance; that is, its net social impact and its financial sustainability. To qualify as an animal in the social enterprise zoo a venture must pass this test. Effectively it probably eliminates many strictly for-profit forms but it does allow for the important possibility that some conventional businesses with important products for social well-being will be found in the social enterprise zoo. In fact, the diagram could be employed to take a first cut at mapping the social enterprise zoo. First it indicates what is in the zoo (denizens of the northeast quadrant) and what is not in the zoo (denizens of the other three quadrants). Second, it suggests that innovative social enterprises may be "pushing the envelope"; that is, working at the frontier with new approaches and technologies that may have the ultimate effect of pushing out the frontier in some direction between due north and due east. Third, it is possible to use the frontier diagram to nominally locate different forms of social enterprise. For example, public sector social enterprises and commercial nonprofit organizations are likely to be towards the top of the diagram in the northeast quadrant but close to the vertical axis (low financial surpluses). Social businesses by contrast are likely to be nearer to the horizontal axis and located farther east. Social cooperatives that allow modest profit distribution and value social impact are more likely to be nearer the middle of the northeast quadrant. Sustainable businesses are likely to be at the far eastern corner of the northeast quadrant where the profit potential is greatest. And so on.

In our diagram note that we have collapsed the complex variety of possible social enterprises into a few generic types or species: commercial nonprofits, social cooperatives, public–private partnerships, social businesses and sustainable businesses, and public sector social enterprises. These are broad categories that contain many variants within (and possibly between) them. For example, benefit corporations may fit somewhere between social businesses per se (which would include L3Cs – low-profit, limited liability companies, for example) and sustainable businesses such as Ben & Jerry's. Similarly, community interest companies may fit between commercial nonprofits and social businesses. Nonetheless, we stipulate these fewer generic categories for two reasons. First, they offer a vocabulary that can be more easily followed throughout the book in discussing broadly similar types of social enterprises. Second they offer a means to cluster the continually emerging variants of social enterprise animals as discussed in the next chapter. The ordering of the clusters inside the frontier in the diagram also provides an orientation to the various balances that different kinds of social enterprises seek to achieve. Thus, commercial nonprofits, though often highly reliant on market revenues, are primarily focused on their social impacts, while sustainable businesses, while socially and environmentally responsible, are primarily concerned with their financial profitability. Public sector social enterprises, largely funded and driven by government, would also emphasize their social impact rather than market success.

The relative locations of these species of social enterprise in the diagram constitute of course only a rough guide. Populations of different social enterprise forms must be analyzed in depth before such generalizations can be defended. Moreover, as the diagram suggests, efficiency can be important. Some forms, arguably social businesses, might be more efficient in their use of resources and hence likely to operate closer to the frontier. Others, perhaps some nonprofits, are less attuned to efficient operations and deployment of their resources. A social enterprise operating near the frontier will be getting more out of its resources, no matter its view of the trade-offs between profits and social impact. Hence a social enterprise more heavily focused on profits but operating near the frontier could conceivably have a stronger social impact than another social enterprise more concerned with social impact but operating well below the efficiency frontier.

Finally, note that we are conceiving social enterprise in terms of alternative organizational types and arrangements rather than as programmatic ventures or innovations per se. The zoo metaphor pushes us to do this – organizations rather than policies, innovations or programs are more like animals. More importantly, this allows us to separate enterprise structure and operations from performance. In particular, achieving innovation or improved programmatic outcomes are what we want our social enterprise animals to do. (That said, Monroe-White and Lecy make an argument in Chapter 10 for classifying social enterprises by the nature of their innovations or theories of social change.)

In sum, the efficiency frontier construct helps us to carve out a conceptual piece of real estate for the social enterprise zoo. The zoo belongs in the northeast quadrant and we argue here that it needn't be restricted further but can conceivably encompass all of the social enterprise animals that live in that quadrant. Alternatively, we could stipulate that only a certain portion or wedge within the northeast quadrant qualifies as a social enterprise (requiring a specified range of ratios between social impact and profitability – Figure 2.2).

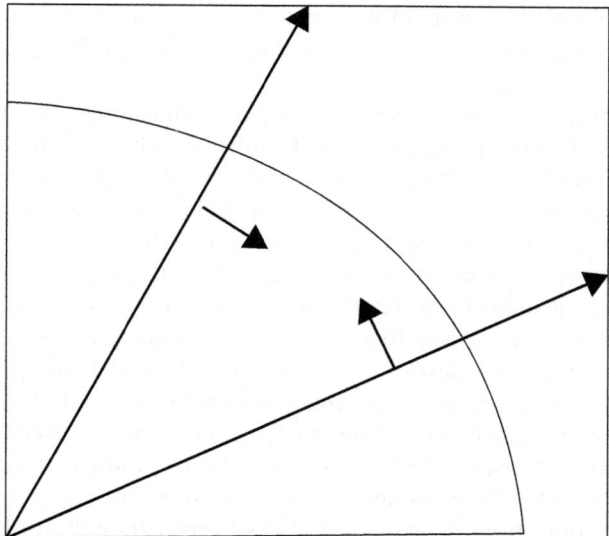

Figure 2.2   Narrowing the social enterprise quadrant

That would be a legitimate policy decision, depending on the preferences of the zookeepers and those to whom the zookeepers are accountable. In addition, the internal design of the zoo, its professional practices and its governance and leadership are further issues that the zoo metaphor compels us to address. Here are a few thoughts about these matters, though we leave the heavy lifting to our authors in subsequent chapters.

Designing the Social Enterprise Zoo

Perhaps the most important design issue in the zoo is how to group the animals and in what kinds of settings. As we have noted, modern zoos have evolved from designs based on clustering similar species (e.g., cats, bears, birds, deer and their fast-of-hoof relatives, fish, reptiles, etc.) close together and often in separated enclosures. In their contemporary versions, zoos have turned their emphasis more to grouping their animals by habitat and accommodating their abilities to roam within relatively unconfined "immersion landscapes" within habitat-defined areas of the zoo (e.g., African plains, rainforests, deserts, wetlands, mountainous environments, bodies of water). The latter model is thought to be supportive of both animal welfare and of educating visitors more closely to the actual behavior of animals in the wild. But zoos do not try to totally emulate the wild; in particular, they generally avoid predation wherein some species exploit others for their food. Other trade-offs may include audience perceptions and tastes as well as the commercial interest of zoo owners.

The application here to social enterprise is interesting. As discussed by Kerlin, Monroe-White, and Zook in Chapter 4, scholars have recognized that, like animals, different forms of social enterprise appear to work better in certain environments – as defined by public policies, social culture, legal context, and other indicators. Thus, as actual zoos have learned, social enterprise animals must be compatible with their habitats as well. Similarly, policymakers (government as zookeeper), rightly or wrongly, want to avoid predation so that one form of social enterprise (e.g., social businesses) does not destroy another (e.g., charitable nonprofits). We say rightly or wrongly because some economic schools of thought, most prominently Schumpeterian competition (Schumpeter, 1942), argue for the benefits of "creative destruction" in order to produce innovation and economic growth. There is merit to this argument but just as actual zoos raise strong objections from interested observers if they allow obvious predation, so too do social enterprise promoters object to unvarnished application of market forces to sort out what social enterprises should survive and which should not.

So the design of the social enterprise zoo around the notion of alternative habitats to accommodate different social enterprise animals must simultaneously sort all of those animals into a limited number of habitats by attending to three-related issues. First, what kinds of potential predators and potential victims must be kept apart in different habitats (or different sections of particular habitats)? Second, what kinds of potentially synergistic animals can be grouped together in the same habitats, like in real zoos, where, for example, birds help elephants and hippos rid themselves of annoying insects? Finally, what types and levels of predation are to be allowed? (Is it OK for seals to prey on fish in their waters? Is it tolerable for large cats to prey on local rodents?) These are issues of ecology discussed by Searing, Lecy, and Andersson in Chapter 5, and Soh, Searing, and Young in Chapter 11. The answers to these questions, contingent on extant varieties of social enterprise, will largely determine the design of the social enterprise zoo as it manifests itself within alternative legal and political jurisdictions.

On the question of professional practices, a primary concern in the physical world of zoos is what to feed each of the animals. In contrast to wildlife preserves, for example, food must often be provided externally, especially for predatory animals that would otherwise hunt their own. For many animals, vegetation is a primary if not exclusive source of nourishment as well. The aardvarks at Chicago's Lincoln Park Zoo are fed a special insectivore chow because, according to the zoo's website, "no one at the zoo would enjoy a 'termite attack'." By design zoos must ensure that sufficient quantities and qualities of appropriate vegetation, explicitly supplied food stocks, and water can support the animals in their various habitats. Along with nutrition, zoos must also attend to the general health needs of their inhabitants, having the necessary veterinary care and medicines required to treat medical problems that may arise or are associated with various life stages, and to prevent outbreaks of diseases that can reasonably be anticipated. Regular monitoring of the health and welfare of its animals is a key function of a zoo's management.

Similar considerations apply in the social enterprise zoo. For instance, some types of social enterprises depend on a surprisingly variable diet of income sources to sustain themselves. Nonprofits are perhaps the most omnivorous in their feeding habits, depending on widely varying mixes of earned revenue, charitable support, government funding and returns on investments, and in-kind income including volunteer labor and gifts. And in fact, the viability and effectiveness of the organization depends largely on how well its financial diet fits its mission (Young, 2007). The variety of income sources may be narrower for other forms of social enterprise, though not so much as might be expected. For-profit social ventures are frequently started with philanthropic or government funding, and often remain dependent on such sources over the long term, even if they achieve sustainability. Similarly, social cooperatives garner public as well as member and philanthropic support while public–private partnerships draw resources from all major sectors – business, government, and philanthropic- and public sector social enterprises draw primarily from government. As considered by Searing and Young in Chapter 8, the social enterprise zoo is thus challenged with discerning how best to nurture its animals through funding combinations appropriate to particular forms and circumstances. Similarly, the monitoring of financial health and program effectiveness of various forms of social enterprise and provision of supports such as consultation, information sharing, and technical assistance, must be based on a sophisticated understanding of the differences among the social enterprise animals, to ensure successful long-term performance in the social enterprise zoo.

Finally, the zoo metaphor suggests that attention be paid to critical issues of management and governance of the social enterprise zoo, as considered by Young and Lecy in Chapter 7, and Calò and Teasdale in Chapter 9, respectively. Real zoos must have expert curatorial staff to make particular selections of animals for the zoo population and they must have central management and governance (zookeepers) to articulate overall policy and to coordinate decision-making and resource allocation. Overall, the zoo must be accountable to an overseeing jurisdiction, whether that be a private board entrusted with the interests of the community and containing various philanthropic, public, and corporate parties, or a hierarchical relationship to a government body responsible for governing the zoo in the context of overall public sector programming; this in addition, of course, to the private marketplace of visitors, customers, and donors.

The world of social enterprise, given its relative youth, is not yet clearly delineated along the lines of management and governance. In some places, such as Japan or parts of Europe, the social enterprise zoo is highly controlled by government, with little private leeway for initiative-taking outside of government policy, either by private organizations or social entrepreneurs pioneering new forms or favoring some forms over others. In other places, like the USA, UK, and much of the less developed world, there is more of a free-for-all with active entrepreneurial curation and near free-market determination of what forms will prosper and which will not. One of the biggest contemporary challenges for social enterprise development is to understand how the governance of the social enterprise zoo works in these various contexts, and, as addressed by Monroe-White and Lecy in Chapter 10 and Tyler in Chapter 12, what differences for social innovation and social impact result. Ultimately a global aspiration may be to evolve an overall model that can better serve the social enterprise zoo of the future in diverse national contexts.

CONCLUSION

To go further with design of the social enterprise zoo requires an empirical base, not just a metaphor, powerful as that may be, for driving the design issue. Design is an exercise in detail as much as application of sweeping principles. We need to know, what are the various animals that have emerged, and continue to emerge, as current and prospective members of the social enterprise zoo? What are the contexts (habitats) in which they are developing or struggling? How are they nurtured (financed) and cared for, or indeed neglected? What roles are curators and zookeepers, that is, the entrepreneurs and governments, actually playing in this evolution? What do we know so far about the interaction among social enterprise forms within existing habitats? Are various species – especially new ones – viable, stable, threatened, threatening, collaborative or competitive with other species? Are things changing as the new forms mature (or die off); are they leading to more or less constructive social innovations or are desired social changes largely unaffected by the frenzy of activity in the social enterprise zoo? While these questions will be addressed piecemeal in subsequent chapters, the bigger picture will take longer to emerge clearly. The design of the social enterprise zoo will continue to be a work in progress for many years, but it is also an ongoing task for scholars and policymakers to scrutinize and incrementally adjust and improve on its current practices and policies over the coming decades.

NOTE

1. See Stanford Graduate School of Business, Center for Innovation, accessed 13 June 2016 at https://www.gsb.stanford.edu/faculty-research/centers-initiatives/csi/defining-social-innovation.

REFERENCES

Battilana, J. and M. Lee (2014), "Advancing research on hybrid organizing – insights from the study of social enterprises," *The Academy of Management Annals*, **8** (1), 397–441.

Benefit Corporation Information Center (2015) [website], accessed 16 June 2016 at http://www.bcorporation.net.

Berens, M.J. (2014), "Death of elephant at Seattle zoo mourned, revives debate," *Seattle Times*, 23 August.

Cooney, K., J. Koushyar, M. Lee, and H. Murray (2014), "Benefit corporation and L3C adoption: a survey," *Stanford Social Innovation Review*, 5 December [blog].

Depedri, S. (2010), "The competitive advantages of social enterprises," in L. Becchetti and C. Borzaga (eds), *The Economics of Social Responsibility*, New York: Routledge, pp. 34–54.

DiMaggio, P. and W.W. Powell (1983), "The iron cage revisited: institutional isomorphism and collective rationality in organizational fields," *American Sociological Review*, **48** (2), 147–60.

Ehrenfeld, J.R. (2008), *Sustainability by Design: A Subversive Strategy for Transforming Our Consumer Culture*, New Haven, CT: Yale University Press.

Hanson, E. (2002), *Animal Attractions: Nature on Display in American Zoos*, Princeton, NJ: Princeton University Press.

Hsu, G., M. Hannan, and Ö. Koçak (2009), "Multiple category memberships in markets: a formal theory of two empirical tests," *American Sociological Review*, **74** (1), 150–69.

Hyson, J. (2000), "Jungles of Eden: the design of American zoos," in M. Conan (ed.), *Environmentalism in Landscape Architecture*, Washington, DC: Dumbarton Oaks, pp. 23–44.

International Labour Organization (2009), "Kenya," accessed 15 June 2016 at http://www.ilo.org/public/english/employment/ent/coop/africa/countries/eastafrica/kenya.htm.

MacFarquhar, N. (2010), "Banks making big profits from tiny loans," *New York Times*, 13 April.

Mair, J. and I. Marti (2006), "Social entrepreneurship research: a source of explanation, prediction and delight," *Journal of World Business*, **41** (1), 36–44.

Quarter, J., L. Mook, and J. Hann (2012), "Non-financial co-operatives in Canada: 1955 to 2005," in L. Mook, J. Quarter, and S. Ryan (eds), *Businesses with a Difference*, Toronto: University of Toronto Press, pp. 40–63.

Newsweek (2015), "Top green companies in the world 2015," accessed 13 June 2016 at http://www.newsweek.com/green-2015/top-green-companies-u.s.-2015.

Santos, F. (2012), "A positive theory of social entrepreneurship," *Journal of Business Ethics*, **111** (3), 335–51.

Schumpeter, J.A. (1942), *Capitalism, Socialism, and Democracy*, London: Routledge.

United Nations (2012), "International Co-operative Alliance statement on the co-operative identity," accessed 15 June 2016 at http://www.un.org/en/events/coopsyear/about.shtml.

Waddock, S. and A. Rasche (2012), *Building the Responsible Enterprise: Where Vision and Values Add Value*, Stanford, CA: Stanford Business Books.

Wagman, B. (2009), "Scientists propose a 'genome zoo' of 10,000 invertebrate species," *Genome 10K*, accessed 13 June 2016 at https://genome10k.soe.ucsc.edu/news/article/1.

Young, D.R. (ed.) (2007), *Financing Nonprofits*, Lanham, MD: AltaMira Press.

Young, D.R. (2014), "The sustainability frontier," in U.P. Jäger and V. Sathe (eds), *Strategy and Competitiveness in Latin American Markets*, Cheltenham, UK and Northampton, MA, USA: Edward Elgar Publishers, pp. 18–43.

Yunus, M. (2010), *Building Social Business: The New Kind of Capitalism that Serves Humanity's Most Pressing Needs*, New York: Public Affairs.

Zahra, S.A., E. Gedajlovic, D.O. Neubaum, and J.M. Shulman (2009), "A typology of social entrepreneurs: motives, search processes and ethical challenges," *Journal of Business Venturing*, **24** (5), 519–32.

3. The ongoing evolution in social enterprise legal forms

Cassady V. Brewer

> I like the duck-billed platypus
> Because it is anomalous.
> I like the way it raises its family,
> Partly birdly, partly mammaly.
> (Ogden Nash, 1953)

INTRODUCTION

The duck-billed platypus (*Ornithorhynchus anatinus*) is indeed extraordinary. Discovered by Western naturalists in the late 1790s/early 1800s,[1] the platypus is semi-aquatic, lays eggs, and has a beak like a duck, yet it also has fur, a tail like a beaver, feet like an otter, and suckles its young. The male even has venomous spurs on its hind feet. Zoologists today classify the platypus as a mammal, but that conclusion was once far from clear (Moyal, 2001).

To get a sense of the initial debate over the classification of the platypus, suspend your knowledge of history for a moment. Instead, imagine that you are an early 1800s (i.e., pre-Darwin) zoologist in Europe. At the time, vertebrate animals fell into four basic categories: mammals, fish, birds, and reptiles (ibid.). Mammals were distinguished by being warm-blooded, producing milk, and giving birth to live young. Fish were distinguished by being cold-blooded and spending their entire lives in water. Birds were warm-blooded like mammals, but were distinguished by laying eggs and not producing milk. Reptiles laid eggs like birds, but were distinguished by being cold-blooded (Hall, 1999).

Aware of the foregoing classifications, you examine the dried specimen of an unknown and unnamed creature from the other side of the world. You have never seen anything quite like the specimen before you. Your initial conclusion is that the creature must be a hoax. You have heard that shrewd taxidermists in foreign lands stitch "the head and trunk of monkeys to the hind parts of fish" to profit from sales to "credulous sailors" (Moyal, 2001).

33

Soon, though, you learn that the animal does indeed exist and that, in addition to its physical oddities, it is warm-blooded and produces milk. It also lays eggs, builds nests, and is amphibious. Now your reaction is one of intense curiosity, and you and other equally curious zoologists earnestly begin studying the platypus and vigorously debating its proper classification in the animal kingdom (ibid.). In fact, as one author has chronicled, the platypus's discovery at the end of the eighteenth century pitted "nation against nation, naturalist against naturalist, and professional against amateur [in a rivalry that] endured for 85 years before the true nature of the platypus was revealed" (Hall, 1999, p. 211).

As mentioned in Chapter 1, there are at least four intellectual frameworks (i.e., cross-subsidy, spectrum, innovation, and EMES – the International Research Network) competing to explain the phenomenon of social enterprise. None of these competing frameworks predominates. Further, no universally accepted legal or other definition of social enterprise has emerged, and no consensus has developed regarding what types of organizations clearly are, or clearly are not, social enterprise organizations. Thus, similar to the way the platypus challenged accepted zoological norms of the time, social enterprise is challenging today's accepted organizational norms. Like the discovery and subsequent study of the platypus, it may be a long time before we understand exactly what makes an organization a "social enterprise."[2]

Admittedly, the "zoo" school of thought set forth in this volume proposes yet another intellectual framework for understanding social enterprise. Unlike existing frameworks, however, the zoo school of thought embraces and complements all of the existing theories, excluding none. Above all, the zoo school of thought recognizes the "chaordic" nature of social enterprise (Hock, 2000; see also Chapter 1). In other words, although one finds chaos in studying social enterprise organizations just as one might find chaos studying animals in the wild, the construct and lens of the "social enterprise zoo" superimposes some order. Specifically, as explained in Chapter 2, we believe that the "social enterprise zoo" comprises six broadly conceived types of "animals" (or cross-breeds thereof): commercial nonprofits, social cooperatives, social businesses, sustainable businesses, public–private partnerships, and public sector social enterprises. This and other chapters of this volume elaborate on these categories as well as other ways of identifying and differentiating the animals in the social enterprise zoo.

Critics will argue that the "zoo" metaphor is not helpful for several reasons. First, due to the breadth of its six categories of animals (as noted above), virtually any organization conceivably may be included or excluded from the "zoo." Moreover, the "social enterprise zoo" is an entirely subjective construct imposed by the observer, not an objective means to differentiate social enterprise organizations. Just about any "animal" can be included or excluded based solely upon the individual observer's perspective – *but maybe that is the point.* As discussed in Chapter 4, social enterprise in the developing world is very different from social enterprise in the industrialized world. Interestingly, the law teaches us that "I know it when I see it" is not necessarily a useless or impractical definition.[3]

In short, we believe that the "zoo" metaphor and our categories of "animals" (as well as other identifiers and differentiators discussed elsewhere in this volume) can be discerning and useful. Furthermore, a basic understanding of the existing and evolving legal forms used to conduct social enterprise supports the zoo metaphor. That is the essential purpose of this chapter.

THE INSTITUTIONAL LOGICS (OR "INSTINCTS") OF CONVENTIONAL LEGAL FORMS

Perhaps similar to the late eighteenth-century guidelines for the classification of vertebrate animals, conventional legal forms[4] generally assume that all organizations fall within and fulfill the legal purposes of one of the three sectors of the economy: government ("public"), for-profit ("private"), and nonprofit ("voluntary"). Any given legal form is primarily adapted to survive and thrive within its associated sector. Among scholars, the propensity of an organization to behave in a certain manner is termed "institutional logic" (Thornton et al., 2012). The law applicable to an organization contributes to the organization's institutional logic (ibid.). Put differently and in line with our zoo metaphor, an organization's legal "instinct" (part of its institutional logic) aligns with its proper place in the larger "environment" of the three sectors of the economy.

Thus, legal form signals and influences several important "instinctual" aspects of an organization. Among other things, legal form signals (1) who may create the organization (formative); (2) how and by whom the organization may be capitalized and financed (financial); (3) how an organization may be taxed (tax); (4) who legally regulates the organization (regulatory); and (5) who controls and governs the organization (governance).

Government

For instance, the public empowers and controls government, and imbues government with its legal purpose.[5] The generally accepted legal purpose ("instinct") of government is to protect and benefit the public. The government fulfills that purpose by enacting and enforcing laws, collecting taxes, and providing security. Furthermore, in carrying out its mandate, a national government typically creates and funds subservient legal entities, such as provinces, states, counties, and municipalities, which are delegated limited power and authority (limited "instinct" if you will) to tax, regulate, and generally govern defined geographical areas.

As part and parcel of its mandate, the government authorizes legal entities formed and controlled by private individuals to conduct certain desirable activities. Generally speaking, when it comes to commercial or humanitarian activities,[6] there are three types of such legal forms: for-profits and cooperatives for the private sector, and nonprofits for the voluntary sector.

Private Sector Legal Forms – Classic For-profits and Cooperatives

Because they primarily serve the private sector, the generally accepted legal purpose ("instinct") of classic for-profit enterprises is to benefit private owners.[7] Classic for-profits fulfill that purpose by allowing private interests to form, own, and control the enterprise. Capital is raised via private debt or equity investment into the enterprise, and revenue is earned by engaging in legally authorized, profitable activities, ultimately creating wealth (or incurring a loss) for private owners. Nonowner stakeholders such as customers, employees, suppliers, and community members may benefit indirectly, but not directly. In fact, some for-profits arguably make money and benefit private owners at the ultimate expense of their customers:

Example   Altria Group, Inc., a publicly traded, for-profit Virginia corporation that, among other businesses, owns three tobacco companies.[8]

Example   Anheuser-Busch InBev, SA/NV, a publicly traded company incorporated under the laws of Belgium that through a number of subsidiaries around the world manufactures and distributes various alcoholic beverages.[9]

Likewise, conventional member-based[10] cooperative enterprises in the private sector use their collective buying, selling, and negotiating power ("instinct") to benefit the individual members of the cooperative, not necessarily nonmembers. Members (not owners) fund and control conventional cooperatives; however, cooperatives typically operate at near break-even levels so that, unlike classic for-profit enterprises, cooperatives normally do not build substantial equity value. Again, certain stakeholders of the cooperative (e.g., employees) may indirectly benefit from the cooperative's existence, but the members are clearly the intended beneficiaries (Lund, 2013):

Example   Land O'Lakes Creameries, Inc., a Minnesota agricultural cooperative corporation doing business in more than 60 countries. Land O'Lakes has over 10 000 employees, 3600 producer-members, and 850 member-cooperatives.[11]

Example   Amul Cooperative, exclusively marketed by Gujarat Cooperative Milk Marketing Federation Ltd., is a dairy producer based in Gujarat, India. The farmer-owned cooperative is reportedly larger than any for-profit dairy company in the world.[12]

There is also a variant on the conventional member-based cooperative known as a "worker cooperative." These cooperatives typically run a for-profit business, but the employees are the members of the cooperative and thereby participate in the profits of the business. Nonemployees and other stakeholders are not directly intended financial beneficiaries of the cooperative. Instead, the member-employees are the financial beneficiaries:

Example   Community Builders Cooperative, LLC, a Massachusetts cooperative-like company legally organized as a worker-owned limited liability company with each worker having an equal vote in the management of the business.[13]

Example   Triangle Wholefoods Collective Ltd., trading as Suma Wholefoods, is an Elland, West Yorkshire, UK cooperative organized as a worker-owned company that strives to eliminate hierarchy and fosters equal pay for its employees.[14]

Conventional Nonprofits

Finally, because they are designed primarily for the voluntary sector, the generally accepted legal purpose ("instinct") of most operating[15] nonprofit organizations is to remedy or alleviate undesirable social, environmental, or economic conditions not addressed by government, by for-profit enterprises, or by conventional cooperatives. The vast majority of these operating nonprofits are subject to the nondistribution constraint:[16] they have no equity owners, but raise capital strictly through pure debt, voluntary contributions, grants, or highly regulated revenue-generating activities. Thereafter, they expend funds and engage in activities designed to counter undesirable conditions (Dehne et al., 2008). Operating nonprofits are most often formed by an individual or small group of individuals who initially serve as officers and directors (or trustees) of the organization. Later, as the operating nonprofit grows in size and scope, it usually adds paid staff and additional voluntary (i.e., unpaid) board members (or trustees) who assume control of the organization from the founder or founders:

Example CARE, Inc., an Atlanta nonprofit corporation that through a network of international affiliates provides goods and services free of charge to individuals and families in the poorest communities in the world.[17]

Example ActionAid International, an African nonprofit association originally formed as Stichting ActionAid International, a Netherlands foundation, that seeks to alleviate and ultimately eliminate poverty and injustice throughout the world.[18]

Until recently, the nonprofit legal form has dominated among social enterprise organizations (Poon, 2011) because the legal "instincts" of the form align closely with a social or environmental mission.

Social Enterprise Organizations

The above-described legal "instincts" associated with conventional for-profits, nonprofits, and cooperatives are well established, widely understood, and commonly accepted (Fourth Sector Mapping Initiative, 2016).[19] Generally speaking though, social enterprise organizations do not follow conventional legal "instincts." For-profit social enterprises, which fall within Chapter 2's typology of social businesses and sustainable businesses, typically adopt a *dual* purpose (albeit to varying degrees): (1) directly benefit private owners and (2) and directly (not indirectly) benefit other stakeholders such as customers, employees, the environment, and community members:

Example Better World Books Marketplace, Inc., a social enterprise incorporated in Indiana, USA, under its for-profit corporation statute, is an online bookseller that also donates books and a portion of its profits to literacy programs all around the world.[20]

Example Grameen Bank, a bank originally established by special act under Indian law and owned predominantly by women who also borrow from the bank, extends credit to the poorest members of society to promote economic development and self-sufficiency.[21]

Social cooperatives, so labeled in Chapter 2, adopt a purpose to benefit members like conventional member-based cooperatives, but they also take on a coextensive purpose of addressing undesirable social, environmental, economic, or other conditions. Thus, social cooperatives may benefit members who are socially or economically disadvantaged (e.g., disabled worker-members, immigrant worker-members), or may adopt a socially beneficial purpose independent of the needs of the members (e.g., the community or the environment), or may do both:

Example   The Cooperative Home Care Associates, Inc., a social cooperative based in New York, creates jobs for otherwise unemployed women by providing home care services to the mentally ill, disabled, or elderly.[22]

Example   European Social Cooperative ESCOOP, a social cooperative based in Italy, provides health, education, training, and other humanitarian services to underprivileged communities throughout Europe.[23]

Nonprofit social enterprises, which in Chapter 2's terms we label commercial nonprofits,[24] may embrace a purpose to address undesirable social, environmental, economic, or other conditions; however, they are not entirely dependent upon voluntary contributions and grants in doing so. Instead, to sustain themselves financially, they primarily or significantly rely upon revenue-generating, commercial activity (i.e., marketing and selling, not giving away, products and services) similar to for-profit enterprises. Nevertheless, the ultimate raison d'être for the revenue-generating activity of these commercial nonprofits is to alleviate undesirable social, environmental, economic, or other conditions, not to generate surplus:

Example   Habitat for Humanity ReStore, Inc., an American nonprofit 501(c)(3) (tax-exempt) organization, helps provide affordable housing to impoverished families by generating revenue from the sale of "gently used" building products to ordinary consumers.[25]

Example   Stichting Oxfam International is a foundation (stichting) registered in The Hague, Netherlands and as a foreign company limited by guarantee in the UK. Oxfam and its 17 affiliates around the world use revenue from the sale of fair-trade and donated property to alleviate poverty and injustice in 90 countries across the globe.[26]

Conventional for-profit, cooperative, and nonprofit legal forms have been and will continue to serve as vehicles for social enterprise organizations.

Thus, the adoption of a particular legal form in and of itself is not determinative of whether an organization should be, or should not be, included
in the social enterprise zoo. In fact, the diversity of conventional legal
forms used for social enterprise arguably supports the need for the zoo
metaphor and its tremendous breadth and flexibility. The legal forms
("animals") within the zoo have the same institutional logic ("instincts") as
identical animals in the wild, but the animals in the zoo behave differently
due to other forces.

Thus, although legal form is not determinative, it is *informative* because
it signals and influences the institutional logic ("instinct") of an organization. Then, to fit within the social enterprise zoo, the organization may
need to amplify, suppress, or otherwise modify its normal, instinctual
behavior. The extent to which applicable law allows or resists such behavior
modification is extremely important to a social entrepreneur's choice of
legal form, *but it is not determinative.*

PUBLIC–PRIVATE PARTNERSHIPS AND PUBLIC SECTOR SOCIAL ENTERPRISES

Before discussing some of the more nuanced aspects of conventional
and evolving legal forms in the social enterprise "zoo," it is important to
address public–private partnerships and public sector social enterprises. As
broadly conceived in Chapter 2, we included public–private partnerships
and public sector social enterprises within our "zoo." From a purely legal
perspective, however, these types of social enterprise organizations are
neither new nor unusual, but easily accommodated by conventional legal
forms. In other words, the institutional logic ("instinct") of public–private
partnerships and public sector social enterprises already falls within the
confines of the social enterprise zoo without the necessity of these organizations altering their normal behavior.

Public–private partnerships, for instance, generally consist of negotiated,
contractual arrangements or joint ventures between or among the government (or an agency or entity thereof) and a conventional for-profit and/or
nonprofit entity. The highly negotiated terms of the arrangement or joint
venture determine the fundamental legal aspects (i.e., formative, financial,
tax, regulatory, governance) of the overall, combined organization. These
types of social enterprise organizations are indeed extraordinarily complicated from a purely legal perspective. Furthermore, successfully navigating
the multiple strands of law (e.g., agency, authority, contract, tort, property,
securities, etc.) applicable to these organizations is exceedingly difficult.
Notwithstanding their legal complexity, however, these organizations do

not raise any *groundbreaking* formative, financial, tax, regulatory, governance, or other such fundamental issues:

Example American Water Works Company, Inc., a public utility company, developed a public–private partnership with the City of Phoenix to design, build, and operate the Lake Pleasant Treatment Plant, which provides water for the city. According to its website, the City of Phoenix offered American Water Works Company a $336 million contract to design, build, and operate the government-owned water plant for 15 years.[27]

Example The state government for Gujarat developed the Chiranjeevi Yojana program, which provides important healthcare services to rural women in India. Specifically, the government pays for the cost of deliveries at selected private sector hospitals, resulting in the saving of numerous maternal and neonatal lives.[28]

As for public sector social enterprises, these organizations typically consist of conventional nonprofit corporations or associations funded and controlled by the government (or an agency thereof). Occasionally though, they consist of conventional for-profit organizations capitalized by government investment or subsidy and controlled by government-appointed representatives. There is nothing particularly special, at least from a legal standpoint, about such government-created and -controlled social enterprise organizations because there are no competing "instincts" as there are in the for-profit/nonprofit social enterprise dynamic (as discussed further below). The legal entity exists and operates entirely at the behest of government:

Nonprofit example Fulton County/City of Atlanta Land Bank Authority, Inc., a Georgia nonprofit corporation created and funded by Fulton County and the City of Atlanta. The Fulton County/City of Atlanta Land Bank Authority, Inc. acquires, holds, and "repurposes to productive use" otherwise nonrevenue-generating and nontax-producing real property located in the City of Atlanta and in Fulton County Georgia, USA.[29]

For-profit example National Railroad Passenger Corporation, a District of Columbia for-profit corporation doing business as Amtrak, which operates a nationwide passenger rail system in the USA. Amtrak, Inc. is dependent upon subsidies from the US government to continue operating. Consequently, the US Department of Transportation owns and controls Amtrak through voting preferred stock. Four former private rail carriers own Amtrak's nonvoting common stock, which has negligible (if any) value.[30]

Another prime example of a public sector social enterprise is Grady Hospital in Atlanta, Georgia, USA. Grady Hospital is actually not one organization but rather a combination of nonprofit entities acting in concert to operate a single hospital. One entity is the Fulton-DeKalb Hospital Authority, Inc. (FDHA), which is actually a "hospital authority" that is established by law and controlled by the governments of Fulton and DeKalb counties in Georgia.[31] FDHA owns the building and real estate where Grady Hospital is located, and the Board of Directors of FDHA consists of members appointed by the Board of Commissioners of each of Fulton and DeKalb counties. Control over the operations of Grady Hospital, however, vests in a separate, independent nonprofit corporation, Grady Memorial Hospital Corporation, Inc. ("Grady Hospital"), a Georgia nonprofit corporation that has applied for and obtained US federal tax-exempt status. Grady Hospital leases the building, land, and all other assets of FDHA for $2.5 million per year. The Board of Directors of Grady Memorial Hospital Corporation, Inc. is separate from the Board of FDHA.

Thus, unlike the for-profit/nonprofit/cooperative legal entity choice, there are no inherent, competing legal "instincts" within public–private partnerships and public sector enterprises. Accordingly, the remainder of this chapter does not address any further legal aspects of public–private partnerships or public sector social enterprises, but instead focuses upon the more nuanced legal aspects of the for-profit, nonprofit, and cooperative forms, including evolving forms, that populate the other four categories of our social enterprise zoo: commercial nonprofits, social cooperatives, social businesses, and sustainable businesses.

ADAPTATION OF CONVENTIONAL FOR-PROFIT LEGAL FORMS

The above examples demonstrate that social enterprise has not been dependent upon a specialized legal form to survive and thrive. On the contrary, in addition to public–private partnerships and public sector enterprises,[32] the commercial nonprofit form of social enterprise has existed for quite some time and has been fairly popular (Poon, 2011; Young, 2013).[33] Social entrepreneurs often choose the nonprofit form because its legal "instinct" of alleviating undesirable social, environmental, or economic conditions is consistent with the purpose of most social enterprise organizations. The competing legal instinct, however, of conventional nonprofit organizations is to shy away from commercial activities involving the sale of goods and services to normal consumers (as opposed to special types of consumers such as students, patrons of the arts and culture, the elderly, the ill, or the financially or physically disadvantaged). This competing legal instinct has led many social entrepreneurs to turn to conventional for-profit legal forms to conduct a social enterprise.

Although less common, using the for-profit legal form for social enterprise is not unprecedented. For instance, private stock companies in the USA and Europe provided affordable housing, operated museums and zoos, and served other public purposes in the 1800s. These private stock companies paid limited dividends to their shareholders (Adam, 2014). Moreover, the cooperative form has been and is used as well, particularly in Italy where the concept of social enterprise cooperatives was recognized as early as 1991 (Galera and Borzaga, 2009; Defourny and Nyssens, 2012).[34]

Recently though, there has been great interest in using privately owned, for-profit legal forms to conduct social enterprise (Brewer et al., 2014). This renewed interest in the conventional for-profit form primarily stems from dissatisfaction with a previously mentioned, fundamental legal characteristic of the nonprofit form: the nondistribution constraint.[35] Except in rare and extraordinary circumstances involving mutual benefit organizations (e.g., homeowners' associations, trade associations, etc.), nonprofits do not issue equity and do not have owners. Legally, a nonprofit may be controlled by individuals or by other organizations through board membership or by some type of voting interest in the nonprofit, but nonprofits neither issue shares nor have shareholders. Generally, the net assets of a nonprofit organization remaining upon liquidation (if any) are required to be passed to another nonprofit or to the government, not to private interests (Brewer, 2015).

Similarly, although not subject to the nondistribution constraint, conventional cooperatives do not offer private equity and capital raising as part of their fundamental legal characteristics (Defourny and Nyssens, 2012). Rather, cooperatives primarily operate to benefit members, not necessarily outside social or environmental stakeholders.

Yet, even though many modern-day entrepreneurs and business leaders fully embrace the *stakeholder*-benefit (as opposed to shareholder- or member-benefit) aspect of social enterprise, they are not willing to forgo *shareholder* benefit entirely. Perhaps even more importantly, many entrepreneurs do not wish to cut off equity (shares) as a way to raise capital to fund their social enterprise (Brewer, 2012). Thus, social entrepreneurs, mindful of the nondistribution constraint and the member-/worker-centric nature of conventional cooperatives, often turn to private, for-profit legal forms to organize their social enterprise. Given, however, the strong, profitmaking legal instinct of these conventional for-profit forms, the result is predictable, especially in the USA where the law is highly polarized between the private sector and the voluntary sector. Social entrepreneurs using the conventional for-profit form often find that they must fight hard against the legally accepted, profit-maximization instinct of the form. Social entrepreneurs in Europe or elsewhere outside the USA arguably face less pressure to maximize profits under conventional for-profit legal forms, particularly under relatively new laws that embrace social enterprise, but the profit versus social purpose tension nevertheless remains (Brakman Reiser, forthcoming).

US LAW AND THE CASE OF *EBAY DOMESTIC HOLDINGS, INC.* V. *NEWMARK*

Recent litigation in the USA underscores the point. The Chancery Court in the State of Delaware is the leading court in the USA for litigating corporate governance disputes. In the 2010 case of *eBay Domestic Holdings, Inc.* v. *Newmark*,[36] eBay became a minority shareholder in Craigslist, the online classified website. Craigslist offers free classifieds, does not sell advertising on its websites, and has relatively few employees. Craigslist primarily makes its very modest revenue from certain online job postings and New York City apartment listings. Nonetheless, Craigslist is the market leader for classified advertising. Historically, however, the company has operated more like a community service than an online auction like eBay. Unbeknownst to Craigslist's controlling shareholder-directors, Craig Newmark and Jim Buckmaster, at the time eBay acquired a minority stake in Craigslist it had the ulterior motive of taking over Craigslist to make the company more profitable, thereby boosting eBay's revenues.

When Newmark and Buckmaster eventually discovered eBay's ulterior motive, they sought to implement a shareholder rights plan that would allow them and their heirs to retain perpetual control of Craigslist and forever preserve its community-service culture. In response, eBay filed suit in Delaware Chancery Court to strike down the shareholder rights plan.

After hearing compelling arguments from both parties, the Delaware Chancery Court ultimately sided with eBay and struck down the shareholder rights plan. Furthermore, in its written opinion, the court made some fairly revealing remarks about Delaware corporate law and the ultimate purpose of a Delaware for-profit corporation:

> I cannot accept as valid. . .a corporate policy that specifically, clearly, and admittedly seeks *not* to maximize the economic value of a for-profit Delaware corporation for the benefit of its stockholders.[37]

And:

> Having chosen a for-profit corporate form, the Craigslist directors are bound
> by the fiduciary duties and standards that accompany that form. . .[includ-
> ing] acting to promote the value of the corporation for the benefit of its
> stockholders. . . The "Inc." after the company name has to mean at least that.[38]

Thus, the *eBay Domestic Holdings, Inc.* v. *Newmark* case reminds us that
adoption of the conventional for-profit form in the USA[39] carries with it
the inherent legal purpose ("instinct") of that form: shareholder wealth
maximization.

On the other hand, *eBay Domestic Holdings, Inc.* v. *Newmark* is a unique
case. First, although Delaware is by far the leading state in the USA with
respect to corporate jurisprudence, Delaware has not adopted a so-called
"constituency statute." A number of other US states have adopted constituency statutes, and consequently the corporate law of those states
expressly allows directors to consider stakeholder interests (e.g., employees) alongside shareholder interests when making decisions regarding the
corporation. The outcome in *eBay Domestic Holdings, Inc.* v. *Newmark*
might have been different if Craigslist had incorporated in a US state with
a constituency statute. That is, the business law of a constituency-statute
state might have allowed Newmark and Buckmaster, as directors, to
consider Craigslist's corporate culture of community service when adopting the shareholder rights plan. In addition, even under Delaware law, if
Newmark and Buckmaster had justified the adoption of the shareholder
rights plan on the basis of preserving or enhancing the long-term value of
Craigslist's shares, instead of expressly disavowing any such motive, the
outcome might have been different.

As illustrated by *eBay Domestic Holdings, Inc.* v. *Newmark*, US business law defaults toward profit maximization as the ultimate purpose
("instinct") of for-profit entities (Strine, 2012). Until recently, then, social
entrepreneurs in the USA leaned toward the nonprofit legal form. The
other private sector legal form, a conventional cooperative, could serve
social entrepreneurs in the USA, but because the primary purpose of US
cooperatives is to benefit either members or workers, they are less accommodating than the nonprofit legal form. Only since 2008 have specialized "hybrid" for-profit legal forms existed in the USA expressly for the
purpose of engaging in social enterprise.[40]

As discussed further below, the conventional for-profit and cooperative laws of Europe and certain other countries are more accommodating
for social enterprise organizations than US law (Orrick, Herrington &
Sutcliffe, LLP et al., 2014 [2016]).

THE "CHAMELEON" ALTERNATIVE IN THE USA: THE LIMITED LIABILITY COMPANY

As established above, US business law naturally resists including a social or environmental mission within a conventional for-profit organization's stated purpose. This has led to the adoption of specialized for-profit legal forms in the USA (discussed further below) expressly designed for social enterprise. Nevertheless, since the early 1990s US business law has authorized a particular type of for-profit legal form easily adaptable to the pursuit of both profits and a social or environmental mission: the limited liability company (LLC) (Brewer, 2012).

LLCs in the USA can be attractive to the social entrepreneur because they offer liability protection like a corporation, but they also permit the existence of a nonbusiness purpose alongside a business purpose. In other words, a social entrepreneur can include within an LLC's governing documents a provision that requires the LLC to pursue social or environmental goals coextensively with profits or even at the expense of profits (Brewer, 2015). Some US jurisdictions go even further to permit nonprofit LLCs (ibid.). On the other hand, LLCs have not attracted as much attention by social entrepreneurs because the US federal income tax treatment of LLCs is complex. Furthermore, because they are generally highly negotiated creatures of contract instead of products of well-understood, pre-existing statutory rules and regulations, many investors prefer the certainty and predictability of US (especially Delaware) corporations over the LLC (Brewer et al., 2014).

EUROPEAN PERSPECTIVE: ADAPTATION OF COOPERATIVE AND FOR-PROFIT FORMS

Perhaps a byproduct of the stronger role of government in fostering public welfare, the law in Europe separating the private sector from the voluntary sector is not as polarized as in the USA (Orrick, Herrington & Sutcliffe, LLP et al., 2014 [2016]; Brakman Reiser, forthcoming). Consequently, the legal obstacles in Europe to forming, capitalizing, and operating a conventional for-profit or cooperative entity that adopts a social (not profit-maximizing) purpose are less challenging (Orrick, Herrington & Sutcliffe, LLP et al., 2014 [2016]; European Social Enterprise Law Association [ESELA], 2015). Less challenging, however, does not mean simple.

Unlike their counterparts in the USA, post-1900 social entrepreneurs in Europe did not routinely adopt the nonprofit legal form. As discussed further in Chapter 9, the nonprofit sector in Europe is not as robust or as independent as in the USA (Defourny and Nyssens, 2012). In addition, under the laws of most European countries, nonprofits are generally restricted from engaging in "trading" (i.e., normal commercial) activities. Instead, the predominant role of European nonprofits is to receive donations and use the proceeds therefrom to perform strictly charitable activities (ibid.). Thus, commercial nonprofits like Goodwill Industries or Habitat for Humanity in the USA are less prevalent in Europe. In addition, most European nonprofit legal forms are subject to the familiar nondistribution constraint imposed upon US nonprofits. As a result, social entrepreneurs in Europe historically have leaned toward the cooperative legal form (Brakman Reiser, forthcoming).

Italy is arguably the first country to recognize social enterprise as a unique way of conceptualizing an organization (Galera and Borzaga, 2009; Defourny and Nyssens, 2012). As Chapter 9 explains, conventional cooperatives were initially the chosen legal form for social enterprise organizations in Italy. The cooperative legal form offers liability protection, the ability to conduct commercial activities, and the legal authority to pursue community (not private) benefit (Brakman Reiser, forthcoming). Then, in 1991 Italy authorized the "social cooperative" as a modification on the cooperative form. Italian social cooperatives are required to pursue "the general benefit" of the community and "the social integration of citizens." Italian social cooperatives generally cannot distribute profits in excess of 2 percent more than the rate paid on Italian Post Service bonds. Additionally, Italian social cooperatives are of two distinct types: Type A provides social services such as healthcare and education, and Type B provides job training and employment, especially for disadvantaged individuals. Special information and financial reporting obligations also apply to Italian social cooperatives (Orrick, Herrington & Sutcliffe, LLP et al., 2014 [2016]; Brakman Reiser, forthcoming).

After Italy's adoption of the social cooperative in 1991, several other European countries followed with their own modified cooperative forms for social enterprise including France ("collective interest cooperative society"); Greece ("social cooperative with limited liability"); Poland ("social cooperative"); Portugal ("social solidarity cooperative"); and Spain ("social initiative cooperative") (ESELA, 2015; Brakman Reiser, forthcoming).

Then, in 2006 Italy was at the forefront again with the passage of legislation defining "social enterprise" under Italian law. The new law permitted most Italian legal forms (including private associations, nonprofit foundations, and noncooperative legal forms) to qualify; however, private companies so qualifying are subject to the nondistribution constraint (Fici, 2006). Thus, within our six categories of "animals" in the zoo (commercial nonprofits, social cooperatives, social businesses, sustainable businesses, public–private partnerships, and public sector social enterprises) an Italian private company qualifying as a "social enterprise" is closer to a commercial nonprofit than a social business or sustainable business.[41]

In 1995, Belgium took a slightly different approach with respect to authorizing legal forms designed for social enterprise. Belgium adopted legislation creating a social purpose company ("Sociétés à Finalité Sociale" or SFS). A Belgian SFS, including a nonprofit, may engage in commercial activity unlike other Belgian nonprofits. Nevertheless, a Belgium SFS, including one formed as a for-profit entity, must limit profit distributions to no more than 6 percent of an investor's contributed capital and upon dissolution must distribute all assets (after payment of creditors and limited returns to investors) to a company or charity that furthers the SFS's social purpose. Belgian SFS companies are also subject to additional reporting requirements (Brakman Reiser, forthcoming). Ultimately, then, designation as a Belgian SFS is not an entirely new legal form, but rather constitutes acceptance of certain legal restraints superimposed upon a standard Belgian legal form.[42] Thus, within the context of our social enterprise zoo, the Belgian SFS could be considered either a commercial nonprofit, a sustainable business, or a social business.

Although Italy may be regarded as the first country to identity social enterprise as unique, the United Kingdom arguably provides the strongest government support to such organizations (Nicholls, 2010). As discussed in Chapter 9, Social Enterprise London, a nongovernmental entity, began to promote the concept of social enterprise and modernization of cooperative law in the UK in 1997. Then, in 2001, a Social Enterprise Unit within the UK's Department of Trade and Industry was established. The Social Enterprise Unit promulgated a definition of social enterprise as "a business with primarily social objectives, whose surpluses are principally reinvested for that purpose in the business or community, rather than being driven by the need to maximize profit for shareholders and owners" (Department of Trade and Industry, 2002, p. 7). Further, effective in 2005, the United Kingdom amended its for-profit companies law to create a distinct for-profit, noncooperative legal form, the community interest company (CIC). At the same time, the UK established the Office of the Regulator of Community Interest Companies. CICs are discussed further below in the category of exclusive, hybrid legal forms for social enterprise.

Last but not least, in 2014, France authorized a new for-profit, noncooperative legal form for social enterprise, the "Enterprise ESS." Prior to 2014 France had authorized social cooperatives, the "Société Coopérative d'Intérêt Collectif" or SCIC, but the Enterprise ESS goes further to accommodate the needs of social entrepreneurs. The Enterprise ESS is a for-profit legal form with a legally mandated social mission. As such, it falls in the category of exclusive, hybrid legal forms for social enterprise like the UK's CIC and is discussed further below.

Necessarily over-generalizing, legal forms used for social enterprise elsewhere in Europe predominantly consist of traditional cooperatives or for-profit business organizations; however, the governance, management, operations, activities, and revenue of the enterprise is directed toward accomplishing a social or environmental mission rather than profit maximization (ESELA, 2015). Conventional European business law is generally more flexible than US business law in this regard (Orrick, Herrington & Sutcliffe, LLP et al., 2014 [2016]; ESELA, 2015).[43]

2014 STUDY OF FOR-PROFIT BUSINESS LAW IN G8 COUNTRIES

Culminating in 2014, and as amended in 2016, the law firm of Orrick, Herrington & Sutcliffe, LLP, and the Thomson Reuters Foundation conducted a study of the availability of legal forms for social enterprise in the G8 countries.[44] The Orrick, Herrington & Sutcliffe, LLP et al. study (2014 [2016]) focused particularly on for-profit legal forms, not adaptations of cooperative or nonprofit forms. The study concludes that the G8 countries fall into three categories with respect to the use of for-profit legal forms for social enterprise:

- The first category of countries (consisting of Japan and Russia) have no specialized for-profit legal forms for conducting social enterprise and a profit-maximization purpose remains paramount in such entities (like conventional US for-profit entities).
- A second category of countries (consisting of the UK, France, Germany, and Italy)[45] also have no *exclusive* for-profit legal form for social enterprise, but the business law of these countries allows a social purpose to be included in a for-profit entity's formative documents. As explained, among these countries, Italy's "social enterprise" designation, Belgium's SFS, and the UK's CIC lead by establishing specific requirements in order for a conventional for-profit organization to be considered a social enterprise.
- The third category of countries (consisting of Canada and the USA, and now Italy and France)[46] authorize exclusive for-profit legal forms for social enterprise. Conventional for-profit legal forms in these countries can also house social enterprise organizations, but

the historical profit-maximization "instinct" of such conventional forms is problematic.

EXCLUSIVE, HYBRID LEGAL FORMS IN THE USA, UK, ITALY, FRANCE AND CANADA

United States

Due to the inadequacy or perceived inadequacy of conventional legal forms, especially in the USA, business law is rapidly evolving to create new, hybrid legal forms better suited to social enterprise. This trend in the law is especially evident with respect to classic for-profit legal forms. Historically, Italy and the United Kingdom have been ahead of the United States in this regard. The USA largely ignored developments in social enterprise law until approximately 2008. Since that time though, various states across the USA seem to be racing to produce new and different hybrid legal forms for social enterprise.[47] These new hybrid legal entities are social enterprise organizations *exclusively*, like the British CIC (discussed above and further below); the French Enterprise ESS (discussed below); and the Italian benefit corporation (discussed below).[48] Ironically, social enterprise innovation in US business law may surpass other jurisdictions in the world precisely because traditional US business law is hostile toward mixing social or environmental purposes with profitmaking purposes.

To some US scholars and practitioners, a conventional or hybrid organization that intentionally and overtly blends the legal norms of for-profit, nonprofit, and cooperative entities is either a distraction or an anathema (Kleinberger, 2010). To some US politicians, such hybrids are "fence sitter[s]" and "a waste of time."[49] Curiously, some in the US nonprofit sector view social enterprise as an existential threat (Dey et al., 2006).

The vast majority of legal observers though, recognize social enterprise as a novel, desirable way of conducting business. Those same observers, however, remain skeptical because the legal infrastructure to identify, regulate, and govern social enterprise is nascent and will take significant time to develop (Brewer, 2012; Tyler et al., 2015; Brakman Reiser, forthcoming).

In short, the legitimization process for US social enterprise law is just beginning.[50] Nonetheless, as of this writing, 39 states in the USA legally authorize hybrid legal forms for conducting social enterprise.[51] Broadly speaking, there are three such hybrid forms: the benefit corporation, the social purpose corporation, and the low-profit limited liability company (L3C).

US benefit corporation

Of the 39 states in the USA enacting some type of social enterprise legal form, 30 of those states plus the District of Columbia have authorized benefit corporations. Maryland was the first state to pass benefit corporation legislation in 2010, and in only five years 29 more states (including Delaware) have followed (Brewer et al., 2014).

Although exclusively designed for social enterprise organizations, a benefit corporation is not an unprecedented legal entity. Instead, it is a variant of a state's regular business corporation.[52] A US benefit corporation is neither subject to an asset lock nor required to limit shareholder distributions. Unlike, however, a regular US business corporation that primarily pursues profits, a benefit corporation must also (1) pursue a "general public benefit"; (2) consider nonfinancial interests of its shareholders and other stakeholders when making decisions; and (3) issue a report on how well it is achieving its overall social and environmental mission (American Bar Association, 2013). The definition of "general public benefit" in the enabling legislation is a "material positive impact on society and the environment."[53] The pursuit of a "general public benefit" is *required*; it is not optional as is the case with regular US corporations that have adopted constituency statute language in their articles of incorporation. Thus, benefit corporations are for-profit corporations that will generate revenue and earn profits, but that will do so in a manner benefitting society *and* the environment as well as shareholders.[54]

The legal mandate to produce a "general public benefit" is the primary distinguishing feature of the benefit corporation.[55] Theoretically (Clark et al., 2013), the general public benefit requirement makes benefit corporations so-called "triple bottom line" (profits, people, *and* planet) companies, not legal entities that either will pursue a social *or* environmental purpose (like social purpose corporations discussed below) *or* will consider other purposes along with profitmaking (like regular corporations subject to a constituency statute). The theory of mandating a triple bottom line, however, has yet to be tested, and weak remedy provisions in most benefit corporation statutes across the USA makes real enforcement of the general public benefit mandate suspect (Brewer et al., 2014; Brakman Reiser, forthcoming).

Perhaps not surprisingly, the general public benefit mandate has also been the chief source of criticism of the benefit corporation. Critics maintain that requiring directors to satisfy such a broad, diverse array of interests (i.e., shareholders, employees, vendors, creditors, the community, and the environment) all at the same time is self-defeating because serving multiple masters is impossible (Murray, 2012). Nonetheless, the purpose of creating a broad public benefit beyond the pecuniary interests of shareholders is central to US benefit corporation legislation.

A US benefit corporation properly falls within the zoo's social business or sustainable business category.

US social purpose corporation

Five states authorize social purpose corporations: California, Florida, Minnesota, Texas, and Washington (Brewer et al., 2014). In essence, the social purpose corporation arguably solves the "multiple masters" problem. That is, a criticism of the benefit corporation is that it requires the directors to consider too many diverse interests in pursuit of its goal of providing an overall "general public benefit." As a result, the critics claim, the benefit corporation will effectively have no master and will accomplish little good. A social purpose corporation, however, will have a focused purpose and mission (e.g., wind energy, not jobs or community benefit), thereby providing clear guidance to directors and increasing the likelihood of success, at least with respect to the chosen social or environmental purpose.

Unlike a benefit corporation, then, a social purpose corporation need only pursue and attempt to accomplish the specific purpose or purposes articulated in its articles of incorporation, rather than a general public benefit. Generally, the specific alternative purpose(s) are as follows: (1) one or more enumerated charitable or public purpose activities that could be carried out by a nonprofit corporation providing public benefits and/or (2) promoting positive short-term or long-term effects (or minimizing adverse short-term or long-term effects) upon any one or more of (a) the corporation's employees, suppliers, customers, and creditors; (b) the community and society; and/or (c) the environment.[56] The specific purpose(s) must be contained in the social purpose corporation's articles of incorporation. Note, however, that (except for California) unless the articles of incorporation explicitly so state, the directors are *not required* to consider the stated social or environmental purpose(s) of the social purpose corporation. In this regard, the social purpose corporation is akin to a regular corporation that has adopted constituency language in its articles of incorporation. Furthermore, some argue that a social purpose corporation is only a "double bottom line" (profits and people *or* planet) company as opposed to a "triple bottom line" company like the benefit corporation.[57]

US social purpose corporations fall within the social business or sustainable business categories in the zoo.

US low-profit limited liability company

Vermont first authorized the low-profit limited liability company (L3C) in 2008.[58] Since that time, only eight other states have passed L3C statutes, and none have passed such legislation since 2011 (Brewer, 2015). Moreover, North Carolina repealed its L3C statute effective 1 January 2014.[59]

The L3C is not so much an outgrowth of for-profit social enterprise as it is an attempt to facilitate and encourage program-related investments (PRIs) in the USA. PRIs are special types of investments made by US tax-exempt private foundations[60] (see also Chapter 8). PRIs are special because they can simultaneously be charitable and profitable. For example, a low interest rate loan from a tax-exempt private foundation to encourage a profitable manufacturer to build a new plant in a job-stricken area can be a PRI.[61]

Knowledgeable scholars, practitioners, and private foundation managers believe that encouraging PRIs is a laudable goal (Lion and Mancino, 2012), and apparently even the US Treasury Department agrees, as evidenced by recently finalized regulations with new examples of PRIs.[62]

Nevertheless, despite the consensus for encouraging PRIs, the L3C has not garnered much support and has been the subject of strong criticism (Bishop, 2010; Callison and Vestal, 2010; Kleinberger, 2010). The American Bar Association's Business Law Section's Committee on Limited Liability Companies, Partnerships, and Unincorporated Entities and Committee on Nonprofit Organizations jointly oppose L3Cs.[63] As noted above, effective 1 January 2014, North Carolina repealed its L3C statute.[64] The L3C also has a number of technical deficiencies and weaknesses (Brewer, 2013). Further passage of L3C statutes across the USA is unlikely.

On the other hand, the L3C receives praise for being the only for-profit hybrid legal form that actually prioritizes charitable and educational purposes over profitmaking purposes. Thus, the argument goes, L3Cs are superior to benefit corporations and social purpose corporations if the social entrepreneur truly desires to elevate mission over profitability (Tyler, 2010).

United Kingdom

As mentioned above, the United Kingdom, along with Italy, is a leading jurisdiction with regard to fostering social enterprise. To wit, in 2005 the United Kingdom amended its companies law to authorize strictly for-profit legal forms to elect to be treated as community interest companies or CICs. A CIC must pursue a "community benefit," must abide by a modified "asset lock" with respect to its capital and payment of dividends, and must involve stakeholders (not just shareholders) in governance. Finally, in 2014, the United Kingdom extended certain tax benefits to CICs and certain other social ventures (Brakman Reiser, forthcoming). Notably though, qualification as a CIC under UK law turns on abiding by the aforementioned superimposed rules regarding community benefit, an asset lock, and stakeholder governance. Thus, the CIC *arguably* is not an entirely new, exclusive legal form for social enterprise distinct from ordinary for-profit legal forms in the UK[65] Nevertheless, in the author's view the UK's CIC should be regarded as new and distinct and therefore falls into the zoo's social business or sustainable business categories.

Canadian Community Contribution Company and Community Interest Company

Like conventional for-profit legal forms in the USA, Canada's conventional for-profit legal forms generally prioritize profitmaking over a social, environmental, or any other purpose (Tobin and Dalton, 2015). Therefore, the province of British Columbia recently established the "community contribution company" (CCC) to serve as a specialized legal form for social enterprise. British Columbia's CCC correlates closely with the US social purpose corporation, although it does not have its roots in US law. Rather, it follows the lead of Britain's CIC. A CCC under British Columbia's new law is at its core a conventional corporation, but it adopts a social purpose in its articles of incorporation. The CCC (or, as it sometimes is called, C3 – but not the same as a US 501(c)(3) tax-exempt organization) is subject to unique reporting and shareholder meeting requirements to demonstrate the entity's commitment to its stated social purpose. The Canadian CCC also must abide by a modified asset lock similar to the United Kingdom's CIC. On the other hand, it does not appear that the CCC has a clear legal mandate to pursue social *and* environmental purposes along with profits. Thus, some commentators would maintain that a Canadian CCC is only a "double bottom line" company (Clark et al., 2013).[66]

Further, the province of Nova Scotia in Canada has proposed the establishment of a CIC legal form for social enterprise. Like the CCC, Nova Scotia's CIC is substantially similar to the United Kingdom's CIC. As such, a Canadian CIC has a modified asset lock, and it is subject to greater degree of government oversight and regulation than a conventional Canadian corporation. As of this writing, however, Nova Scotia's CIC law had not become effective (Tobin and Dalton, 2015).

Both the existing Canadian CCC and the promised CIC fall within the zoo's social business and sustainable business categories. Otherwise, social entrepreneurs in Canada turn to conventional legal forms to conduct a social enterprise (ibid.).

Italian Benefit Corporation

As mentioned above, Italy very recently (January 2016) passed benefit corporation legislation.[67] Italy's new social enterprise legal form, "Società

Benefit," supplements its pre-existing social cooperative legal form. The Italian Società Benefit appears substantially similar to US benefit corporations. Thus, it would fall within the zoo's category of a social business or a sustainable business. Only time will tell if Italy's Società Benefit will eclipse social cooperatives as the preferred legal form for social enterprise in Italy.

France's Enterprise ESS

Late in 2014, France enacted two pieces of legislation relating to social enterprise. In one statute similar to Italy's 1991 legislation, France authorized a cooperative legal form (the "Société Coopérative d'Intérêt Collectif" or SCIC) that may have both a commercial purpose and a *"utilité sociale"* purpose. A *utilité sociale* purpose is defined as assisting vulnerable persons or activities in order to remedy discrimination or inequalities in society. With another statute, France created a new, private share interest, noncooperative legal form designated as an "Enterprise de l'Economic Sociale et Solidaire" or Enterprise ESS. The Enterprise ESS is the for-profit, noncooperative counterpart to the SCIC, and an Enterprise ESS is likewise limited to a *utilité sociale* purpose that accompanies its otherwise commercial purpose.

Although the French Enterprise ESS is a hybrid for-profit legal entity similar to the US benefit or social purpose corporation, an important distinction is that the *utilité sociale* purpose does not extend to an environmental mission. Thus, unlike the US hybrid legal forms, France's Enterprise ESS has a more limited purpose and presumably would not be used by a social enterprise organization primarily focused upon remedying environmental problems.

THIRD-PARTY CERTIFICATIONS FOR SOCIAL ENTERPRISE ORGANIZATIONS

In addition to the emergence of unique social enterprise legal forms across jurisdictions, third-party, nongovernmental certifications for these organizations are growing. The leading third-party certifier is B Lab (a Pennsylvania-based nonprofit organization). B Lab offers to certify as "B Corps" those for-profit organizations serving social and environmental purposes along with generating profits and shareholder value. Importantly, the B Lab certification turns on serving both social *and* environmental purposes along with generating profits. In other words, assuming they are fulfilling their stated purposes, B Lab generally rates so-called "triple bottom line" companies higher than "double bottom line" companies. Such rating aligns with the benefit corporation versus social purpose corporation distinction under state law in the USA. Perhaps not surprisingly, B Lab plays a prominent role in promoting benefit corporation legislation across the USA and, more lately, outside the USA. Some view B Lab's role in enacting benefit corporation legislation as helpful and important (Clark et al., 2013), while others view B Lab's role as nothing less than officious intermeddling (Callison, 2012; Lidstone, 2014). B Lab does make it clear on its website that "benefit corporations" and "B Corps" are not the same.[68]

To earn B Corp status, a *for-profit* business organization[69] must achieve and maintain a certain score on a scale developed by B Lab.[70] Scoring depends upon numerous factors such as facilitating employee ownership, providing retirement and health plans, encouraging sustainability and other environmentally friendly practices, and serving the community. B Lab monitors and audits its B Corps to ensure that they continue to meet the requirements for certification. B Lab generates revenue to conduct its activities through charitable contributions (i.e., B Lab is a US tax-exempt nonprofit) as well as yearly licensing fees imposed upon B Corps. Annual sales revenue determines a B Corp's yearly license fee.

B Corps do not have any legally recognized status. Moreover, there is no US federal or state government oversight or involvement in B Lab's certification process. Rather, B Corp certification is akin to a good business seal of approval as determined by B Lab.

Furthermore, despite their name, B Corps are not strictly limited to *incorporated* for-profit organizations. All US for-profit legal entities (including regular corporations, benefit corporations, social purpose corporations, LLCs, and L3Cs) may qualify as B Corps. Certification is available for non-US for-profit legal entities as well.

Other third-party certifications similar to B Lab's exist, but they have not been as popular or successful as B Corp certification.

CONCLUSION

Legal form is not and may never be the bellwether of social enterprise organizations. The social entrepreneur must choose among many diverse legal forms, including emerging forms, based upon local law as well as other considerations such as tax treatment, governance, financing, and ownership. These and other considerations are discussed further elsewhere in this book. Legal form is, however, a critically important part of understanding social enterprise organizations. Finally, the zoo metaphor proposed in this book is a useful tool through which to organize and study social enterprise organizations. The zoo metaphor easily embraces the vast diversity of legal forms used by social entrepreneurs while at the same time proposing categories or "species" (commercial nonprofits, social cooperatives, social businesses, sustainable businesses, public–private partnerships, and public sector social enterprises) through which to study social enterprise.

NOTES

1. Apparently, the actual year in which John Hunter, the second Governor of the English colony of New South Wales in Australia, first observed the platypus is not settled, but must have been either 1797 or 1798 (compare Moyal, 2001 at p. 4 with Hall, 1999 at p. 211). British naturalist, Dr. George Shaw, first named the platypus in 1799 (Hall, 1999; Moyal, 2001).
2. Yaso Thiru similarly suggested in 2011 that social enterprise compares to the platypus (Thiru, 2011). To be clear, however, we are not asserting that social enterprise is a breed of animal unto itself like a platypus. Quite the opposite: we assert that many distinct "animals" populate the social enterprise zoo. We are, however, suggesting that the historical process of the discovery and ultimate understanding of the nature of the platypus is similar to the current, ongoing process of the discovery and understanding of social enterprise.
3. Justice Potter Stewart famously used this phrase regarding whether speech (including art, music, and film) is so offensive as to be "obscene" such that it can legally be restricted in the USA despite the First Amendment's general protection of free speech. See Jacobellis v. Ohio, 378 US 184 (1964). Legal efforts in the USA to differentiate between "obscenity," which can be severely curtailed and even banned, versus "speech," which ordinarily cannot be curtailed or banned, have always been controversial and no clear definition of what constitutes an "obscenity" has ever emerged. Nevertheless, the rule remains: speech (including art, music, and film) that is considered "obscene" can be restricted and possibly banned under US law notwithstanding the US Constitution's First Amendment guarantee of free speech.
4. For readers needing a capsule summary of the fundamental legal and tax aspects of conventional forms, see the Appendix to this chapter. Of course, the Appendix provides general legal information only and is not a substitute for legal representation or advice.
5. Of course, one might quibble with this point, especially for undemocratically elected governments, but even autocrats derive their power from the ability to control the public.
6. We are putting aside here activities and arrangements such as trusts and estates that hold assets for the benefit of others, but which do not directly engage in any activity other than managing those assets. See also the related discussion below regarding private foundations and donor-advised funds.
7. The generally accepted profit-maximization norm in the for-profit sector has not always dominated. For instance, prior to the 1900s, for-profit stock companies paying limited dividends – so called "philanthropy and 5 percent" companies – were formed in the USA and Europe, particularly Germany, to provide affordable housing, museums, zoos, and other public benefits (Adam, 2014).
8. See http://www.altria.com/Pages/default.aspx, accessed 14 June 2016.
9. See http://anheuser-busch.com, accessed 14 June 2016.
10. To be distinguished from social cooperatives, which are explained further below.
11. See http://www.landolakes.com, accessed 14 June 2016.
12. See http://www.amul.com, accessed 14 June 2016.
13. See http://communitybuilderscooperative.com, accessed 14 June 2016.
14. See http://www.suma.coop, accessed 14 June 2016.
15. We use the term "operating" here to distinguish nonprofits that directly engage in

charitable or other beneficial activities from pure grant-making nonprofits (e.g., private foundations and donor-advised funds) that do not directly engage in such activities but that financially support operating nonprofits.

16. Some jurisdictions may refer to an "asset lock," which is substantially equivalent to the nondistribution constraint. Others, such as the UK's community interest company (CIC, discussed below), have a modified asset lock.

17. See http://www.care.org/, accessed 14 June 2016.

18. See http://www.actionaid.org, accessed 14 June 2016.

19. As further support for the foregoing assertions in this chapter, the Appendix provides high-level legal and tax information concerning conventional for-profit, cooperative, and nonprofit forms of organizations across multiple jurisdictions around the world.

20. See http://www.betterworldbooks.com, accessed 14 June 2016.

21. See http://www.grameen-info.org, accessed 14 June 2016.

22. See http://www.chcany.org, accessed 14 June 2016.

23. See http://www.escoop.eu, accessed 14 June 2016.

24. We use the term "commercial" here to distinguish operating nonprofits that sell goods or services as part of performing their charitable or other mission (e.g., Habitat for Humanity) from nonprofits that do not engage in any such commercial activity in connection with performing their mission (e.g., a local homeless shelter sponsored by a church). Some nonprofits, more commonly known as foundations or donor-advised funds, usually do not engage in charitable activities directly but instead grant funds to operating nonprofits. In many jurisdictions, there are elaborate rules differentiating and regulating foundations and donor-advised funds, and the term "commercial nonprofits" as used herein is not meant to include such pure-granting organizations.

25. See http://www.habitat.org/restores, accessed 14 June 2016.

26. See https://www.oxfam.org/, accessed 14 June 2016.

27. See http://www.amwater.com, accessed 14 June 2016.

28. See http://www.nhp.gov.in/sites/default/files/pdf/chiranjeevi-yojana-details.pdf, accessed 30 June 2016.

29. See http://fccalandbank.org, accessed 14 June 2016.

30. See http://www.amtrak.com/home and Amtrak, Inc.'s Annual Report: Fiscal Year 2013 (by Ernst & Young, LLP), accessed 14 June 2016 at https://www.amtrak.com/ccurl/1000/237/Amtrak-Annual-Report-2013.pdf.

31. See Hospital Authorities Law, Official Code of Georgia Annotated §31-7-70 et. seq., especially §31-7-74.1 (2015). For further information, see http://www.thefdha.com/about/board-of-trustees.html, accessed 14 June 2016. See also Fulton DeKalb Hospital Authority website (2016), "History," accessed 29 June 2016 at http://thefdha.org/history.html.

32. See the discussion above regarding government-formed social enterprises and public–private partnerships.

33. For instance, one might point to the Middle Ages when monasteries began making and selling wine, cheese, and beer as the origin of the commercial nonprofit form of social enterprise. Or, perhaps one might point to Toynbee Hall (ca. 1884 London) and Hull House (ca. 1889 Chicago), both part of the "settlement house" movement, intended to allow middle class and poor individuals to live and work together with the hope of alleviating poverty. Or, one could certainly point to Morgan Memorial Goodwill Industries (ca. 1895 Boston) where Reverend Edgar J. Helms went door-to-door in Boston's wealthiest neighborhoods collecting donated goods in burlap bags and then hiring unemployed immigrants to refurbish and sell the goods at a profit (Doeringer, 2010).

34. Other jurisdictions with specialized cooperative legal forms for social enterprise include France, Greece, and Poland.

35. Also sometimes referred to outside the USA as an "asset lock."

36. eBay Domestic Holdings, Inc. v. Newmark, 16 A.3d 1 (Del. Ch. 2010).

37. Ibid. at 35.

38. Ibid. at 34.

39. But see the discussion below regarding Delaware's post-2010 adoption of benefit corporation law.
40. See the discussion below of the emerging US hybrid legal forms for social enterprise.
41. As of the submission of the manuscript for this chapter in early 2016, Italy had passed a new "benefit corporation" law, which is discussed further below. Italian "benefit corporations" are apparently not subject to the nondistribution constraint unless they seek to qualify as a "social enterprise" under Italian law. Therefore, an Italian "benefit corporation" not qualifying as a "social enterprise" under Italian law falls within the zoo's category of either a social business or a sustainable business.
42. Similar legal designations exist (or are contemplated under proposed legislation) in Denmark, Luxembourg, and Finland (ESELA, 2015).
43. The European Social Enterprise Law Association has published a thorough report on EU legal entities appropriate for a social enterprise organization (see ESELA, 2015). Furthermore, for a useful website tracking European social enterprise law, see http://esela.eu/maps/, accessed 14 June 2016.
44. Canada, France, Germany, Italy, Japan, Russia, United Kingdom, and United States.
45. But as discussed further below, the original study concluded prior to France's adoption of the Enterprise ESS late in 2014 and Italy's adoption of a benefit corporation statute in 2016. Moreover, due to its CIC legal form, the author would have included the UK in the study's third category along with the USA, Canada, France, and Italy; however, the Orrick Herrington & Sutcliffe, LLP et al. study concludes that the UK's CIC is merely an adaptation of pre-existing for-profit legal forms in the UK, not an exclusive legal form for social enterprise.
46. See note 44 above.
47. Business law in the USA is predominantly the product of state law, not federal law (Brewer et al., 2014). See the Social Enterprise Law Tracker website (http://socentlaw-tracker.org/#/map, accessed 14 June 2016) for up-to-date information on US states adopting hybrid legal forms for social enterprise.
48. Italy just very recently (January 2016) joined the USA, the UK, and France in creating a hybrid form of noncooperative legal entity exclusively designed to house social enterprise organizations. This new Italian form is distinct from the social cooperative that Italy authorized in 1991. See the further discussion in the text at note 67.
49. Governor Paul LePage in comments made in connection with vetoing benefit corporation legislation in Maine. See https://twitter.com/socentlaw_track/status/61338337 2891627520, accessed 14 June 2016.
50. This process in the USA of first ignoring, then heavily criticizing, and then legitimizing social enterprise law has familiar overtones. As trade unionist Nicholas Klein said in a 1918 address to the Amalgamated Clothing Workers of America in Baltimore: "First they ignore you. Then they ridicule you. And then they attack you and want to burn you. And then they build monuments to you. And that is what is going to happen to the Amalgamated Clothing Workers of America." See http://www.csmonitor.com/USA/Politics/2011/0603/Political-misquotes-The-10-most-famous-things-never-actually-said/First-they-ignore-you.-Then-they-laugh-at-you.-Then-they-attack-you.-Then-you-win.-Mohandas-Gandhi, accessed 14 June 2016. Mahatma Ghandi is popularly credited with saying something similar ("First they ignore you, then they laugh at you, then they fight you, then you win"), but apparently he did not (ibid.).
51. See the Social Enterprise Law Tracker website cited in note 47.
52. In Darwinian terms, one might say a "mutation" of a state's regular business corporation.
53. Each state has its own version of benefit corporation legislation. Therefore, the definition of "general public benefit" may vary slightly from state to state.
54. For a comprehensive overview of benefit corporations, see American Bar Association (2013).
55. Again, although some may disagree, in the author's view the legal mandate to produce a general public benefit distinguishes the benefit corporation from the UK's CIC and

Belgium's SFS. That is why the author of this chapter refers to the benefit corporation as a legal entity exclusively designed for social enterprise.

56. See, e.g., Cal. Corp. Code §2602(b)(2).
57. Neither the phrase "double bottom line" nor "triple bottom line" has any meaning whatsoever in established US business law.
58. See Vt. Stat. Ann. tit. 11, §3001(27) (2015).
59. See S.B. 439, 2013–2014 NC General Assembly.
60. See US Internal Revenue Code §4944(c) (2016).
61. See US Treas. Reg. §53.4944-3(b) exs. 4 & 5.
62. Treas. Reg. §53.4944-3(b) exs. 11–19.
63. Letter from Linda J. Rusch, Chair, Am. Bar Ass'n Bus. Law Section, to Steve Simon, Assistant Minority Leader, Minn. House of Representatives (Apr. 19, 2012): see Kleinberger (2012).
64. See S.B. 439, 2013–2014 NC General Assembly.
65. See the text accompanying notes 44 through 46 regarding the Orrick Herrington & Sutcliffe, LLP et al. study that categorizes the UK's CIC as a nonexclusive form of legal entity for social enterprise. Practically speaking, however, the author believes that the UK's CIC is an exclusive form for social enterprise because it must abide by superimposed rules not applicable to regular for-profit legal forms in the UK.
66. See the text accompanying note 53 above.
67. See The Blog: Voice of the B Corporation Community (2015), "Italian parliament approves benefit corporation legal status," 22 December, accessed 14 June 2016 at http://bcorporation.eu/blog/italian-parliament-approves-benefit-corporation-legal-status.
68. See http://benefitcorp.net/businesses/benefit-corporations-and-certified-b-corps, accessed 14 June 2016.
69. Nonprofit organizations are not eligible to be certified as B Corps.
70. See http://bimpactassessment.net/, accessed 14 June 2016.

REFERENCES

Adam, T. (2014), "Profit and philanthropy: stock companies as philanthropic institutions in nineteenth century Germany," *Voluntas*, **25** (2), 337–51.

American Bar Association (ABA) Business Law Section Corporation Laws Committee (2013), "Benefit corporation white paper," *The Business Lawyer*, **63** (4), 1083–110, accessed 2 February 2016 at http://apps.americanbar.org/dch/committee.cfm?com=CL270000.

Bishop, C.G. (2010), "The low-profit LLC (L3C): program related investment by proxy or perversion?," *Arkansas Law Review*, **63** (2), 243–67.

Brakman Reiser, D. (forthcoming), "Alternative business organizations and social enterprise," in E. Heath, B. Kaldis and A. Marcoux (eds), *Routledge Companion to Business Ethics*, London and New York: Routledge.

Brewer, C.V. (2012), "A novel approach to using LLCs for quasi-charitable endeavors (A/K/A 'social enterprise')," *William Mitchell Law Review*, **38**, 678–736.

Brewer, C.V. (2013), "Seven ways to strengthen and improve the L3C," *Regent University Law Review*, **25** (2), 329–50.

Brewer, C.V. (2015), "Nonprofit and charitable uses of LLCs," *Research Handbook on Partnerships, LLCs and Alternative Forms of Business Organizations*, Cheltenham, UK and Northampton, MA, USA: Edward Elgar Publishing, pp. 227–51.

Brewer, C.V., E.S. Minnigh, and R.A. Wexler (2014), "Social enterprise by non-profits and hybrid organizations," *Tax Management Portfolio*, No. 489-1st.

Callison, W.J. (2012), "Putting new sheets on a procrustean bed: how benefit corporations address fiduciary duties, the dangers created and suggestions for change," *American University Business Law Review*, **2** (1), 85–114.

Callison, J.W. and A.W. Vestal (2010), "The L3C illusion: why low-profit limited liability companies will not stimulate socially optimal private foundation investment in entrepreneurial ventures," *Vermont Law Review*, **35**, 273–96.

Clark, W.H., Jr., Drinker Biddle & Reath LLP, and L. Vranka (2013), *The Need and Rationale for the Benefit Corporation: Why it is the Legal Form that Best Addresses the Needs of Social Entrepreneurs, Investors, and, Ultimately, the Public*, White Paper, accessed 2 February 2016 at http://benefitcorp.net/policymakers/benefit-corporation-white-paper.

Defourny, J. and M. Nyssens (2012), "Conceptions of social enterprise in Europe: a comparative perspective with the United States," in B. Gidron and Y. Hasenfeld (eds), *Social Enterprises: An Organizational Perspective*, London: Palgrave Macmillan.

Dehne, A., P. Friedrich, and C. Nam (2008), "Taxation of nonprofit associations in an international comparison," *Nonprofit and Voluntary Sector Quarterly*, **37** (4), 709–29.

Department for Trade and Industry (2002), *Social Enterprise: A Strategy for Success*, accessed 2 February 2016 at http://webarchive.nationalarchives.gov.uk/20070108124358/http://cabinetoffice.gov.uk/third_sector/documents/social_enterprise/se_strategy_2002.pdf.

Dey, P., C. Stayaert, and D. Hjorth (eds) (2006), *The Rhetoric of Social Entrepreneurship: Paralogy and New Language Games in Academic Discourse*, Cheltenham, UK and Northampton, MA, USA: Edward Elgar Publishing.

Doeringer, M.F. (2010), "Fostering social enterprise: a historical and international analysis," *Duke Law Review*, **20** (2), 291–329.

European Social Enterprise Law Association (ESELA) (2015), *Social Enterprise in Europe: Developing Legal Systems Which Support Social Enterprise Growth*, accessed 14 June 2016 at http://esela.eu/wp-content/uploads/2015/11/legal_mapping_publication_051015_web.pdf.

Fici, A. (2006), "The new Italian law on social enterprise," accessed 2 February 2016 at http://www.oecd.org/cfe/leed/37508649.pdf.

Fourth Sector Mapping Initiative (FSMI) (2016), "Background and need," accessed 29 June 2016 at http://www.mapping.fourthsector.net/#!about-fsmi/cee5.

Galera, G. and C. Borzaga (2009), "Social enterprise: an international overview of its conceptual evolution and legal implementation," *Social Enterprise Journal*, **5** (3), 210–28.

Hall, B.K. (1999), "Thinking of biology: the paradoxical platypus," *BioScience*, **49** (3), 211–18.

Hock, D. (2000), *Birth of the Chaordic Age*, San Francisco, CA: Berrett-Koehler Publishers, Inc.

Kleinberger, D.S. (2010), "A myth deconstructed: the 'emperor's new clothes' on the low-profit limited liability company," *The Delaware Journal of Corporate Law*, **35** (3), 879–910.

Kleinberger, D.S. (2012), "ABA Business Law Section on behalf of its committees on LLCs and nonprofit organisations, opposed legislation for low profit limited liability companies (L3Cs)," *William Mitchell College of Law Legal Studies Research Paper Series*, Paper No. 2012-05.

Kleinberger, D.S. and J.W. Callison (2010), "When the law is understood: L3C no," *William Mitchell College of Law Legal Studies Research Paper Series*, Paper No. 2010-07.

Lidstone, H.K. (2014), "The long and winding road to public benefit corporations in Colorado," *The Colorado Lawyer*, **43** (1), 39–50.

Lion, O. and D.M. Mancino (2012), "PRIs – new proposed regulations and the new venture capital," *Taxation of Exempts*, September/October, 3.

Lund, M. and L. Pitman (eds) (2013), *Cooperative Equity and Ownership: An Introduction*, Madison, WI: University of Wisconsin-Madison Center for Cooperatives.

Moyal, A. (2001), *Platypus: The Extraordinary Story of How a Curious Creature Baffled the World*, Washington, DC: Smithsonian Books.

Murray, H.J. (2012), "Choose your own master: social enterprise, certifications, and benefit corporation statutes," *American University Law Review*, **2** (1), 2–53.

Nash, O. (1953), *The Private Dining Room and Other New Verses*, London: J.M. Dent.

Nicholls, A. (2010), "The legitimacy of social entrepreneurship: reflexive isomorphism in a pre-paradigmatic field," *Entrepreneurship Theory and Practice*, **34** (4), 611–33.

Orrick, Herrington & Sutcliffe, LLP, UnLtd, and Thomson Reuters Foundation (2014 [2016]), *Balancing Purpose and Profit*, accessed 29 June 2016 at http://www.trust.org/publications/i/?id=2435372d-3e6d-42d7-a726-a1fe21cba400, as amended 2016, Thomson Reuters Foundation.

Poon, D. (2011), "The emergence and development of social enterprise sectors," *Social Impact Research Experience Journal*, **11**, accessed 14 June 2016 at http://repository.upenn.edu/cgi/viewcontent.cgi?article=1010&context=sire.

Strine, L.E. (2012), "Our continuing struggle with the idea that for-profit corporations seek profit," *Wake Forrest Law Review*, 47, 135–72.

Thiru, Y. (2011), "Social enterprise education: new economics or a platypus?," in G.T. Lumpkin and J.A. Katz (eds), *Social and Sustainable Entrepreneurship (Advances in Entrepreneurship, Firm Emergence and Growth, Volume 13)*, Bingley, UK: Emerald Group Publishing Limited, pp. 175–200.

Thornton, P.H., W. Ocasio, and M. Lounsbury (2012), *The Institutional Logics Perspective: A New Approach to Culture, Structure and Process*, Oxford: Oxford University Press.

Tobin, D.J. and L. Dalton (2015), "The rise of the for-profit, socially responsible corporation in Canada," *Blaney McMurtry LLP*, 29 May, accessed 2 February 2016 at http://www.blaney.com/articles/rise-profit-socially-responsible-corporation-canada.

Tyler, J. (2010), "Negating the problem of having 'two masters': a framework for L3C fiduciary duties and accountability," *Vermont Law Review*, **35** (1), 117–62.

Tyler, J., E. Absher, K. Garman, and A. Luppino (2015), "Producing better mileage: advancing the design and usefulness of hybrid vehicles for social enterprise ventures," *Quinnipiac Law Review*, **33** (2), 235–337.

Young, D.R. (1983 [2013]), *If Not for Profit, for What?*, Digital Reissue, Georgia State University Library, accessed 18 June 2016 at http://scholarworks.gsu.edu/facbooks2013/1/.

APPENDIX: FUNDAMENTAL LEGAL ASPECTS

Conventional For-profit Entities

Jurisdictions around the world typically authorize the formation and operation of specialized legal entities designed to engage primarily in for-profit activities for the pecuniary benefit of private owners. These for-profit entities normally have private owners, managers, and investors, and they primarily engage in business or investment activities strictly for the financial benefit of their private owners, managers, and investors.

Generally speaking (and of course subject to notable exceptions), these legal entities have two variable attributes even though they may be labeled differently from jurisdiction to jurisdiction. The two variable attributes are (1) either full or partial protection of the owners of the entity from legal liability to third parties for the activities of the for-profit; and (2) either entity-level income tax treatment or so-called "flow-through" income tax treatment (meaning the owners, not the entity itself, are subject to tax on the entity's income).

Well-advised for-profit entrepreneurs, including social entrepreneurs, will ordinarily choose a legal entity that offers robust liability protection; however, this choice often comes with increased tax costs. Entrepreneurs who are tax sensitive thus may choose a "flow-through" legal entity – that is, one that is not separately taxed in addition to taxes required to be paid by the owners. But, flow-through legal entities do not always offer robust liability protection and, even where they do, the applicable tax rules are typically complex and administratively burdensome. Regardless, no for-profit legal form is perfect for every circumstance whether the entrepreneur is interested purely in making a profit or is a social entrepreneur for whom profitmaking is not paramount.

Conventional Operating Nonprofits

In addition to for-profit legal entities, most jurisdictions around the world also authorize the formation and operation of nonprofit and often tax-exempt legal entities. The principal distinguishing legal feature of such nonprofit entities is generally the so-called "nondistribution constraint" (also known as an "asset lock" outside the USA). Specifically, the nonprofit has no private equity owners, and the nonprofit's earnings after payment of expenses either accumulates or is distributed to third-party beneficiaries. If the nonprofit is also tax exempt, then it usually is highly regulated and may engage only in limited categories of activities, with the broadest category being "charitable" activities. Moreover, the earnings of the nonprofit may become taxable, or the nonprofit may lose its exempt status, if its activities stray too far from the entity's basis for its tax exemption. Finally, some very specific and highly favored types of qualified tax-exempt entities allow donors to take an income tax deduction for contributions to the organization.

Entrepreneurs and social entrepreneurs not interested in private ownership of an enterprise thus may choose the nonprofit legal form. The nonprofit may or may not qualify for tax-exempt status depending upon whether its activities fall within one or more of the permitted categories. Further, the nonprofit may or may not allow donors to take an income tax deduction for contributions depending upon whether it qualifies for such highly favored status. Regardless, social entrepreneurs choosing the nonprofit form generally understand that they are relinquishing (1) private ownership and (2) unfettered legal control over the entity.

Nonprofits (as well as trusts) can serve as pure grant-making foundations as well, but these nonprofits ordinarily do not engage in any type of commercial activity. Instead, foundation nonprofits (which almost always are tax exempt) generally invest their assets to achieve a market-rate return in order to make grants to operating nonprofits or, occasionally, to deserving individuals.

Conventional Cooperatives

Many jurisdictions around the world authorize cooperative enterprises. Cooperatives operate commercially for the collective benefit of their members, but ordinarily do not accumulate excess surplus. Instead, cooperatives share their limited net earnings with their members in the form of member discounts or services.

Cooperatives normally offer liability protection because they legally exist as conventional for-profit corporations, nonprofit corporations, or some other form of limited liability entity; however, cooperatives elect into special statutory, regulatory, and tax regimes that impose limitations on their activities and investments. Furthermore, cooperatives usually do not have investor-owners. Rather, they have member-owners. These member-owners can be individuals or businesses. In so-called worker cooperatives, the members are employees of the cooperative and thereby benefit. In addition, cooperatives tend to be highly democratic – one vote per member – not controlled based upon proportionate number of shares or other units of ownership.

Entrepreneurs and social entrepreneurs choosing the cooperative form understand that although the entity may engage in commercial activity, they do not hold equity in a cooperative like private owners and investors, and they relinquish decision-making power to members acting collectively.

PART II

How the zoo functions

4. Habitats in the zoo

Janelle A. Kerlin, Thema Monroe-White, and Sandy Zook

INTRODUCTION

Many types of natural habitats are found throughout the world. Every such habitat has unique characteristics that allow it to support specific plant and animal life. Some habitats contain animals not found elsewhere in the world while others are not able to support certain species that are considered commonplace most everywhere else. The same can be said of habitats for social enterprise in different countries if we think of macro-level institutional factors as elements of the habitat (i.e., water, soil, and weather) that give rise to the legal forms and financing mechanisms (plant life) that shape the kinds of social enterprises (animals) that emerge and their relationships (organizational ecology, adaptability, and resilience) with the environment. For social enterprises, these macro-level elements include large socioeconomic factors such as governance style, size of the economy, type of civil society and dependence on international aid that shape the role of government (see Chapter 9) and the types of legal forms and financing mechanisms (see Chapter 8), organizational ecologies (see Chapter 5), and need for adaptable and resilient social enterprise animals (see Chapter 11).

Natural habitats not only influence the presence of specific animals and their numbers, but animals may also evolve over time in response to changes in the elements of their habitat. We have found a similar dynamic process among social enterprises, where changes in specific elements of a habitat may precipitate an adaptive response in a social enterprise sector. For example, changes in the form of government in Chile and Spain led to shifts in the nature of the economy, civil society, and other institutional factors, which in turn led to changes in the social enterprise sector (Fisac-Garcia and Moreno-Romero, 2015; Gatica, 2015). Though this chapter takes a country-level approach, we acknowledge that distinct habitats can be found below the country level as well. Indeed, Fisac-Garcia and Moreno-Romero (2015) also found that in Spain, regional differences in governance have resulted in the emergence of different regional social enterprise habitats across the country.

This chapter takes a macro-institutional approach to identifying the country habitats that influence social enterprise. Indeed, research has increasingly demonstrated that countries appear to actualize social enterprise differently in response to differences in their institutional contexts (see Borzaga and Defourny, 2001; Dacanay, 2004; Kerlin, 2006, 2009; Nyssens, 2006; Defourny and Nyssens, 2008, 2010; Grant, 2008; Nielsen and Samia, 2008; Amin, 2009; Galera and Borzaga, 2009; Bacq and Janssen, 2011; Cooney, 2011, 2012; Defourny and Kim, 2011; Mook et al., 2012; Spear, 2012). In this chapter we consider Kerlin's (2013) macro-institutional social enterprise (MISE) framework, which examines country-level institutional habitats for social enterprise, as well as various qualitative and quantitative work that supports this approach. We then explore the intermediate factor of entrepreneurial opportunity and its influence on the levels of social enterprise among countries and differences in types of social enterprise activities across broad income divides. The results of this research support the idea that macro-institutional approaches to studying social enterprise habitats can help explain the incidence of a broad range of social enterprise "animals" and their prevalence and relationships in different habitats.

SOCIAL ENTERPRISE HABITATS AND THEIR MACRO-LEVEL INSTITUTIONS

Drawing on the theory of historical institutionalism (Thelen, 1999), the MISE framework seeks to explain how institutional context influences social enterprise by examining how formal and informal institutions create causal paths that both shape and constrain newer institutions (Kerlin, 2013). It proposes that the more prominent institutional mechanisms of influence shaping social enterprise include a mixture of international influences, culture, form of government, model of civil society, and stage of economic development (Figure 4.1) (ibid.). From here, Kerlin (2013) builds a preliminary typology of social enterprise country models based on the varying characteristics of these national-level variables and social enterprises in different countries. This overall approach aligns with Salamon et al. (2000) and Salamon and Sokolowski's (2010) social origins approach and similar research that connects national trends in entrepreneurship with government and society (Baumol, 1990; Bosma and Levie, 2010). Importantly, the MISE framework allows countries to retain the unique conceptualizations and practice of social enterprise that stem from their habitats. The framework therefore does not adhere to or support the

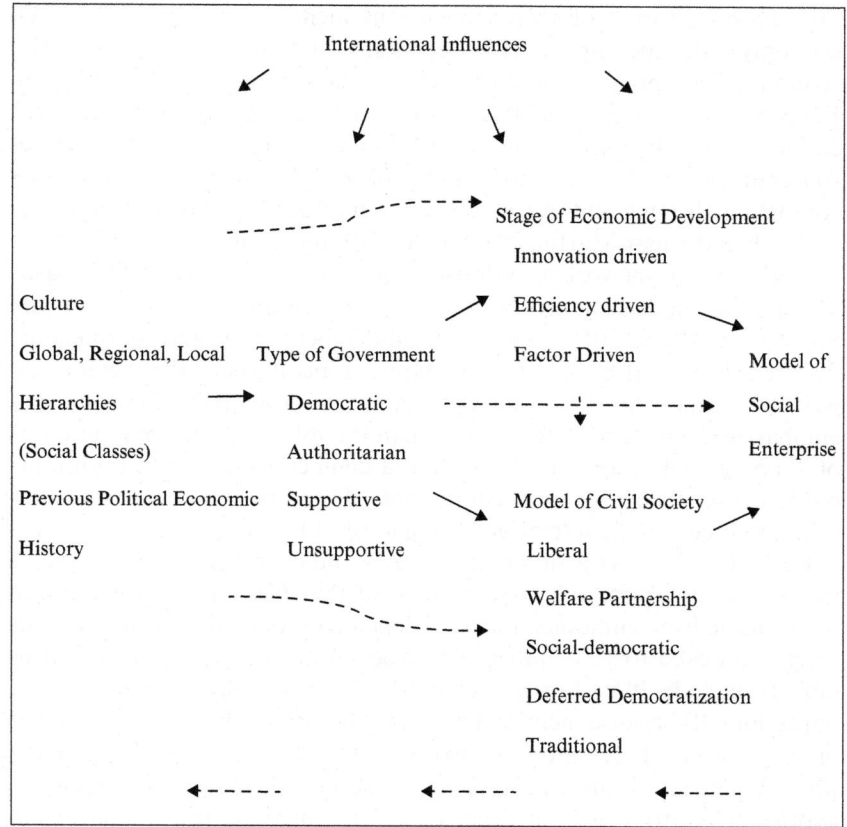

Figure 4.1   A macro-institutional framework for understanding social enterprise country models

creation of a strict universal definition of social enterprise (Kerlin, 2009, 2013). Indeed, one of the purposes of the framework is to help overcome difficulties that can arise in cross-regional communication when a common definition is not in use.

As shown in Figure 4.1, the MISE framework proposes that the type of civil society and economic stage of development in a country are two of the most influential factors determining key characteristics of a given social enterprise sector (Kerlin, 2013). MISE uses the World Economic Forum's (WEF) Global Competitiveness Index (GCI), which calculates the relative economic competitiveness of a country using 12 measures to construct a typology of economic development (Schwab and Sala-i-Martin, 2011). Countries are then classified into groups or stages according to their scores on each of these dimensions including: factor-driven (FD) economy, efficiency-driven (ED) economy and innovation-driven (ID) economy. Entrepreneurship varies within these three economy types. In FD economies entrepreneurship is primarily necessity based through self-employment, while small and medium-sized manufacturing dominates ED countries, and ID countries are typically wealthier, with enterprises competing through the introduction of innovative goods and processes (Schwab and Sala-i-Martin, 2011; Monroe-White et al., 2015).

The MISE framework also draws on a definition of civil society based on the five models of civil society sectors developed by Salamon and Sokolowski (2009, 2010): liberal, social-democratic, welfare partnership, deferred democratization, and traditional. Liberal, social-democratic and welfare partnership are primarily found in developed countries that emphasize the welfare state more so than the role of government in terms of shaping civil society (ibid.). Deferred democratization and traditional models of civil society are predominantly found in less-developed countries and focus on the role of government (ibid.).

Kerlin (2013) uses the different economy and civil society types to create five social enterprise country models: sustainable subsistence, autonomous mutualism, enmeshed focused, dependent focused and autonomous diverse matched to 12 countries. Monroe-White et al. (2015) expand this table to include 30 countries (Table 4.1). Note that several countries are borderline (B) because their model of civil society is in between two models of civil society. There are also two transitional social enterprise models where countries are in transition from one model of social enterprise to another. Countries are not expected to stay in these transitional situations long and thus their current places in the table are not considered permanent model types. For example, the Slovak Republic, Hungary, the Czech Republic, and South Africa are categorized as transitional, indicating that the habitats of these countries are changing. As mentioned earlier, this is similar to the transitions Chile and Spain experienced in the twentieth century that led to adaptations in their social enterprise sector (Fisac-Garcia and Moreno-Romero, 2015; Gatica, 2015). Table 4.2 outlines the five models of social enterprise and the primary attributes of each model.[1]

COMPARATIVE QUALITATIVE STUDIES OF COUNTRY HABITATS FOR SOCIAL ENTERPRISE

Thus far, qualitative support for the MISE framework has included studies from overarching regional and country-level research on East-Central

Table 4.1   Models of social enterprise: expanded to 30 countries

Civil Society	Economy Type		
	Factor driven	Efficiency driven	Innovation driven
Liberal	–	–	Autonomous diverse: United States, United Kingdom, Switzerland (B)
Welfare partnership	–	–	Dependent focused: France, Israel, Netherlands, Belgium, Denmark (B), Italy, Germany, Japan (B), Spain (B)
Social-democratic	–	–	Enmeshed focused: Sweden, Austria, Norway, Finland (B)
Deferred democratization	–	Autonomous mutualism: Argentina (B), Ukraine, Brazil, Peru, Chile (B), Romania (B), Russia, Colombia (B)	Transitional model: Slovak Republic, Hungary (B), Czech Republic (B)
Traditional	Sustainable subsistence: Zimbabwe, Uganda	Transitional model: South Africa (B)	–

Note: B = borderline country for model of civil society.

Source: From Kerlin (2013).

Europe, Southeast Asia, Western Europe, Argentina, Australia, Austria, Chile, Japan, South Korea, Spain, Sweden, United States, Zimbabwe, and Zambia (Kerlin, 2009, 2013; Lehner, 2011; Fisac-Garcia and Moreno-Romero, 2015; Gatica, 2015; Jeong, 2015; Mason and Barraket, 2015). Here, we review some of the qualitative research found in Kerlin (2013) on Zimbabwe, Argentina, Italy, Sweden, and the United States to provide examples of how institutions in different country habitats can

Table 4.2   Social enterprise models and attributes

Model of Social Enterprise	Attributes
Sustainable subsistence model	Factor-driven stage of economic development: low GDP per capita that necessitates need-based entrepreneurship Traditional civil society model: builds on traditional forms of social interaction in small village groups Associated with African and Southeast Asian societies Characterized by individualized small group efforts of entrepreneurs to provide poverty relief through subsistence self-employment Activities supported by international aid and often appear as microfinance-supported projects due to the need to provide a sustainable form of assistance and improve small-scale economic development
Autonomous mutualism	Efficiency-driven stage of economic development: higher GDP per capita and more possibility for drawing on larger pooled resources for entrepreneurship, either formally or informally Deferred democracy civil society model: social enterprises work autonomously from and sometimes in opposition to the state to address perceived deficiencies in state policies Primarily found in South American and East-Central European countries Larger social enterprise sector than sustainable subsistence model Consists of small and medium-sized businesses filling gaps left by economic markets and government welfare programs Social enterprise most likely to participate in and be viewed as a form of social activism in this model because of tradition of civil society working in opposition to an authoritarian state
Dependent focused	Innovation-driven stage: availability of a high degree of wealth necessary to support a large welfare state, as well as government policies and other institutions supportive of innovative entrepreneurship Welfare partnership: unusually large civil society sector heavily engaged in service and supported by government Primarily found in continental Western Europe Typically smaller social enterprise sector due to a large welfare state: relies on state subsidies for implementation

Table 4.2   (continued)

Model of Social Enterprise	Attributes
Autonomous diverse	Innovation-driven stage: may have greater supply and demand for diverse social enterprise services compared to enmeshed focused and autonomous diverse models due to society's desire for particular goods and services and ability to pay Liberal model of civil society: autonomous from the state Primarily associated with the United States and Australia Autonomy from state limits subsidies available and encourages use of social enterprise as an income generator for organizations that may be independent from programming for participants Highly supportive environment for innovative entrepreneurialism and a high level of wealth that supports private philanthropy for social enterprise
Enmeshed focused	Innovation-driven stage: availability of a high degree of wealth necessary to support a large welfare state, as well as government policies and other institutions supportive of innovative entrepreneurship Social-democratic model: large state presence and support for social welfare spending and relatively small NGO employment sector Primarily found in continental Western Europe Similar to dependent focused, but there are fewer and less diverse kinds of social enterprises, many of which have close ties with specific public policies that may have spurred their development

influence social enterprise country models according to the MISE framework. Table 4.3 shows the socioeconomic data for the five countries used in tracking large-scale differences across the five institutions relevant to social enterprise. Table 4.4 draws on currently available empirical evidence to show the differences in characteristics of social enterprise for the same five countries.[2]

Zimbabwe

Zimbabwe has a long and varied history of pre-colonial, colonial, and then authoritarian restrictions that interrupted and limited the development of the economy and civil society and helped shape the present state – a largely authoritarian-run "democracy." However, cultural indicators show that

Table 4.3 *Socioeconomic data for five countries*[a]

	Culture[b]		Welfare State[c,d]	Governance[e]			Economy[f]	GCI[i] ranking (1= most competitive)	Civil Society[g]	Intl Aid[h]
				(Percentile rank/governance score)						
	In-group collectivism (practices)	Uncertainty avoidance (values)	Public spending on health/education (% of GDP)	Regulatory quality (0–100/ –2.5 to +2.5)	Rule of law (0–100/ –2.5 to +2.5)	Control of corruption (0–100/ –2.5 to +2.5)	Economic development stage		Sector model (B = borderline)	Per capita (in US$)
Zimbabwe	5.57	4.73	5.16	1.4/–2.29	0.9/–1.91	1.9/–1.49	Factor	136	Traditional (B) (assumed)	52
Argentina	5.51	4.66	9.94	21/–0.9	29.7/–0.66	38.1/–0.49	Efficiency	87	Deferred (B) democratization	3
Italy	4.94	4.47	10.60	77.6/+0.9	62.7/+0.39	59/+0.05	Innovation	48	Welfare partnership (B)	–
United States	4.25	4	12.43	89.5/+1.36	91.5/+1.53	85.2/+1.18	Innovation	4	Liberal	–
Sweden	3.66	3.60	13.68	96.7/+1.66	99.5/+1.93	98.6/+2.23	Innovation	2	Social-democratic	–

Notes:

a. The information in Table 4.3 largely draws on datasets from 2010–11 to be consistent with data used in Monroe-White's quantitative analysis as well as the qualitative discussion in Kerlin's 2009 book on social enterprise in different countries and regions also used in this chapter.

b. *Source:* The Global Leadership and Organizational Behavior Effectiveness (GLOBE) Research Project is a study of 62 cultures/countries reported in *Culture, Leadership, and Organizations: The GLOBE Study of 62 Societies* (House et al., 2004). The study examines culture through nine different dimensions each in terms of practices and values. This chapter uses the study's findings for two dimensions: in-group collectivism in societal practices, which is "the degree to which individuals express pride, loyalty, and cohesiveness in their organizations or families" (p. 12) (on a scale of 1–7 where higher scores indicate greater in-group collectivism in practice) and uncertainty avoidance in societal values, which is "the extent to which members of an organization or society *should* strive to avoid uncertainty by relying on established social norms, rituals, and bureaucratic practices" (p. 11) (on a scale of 1–7 where higher scores indicate greater uncertainty avoidance). Findings for both dimensions correlate with findings for similar dimensions in Geert Hofstede's (1980, 2001) pioneering work, *Culture's Consequences.* Thus work based on Hofstede's dimensions and findings is also likely to hold true for GLOBE findings in these areas.

c. *Sources:* World Bank (2010b), *World Development Indicators.* Education spending data are from the United Nations Educational, Scientific, and Cultural Organization (UNESCO) Institute for Statistics. Health spending data are from the World Health Organization, *World Health Report* and updates and from the OECD for its member countries, supplemented by World Bank poverty assessments and country and sector studies. Education and health spending data are from 2007 except Zimbabwe with data from 2001. Accessed 16 June 2016 at http://databank.worldbank. org/ddp/home.do.

d. *Definition:* Public expenditure on education consists of current and capital public expenditure on education plus subsidies to private education at the primary, secondary, and tertiary levels. Public health expenditure consists of recurrent and capital spending from government (central and local) budgets, external borrowings and grants (including donations from international agencies and nongovernmental organizations), and social (or compulsory) health insurance funds.

e. *Source:* The World Bank (2010a), *Worldwide Governance Indicators* report provides six governance indicators for 212 of the world's countries and territories. Four of these indicators are referred to in this chapter: government effectiveness is the quality of public services, the capacity of the civil service and its independence from political pressures, and the quality of policy formulation. Regulatory quality is the ability of the government to provide sound policies and regulations that enable and promote private sector development. Rule of law is the extent to which agents have confidence in and abide by the rules of society, including the quality of contract enforcement and property rights, the police, and the courts, as well as the likelihood of crime and violence. Control of corruption is the extent to which public power is exercised for private gain, including both petty and grand forms of corruption, as well as "capture" of the state by elites and private interests (accessed 16 June 2016 at http://info.worldbank.org/governance/wgi/index.aspx#countryReports).

f. *Sources:* World Economic Forum's *2010–11 Global Competitiveness Report* (Schwab, 2010), in addition to a competitiveness ranking of 139 countries, provides a typology of stages of economic development largely based on GDP per capita (Sala-i-Martin et al., 2010).

g. *Source:* Johns Hopkins Comparative Nonprofit Sector Project. Based on two decades of empirical research in over 40 countries, Salamon and Sokolowski's (2010) models of civil society sectors distinguish five types based on differences in empirical data across five dimensions: workforce size, volunteer share, government support, philanthropic support, and expressive share. Zimbabwe was not included in the Johns Hopkins project; however, its civil society characteristics largely match other African countries that belong in the traditional model thus Zimbabwe's alignment with this model is assumed.

h. *Sources:* World Bank (2010b), *World Development Indicators.* International aid data is from the Development Assistance Committee (DAC) of the Organisation for Economic Co-operation and Development (OECD), and population estimates from the World Bank. Data are from 2010. *Note:* International aid per capita includes net official development assistance (loans and grants from DAC member countries, multilateral organizations, and non-DAC donors) divided by the mid-year population estimate. Italy, Sweden, and the United States did not receive international aid (data accessed 16 June 2016 at http://databank.worldbank.org/ddp/home.do?Step=12&id=4&CNO=2).

i. Global Competitiveness Index.

Table 4.4   Social enterprise characteristics for five countries

	Outcome Emphasis	Common Form	Variation in Types of Activities	Reliance on Commercial Revenue	Government Involvement		Civil Society Presence
					SE policies/ subsidies	SE legal form	
Zimbabwe[a] *Sustainable subsistence*	Individual self-sustainability	Microfinance/ nonprofit	Low	High	No	No	Moderate (works w/intl aid)
Argentina[b] *Autonomous mutualism*	Group self-sufficiency	Cooperative/ mutual benefit	Moderate	High	No	No	Strong
Italy[c] *Dependent focused*	Social benefit	Cooperative	Low	Moderate–low (reliant on govt subsidies)	High	Yes	Moderate (partnered w/ govt)
United States[d] *Autonomous diverse*	Organizational sustainability	Nonprofit/ business	High	Moderate (mixed w/charity & govt revenue)	No	No	Strong
Sweden[e] *Enmeshed focused*	Social benefit	Cooperative/ business[f]	Low	Low (very reliant on govt subsidies)	Very high	No	Low (highly partnered w/ govt)

Notes:

a. *Source:* Masendeke and Mugova (2009).
b. *Source:* Roitter and Vivas (2009).
c. *Sources:* Borzaga and Santuari (2001); Nyssens (2009).
d. *Source:* Kerlin and Gagnaire (2009).
e. *Sources:* Stryjan (2001, 2004); Spear and Bidet (2005); Gawell et al. (2009).
f. While government-supported social cooperatives have been the dominant social enterprise form in Sweden, recently some businesses with a social purpose have appeared that are less engaged with government (Gawell et al., 2009).

citizens have a strong tradition of supportive collective activity. According to the GLOBE analysis, Zimbabweans rate the highest of the five countries in terms of in-group collectivism (House et al., 2004). Here, collectivism is theorized to support social innovation and enterprise through the generation of "variety through group-based, incremental improvements and changes" and the leveraging of "their own resources by harnessing 'clanlike' affiliations" (Tiessen, 1997, p. 368). Given the current instability in Zimbabwe, a feeling or need for more uncertainty avoidance aligns with the situation in the country (House et al., 2004).

Indeed, World Governance Indicators and the Global Competitiveness Index (GCI) in Table 4.3 show that Zimbabwe has one of the poorest institutional environments in the world. In 2009 it had a GDP per capita of $375 and is currently categorized as a factor-driven economy (Schwab, 2010, p. 350). Given its high poverty level, the country receives international aid estimated at $52 per person in 2010 (World Bank, 2010a). In terms of civil society, in 2010 the Zimbabwe National Association of Non-Governmental Organizations (NANGO) described government suspicion, mistrust of the sector, and recent victimization of civil society through arrests and intimidation as well as restrictions on its freedom of expression in the independent media (NANGO, 2010). Zimbabwe's civil society sector model best aligns with countries belonging to the traditional model though it is a borderline case because government repression likely limits volunteer participation (Salamon and Sokolowski, 2010).

The failure of political and economic institutions and a weak civil society in Zimbabwe have led to a necessity-driven type of social enterprise characterized by microfinance supported by international aid. As such, immediate outcomes for social enterprise are focused on individual self-sustainability and the maintenance of livelihoods. Indeed, Masendeke and Mugova (2009) report that high levels of unemployment and the negative social impact of structural adjustment reforms promoted by international financial institutions have led to the recent movement towards social enterprise solutions. Not surprisingly, given the high collectivism rating, descriptions of social enterprise in Zimbabwe do indeed have a strong emphasis on collective microfinance forms of social enterprise that receive initial direction and support from international aid (ibid.). With little recourse to welfare state or philanthropic support, social enterprise in Zimbabwe is heavily reliant on commercial revenue. With its habitat of high poverty, lack of a supportive state, and need for sustainable livelihoods, Zimbabwe's situation most closely aligns with the sustainable subsistence social enterprise model.

Argentina

Argentina transitioned from authoritarian to democratic rule in 1983. That event, as well as structural adjustment programs in the late 1990s and the 2001 economic crisis, had a dramatic effect on government policies, the economy, and civil society. Culturally, Argentina has a moderate risk avoidance rating and a high collectivism orientation, the latter manifesting itself in many forms of mutual association that have long traditions. Reflective of recent events, Worldwide Governance Indicators for 2010 (see Table 4.3) show Argentina has experienced declines in a number of areas since 1996 (World Bank, 2010a). The 2010–11 *Global Competitiveness Report* finds that economic factors in Argentina have only recently improved in some respects (Schwab, 2010). The report, which places the country in the efficiency-driven stage of economic development, puts GDP per capita in at $7726 in 2009 (Schwab, 2010, p. 80).

According to Salamon and Sokolowski (2010), Argentina has a borderline deferred democratization civil society sector model. The recent changes in government and the economy have encouraged a restructuring of the relationship between civil society and the state. With the return of democracy in 1983, many associations were restored, though they were largely tied to the welfare state. Structural adjustment reforms in the 1990s, however, brought privatization and a dismantling of the welfare state, dramatically changing the landscape for civil society (Jacobs and Maldonado, 2005). When coupled with the 2001 economic crisis, the situation encouraged a (re)turn to mutual forms of civil society organizations (Roitter and Vivas, 2009).

With little recourse to the state or the economy during economic downturns, social enterprise in Argentina has developed in part around mutual benefit forms of organization that have a historical legacy in the country including cooperatives, mutual benefit associations, and cooperative recuperated companies.[3] Thus the immediate outcome emphasis of social enterprise is group self-sufficiency. Indeed, higher levels of GDP than Zimbabwe likely make it possible for groups to aggregate resources for mutual benefit and reduce reliance on international assistance. Interestingly these larger-scale social enterprise structures, at times including entire factories, align with the aggregation of production reflective of the efficiency-driven economic stage Argentina is currently in. With little support from the welfare state, philanthropy or even international aid, social enterprise is characterized by the larger presence of civil society. The institutional context and its connection to social enterprise in Argentina thus best aligns with the autonomous mutualism social enterprise model.

Italy

With the start of the twenty-first century, Italy experienced greater overall political and economic stability than in previous decades, though problems of corruption persist. Similar to other Western European countries, Italy has a strong welfare state. Culturally, however, unlike other West European countries that value low uncertainty avoidance and have low collectivism, Italy values moderate uncertainty avoidance and practices moderate in-group collectivism. Worldwide Governance Indicators consistently rank Italy in the 60th and 70th percentile on a number of important indicators (see Table 4.3) (World Bank, 2010a). Categorized as an innovation-driven economy, the Global Competitiveness Index ranked Italy 48 out of 139 countries in 2010. In 2009 Italy had an average GDP per capita of $35435 (Sala-i-Martin et al., 2010, p. 27).

The civil society sector in Italy is considered to be a borderline welfare partnership model (Salamon and Sokolowski, 2010). Historically, the foundation for civil society in Italy was city corporations or guilds among other entities.[4] These were self-managed forms of mutual assistance that had legal and financial autonomy. More recently the development of the welfare state meant many service-oriented civil society organizations became public entities. In the 1980s, however, budget restrictions and dissatisfaction with welfare state services spurred the development of new forms of civil society organizations, including social cooperatives (Barbetta et al., 2004).

The rise of social enterprise in Italy provides an example of a re-emerged collective civil society tradition in the form of social cooperatives.[5] As Barbetta et al. (2004) note, social cooperatives "revitalized the mutuality sentiments of the guild, and at the same time sought to merge market means with charitable purpose" (p. 251). Initially a civil society response to a crisis of unemployment among hard-to-employ populations, the success of social cooperatives brought the attention and support of the welfare state that used them to help further its policy agenda in the area of work integration for the hard to employ. Thus immediate outcomes for social enterprise in Italy focus on social benefit and social cooperatives have a reliance on government subsidies and supportive policies. Indeed, in 1991 Italy became the first country in Western Europe to pass legislation designating a legal form for social enterprise known as "Type B" social cooperatives (Borzaga, 1996; Borzaga and Santuari, 2001; Nyssens, 2009). Given the mutual dependence of the welfare state and social cooperatives and the focus on work integration, the Italian case best aligns with the dependent focused model of social enterprise.

United States

In the United States, the stability and strength of its institutions over
long periods of time have supported innovation and high economic
growth, though the 2008–09 economic recession brought new challenges.
Compared to West European countries, the USA has a small welfare state
but similarly rates low on uncertainty avoidance and low on collectivism,
both indicating a culture that drives innovation through the generation of
variety. On government performance, the USA slipped into the high 80th
percentile in 2010 after a decade in the 90th percentile on a number of
factors due to the economic recession. Similarly, according to the 2010–11
Global Competitiveness Report, the USA ranked 4th of 139 countries,
down from second place in 2009–10 and first place in 2008–09 (Sala-i-
Martin et al., 2010). In the innovation-driven stage, its domestic economy
remains the world's largest with a 2009 GDP per capita of $46381
(Schwab, 2010, p. 340).

According to Salamon and Sokolowski (2010), the civil society sector
in the United States belongs to the liberal model and is characterized by
its large size, diverse activities, volunteer support, and autonomy from
the state. Over the past few decades, it has experienced dramatic growth,
making it difficult for traditional forms of nonprofit revenue (philanthropy
and government) to keep up with the increased demand. Kerlin and
Gagnaire (2009) suggest that this situation may have been a factor in a 20-
year increase in commercial revenue supporting nonprofits (see also Kerlin
and Pollak, 2011).

Like civil society, social enterprise in the USA is characterized by its
autonomy from government, reflecting limited involvement of the welfare
state and the diversity of its forms. In addition to for-profit forms of social
enterprise, it also has a growing foundation in the increasing number of
nonprofits that are pursuing commercial activities as a revenue maintenance and growth strategy due to stagnation in government and philanthropic sources (see above). Unlike most other countries, social enterprise
in the USA sometimes emphasizes revenue generation without a programming component, though it can also provide both. Thus, the immediate
outcome for social enterprise is often organizational sustainability, which
then supports social benefit. Still, innovation and effective governance in
the USA also generates wealth that supports social enterprise development through private philanthropy and government funding. On balance,
however, the result is a moderate though increasing reliance of social enterprise on commercial revenue. Given this institutional context, the social
enterprise habitat in the USA aligns with the autonomous diverse model.

Sweden

Sweden is known for its strong, stable institutions that include a healthy economy and a large welfare state that offers a high degree of social protection. Though the last few decades have witnessed a divestiture of some state responsibilities, this pattern is ongoing. Culturally, Sweden scores the lowest among the five countries on both in-group collectivism and uncertainty avoidance, the latter perhaps assisted by state social protections.

Sweden ranks among the highest in the world on both governance and economic factors. As the governance figures show in Table 4.3, its rankings are among the highest in government effectiveness, regulatory quality, rule of law, and control of corruption. Sweden's economy moved from 4th to 2nd in the 2010 Global Competitiveness Index, replacing the United States in the number 2 position. This ranking can be attributed, among other variables, to highly efficient and transparent public institutions, trust in public officials, innovation, and a low level of corruption. The country falls into the innovation-driven economic stage and had a GDP per capita of \$43 986 in 2009 (Schwab, 2010, p. 310).

Sweden has a social-democratic model of civil society characterized by low diversity but a high degree of volunteering (Lundstrom and Wijkstrom, 1995; Salamon and Sokolowski, 2010). The prominence of the welfare state in Sweden means that service delivery in certain areas such as health, education, and social welfare is almost entirely provided by the state. According to some theorists this has led to a smaller nonprofit sector that is focused on activities such as culture, adult education, and sports. However, for those few social service nonprofits that work within the state's social welfare domain there is a high degree of financial and in-kind state support (Wijkstrom, 2000). Indeed, cooperation is so close that "it can be difficult to separate these entities one from the other" (Lundstrom and Wijkstrom, 1995, p. 22).

The dominance of the welfare state in Sweden has led to fewer social enterprises (compared to other developed countries) operating in fewer spheres of activity. Because many of the work integration social enterprises that dominate social enterprise activity in Sweden fall into the welfare state's sphere of activity (notably some nonprofits), these enterprises have close ties with specific public policies and government institutions that in some cases spurred their development. These include social work cooperatives and community development businesses. Thus, in Sweden, social enterprise in many ways is a labor market policy tool that the welfare state uses to address problems of unemployment (Stryjan, 2001, 2004; Levander, 2010). Innovation and effective governance have supported a strong economy that in turn supports a strong welfare state. We also note the emergence in Sweden of some businesses with a social purpose that appear to be less engaged with government (Gawell et al., 2009). Overall, however, the macro-level institutions in Sweden that have helped shape social enterprise align Sweden with the enmeshed focused model.

The five case studies illustrate how macro-level institutions (or at times the lack of them) in various habitats, including culture, the state, the economy, and civil society, put pressure on social enterprise organizations to fulfill particular functions and be structured in specific ways. Thus, the resulting types of social enterprises fit their particular habitats in terms of needs as well as the institutional structures of each country. As supported by the theory of historical institutionalism, it can be expected that these socio-economic institutions will change over time due to shifts in power relations and other sector dynamics and that social enterprise models for different countries will therefore change over time as well (see Fisac-Garcia and Moreno-Romero, 2015; Gatica, 2015).

LARGE-SCALE QUANTITATIVE ANALYSIS ON HABITATS AND SOCIAL ENTERPRISE PRESENCE

The MISE framework is also supported by recent quantitative analysis reported in Monroe-White et al. (2015). This study extended Kerlin's (2013) work by drawing on large socioeconomic datasets and logistic hierarchical linear modeling to examine if the size of the social enterprise sector, as defined by the number of social enterprises in relation to the number of traditional for-profit enterprises in a country, varies by country and if this variation can be explained by the national-level variables identified by Kerlin (2009, 2013).[6] This statistical analysis drew on information on social enterprise organizations and national-level institutions in 54 countries. The social enterprise/entrepreneur dependent variable was based on the 2009 Global Entrepreneurship Monitor (GEM) Adult Population Survey, which captures, among other things, existing national differences in entrepreneurial behavior and characteristics of entrepreneurs aged 18 to 64. National-level predictor variables were drawn from Kerlin (2009, 2013). Data on these independent variables were derived from the World Bank's World Development Index, The World Economic Forum's Global Competitiveness Index, the GLOBE survey on culture, and the OECD Development Assistance Committee's data on international aid by country.

As reported in Monroe-White et al. (2015), the study found that almost half the variance in the size of a country's social enterprise sector can be attributed to country-level institutional factors. Specifically, the study found that the size of the social enterprise sector within a given country can vary significantly according to economic competitiveness, size of the welfare state, and in-group collectivism (ibid.) consistent with some of the basic assumptions of the MISE framework.

ENTREPRENEURIAL OPPORTUNITIES AS INTERMEDIATE FACTORS

Recent quantitative research by Monroe-White (2014) also finds that intermediate factors such as the presence of different kinds of entrepreneurial opportunities in a given habitat can influence social enterprise (see also Shane and Venkataraman, 2000; Baron, 2006; Alvarez and Barney, 2007; Ozgen and Baron, 2007; Shane, 2007; Dyer et al., 2008). For social entrepreneurs, opportunities are defined broadly to encompass both profit and nonprofit goals. Unlike profit-maximizing entrepreneurs (Drucker, 1985) however, social entrepreneurs seek out opportunities to respond to "wicked" and "intractable" social and environmental problems (Zahra et al., 2008; Cannatelli et al., 2012). According to Nicholls and Murdock (2012), these problems arise through failures in the private market, the public sector, and/or lack of scale in, or fragmentation across, civil society. To better understand the relationship between entrepreneurial opportunity and social enterprise, Monroe-White (2014) drew on large, multinational datasets to test if greater commercial, social, and environmental opportunities influence the size of social enterprise sector (see note 6). She hypothesized there will be a greater number of social enterprise organizations in countries with greater economic market strength and greater unmet social and/or environmental needs.

Specifically, through regression analysis, she explored the relationship between the size of the social enterprise sector within a country and four opportunity variables: human development (HDI), environmental opportunities (EPI), gross national income (GNI), and income inequality (GINI).[7] Her model included 38 countries and 16 230 businesses (comprising conventional businesses, social organizations, and social enterprises as described in note 6).[8] Total country population was included as a control variable.

Results indicated that 30.9 percent of the variance in organization type can be accounted for by country-level characteristics. Moreover, an organization in a country with average human development scores, environmental opportunities, and commercial opportunities is highly unlikely to be a social enterprise. In fact, organizations were 50 times more likely to be a conventional or social organization than a social enterprise in countries with average characteristics. Human development scores were also a significant predictor of an organization being a social enterprise. That is, as human development scores increase, the likelihood of an organization being a social enterprise within a country also increases. Since human development scores are measured as a percentage, for every 1 percent increase in HDI, the odds of an organization being a social enterprise increases 24.8 times. This result strongly supports the idea that social enterprise organizations are more likely in countries with strong institutions and fewer social needs, supporting earlier findings that social enterprise is a privileged activity (Bosma and Levie, 2010).

SOCIAL ENTERPRISE ACTIVITIES ACROSS BROAD INSTITUTIONAL DIVIDES

Though strong institutions appear to support more robust social enterprise sectors, Kerlin's social enterprise country models above suggest that the lack of institutions in some country habitats also gives rise to particular needs that are filled by specific social enterprise activities. Thus, regardless of the scale of social enterprise, specific roles and activities for social enterprise would be found in some countries and not in others. To test this idea, we further explored whether the actual activities of social enterprises varied with large differences in the presence of important institutions. Drawing on preliminary work by Monroe-White (2014), we therefore examined the industry sectors where social enterprise organizations are clustered in high-income countries versus middle- and low-income countries. Because we used GEM data on social enterprises, the sample of organizations was limited to organizations that voluntarily answered questions regarding the purpose of the organization. Thus, though this data may not be fully representative of the social enterprises operating within a country, it still provides preliminary insights into the industries in which these organizations operate across broad country groupings by level of income.

We used the International Classification of Non Profit Organizations (ICNPO) (Salamon et al., 2003) to classify social enterprises that responded to the purpose question in the GEM survey. ICNPO categories are as follows: (1) culture and arts, (2) education and research, (3) health, (4) social services, (5) environment, (6) development and housing, (7) law, advocacy and politics, (8) philanthropic intermediaries and voluntarism promotion, (9) international, (10) religion, (11) business and professional associations, and unions or (12) other, not elsewhere classified.[9]

After coding, 32 countries with available data were sorted using the 2009 World Bank's Global Development Finance categories for lower-, middle- and high-income countries. Using this classification system, we identified one low-income country, 17 middle-income countries and 14 high-income countries. Countries were then sorted into two groups: low/middle income countries and high-income countries. Of the social enterprises in this sample, 80 percent (n = 870) were operating in high-income countries, while 20 percent (n = 223) were in low- and middle-income countries. With this delineation, we found that social enterprises operating in high-income countries were more likely to identify more than one industry sector in which enterprises have a social impact.

As Figure 4.2 shows, based on our sample, social enterprises in all 32 countries were primarily clustered in the arts and social service sectors with over half of social enterprise organizations working, at least partially, in these two sectors. Significantly though, a larger portion of organizations in high-income countries operated in the arts sector while social enterprises in low- and middle-income countries were concentrated more in social services. However, there were no discernible differences across education, development and housing, health services, environment, law, philanthropy and volunteerism or religion. No lower- or middle-income countries reported social enterprises working in the international or

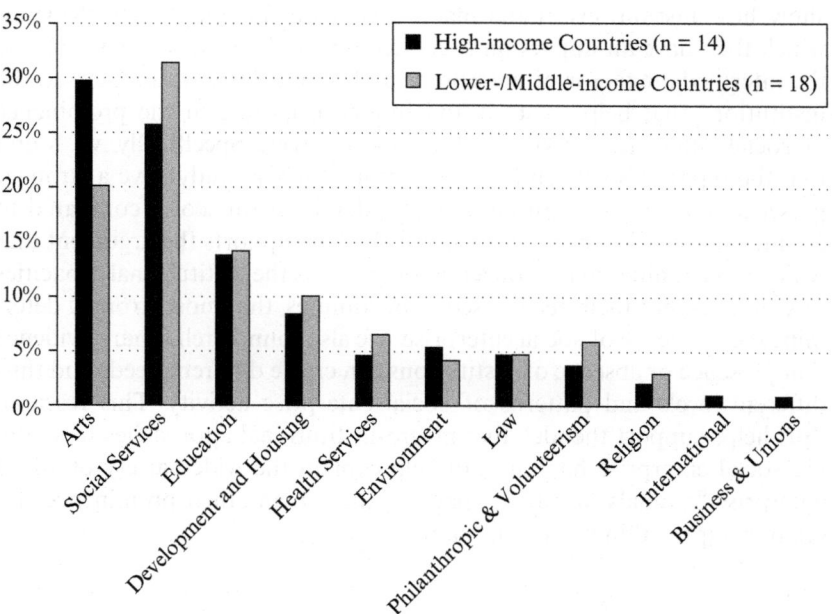

Figure 4.2   The relative presence of social enterprise industry sectors across the income divide

business and unions sectors. These findings are highly preliminary especially given the lack of data on low-income countries. Indeed, given more information we would expect to see more variation across extreme income differences. Nonetheless, these findings indicate more of a focus on social services in countries that are not classified as high income, supporting the idea that countries lacking specific institutions in their habitats will develop differing social enterprise roles broadly construed.

CONCLUSION

In this chapter we examined the role of habitat in shaping social enterprise at the country level. In particular, we drew on Kerlin's (2013) macro-institutional social enterprise (MISE) framework to help explain how prominent, macro-level institutions can influence many different facets of social enterprise discussed in this book. Our focus on macro-level institutions here is not meant to diminish the role of other contextual elements such as micro-level institutions and actors who also play an important part in shaping social enterprise (Nicholls, 2010). Our point was to focus on the macro aspect as one of the many different factors at play but also show how institutions at the macro-level can influence other elements, which then have an impact on social enterprise. Indeed, we also explored the intermediate factor of entrepreneurial opportunity with an eye to the institutions that help create it and influence its role in the prominence of social enterprise activity in different countries. Specifically, we found that the types of social enterprises captured in this study have a stronger presence in countries with high human development scores compared to countries with greater unmet social need. This supports the argument that while opportunities matter on a micro-level, it is the institutional capacities of countries, not their need-based opportunities, that most strongly determine the incidence of social enterprise. We also found preliminary evidence that presence or absence of institutions can create different needs and thus different levels and patterns of social enterprise activity. This research thus helps support the idea that macro-institutional approaches to studying social enterprise habitats can help explain the wide variety of social enterprise "animals" in various parts of the zoo and their prominence and relationships within particular habitats.

NOTES

1. Jeong (2015) has proposed a sixth model of social enterprise, strategic diverse, based on the development of social enterprise in South Korea. The strategic-diverse model is characterized by a moderate-sized civil society in comparison with its stage of economic growth. South Korea's governance is influenced by both Europe and the United States, using policy to encourage social enterprise development to compensate for the lack of a welfare state.
2. Information on country-level case studies of social enterprise was drawn from the writings of social enterprise researchers from each of the countries in question. See cited references.
3. Failed companies that have been reorganized into self-managed cooperatives at times in opposition to local authorities. Roitter and Vivas (2009) find that 170 recuperated companies have emerged in Argentina since the end of the 1990s.
4. Putnam (1993) provides an in-depth study of civil society in Italy and notes strong regional variation between northern and southern parts of the country.
5. Social cooperatives, common in Western Europe, are characterized by multi-stakeholder ownership and democratic management involving workers, managers, volunteers, customers, donors, and public authorities.
6. Using the 2009 Global Entrepreneurship Monitor (GEM) data, three types of organizations were identified: conventional business, social organization, and social enterprise. Conventional businesses are those that sell goods and/or services without an explicit social purpose. Social organizations are traditional nonprofits, nonprofit equivalents, or social organizations with an explicit social purpose that do not generate revenue from sales. Third, social enterprises are organizations with an explicit social purpose that also generate revenue from sales. Using the definition of social enterprise from Kerlin (2013) an organization is defined as a social enterprise if the respondent indicated that their organization generated revenue from sales and that they are the current founder and/or owner-manager of an existing organization with an explicit social purpose. These classifications were used to compare social enterprises to non–social enterprise organizations (i.e., conventional and/or social).
7. Commercial opportunity, or the market strength of a country, was measured using the World Bank's gross national income (GNI) per capita and social opportunity was measured by the Human Development Index (HDI) (created by the World Bank to measure quality of life). HDI is a composite index measuring average achievement in three basic dimensions of human development – health conditions, knowledge attainment, and standard of living. For environmental opportunity, the Environmental Performance Index (EPI) was used, which ranks countries on their environmental public health and ecosystem vitality (De Sherbinin et al., 2013). Income inequality was measured using the GINI Index because of its significant influence on economic development (Sen, 1992).
8. Variance inflation factors (VIFs) ranged from 1.69 to 3.39, indicating no multicollinearity issues.
9. The GEM interview protocol allowed owner/manager/founders of social organizations and social enterprises to specify the kinds of products or services they provide in the form of an open-ended response to a single question. Answers allowed respondents to specify their enterprises' primary area of focus. Responses were transcribed and later translated into English for comparative analysis. In all, 1093 owner/manager/founders of social enterprises responded to this question; of these, a total of 1050 were provided by owner/manager/founders of social enterprise organizations; this led to a 96 percent overall response rate for this item. Open-ended responses were entered into Microsoft Excel as matrix displays, and were coded using thick descriptions (Miles and Huberman, 1994). One or more ICNPO codes were assigned to "chunks" of data (phrases, sentences or paragraphs) that conveyed a meaningful idea or set of ideas (Krippendorff, 2012) prior to analysis. Each entry was carefully analyzed due to misspellings generated by the GEM interviewers and/or English-language translators. In an effort to ensure the reliability of

coding, codes were double-checked for accuracy prior to analysis. In instances where the appropriate code could not be determined (most likely due to lack of sufficient information), responses were coded as "Don't Know" and excluded from the analysis.

REFERENCES

Alvarez, S.A. and J.B. Barney (2007), "Discovery and creation: alternative theories of entrepreneurial action," *Strategic Entrepreneurship Journal*, **1** (1–2), 11–26.

Amin, A. (ed.) (2009), *The Social Eonomy: International Perspectives on Economic Solidarity*, New York: Zed Books.

Bacq, S. and F. Janssen (2011), "The multiple faces of social entrepreneurship: a review of definitional issues based on geographical and thematic criteria," *Entrepreneurship and Regional Development*, **23** (5–6), 373–403.

Barbetta, G.P., S. Cima, and Z. Nereo et al. (2004), "Italy," in L. Salamon and S. Sokolowski (eds), *Global Civil Society. Dimensions of the Nonprofit Sector, Volume 2*, Bloomfield, CT: Kumarian Press.

Baron, R.A. (2006), "Opportunity recognition as pattern recognition: how entrepreneurs 'connect the dots' to identify new business opportunities," *Academy of Management Perspectives*, **20** (1), 104–19.

Baumol, W.J. (1990), "Entrepreneurship: productive, unproductive and destructive," *Journal of Political Economy*, **98** (5), 893–921.

Borzaga, C. (1996), "Social cooperatives and work integration in Italy," *Annals of Public and Cooperative Economics*, **67** (2), 209–34.

Borzaga, C. and J. Defourny (2001), *The Emergence of Social Enterprise*, London: Routledge.

Borzaga, C. and A. Santuari (2001), "Italy: from traditional co-operatives to innovative social enterprises," in C. Borzaga and J. Defourny (eds), *The Emergence of Social Enterprise*, New York: Routledge.

Bosma, N. and J. Levie (2010), *Global Entrepreneurship Monitor 2009 Global Report*, accessed 16 June 2016 at http://www.gemconsortium.org/report.

Cannatelli, B., A.G. Masi, and M. Molteni (2012), "Green technology implementation in developing countries: opportunity identification and business model design," in A. Nicholls and A. Murdock (eds), *Social Innovation: Blurring Boundaries to Reconfigure Markets*, New York: Palgrave Macmillan.

Cooney, K. (2011), "An exploratory study of social purpose business models in the United States," *Nonprofit and Voluntary Sector Quarterly*, **40** (1), 185–96.

Cooney, K. (2012), "Mission control: examining the institutionalization of new legal forms for social enterprise in different strategic action fields," in B. Gidron and Y. Hasenfeld (eds), *Social Enterprise: An Organizational Perspective*, New York and London: Palgrave Macmillan.

Dacanay, M. (2004), "Creating a space in the market: social enterprise stories in Asia," paper at the Asian Institute of Management and Conference of Asian Foundations and Organizations, Makati City, Philippines.

Defourny, J. and S.Y. Kim (2011), "Emerging models of social enterprise in Eastern Asia," *Social Enterprise Journal*, **7** (1), 86–111.

Defourny, J. and M. Nyssens (2008), "Social enterprise in Europe: recent trends and developments," *Social Enterprise Journal*, **4** (3), 202–28.

Defourny, J. and M. Nyssens (2010), "Conceptions of social enterprise and social entrepreneurship in Europe and the United States: convergences and divergences," *Journal of Social Entrepreneurship*, **1** (1), 32–53.

De Sherbinin, A., A. Reuben, M.A. Levy, and L. Johnson (2013), *Indicators in Practice: How Environmental Indicators are Being Used in Policy and Management Contexts*, New Haven, CT and New York: Yale and Columbia Universities.

Drucker, P.F. (1985), *Innovation and Entrepreneurship: Practice and Principles*, New York: Harper & Row.

Dyer, J.H., H.B. Gregersen, and C. Christensen (2008), "Entrepreneur behaviors, opportunity recognition, and the origins of innovative ventures," *Strategic Entrepreneurship Journal*, **2** (4), 317–38.

Fisac-Garcia, R. and A. Moreno-Romero (2015), "Understanding social enterprise country models: Spain," *Social Enterprise Journal*, **11** (2), 156–77.

Galera, G. and C. Borzaga (2009), "Social enterprise: an international overview of its conceptual evolution and legal implementation," *Social Enterprise Journal*, **5** (3), 210–28.

Gatica, S. (2015), "Understanding the phenomenon of Chilean social enterprises under the lens of Kerlin's approach: contributions and limitations," *Social Enterprise Journal*, **11** (2), 202–26.

Gawell, M., B. Johannisson, and M. Lundqvist (eds) (2009), *Entrepreneurship in the Name of Society*, Stockholm: Knowledge Foundation.

Grant, S. (2008), "Contextualising social enterprise in New Zealand," *Social Enterprise Journal*, **4** (1), 9–23.

Hofstede, G. (1980), *Culture's Consequences: International Differences in Work-Related Values*, Thousand Oaks, CA: SAGE.

Hofstede, G. (2001), *Culture's Consequences: Comparing Values, Behaviors, Institutions, and Organizations Across Nations*, Thousand Oaks, CA: SAGE.

House, R.J., P.J. Hanges, and M. Javidan et al. (2004), *Culture, Leadership, and Organizations: The GLOBE Study of 62 Societies*, Thousand Oaks, CA: SAGE.

Jacobs, J.E. and M. Maldonado (2005), "Civil society in Argentina: opportunities and challenges for national and transnational organisation," *Journal of Latin American Studies*, **37** (1), 141–72.

Jeong, B. (2015), "The developmental state and social enterprise in South Korea: a historical institutionalism perspective," *Social Enterprise Journal*, **11** (2), 116–37.

Kerlin, J. (2006), "Social enterprise in the United States and Europe: understanding and learning from the differences," *Voluntas*, **17** (3), 247–63.

Kerlin, J. (ed.) (2009), *Social Enterprise: A Global Comparison*, Lebanon, NH: Tufts University Press.

Kerlin, J. (2013), "Defining social enterprise across different contexts: a conceptual framework based on institutional factors," *Nonprofit and Voluntary Sector Quarterly*, **42** (1), 84–108.

Kerlin, J. and K. Gagnaire (2009), "United States," in J. Kerlin (ed.), *Social Enterprise: A Global Comparison*, Lebanon, NH: Tufts University Press.

Kerlin, J. and T. Pollak (2011), "Nonprofit commercial revenue: a replacement for declining government grants and private contributions?" *American Review of Public Administration*, **41** (6), 686–705.

Krippendorff, K.H. (2012), *Content Analysis: An Introduction to its Methodology*, 3rd edition, Thousand Oaks, CA: SAGE.

Lehner, O.M. (2011), "The phenomenon of social enterprise in Austria: a triangulated descriptive study," *Journal of Social Entrepreneurship*, **2** (1), 53–78.

Levander, U. (2010), "Social enterprise: implications of emerging institutionalized constructions," *Journal of Social Entrepreneurship*, **1** (2), 213–30.

Lundstrom, T. and F. Wijkstrom (1995), "Defining the nonprofit sector: Sweden," *Working Papers of the Johns Hopkins Comparative Nonprofit Sector Project*, No. 16, Baltimore, MD: The Johns Hopkins Institute for Policy Studies.

Masendeke, A. and A. Mugova (2009), "Zimbabwe and Zambia," in J. Kerlin (ed.), *Social Enterprise: A Global Comparison*, Lebanon, NH: Tufts University Press.

Mason, C. and J. Barraket (2015), "Understanding social enterprise model development through discursive interpretations of social enterprise policymaking in Australia (2007–2013)," *Social Enterprise Journal*, **11** (2), 138–55.

Miles, M.B. and A.M. Huberman (1994), *Qualitative Data Analysis: An Expanded Sourcebook*, 2nd edition, Thousand Oaks, CA: SAGE.

Monroe-White, T.K. (2014), "A cross-country investigation of social enterprise innovation: a multilevel modeling approach," doctoral thesis, Atlanta, GA: Georgia Institute of Technology.

Monroe-White, T., J. Kerlin, and S. Zook (2015), "A quantitative critique of Kerlin's macro-institutional social enterprise framework," *Social Enterprise Journal*, **11** (2), 178–201.

Mook, L., J. Quarter, and S. Ryan (eds) (2012), *Businesses with a Difference: Balancing the Social and the Economic*, Toronto: University of Toronto Press.

National Association of Non-Governmental Organizations (NANGO) (2010), "Early warning system report reporting period October 2009–February 2010," accessed 16 June 2016 at http://civicus.org/csw_files/EWS_Q1_Report_Zimbabwe.pdf.

Nicholls, A. (2010), "The legitimacy of social entrepreneurship: reflexive isomorphism in a pre-paradigmatic field," *Entrepreneurship Theory and Practice*, **34** (4), 611–33.

Nicholls, A. and A. Murdock (2012), *The Nature of Social Innovation. Social Innovation*, Basingstoke, UK and New York: Palgrave Macmillan.

Nielsen, C. and P. Samia (2008), "Understanding key factors in social enterprise development of the BOP: a systems approach applied to case studies in the Philippines," *Journal of Consumer Marketing*, **25** (7), 446–54.

Nyssens, M. (2006), *Social Enterprise: At the Crossroads of Markets, Public Policies and Civil Society*, London: Routledge.

Nyssens, M. (2009), "Western Europe," in J. Kerlin (ed.), *Social Enterprise: A Global Comparison*, Lebanon, NH: Tufts University Press.

Ozgen, E. and R.A. Baron (2007), "Social sources of information in opportunity recognition: effects of mentors, industry networks, and professional forums," *Journal of Business Venturing*, **22** (2), 174–92.

Putnam, R. (1993), *Making Democracy Work: Civic Traditions in Modern Italy*, Princeton, NJ: Princeton University Press.

Roitter, M. and A. Vivas (2009), "Argentina," in J. Kerlin (ed.), *Social Enterprise: A Global Comparison*, Lebanon, NH: Tufts University Press.

Sala-i-Martin, X., J. Blanke, and M. Hanouz et al. (2010), "The Global Competitiveness Index 2010–2011: looking beyond the global economic crisis," in K. Schwab (ed.), *The Global Competitiveness Report 2010–2011*, Geneva:

World Economic Forum, accessed 16 June 2016 at http://www3.weforum.org/docs/WEF_GlobalCompetitivenessReport_2010-11.pdf.

Salamon, L.M. and S.W. Sokolowski (2009), "Bringing the 'social' and the 'political' to civil society: social origins of civil society sector in 40 countries," paper presented at the 38th Annual Conference of the Association for Research on Nonprofit Organizations and Voluntary Action, 19–21 November, Cleveland, OH.

Salamon, L.M. and S.W. Sokolowski (2010), "The social origins of civil society: explaining variations in the size and structure of the global civil society sector," paper presented at the 9th International Conference of the International Society for Third Sector Research, 7–10 July, Istanbul, Turkey.

Salamon, L., S.W. Sokolowski, and H.K. Anheier (2000), "Social origins of civil society: an overview," *Working Papers of the Johns Hopkins Comparative Nonprofit Sector Project*, No. 38, Baltimore, MD: The Johns Hopkins Center for Civil Society Studies.

Salamon, L.M., S.W. Sokolowski, and R. List (2003), *Global Civil Society: An Overview*, Baltimore, MD: Johns Hopkins Center for Civil Society Studies.

Schwab, K. (ed.) (2010), *The Global Competitiveness Report 2010–2011*, Geneva: World Economic Forum, accessed 16 June 2016 at http://www3.weforum.org/docs/WEF_GlobalCompetitivenessReport_2010-11.pdf.

Schwab, K. and X. Sala-i-Martin (eds) (2011), *The Global Competitiveness Report 2011–2012*, Geneva: World Economic Forum.

Sen, A. (1992), *Inequality Reexamined*, Oxford: Oxford University Press.

Shane, S. (2007), *A General Theory of Entrepreneurship: The Individual–Opportunity Nexus*, Cheltenham, UK and Northampton, MA, USA: Edward Elgar Publishing.

Shane, S. and S. Venkataraman (2000), "The promise of entrepreneurship as a field of research," *Academy of Management Review*, **25** (2), 217–26.

Spear, R. (2012), "Social entrepreneurship: a comparative perspective," in L. Mook, J. Quarter, and S. Ryan (eds), *Businesses with a Difference: Balancing the Social and the Economic*, Toronto: University of Toronto Press.

Spear, R. and E. Bidet (2005), "Social enterprise for work integration in 12 European countries: a descriptive analysis," *Annals of Public and Cooperative Economics*, **76** (2), 195–231.

Stryjan, Y. (2001), "Sweden: the emergence of work-integration social enterprises," in C. Borzaga and J. Defourny (eds), *The Emergence of Social Enterprise*, New York: Routledge.

Stryjan, Y. (2004), "Work integration social enterprises in Sweden," *Working Papers Series*, No. 04/02, Liège: EMES International Research Network.

Thelen, K. (1999), "Historical institutionalism in comparative politics," *Annual Review of Political Science*, **2** (1), 369–404.

Tiessen, J.H. (1997), "Individualism, collectivism, and entrepreneurship: a framework for international comparative research," *Journal of Business Venturing*, **12** (5), 367–84.

Wijkstrom, F. (2000), "Changing focus or changing role? The Swedish nonprofit sector in the 1990s," *German Policy Studies*, **1** (2), 161–88.

World Bank (2010a), *Worldwide Governance Indicators – Country Data Report*, accessed 16 June 2016 at http://info.worldbank.org/governance/wgi/index.aspx#countryReports.

World Bank (2010b), *World Development Indicators*, World Bank World

Databank, accessed 16 June 2016 at http://databank.worldbank.org/ddp/home.
do?Step=12andid=4andCNO=2.
Zahra, S.A., H.N. Rawhouser, and N. Bhawe et al. (2008), "Globalization of
social entrepreneurship opportunities," *Strategic Entrepreneurship Journal*, **2** (2),
117–31.

5. Ecologies within the habitats of the zoo

Elizabeth A.M. Searing, Jesse D. Lecy, and Fredrik O. Andersson

INTRODUCTION

Long gone are the zoos of old where animals were kept in cages and displayed separately. The modern zoo is a complex organization incorporating education, conservation, and research (Scott, 2012). Animals are generally united in habitats that include or reflect natural ecosystems. At the Oregon Zoo in Portland, for example, the Africa Savanna habitat contains zebra, gerenuk, hooded vultures, lesser kudu, and occasionally other animals. This is not simply a cosmetic mimicry of wild conditions, however; the impact that animals have on each other and their environment stems from complex systems of competition for resources, population dynamics, natural forces of selection, and social order that emerge to maintain balance.

The complexity of organizational ecology is similar to the natural world, with networks of individuals and environmental characteristics that are both dynamic and unique. The emergence of several new species within the social enterprise zoo signals that the social enterprise context contains resources sufficient to sustain growth and innovation of new organizational types. The new species consist of both types of social enterprise, with many subsisting on the common pool of earned income that sustains prototypical for-profits and nonprofits, but also with some angling to capture specialized resources such as program-related investments or social impact bonds. How does the emergence of new organizational forms impact the social enterprise ecosystem, and what does it mean for the future of all species that live there?

Using insights from organizational ecology, we explore the species-level dynamics that dictate daily life in the niches of the social enterprise zoo. First, we describe organizational ecology and the organizational niches of social enterprise. Next, we introduce the three phases of niche development and the two case studies that are used throughout the study to illustrate the concepts. In the analysis, each phase contains descriptive information on the state of resources and competition unique to that phase for both the case studies and the niche as a whole. Finally, we conclude and offer potential suggestions for how to facilitate the ongoing health of the ecosystem.

LITERATURE AND CONTEXT

Defining Organizational Ecology

Organizational ecology is the study of the dynamics of the system in which organizations find themselves. The primary tenet uniting various interpretations and applications of the field is that processes of evolution and selection that are found in the biological world are also present in the organizational world (Singh and Lumsden, 1990). Within a certain market niche, a variety of organizational types and sizes will divide available resources using different means: acquisition, forming alliances, fighting enemies, reproduction, and encouraging innovative behavior. The success of such tactics will be determined by localized factors such as resource availability, the density of organizations in the niche, and other systemic elements. Importantly, the focus on organizational ecology is not solely on the individual traits of the organizations or on the external factors that surround them. Instead, it is a systemic approach to studying a dynamic process over time.

Organizational ecology as a field shares several elements with other fields of study. Population ecology is often folded into organizational ecology, and they are occasionally referred to interchangeably (Baum and Oliver, 1991). There are differences, however. First, organizational ecology originally stemmed from studies in population ecology (Singh and Lumsden, 1990; Hannan and Freeman, 1993). Population ecology encompasses several fields beyond organizations while remaining largely in the realm of macro-level analysis. Organizational ecology has seeped into other levels of analysis as well, such as community ecology (Astley, 1985) and individual firm survival (Hager et al., 2004; Lecy, 2010). Community ecology is specifically focused on "the emergence and disappearance of organizational forms" (Carroll, 1984, p. 74), which are the potential bookends to the phases of ecological niche development contained in this study. Therefore, organizational ecology should be considered an offshoot of population ecology, albeit a mature and successful one.

The Organizational Niche of Social Enterprise

An organizational niche is a specific geographic market or a segment of a market that an organization can "occupy" through stable business relationships. A wide variety of organizational niches exist, and there is a healthy literature describing particular industries in the nonprofit and for-profit sectors. The social enterprise organizational niche overlaps with these other two domains but is notable for a couple of reasons. First, argued in this text, the issue of boundary definition in a difficult and complex one. There is a challenge defining not only which animals belong in the zoo, but also determining the boundaries of the niches within the zoo. Similar to the groupings and boundaries of more traditional zoos, there can be several different criteria by which to organize and describe the niche, such as organizational type or preferred diet.

One of the unique benefits of the "zoo" typology offered in this book is its versatility in defining boundaries of inclusion in the social enterprise space. How to define the animals within the zoo can adapt according to the question being asked. Legal form is useful in that it signals that an official public action has been taken to signal a social purpose (incorporating as a nonprofit or low-profit limited liability company [L3C] for example).[1] The influence of legal form on other operational details means that this is often a good way to sort the zoo animals. However, organizations often go through several phases before incorporating, if they choose to do so; further, taking an international perspective requires attention to the historical-institutional background of the legal framework and makes even comparison between legal forms difficult. Therefore, legal form is a potential way to sort the animals, but not necessarily the best way.

A second way to sort animals is by what they eat. Does the organization stick closely to earned market income, or does it also bring in grant money? The presence of a grant does not require that the organization be nonprofit; there are funds specifically for for-profit social enterprise, whether program-related investments (PRIs) from larger foundations or seed grants from universities and government programs to support start-ups. From the ecological vantage point, however, information about food supply can help locate an organization within a niche and identify possible competition or cooperation with other organizations vying for the same resources. In this way, resources can shed light on the boundaries of the zoo.

The ability to classify social enterprise animals in different ways is also useful in discussing organizational fitness. The success of alternative organizational species in a niche has a great deal to do with the synergy between organizational and environmental traits. The giraffe's long neck, for example, is not due to repeated stretching, as Lamarck guessed – it

can be attributed to the tendency of those longer-necked giraffes to be
better fed and more prolific than their shorter brethren (Prothero and
Schoch, 2002). Over time, the fitness of the giraffe for its niche sharp-
ened. This is even more remarkable when you think that the modern
giraffe is actually one of the few surviving descendants of what used
to be a far more varied giraffe "zoo" in prehistoric times (Mitchell and
Skinner, 2003). This is the original logic behind the L3C corporate form:
the L3C was designed to provide a distinct advantage in attracting and
utilizing PRIs (Brewer, 2013). Should this conduit work as planned and
the L3C find itself in a niche rich in this resource, the social enterprise
type would have an advantage over other organizations competing for
the same resources. If PRIs prove to be scarce, however, the L3C may
find itself endangered.

METHODOLOGY

This chapter examines the organizational ecology literature in the social
enterprise context, employing two case studies to illustrate the stages of
organizational niche development. In the first phase, a new organizational
species emerges from the landscape. This "emergence" entails a struggle
for legitimacy and access to resources for the new organizational type,
resulting in a high failure rate. In the second phase, "expansion," legitimacy is achieved through success and recognition of early organizations
and additional resources become available, attracting a large number of
new enterprise start-ups. As the market becomes saturated and crowded,
however, competition for resources becomes fierce and the failure rate of
organizations increases. The fledgling industry achieves "maturity" and is
relatively stable for a time. The stages of niche development are illustrated
in Figure 5.1.

The first case study details the emergence and evolution of microfinance
as a method of poverty alleviation. The purpose of microfinance is to
provide banking services and small loans to less affluent clients that have
been historically excluded from banking and lending services (Mersland
and Strøm, 2010). The concept of microcredit is not new: savings groups
have existed in various cultural contexts for centuries, and even scholars
from the Enlightenment in the seventeenth and eighteenth centuries recognized that charitable giving has limited benefits in eliminating poverty
(Dees, 2007). For example, informal Irish group loan funds thrived during
the eighteenth and nineteenth centuries, enduring even times of harsh
famine (Hollis and Sweetman, 2001, 2004). There were also the communal savings funds of seventeenth-century Germany, the box clubs of

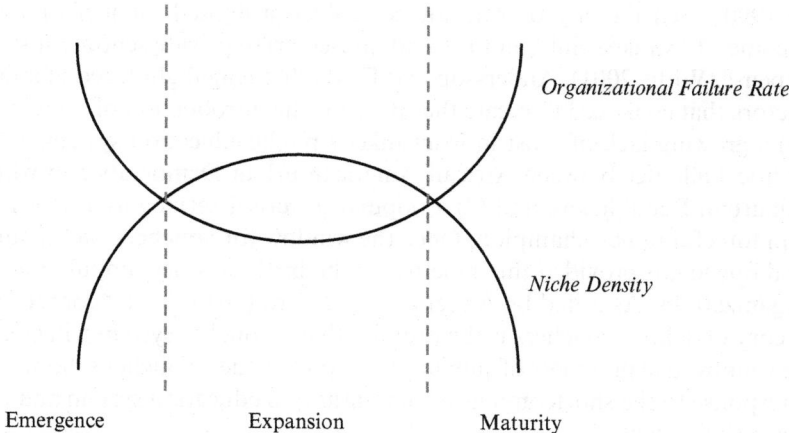

Organizational Failure Rate

Niche Density

Emergence   Expansion   Maturity

Figure 5.1   Stages of niche development

eighteenth-century England, and rotating savings and credit organizations (ROSCAs) such as *hui* in China and *chit* funds in India (Tsai, 2004; Seibel, 2005, 2010). Microfinance in its modern formalized context, however, has only existed for a few decades. Seibel (2010, p. 3) calls this 1970s' phenomenon the "microcredit revolution." One of the hallmarks of the revolution is the explicit inclusion of other aspects of the local cultural fabric. For example, microfinance often targets a particular marginalized group, such as women (Bloom and Dees, 2008); this approach often deliberately integrates the program with traditional cultural norms. This attempt to enact systemic change on the economic and cultural level has become a hallmark of the movement, with both proponents and detractors (Bloom and Dees, 2008; Karim, 2011). The rich history of the microfinance movement, including recent attempts both to undermine the field and improve its practices, provides a useful example of an organizational species that has thrived and survived in a niche that can be viewed as microcosm of the social enterprise zoo as a whole.

The second case study is the development of voucher schools, specifically in the Milwaukee context. The idea of school vouchers as a novel approach for refining public education dates back to the thinking of Milton Friedman in the 1950s (Friedman, 1955). Friedman viewed vouchers as a way to fundamentally change the organizational vehicles that delivered public education in the United States, from rigid and bureaucratic public agencies to social enterprises operating in an educational market with strong emphasis on customer satisfaction and service. However, it would take more than three decades before the first voucher program emerged in 1990 when the city of Milwaukee enabled a limited number of low-income Milwaukee children to attend nonsectarian private schools at state expense (Witte, 2001). Andersson and Ford (2015) highlight three enabling factors that coalesced to create the space for the introduction of vouchers: (1) a growing lack of trust in Milwaukee's public education system, (2) a political alliance between African-American urban Democrats and white nonurban Republicans, and (3) a popular governor serving as a powerful and forceful policy champion. Once the window for vouchers was created and opened, it provided the impetus for the birth of a new population of organizations. As noted by Andersson and Ford (2015, p. 5), "core to the theory of school vouchers is the promise that a voucher system will create new innovative providers of public education (i.e., new voucher schools) as a response to the shortcomings of the status quo education system and the desires of parents."

This window of opportunity has created a population of more than 100 mostly religious private voucher schools serving more than 20 percent of Milwaukee's K-12 student population. No longer limited to only low-income students or nonsectarian schools, almost 25 000 Milwaukee students from families earning up to 300 percent of the federal poverty level are enrolled in a voucher school (Ford, 2016). At the same time, many schools have also exited the Milwaukee voucher market since its inception (Ford, 2011).

ANALYTICAL OVERVIEW: RESOURCES AND RELATIONSHIPS

Within each phase, we explore two elements that are central to organizational ecology theory: resource availability and relationships among organizations. The social enterprise niche can offer an array of resources. It is true that many social enterprises rely heavily on earned income derived from market activities; depending on your definition, this may be a prerequisite for classification as a social enterprise (Social Enterprise UK, 2012). However, it is also true that many types of resources that are traditionally available to nonprofits are available to for-profits in the right circumstances. Though this practice is neither risk-free nor widely popular, PRIs are becoming increasingly common and are an interesting example of what would originally have been thought of as a very specialized food source available to nonprofits ("foundation grants"), but is now being sought by for-profit firms as well (see Chapter 8).

The complex nature of relationships between organizations is a central component of organizational ecology and a prime determinant of which animals fit into which niche (Aldrich, 1990). Barnett and Amburgey (1990) contended that the nature of such relationships depend on whether each organization's survival is positively or negatively related to others. Direct or indirect competition occurs when life expectancy is inversely related between organizations, while cooperation occurs when life expectancy between two or more organizations is positively correlated (Hannan and Freeman, 1989). Therefore, even in a resource shortage, if the odds of one enterprise making it through goes up if it bands together with another, it will cooperate.

Competitive strength can be due to a host of different factors, both institutional and environmental. Large organizations often have disproportional influence on the dynamics around them (Barnett and Amburgey, 1990), though this is often due to cultivated advantages that have allowed them to dominate the niche as individual organizations (Foster and Fine, 2007). Many types of "competitive edge" can also be attributed to species characteristics that help organizations gain and maintain niche domination. Financially, these can include the ability to use equity to secure funds, in the case of for-profit companies (Zietlow, 2001; Ridley-Duff, 2008) or to use of resources such as volunteerism and community effort to provide additional value, in the case of nonprofits (Evers, 2001). Indeed, there is a substantial literature on mixed markets that emphasizes differentiation on such characteristics, highlighting the comparative advantages of different types of organizations for achieving greater effectiveness or higher quality (Barman, 2002; Goering, 2008).

Cooperation and strategic linkages also play a crucial role in the functioning of the ecosystem. Social enterprises that were founded as components of strategic partnerships, for example as an element in system with other organizations or in connection with a supporting foundation, can immediately reap the benefits of more stable resources and potentially enhanced legitimacy (Baum and Oliver, 1996; Pfeffer and Salancik, 2003); however, as Baum and Oliver (1991) discovered, both individual enterprises and the linkages between enterprises are subject to potentially restrictive institutional forces, as well.

There are potential benefits to cooperating with other organizations of various sizes, large and small. Organizations that have strong social networks generally have a much better chance at survival than organizations that do not have a similar support network (Hager et al., 2004; Galaskiewicz et al., 2006); Searing (2014b) discovered that more successful organizations had larger social networks, despite all organizations in the study belonging to the same incubator. Further, cooperation allows loosely structured networks of services to emerge, where any given enterprise can specialize in a particular product or method of service delivery, and can refer clients or customers to other members of the network for complementary needs.

EMERGENCE

Emergence represents the genesis of a new industry, often created through pioneering firms. A new industry is prone to risk and is thus viewed skeptically by entrepreneurs and investors until it can prove that it is profitable and stable; thus legitimacy is a primary concern at this early stage. Innovative, new organizations have a difficult time raising capital and attracting talent. The evolutionary dynamic that drives emergence is known as "speciation," the development of a new species in response to the unique circumstances within the niche. Similar to biological processes, speciation can be very fast if a new idea or mutation has the ability to propagate quickly in an environment, or it can be something that has evolved slowly over time to the point that it no longer resembles its forbears in a significant way. Often, it is a combination of the two scenarios depending on how the new organizational form emerges; for example, informal lending practices evolved slowly for centuries, but the legalization of microbanks led to a rapid evolution of legal forms of microfinance.

Resources and Relationships: Liabilities of Smallness and Newness

The social enterprise niche is particularly susceptible to two potentially fatal conditions described in the organizational ecology literature: the liabilities of smallness and newness. The "liability of newness" describes the increased likelihood that a young organization or population will die off compared to a larger one of similar characteristics. Stinchcombe (1965) originally suggested that this was for one of four reasons. New firms will not have had the time to develop routines and learning-by-doing; similarly, they will likely be unable to provide money or time for employees to receive training either in-house or externally. The networks of new firms will also likely be more anemic than those of older firms, suggesting that organizational allies and relationships with clients and other resource providers may be scarcer. These traits will likely improve over time as an organization (or type of organization) builds expertise and legitimacy, improving its chances at survival (Singh et al., 1986). For example, funding is often difficult for a young organization due to the lack of a track record and, depending on the corporate form, potentially a lack of collateral. This difficulty also applies to species of organizations. There may be an initial rush of interest in investing in the first organization of a certain new social enterprise type, but what about the 15th? How much money would an investor be willing to risk if there is no history of what success or dissolution looked like for that organizational form?

Similar arguments sustain the "liability of smallness." Small organizations often have little organizational slack, which increases their financial vulnerability (Tuckman and Chang, 1991). Further, Frumkin (2002) suggests many of the same reasons that underlie the liability of smallness in nonprofits apply to newness: lack of connections to outside resources, inability to attract experienced human resources, and an inadequate starting endowment compared to for-profit enterprises. However, both liabilities need not be found concurrently. Even when they are, empirical studies have shown that both factors are significant in predicting organizational closure (Hager et al., 2004). Therefore, in designing or analyzing the ecological niche of a social enterprise, attention must be given to whether smaller and/or newer organizations should receive special accommodations in order to achieve longer-term social good.[2] Whether the topic of discussion is benefit corporations or bear cubs, the small and new are more likely to meet their demise than larger and more experienced inhabitants of the niche.

These ideas are especially relevant to the social enterprise zoo since the phenomenon is relatively new and the vast majority of social enterprises are small. Although the idea of simultaneously pursuing market success and social good at the same time has been around for some time, the concept of social enterprise has emerged full blown only in the last two to three decades (Young, 1983; Dees, 1998; Zietlow, 2001). In the USA there are a growing number of states with one or more dedicated forms of for-profit social enterprise (Brewer, 2015), but these forms are new and thus lack legitimacy (see Chapter 3). Therefore, many social enterprises must struggle for both individual and institutional legitimacy and survival.

Case Study 1: Microfinance

In the early 1990s, microlending organizations diversified into additional financial services such as banking; this expansion into microfinance opened needed access to safe savings repositories to clients and helped diversify risk for these institutions. Uptake was slow: not only were the targets of many programs rural women, who traditionally did not hold formal occupations, but transaction costs were high and repayment rates were expected to be low. Not only were clients not sure of the new services, but the institutions providing such services were scarce and often highly specialized. But the social component of lending circles, the employment of local representatives, and high repayment rates led to sustainable and even profitable operations. The movement began to gather steam in 1997 during the first Microcredit Summit, where a mixed group of nonprofits and policy experts pledged large amounts of resources to expanding microcredit services to a worldwide audience. The international attention plus the increase in resources secured the legitimacy needed to attract even larger amounts of both to the movement.

Case Study 2: Voucher Schools

In 1990, the Milwaukee Parental Choice Program (MPCP) started as a groundbreaking policy experiment providing opportunities for social entrepreneurs to create a new form of social enterprise: private voucher schools. During the early years of the program, there were several restrictions in place regulating the type of student that could be enrolled as a voucher student and regulations controlling what types of schools were eligible for voucher funding; hence, only a handful of new organizations were born during this time. So even though there were opportunities to grab early market shares in an emerging population not even close to reaching the environment's carrying capacity, density remained low for the first eight years. As suggested by population ecology, being an early entrant can indeed be difficult and demanding due to the lack of legitimacy of the new organizational form, and it is worth noticing that none of the voucher school start-ups from the early 1990s are still operating today. Andersson and Ford (2015, p. 7) illuminate this lack of legitimacy by highlighting how attempts to expand, liberalize, and evolve the MPCP were instantaneously confronted and disputed in court "causing the program to continue its marginal trajectory." Clearly, voucher schools were not instantly viewed as legitimate social enterprises, meaning key resources had to be deployed and exhausted to make justifications and explanations of the organizational form rather than being focused on how to build and sustain the actual social enterprise. Thus, it is when the voucher school form starts attaining legitimacy, reducing the need for such justification and explanation, that one would expect to see a rise in density.

EXPANSION

Following the initial legitimation of the new organizational type, the chances of survival for both the species and the individual organizations begins to increase. Failure rates of new organizations drop as capital and human resources become easier to attract. As seen in Figure 5.1, the failure rate drops below the entry rate, causing a boom in the density of organizations. Rather than relying on each other to help legitimize the species, organizations begin to compete amongst themselves for resources, which are currently plentiful. However, the beginnings of competitive resource extraction methods begin to take shape.

Resources and Relationships: Specialists and Generalists

Sustainable resource extraction is achieved strategically by two different types of organizations: generalists and specialists. Organizational ecology theory predicts that the dominance of each type will be cyclical relative to environmental conditions. Specialists are efficient at exploiting a specific resource; this gives them an advantage when this resource is plentiful. Generalists that can survive on almost any type of food, however, will dominate during times of change, for example, food shocks, since they are able to adapt to the most plentiful resource around them. This logic is akin to portfolio theory and revenue diversification in nonprofit finance (Kearns, 2007; Carroll and Stater, 2009; Frumkin and Keating, 2011). If you can eat meat *and* vegetation, then you will be able to survive when one or the other becomes scarce; similarly, if you can survive on, say, user fees from an educational homeownership program if something happens to your major fundraising event for the year, then you will be better equipped to survive than an organization solely reliant on donors. However, studies in nonprofit revenue theory have found that diversification helps stave off organizational closure, but potentially hinders growth (Chang and Tuckman, 2010; Chikoto and Neely, 2013). Ecologically, this is expected – organizational types that are more adept at a particular type of resource extraction will thrive in comparison to the generalist when this resource is plentiful or extraction methods are particularly efficient. So the process is cyclical: generalists are dominant, then specialists gain, then a resource shock hits and the generalists regain control.

The new breeds of for-profit social enterprises all have different approaches to the specialist/generalist approaches. The low-profit limited liability corporation (L3C) is designed to be a specialist, with language in their founding documents designed to facilitate the attraction of PRIs. Should these L3Cs exist in a niche where PRIs are abundant, then they will have a distinct advantage in their extraction compared to other organizations, and the species will thrive. On the other hand, if foundations are reluctant to give PRIs, then the L3Cs will not have that competitive edge and will need to rely on other resources.

Case Study 1: Microfinance

The first step toward legitimacy of microfinance came with the Microcredit Summit; the legitimization and recognition of microfinance as a worldwide movement, however, came in the mid-2000s with several international distinctions. First, the United Nations declared 2005 to be the "Year of Microcredit"; the next year Muhammad Yunus won the Nobel Peace Prize for his work in microcredit and microfinance (Yunus, 2006; Counts, 2008). Yunus effectively publicized his work with Grameen Bank so that it could provide a template for other organizations and other contexts; this led not only to an increase in funding, but also institutional propagation and the population of the niche (Davis et al., 2010; Karim, 2011). These successes led Rosengard (2004) to consider microfinance a resoundingly successful example of how funding helps to legitimize new organizations, in this case social enterprises. It became easier for new microfinance firms to organize and the total number of firms began expanding rapidly.

Case Study 2: Voucher Schools

The take-off for voucher schools occurred in the late 1990s when an injunction was lifted allowing religious schools to enter the population for the first time (Witte, 2001). The widening of the opportunity window led to a rapid growth in the number of voucher participating schools, and in only a few years the voucher population went from being a fringe to a major player in the education market in Milwaukee (Ford, 2011). As the number of social entrepreneurs successfully forming new voucher schools started growing, new social entrepreneurs were also tempted and many decided to enter the market. These new social entrepreneurs also had the benefit of learning from the experiences of earlier social entrepreneurs in building and adopting ways of organizing a voucher school. Thus, as legitimacy for the voucher school form increased, so did the density of the school voucher population, which reached its peak around 2002/03.

MATURITY

As more entrepreneurs hear of the abundant resources available to social entrepreneurs, the niche becomes increasingly crowded. This increase in population causes intense competition for resources of all kinds. As seen in Figure 5.1, maturation of the industry occurs as the density of organizations decreases as organizations within the niche increasingly starve or exit for other reasons. Those organizations that remain have evolved some kind of competitive edge, whether this is through efficient methods, extensive social networks, or resource specialization. In the broader social enterprise context, this phase could occur once a specific type of social enterprise form has emerged, but after the original hype wears down and investors disperse. This phase, however, often highlights the constraints necessary to overcome in order to spur additional innovations in either financing or organizational adaptations or speciation, causing either a shift in the niche or the birth of a new one altogether. Will a resurgence of new organizational species emerge to directly address the weaknesses in the status quo form? Will the innovations instead be driven by new financing methods, causing a shift in those organizations that can "adapt" to that type of resource?

Resources and Relationships: Competition and Saturation

In the maturity phase, the niche has been saturated with competitors drawn by the rich resources to the point where resources become scarce. In the case of social enterprise, funding and clients may then decide to pursue their objectives not only in other niches, but also in other sectors entirely. Those individuals in need of the services of thrift stores, hospitals, or a college education may then choose from a wide variety of corporate forms and enterprises, possibly leading to a brutal competitive environment over funds.

However, finances are not the only scarce resource fought over in the social enterprise environment. Human resources are another. For example, for-profit executives have often been recruited to run nonprofit organizations, though the desirability of this is often debated in discussions on executive pay (Oster, 1998; Barragato, 2002; Frumkin and Keating, 2010) and the commercialization of the nonprofit sector (Dees, 1998; Young and Salamon, 2002; Guo, 2006). Each sector poaches administrative, financial, or subject matter specialist talent from other sectors.

Even clients are contended, even if the goods and services supplied are at least partially public. Markets mixed between for-profits and nonprofits such as hospitals and daycare can be highly competitive. If not the teeth and claws engaged in competition in the wild, these competitors deploy product differentiation (Hansmann, 1987), cross-subsidization (James, 1983; Oster, 2010), and occasionally anti-competitive or collusive behavior in order to win the war for clients (Searing, 2014a). The success of these tactics constitute the efficacy of "resource extraction," an ecological term describing the ability to remove and use resources from the environment. The more effective the resource extraction, the more successful the organizational species (or individual enterprise) will be in its niche.

Despite intensifying competition and contention in the system between allies and enemies, there are both benefits and drawbacks to any sort of increase in the population. This is called "density dependence" (Aldrich, 1990; Barnett and Amburgey, 1990). The foundings and successes of current organizations are highly dependent on the fates of previous organizations, and this ebbs and flows as dead organizations free up resources for new ones to emerge (Carroll and Delacroix, 1982; Delacroix and Rao, 1994). The increased legitimization of the field means that, despite the higher rate of individual casualties, the species may still be in good health.

There are also sociological forces at work. As mentioned previously, new organizations or species suffer from a lack of legitimacy, which can keep cautious investors, clients, or other resources away. Therefore, in the beginning stages, an increase in the number of organizations in a niche can signal legitimacy and increase the overall level of resource availability, regardless of the degree of competition (Barnett and Amburgey, 1990). However, as the niche becomes more crowded, gains received from additional legitimacy may wane due to the increased exposure of the niche and increased competition for resources (Hannan and Freeman, 1988). This in turn causes an increase in the mortality rate of organizations as resources become scarcer.

Case Study 1: Microfinance

The maturation of the microfinance movement is evident in the emergence of several trends: a market that is becoming crowded and competitive, growing criticism of microfinance practices, and the development of innovations within the industry. Even in 2002, there were suspicions that practices that set microfinance institutions apart had begun to fade (Cohen, 2002). This led to a critique that microfinance has become too commercialized with microfinance banks becoming the loan sharks that they had originally been designed to replace (Epstein and Smith, 2007; Lewis, 2008). Recent empirical evidence has also cast doubt on the efficacy of microfinance as a poverty alleviation tool (Crépon et al., 2011; Banerjee et al., 2013), and other authors have found evidence of undesirable externalities such as an increase in child labor at the cost of school attendance in agricultural communities (Maldonado and González-Vega, 2008).

These developments are evidence that the field of microfinance has grown large enough that there is heterogeneity of type, quality, and complexity in microfinance banks; the niche has become quite crowded. Also, the critical tone shows that the industry has gained enough legitimacy to become the norm. For example, microfinance is now being used as a tool to legitimize certain practices, such as corporate social responsibility

(Chiu, 2014). Failure rates increase in this phase not because of a lack of legitimacy of the organizational form, but because of the difficulty new organizations have in establishing advantage and securing sufficient resources with so many competitors.

The competitive, mature market can also catalyze innovation, such as the development of dedicated social impact funds and microfinance collateralized debt obligations (Byström, 2008). Micro-insurance targets the diversification of risk, such as that found in agricultural occupations, rather than access to capital outright. Finally, crowdfunding can also be seen as an improvement on microfinance as a means of circumventing a traditional lack of access to finance by small lenders (Coleman, 2007). These critiques and innovations signal the maturity of the species within the niche and the creation of new opportunities and innovations.

Case Study 2: Voucher Schools

As posited by population ecology theory, at some point the relationship between density and the founding rate changes and the number of exits start to grow. This is in part due to the fading of the legitimation effects of new entrants but, more importantly, competitive pressures become manifest and start generating impacts that do not exist at relatively low densities. Today there are only a handful of new voucher schools entering the Milwaukee education market annually, and failure rates have increased again. These exits can be linked to changes in the institutional framework surrounding the voucher program that were put in place to ensure greater accountability and to offer ways to shut down deficient schools. Andersson and Ford (2015) describe how growing legitimacy was also followed by growing public scrutiny as stories of troubled voucher schools emerged in the media and major institutional voids were detected, perhaps the worst being the presence of a convicted rapist at the helm of one voucher school. Another factor behind increasing exits is that the greater density of voucher schools not only increases competition among all educational market actors, but also within the voucher school population itself.

IMPLICATIONS AND CONCLUSIONS

An ecological lens can add insight into both nascent and existing social enterprise fields. Individual organizations will emerge and die, perhaps more often than in other industries because a large percentage of social enterprises are young and new. In early stages new species will struggle with legitimacy and identifying stable niches. Success of pioneers leads to replication of the organizational model and expansion of the industry, which in turn leads to resource constraints and heightened competition. New corporate species such as benefit corporations, social purpose organizations, and L3Cs struggle not only to establish credibility for their own individual establishments, but also to familiarize investors and clients with the benefits and attributes of their new corporate form. Often, this will entail comparison between themselves and other new or established social enterprise forms available in their niche, which is populated by a variety of animals of other forms and in other sectors. On a broader scale, there are still individuals and investors waiting to see whether profit can be made at the same time social good is accomplished, so that the idea of "social enterprise" continues to struggle for legitimacy.

These struggles are all knit together in a complex ecological system that includes organizations, resources, institutions, and a host of other factors that influences the ebb and flow of enterprises within every habitat of the social enterprise zoo. Zookeepers, resource providers, social entrepreneur/ curators and students of the social enterprise zoo must therefore direct their efforts toward understanding the complex system as a whole rather than simply burrowing into the specifics of a particular organizational animal or species. Zoos have become places for complexity, not cages, hence this metaphor can guide thinking about social enterprise, especially in terms of policy. The flourishing of organizational species within the zoo depends not only on individual organizations, but also on the health of its ecosystems as a whole. Encouraging the discussion and propagation of social enterprises, including the establishment of commonly accepted performance metrics, will help to establish the legitimacy of what many scholars and investors still view with curious trepidation as they peruse the zoo.

NOTES

1. This is excluding research on elements such as nascent entrepreneurship, however, where the incorporation or even the activity may not have begun yet.
2. An example of this would be wind energy subsidies, which are designed to offset the development of a technology with potential long-term savings by subsidizing the industry until economies of scale and legitimacy barriers have made the industry viable.

REFERENCES

Aldrich, H.E. (1990), "Using an ecological perspective to study organizational founding rates," *Entrepreneurship Theory and Practice*, **14** (3), 7–24.
Andersson, F.O. and M.R. Ford (2015), "Social entrepreneurship through an

organizational ecology lens: examining the emergence and evolution of the voucher school population in Milwaukee," *Voluntas*, 1–21, doi: 10.1007/s11266-015-9576-0.

Astley, W.G. (1985), "The two ecologies: population and community perspectives on organizational evolution," *Administrative Science Quarterly*, 30 (2), 224–41.

Banerjee, A.V., E. Duflo, R. Glennerster, and C. Kinnan (2013), "The miracle of microfinance? Evidence from a randomized evaluation," *NBER Working Papers*, No. 18950.

Barman, E.A. (2002), "Asserting difference: the strategic response of nonprofit organizations to competition," *Social Forces*, 80 (4), 1191–222.

Barnett, W.P. and T.L. Amburgey (1990), "Do larger organizations generate stronger competition?," in J.V. Singh (ed.), *Organizational Evolution: New Directions*, Newbury Park, CA: SAGE.

Barragato, C.A. (2002), "Linking for-profit and nonprofit executive compensation: salary composition and incentive structures in the US hospital industry," *Voluntas*, 13 (3), 301–11.

Baum, J.A. and C. Oliver (1991), "Institutional linkages and organizational mortality," *Administrative Science Quarterly*, 38 (2), 187–218.

Baum, J.A. and C. Oliver (1996), "Toward an institutional ecology of organizational founding," *Academy of Management Journal*, 39 (5), 1378–427.

Bloom, P.N. and G. Dees (2008), "Cultivate your ecosystem," *Stanford Social Innovation Review*, 6 (1), 47–53.

Brewer, C.V. (2013), "Seven ways to strengthen and improve the L3C," *Regent University Law Review*, 25, 329.

Brewer, C.V. (2015), "Social enterprise entity comparison chart," accessed 16 June 2016 at http://papers.ssrn.com/sol3/papers.cfm?abstract_id=2304892.

Byström, H.N.E. (2008), "The microfinance collateralized debt obligation: a modern Robin Hood?," *World Development*, 36 (11), 2109–26.

Carroll, D.A. and K.J. Stater (2009), "Revenue diversification in nonprofit organizations: does it lead to financial stability?," *Journal of Public Administration Research and Theory*, 19 (4), 947–66.

Carroll, G.R. (1984), "Organizational ecology," *Annual Review of Sociology*, 10 (1), 71–93.

Carroll, G.R. and J. Delacroix (1982), "Organizational mortality in the newspaper industries of Argentina and Ireland: an ecological approach," *Administrative Science Quarterly*, 27 (2), 169–98.

Chang, C.F. and H.P. Tuckman (2010), "Income diversification," in D.R. Young and B.A. Seaman (eds), *Handbook of Research on Nonprofit Economics and Management*, Cheltenham, UK and Northampton, MA, USA, pp. 5–17.

Chikoto, G.L. and D.G. Neely (2013), "Building nonprofit financial capacity: the impact of revenue concentration and overhead costs," *Nonprofit and Voluntary Sector Quarterly*, doi: 10.1177/0899764012474120.

Chiu, T.-K. (2014), "Putting responsible finance to work for Citi microfinance," *Journal of Business Ethics*, 119 (2), 219–34.

Cohen, M. (2002), "Making microfinance more client-led," *Journal of International Development*, 14 (3), 335–50.

Coleman, R.W. (2007), "Is the future of the microfinance movement to be found on the Internet?," paper presented at the International Trade and Finance Association Conference.

Counts, A. (2008), *Small Loans, Big Dreams: How Nobel Prize Winner Muhammad*

Yunus and Microfinance are Changing the World, Hoboken, NJ: John Wiley and Sons.

Crépon, B., F. Devoto, E. Duflo, and W. Parienté (2011), "Impact of microcredit in rural areas of Morocco: evidence from a randomized evaluation," Working Paper, Massachusetts Institute of Technology.

Davis, K., L. Maxwell, and J. Horton (2010), "Banking for better lives: the impact of micro-finance on women and their households," *Journal of Business Administration Online*, **9** (2).

Dees, J.G. (1998), "Enterprising nonprofits," *Harvard Business Review*, **76** (1), 54–69.

Dees, J.G. (2007), "Taking social entrepreneurship seriously," *Society*, **44** (3), 24–31.

Delacroix, J. and H. Rao (1994), "Externalities and ecological theory: unbundling density dependence," in J.A.C. Baum and J.V. Singh (eds), *Evolutionary Dynamics of Organizations*, New York: Oxford University Press, pp. 255–68.

Epstein, K. and G. Smith (2007), "The ugly side of microlending," *Business Week*, 13 December.

Evers, A. (2001), "The significance of social capital in the multiple goal and resource structure of social enterprises," in C. Borzago and J. Defourny (eds), *The Emergence of Social Enterprise*, London and New York: Routledge.

Ford, M. (2011), "School exits in the Milwaukee Parental Choice Program: evidence of a marketplace?," *Journal of School Choice*, **5** (2), 182–204.

Ford, M.R. (2016), "Changes in school enrollment patterns after the first-time release of school-level test scores in Milwaukee's school voucher program: a first look," *Education and Urban Society*, **48** (5), 460–78.

Foster, W. and G. Fine (2007), "How nonprofits get really big," *Stanford Social Innovation Review*, **5** (2), 46–55.

Friedman, M. (1955), *The Role of Government in Education*, Brunswick, NJ: Rutgers University Press.

Frumkin, P. (2002), "Service contracting with non-profit and for-profit providers: on preserving a mixed organizational ecology," paper for the Institute for Government Innovation, John F. Kennedy School of Government, Harvard University.

Frumkin, P. and E.K. Keating (2010), "The price of doing good: executive compensation in nonprofit organizations," *Policy and Society*, **29** (3), 269–82.

Frumkin, P. and E.K. Keating (2011), "Diversification reconsidered: the risks and rewards of revenue concentration," *Journal of Social Entrepreneurship*, **2** (2), 151–64.

Galaskiewicz, J., W. Bielefeld, and M. Dowell (2006), "Networks and organizational growth: a study of community based nonprofits," *Administrative Science Quarterly*, **51** (3), 337–80.

Goering, G.E. (2008), "Welfare impacts of a non-profit firm in mixed commercial markets," *Economic Systems*, **32** (4), 326–34.

Guo, B. (2006), "Charity for profit? Exploring factors associated with the commercialization of human service nonprofits," *Nonprofit and Voluntary Sector Quarterly*, **35** (1), 123–38.

Hager, M.A., J. Galaskiewicz, and J.A. Larson (2004), "Structural embeddedness and the liability of newness among nonprofit organizations," *Public Management Review*, **6** (2), 159–88.

Hannan, M.T. and J. Freeman (1988), "The ecology of organizational mortality:

American labor unions, 1836–1985," *American Journal of Sociology*, **94** (1), 25–52.

Hannan, M.T. and J. Freeman (1989), *Organizational Ecology*, 1st edition, Cambridge, MA: Harvard University Press.

Hannan, M.T. and J. Freeman (1993), *Organizational Ecology*, reprint, Cambridge, MA: Harvard University Press.

Hansmann, H. (1987), "Economic theories of nonprofit organization," in W.W. Powell (ed.), *The Nonprofit Sector: A Research Handbook*, 1st edition, New Haven. CT: Yale University Press.

Hollis, A. and A. Sweetman (2001), "The life-cycle of a microfinance institution: the Irish loan funds," *Journal of Economic Behavior and Organization*, **46** (3), 291–311.

Hollis, A. and A. Sweetman (2004), "Microfinance and famine: the Irish loan funds during the Great Famine," *World Development*, **32** (9), 1509–23.

James, E. (1983), "How nonprofits grow: a model," *Journal of Policy Analysis and Management*, **2** (3), 350–65.

Karim, L. (2011), *Microfinance and its Discontents: Women in Debt in Bangladesh*, Minneapolis, MI: University of Minnesota Press.

Kearns, K. (2007), "Income portfolios," in D.R. Young (ed.), *Financing Nonprofits: Putting Theory into Practice*, Lanham, MD: AltaMira Press, pp. 291–314.

Lecy, J. (2010), "Sector density, donor policy, and organizational demise: a population ecology of international nonprofits," doctoral dissertation, Syracuse University, Syracuse.

Lewis, J.C. (2008), "Microloan sharks," *Stanford Social Innovation Review*, **6** (3), 54–60.

Maldonado, J.H. and C. González-Vega (2008), "Impact of microfinance on schooling: evidence from poor rural households in Bolivia," *World Development*, **36** (11), 2440–55.

Mersland, R. and R.Ø. Strøm (2010), "Microfinance mission drift?," *World Development*, **38** (1), 28–36.

Mitchell, G. and J. Skinner (2003), "On the origin, evolution and phylogeny of giraffes Giraffa camelopardalis," *Transactions of the Royal Society of South Africa*, **58** (1), 51–73.

Oster, S.M. (1998), "Executive compensation in the nonprofit sector," *Nonprofit Management and Leadership*, **8** (3), 207–21.

Oster, S.M. (2010), "Product diversification and social enterprise," in B.A. Seaman and D.R. Young (eds), *Handbook of Research on Nonprofit Economics and Management*, Cheltenham, UK and Northampton, MA, USA.

Pfeffer, J. and G. Salancik (2003), *The External Control of Organizations: A Resource Dependence Perspective*, Stanford, CA: Stanford University Press.

Prothero, D.R. and R.M. Schoch (2002), *Horns, Tusks, and Flippers: The Evolution of Hoofed Mammals*, Baltimore, MD: Johns Hopkins University Press.

Ridley-Duff, R. (2008), "Social enterprise as a socially rational business," *International Journal of Entrepreneurial Behavior and Research*, **14** (5), 291–312.

Rosengard, J.K. (2004), "Banking on social entrepreneurship: the commercialization of microfinance," *Mondes en développement*, **126** (2), 25–36.

Scott, J. (2012), "The role of modern zoos in wildlife conservation: from the WCS to the wild," *Student Theses 2001–2013*, Paper No. 22, accessed 16 June 2016 at http://fordham.bepress.com/environ_theses/22/.

Searing, E.A.M. (2014a), "Charitable (anti)trust: the role of antitrust regulation in the nonprofit sector," *Nonprofit Policy Forum*, **5** (2), 261–88.

Searing, E.A.M. (2014b), "Judging a book by its cover: the role of corporate form in social enterprise start-ups," accessed 16 June 2016 at http://ssrn.com/abstract=2534782.

Seibel, H.D. (2005), "Does history matter? The old and the new world of microfinance in Europe and Asia," Working Paper, University of Cologne.

Seibel, H.D. (2010), "Old and new worlds of microfinance in Europe and Asia," *Southeast Asia's Credit Revolution: From Moneylenders to Microfinance*, London: Routledge, pp. 40–57.

Singh, J.V. and C.J. Lumsden (1990), "Theory and research in organizational ecology," *Annual Review of Sociology*, **16**, 161–95.

Singh, J.V., D.J. Tucker, and R.J. House (1986), "Organizational legitimacy and the liability of newness," *Administrative Science Quarterly*, **31** (2), 171–93.

Social Enterprise UK (2012), "About social enterprise," accessed 16 June 2016 at http://www.socialenterprise.org.uk/about/about-social-enterprise#what%20are%20ses.

Stinchcombe, A.L. (1965), "Social structure and organization," in J.G. March (ed.), *Handbook of Organizations*, Chicago, IL: Rand McNally, pp. 142–93.

Tsai, K.S. (2004), "Imperfect substitutes: the local political economy of informal finance and microfinance in rural China and India," *World Development*, **32** (9), 1487–507.

Tuckman, H.P. and C.F. Chang (1991), "A methodology for measuring the financial vulnerability of charitable nonprofit organizations," *Nonprofit and Voluntary Sector Quarterly*, **20** (4), 445–60.

Witte, J.F. (2001), *The Market Approach to Education: An Analysis of America's First Voucher Program*, Princeton, NJ: Princeton University Press.

Young, D.R. (1983), *If Not for Profit, for What?*, Lexington, MA: Heath.

Young, D.R. and L.M. Salamon (2002), "Commercialization, social ventures, and for-profit competition," in L.M. Salamon (ed.), *The State of Nonprofit America*, Washington, DC: Brookings Institution Press, pp. 423–46.

Yunus, M. (2006), "Nobel lecture," paper presented at The Nobel Peace Prize, Oslo, Norway, 10 December.

Zietlow, J.T. (2001), "Social entrepreneurship: managerial, finance and marketing aspects," *Journal of Nonprofit and Public Sector Marketing*, **9** (1–2), 19–43.

6.   Changes over the life cycles of social enterprise animals

Jesse D. Lecy and Elizabeth A.M. Searing

INTRODUCTION

Caring for a newborn can be disorienting, frustrating, and downright difficult, and this is true whether the new arrival is human, canine, or a social enterprise. The needs of a new entity can be very different from those in later and more fully developed stages of life. It is widely accepted among organizational scholars that just as biological organisms pass through various stages of development – gestation, birth, infancy, adolescence, and adulthood – organizations also pass through various stages of life (Scott, 1971; Dodge and Robbins, 1992). The needs of an organism or organization will vary greatly depending upon its stage of development (Adizes, 1979; Quinn and Cameron, 1983); even more importantly, organisms and organizations are vulnerable to different ailments at each stage. Those in charge of the social enterprise zoo will benefit from knowledge of the idiosyncrasies of development for those in their care.

This chapter highlights important considerations for each stage of the social enterprise life cycle and implications of the sector context. We compare the literatures of the two sectors (for-profit and nonprofit) in order to highlight common lessons that emerge from both fields of research; additionally, we discuss any variation we might expect across organizational form. This comparison occurs through the organizational life cycle stages and is illustrated throughout with data and empirical examples. We conclude with practical thoughts and implications on caring for the social enterprise zoo animals at each stage.

METHODOLOGY

This study takes a dual-pronged approach in applying the theoretical lens of life cycle theory to the social enterprise zoo. First, we examine the distinct life cycle literatures within for-profit and nonprofit fields. In particular, the five general phases of the life cycle are reviewed – nascent and emerging organizations; newly formed organizations; professionalizing organizations, scaling organizations; and large, mature organizations – with a view towards identifying within each phase the similarities and differences between the two sectors. We then focus specifically on the nonprofit variety of social enterprise for purposes of understanding the life cycle on a species level. Nonprofit organization–level information is analyzed to reveal empirical patterns in a progression along the five-stage model of the life cycle over a ten-year period. The implications of these findings for social enterprise are then discussed, with existing literature and empirical support where available. Potential divergences from the nonprofit empirical model for for-profit enterprises are also presented, and limitations and further research are discussed.

THE ORGANIZATIONAL LIFE CYCLE

There is a fairly large literature on organizational life cycles within both the for-profit and nonprofit literatures (Lippitt and Schmidt, 1967; Quinn and Cameron, 1983; Smith et al., 1985; Walsh and Dewar, 1987; Dibrell et al., 2011). It has proven to be an enduring metaphor because it offers insight into the process of organizational growth, which occurs in stages. Just as an organism reaches specific milestones along the maturation process – walking, speech, puberty, adulthood – organizations tend to exhibit predictable behaviors at specific stages of development and tend to move through the life stages in order (Levie and Hay, 1998). It also has high face validity as most directors are able to easily place their organization within categories described by a life cycle framework (Eggers et al., 1994). Although a wide range of models have been proposed, they all share the same basic elements: an organization is born, begins life as a vulnerable infant, transitions into more self-sufficient adolescent, and eventually reaches adulthood (Quinn and Cameron, 1983; Dodge and Robbins, 1992; Gupta and Chin, 1994).

The metaphor has proved useful because it highlights certain behavioral traits and proficiencies of organizations at each stage of life. Or as stated by Gupta and Chin (1994, p. 270):

> Since organizations are in a continuous process of adaption, and organizations exhibit a unique set of characteristics in each developmental stage; having the ability to recognize an organization's particular stage of development would help the formulation of its strategies, identification of risk and opportunities, and management of organizational change.

New organizations are innovative and adaptive, but they do not have great capacity to manage people or standardize quality in products or services effectively, for example. Larger organizations are capable of using sophisticated systems to benefit from economies of scale, but they can also become more managerially rigid and locked into relationships that make them inflexible. Understanding the characteristics associated with specific stages, as well as the dynamics of passing from one stage to another, can offer insight into how organizations grow and evolve as they attempt to scale. This issue of growth and scaling is an especially salient issue in the pursuit of social enterprise impact.

The number of stages varies from two to ten depending upon the proposed framework and the research domain, and the milestones that delineate the transition to a new stage also vary by study and industry (Gupta and Chin, 1994). These differences arise partly because of nuances in how life stages are conceptualized, but partly from variation across different industries and markets. Charter schools that serve poor populations are an important form of social enterprise, but because of natural limits to the size of a school and the regulatory environment they may only need to pass through one or two life cycle stages on the way to maturity. TOMS shoe store, on the other hand, has a multinational manufacturing base and national retail footprint that requires a complex supply chain, sophisticated marketing, and flexible human resource systems. An organization with this size and scope will pass through more stages of development before reaching maturity.

Phelps et al. (2007) conducted a thorough review of 40 years of the life cycle literature in order to examine the important dimensions of the research domain such as the number of stages proposed by different scholars and the development of theoretical and empirical branches of research. They find that most scholars use taxonomies that emphasize three to five stages of the organizational life cycle (Figure 6.1). The review demonstrates how this research domain has evolved from a primarily theoretical field to a largely empirical endeavor, with little convergence to a specific set of stages as the domain matures. This evolution is nicely summarized in Figure 6.2.

TRANSITIONS THROUGH LIFE CYCLES

Biological animals and organizational animals differ in a few key respects. The growth process is deterministic for animal species. It can be stunted at certain stages, but they are biologically programmed to grow according to a specific schedule and achieve a given size. With most organizations, however, there is no predetermined end point. Some elect to pass through all stages of growth and are able to achieve significant scale, while others

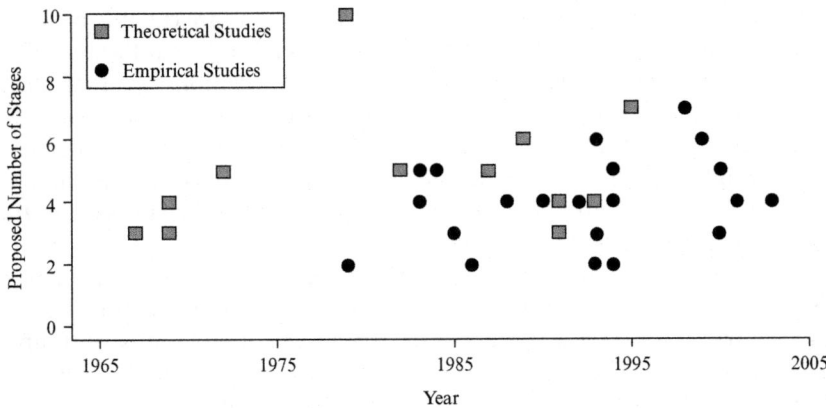

Source: Adapted from Phelps et al. (2007).

Figure 6.1   Number of stages in the life cycle literature

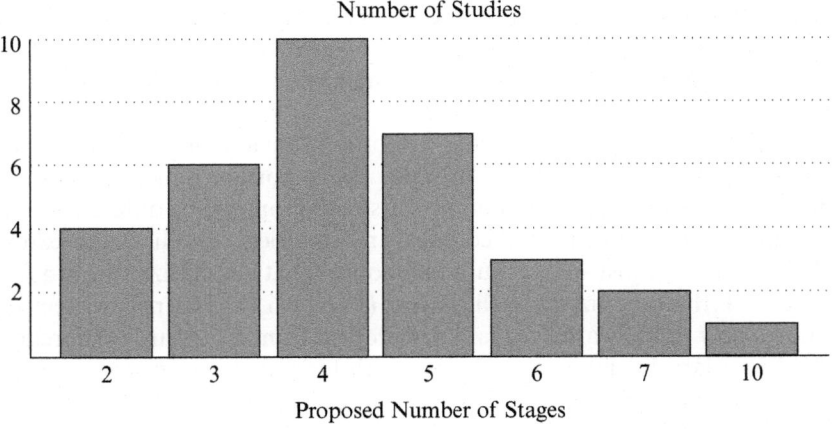

Figure 6.2   Analysis of 40 years of life cycle research

stay informal, small or medium sized either by choice or circumstance. Those that do reach the adult stage do so at different rates. More so, animals cannot move backwards in the growth process (from adulthood to adolescents, for example). Organizations can and do, however, downsize.

Similarly, the life stage of an animal is closely related to the age of an organism. Human toddlers are between 12 and 36 months of age, and puberty typically arrives between ages 11 and 15 years. But since the complexity of an organization is often more related to size than age, organizational life cycles are better characterized by size. In the for-profit literature, size is often measured by either the level or growth of number of employees or revenues (often simply called "sales") (Levie and Hay, 1998); in the nonprofit literature, because of the complications of volunteer participation, size is usually measured by revenues or expenses (Steinberg, 1986; Searing, 2015). Although size and age are correlated, an organization can spend an indefinite amount of time at a specific size without progressing, so age of an organization can sometimes be misleading.

Additionally, most species tend to have a large and stable adult population that nurtures a smaller group of more vulnerable adolescents. In a population of organizations, on the other hand, the majority of individuals will be small, with the adult population being the minority. The height and weight of all 20-year-old elephants in reality will follow a normal distribution centered on a species average, whereas organizations will follow a right-skewed distribution with many small organizations. The zoological analogy would be that for every adult elephant, we would expect to find hundreds of elephants that are 3ft tall. Although we do not have good systematic data on social enterprise organizations across corporate forms, nonprofit data can be insightful in this regard. If we look at the size distribution of US nonprofits in 2010 (measured by annual revenue), we can observe the expected pattern of a large number of small organizations (Figure 6.3). Most organizations are small (less than $200k in revenues a year). Only 18 percent of nonprofits have revenues above $1 million a year, but they accumulate 97 percent of all sector revenues.

Although there are 367 000 nonprofits that file IRS 990 tax forms in 2010 with reported revenues up to $35 billion a year ($3.6 billion if you exclude hospitals and universities), a whopping 82 percent of these have revenues less than $1 million, 58 percent have revenues less than $200k, and 43 percent have revenues less than $100k. In other words, the vast majority of active nonprofits are small. Conversely, 97 percent of nonprofit revenues accrue to the 18 percent of nonprofits with revenues above $1 million a year. The remaining 82 percent of nonprofits compete for only 3 percent of total sector revenues.

These data demonstrate the principle that there is not a typical mid-range size of organization from which small and large organizations deviate. Instead, the majority of organizations are small to medium sized, but there is a modest set of very large organizations. Although the analysis here is restricted to nonprofit organizations, this general distribution is typical across most organizational sectors (Hurst and Pugsley, 2011). Social enterprise populations can be expected to follow a similar pattern – at any

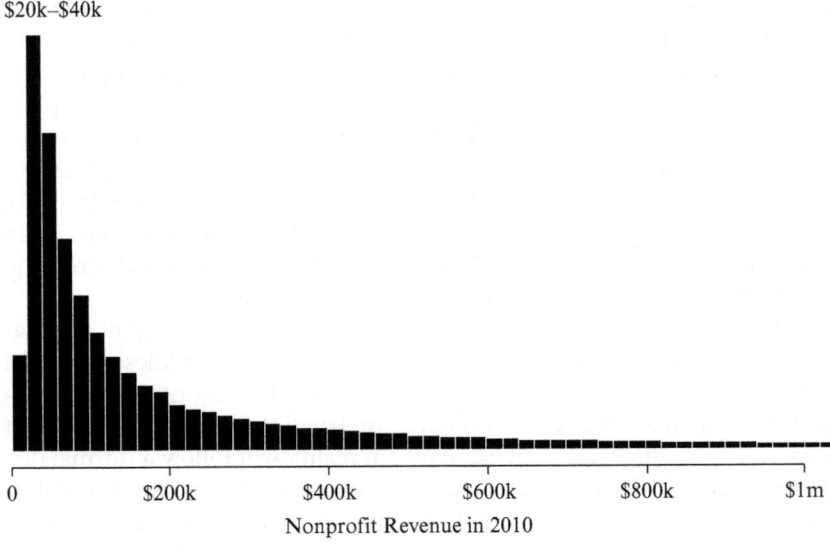

$20k–$40k

0            $200k $400k $600k $800k $1m

Nonprofit Revenue in 2010

*Figure 6.3   Size and distribution of nonprofits that filed IRS tax forms in
2010*

given time we anticipate many small organizations and a handful of large,
dominant ones. And over a period of time, most organizations will be in
the early stages of organizational life cycles, and only a small proportion
will have reached maturity.

Another way of examining this same relationship is by looking at
organizational age. Similar to the population pyramid within any country,
the age of organizations within a given sector will follow a distinctive
pattern with many young organizations and a declining number of older
organizations (Figure 6.4). This pattern is driven by two factors – as the
economy expands there is an increase in the total number of nonprofits
started each year. In the 1990s, for example, there were approximately
25 000 new nonprofits started each year, whereas by 2010 there were more
than 50 000. Since more organizations were started in the recent past, we
expect to see a large number of younger organizations than older ones. But
the pyramid is also driven by the death of organizations at all stages, which
means that, similar to human populations, many existing organizations
are not likely to live to see old age. In the for-profit sector, even though
enterprises emerge in much larger numbers, the mortality rate is also high:
only 60 percent of start-ups survive until age 3 (Gage, 2012). This still
represents a sizable net inflow of new organizations, however. Because of
these dynamics, growing industries will tend to have a very broad base and

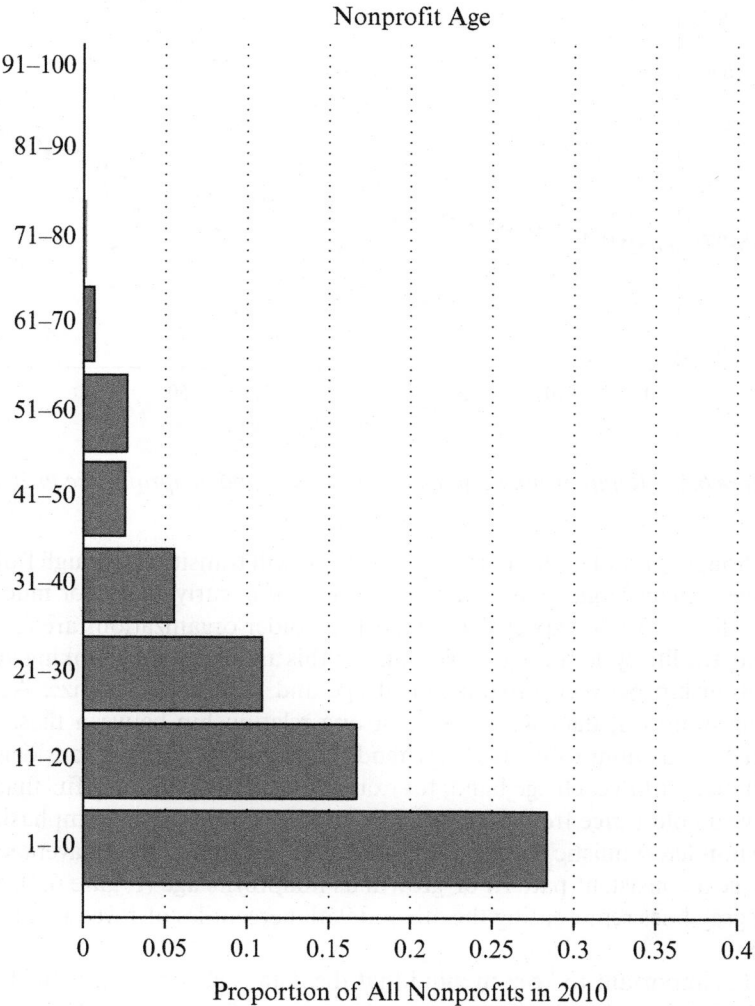

Figure 6.4   The organizational age pyramid in 2010

a narrow peak. We expect the social enterprise population to be even more dominated by young organizations than the greater economy due to the groundswell of attention given in the last decade to social enterprise, and the creation of new corporate forms specifically for social enterprises, for example in the UK (community interest companies [CICs]), Italy (social cooperatives), and many states in the USA (limited-liability corporations [LLCs] and benefit corporations, among others).

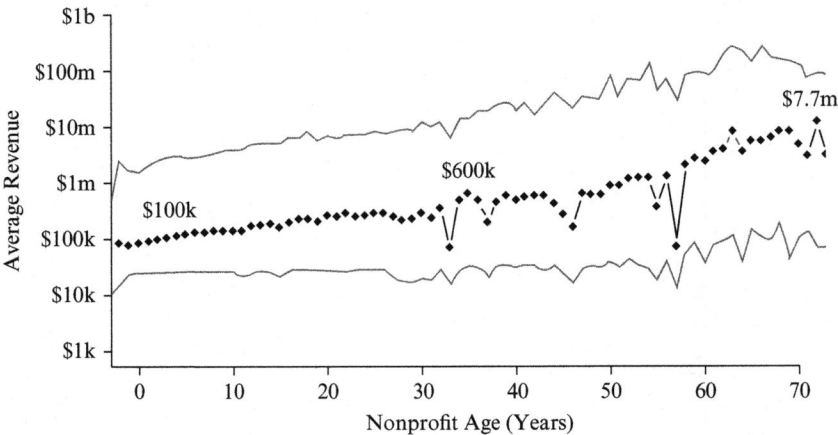

Figure 6.5   Relationship between nonprofit age and nonprofit size in 2010

Although it is not certain that organizations will transition through full life cycles – many organizations remain small and in early stages for much of their lives – we do expect that, on average, older organizations are further along the life cycle spectrum. We can test this assumption by looking at the relationship between organizational age and organizational size. Again, using nonprofit data we do see a strong relationship between these two variables: as nonprofits age, they tend to get larger. There is considerable variance within each age band; for example, revenue of nonprofits that are 70 years old range from $25k to close to $100 million, again emphasizing the nondeterministic nature of organization life cycles. But on average, we do see a consistent pattern of growth as nonprofits age (Figure 6.5), with the gray lines representing the 5th and 95th percentiles of revenues at each age.

It is important to keep in mind that the data is clustered near the lower end of the age distribution – almost 65 percent of nonprofits are less than 20 years old. This is partly what drives the clustering of organizational revenues between $25k and $200k.

A LIFE CYCLE EXAMPLE

Good empirical organizational data on for-profit social enterprises is limited: organizational forms like L3Cs and benefit corporations are new, and thus there are not many cases to observe; additionally, the ones that exist are mostly only a few years old. Though many social enterprises have incorporated as more traditional LLCs or for-profit corporations, they are difficult to identify systematically within corporate databases since most states do not have a code to designate a company as a social enterprise. Finally, the B-Corp certification from B-Lab is self-elected rather than a corporate form. The designation tends to favor wealthier, more established companies that can afford the certification process. As a result, a systematic analysis of the life cycle using for-profit data is difficult. Nonprofit financial data, on the other hand, is in the public domain and thus can be useful for constructing panels with large samples. Although not all nonprofits are necessarily socially enterprising (e.g., generate a significant amount of revenue through earned income sources), it is still instructive to look at how nonprofits pass through the organizational life cycles as the framework is largely generalizable to the broader social enterprise space.

In this section we examine life cycle transitions in nonprofits using a five-stage model:[1]

1. *Nascent stage.* The enterprise is being organized but has not yet been formally incorporated.
2. *Newborn.* The organization has been formally incorporated but has less than $100k in revenues and no full-time employees.
3. *Adolescent.* The organization has hired its first full-time employee and has begun the process of formalizing management and governance processes. Revenues range between $100k and $1 million.
4. *Young adult.* The organization has achieved a stable program model, has multiple staff, and has some formal organizational processes in place. It begins the process of scaling to reach a size where it can achieve more impact and is not vulnerable to small shocks. Revenues range between $1 million and $10 million.
5. *Mature organization.* The organization has become large, has a professional staff, a strong governance structure, and a stable revenue base. Revenues over $10 million.

These life stages and revenue cut-points are meant as general categories. The actual transition points between life stages will vary by subsector, but this global perspective allows us to highlight patterns of movement between stages over time. Using the Core Trend IRS 990 file available from the National Center for Charitable Statistics (NCCS), we analyze revenue data from 2000 and 2010 to examine the rate of transitions between each of these life stages over a ten-year period. Revenues have been adjusted for inflation, and the data include nonprofits from all subsectors of nonprofit activity.

Table 6.1   Changes in nonprofit size over a ten-year period

2000	$0–100k	$100k–1m	$1m–10m	Over $10m	Dead	Total Cases
Not yet formed	0.59	0.34	0.07	0.01	–	177 900
$0–100k	**0.44**	0.19	0.01	0.00	0.36	97 605
$100k–1m	0.10	**0.56**	0.13	0.00	0.22	101 976
$1m–10m	0.01	0.09	**0.64**	0.12	0.14	36 659
Over $10m	0.00	0.01	0.07	**0.81**	0.10	9 998

Table 6.1 is a transition matrix, where the rows represent the nonprofit status in the year 2000, and the columns represent the status in 2010. Each cell represents the probability of an organization starting in one stage in the year 2000 (the row category), and ending in another stage in the year 2010 (the column category). The highlighted diagonal represents the cases where an organization stays in the same category throughout the decade. As an example, an organization that has revenues between $100k and $1 million in 2000 has a 56 percent chance of being in the same stage of life in 2010, and a 13 percent chance of growing into the next stage (revenues between $1 million and $10 million). There is also a 10 percent chance that the same organization shrinks over the ten-year period, and a 22 percent chance that it ceases operating. The cells in each row will sum to one, representing all possible outcomes for an organization starting from the given stage in 2000, including organizational demise.[2] Analyzing data in this fashion is instructive in several ways. We learn the following:

Growth inertia is prevalent across all sizes of organization   This is evidenced by the most likely outcome for a nonprofit at any given stage that it is to be at the same stage ten years later. Unlike animals that pass through life stages rather quickly, nonprofits might spend many years at a specific stage and might never leave that stage. Similarly, when we do see transitions nonprofits are almost equally as likely to grow as they are to shrink. Medium-sized nonprofits (revenues between $1 million and $10 million) have a 12 percent chance of being larger ten years later, and a 9 percent chance of being smaller. For small nonprofits it is a 13 percent chance of growing, 10 percent chance of shrinking.

Inertia has long been a topic of the behavioral (Cyert and March, 1963) and ecological streams of organizational research (Carroll, 1984;

Hannan and Freeman, 1993). In order for an organization to survive, it must encode behavior in routines and policies so that it can perform standard tasks in a consistent manner. Once these routines are established they can be difficult to change, thus creating inertia within an organization.

Growth is slow   Those organizations that do grow transition only to the adjacent size category. There are almost no examples of organizations that leaped more than one size category in ten years with the exception of start-ups. The typical growth trajectory is steady, not punctuated. Some for-profit industries might diverge from this pattern in that nonprofits have additional capital constraints. Since nonprofits lack ownership rights or claims on profits that can be bought and sold, they have underdeveloped capital markets, which may curtail rapid growth. As an example, the average 2012 venture capital investment ranged between $7 million (Series A) and $39 million (Series D) (Morris, 2012), whereas the average foundation grant is less than $150000 (The Foundation Center, 2016).[3] Most social businesses would not have access to aggressive growth financing like venture capital because of their dual emphasis on both profit and social good, but they may have better access to growth capital than the typical nonprofit.

   The exception is the group of new nonprofits: those that were formed between 2000 and 2010. The majority start out small (59 percent), but there are 7 percent that breach the $1 million in revenues mark quickly, and 1 percent (roughly 1700 organizations) that achieve over $10 million in revenues within their first decade of operation. Some of this fast growth might be accounted for by things like mergers or the creation of a new nonprofit shell entity, such as a community development corporation, for a pre-planned or a spin-off project. But some will be the result of efforts by ambitious and successful new nonprofits. Eisenhardt and Schoonhoven (1990) observe the same pattern in data from technology start-ups with most firms growing modestly, but a handful with strong start-up teams and favorable markets experiencing meteoric growth.

Growth is hard   For organizations at all sizes there is a higher probability of closing than there is of passing to the next life stage (14 percent chance of growth versus 12 percent chance of shrinkage for medium-sized nonprofits, 22 percent versus 13 percent for small nonprofits). Growth is especially difficult for new organizations; they are almost twice as likely to close down as they are to grow (36 percent versus 19 percent). Failure can be even more prevalent in competitive for-profit markets; indeed, nonprofits have historically lower closure rates (Harrison and Laincz, 2008).

Nowhere to go but (closing) down   For those organizations that reach the stage of mature adulthood with revenues over $10 million, it is significant to note that they are more likely to close down completely (10 percent) than they are to shrink in size (9 percent). With median net assets of $14 million, one would expect that this group would be able to scale down gracefully if necessary. But once an organization has reached a large scale there are typically sunk infrastructure costs and stakeholder expectations that require the organization to maintain its size. If it begins to falter it might try to engineer organizational changes, which in turn can introduce instability that can lead to demise (Kotter, 1995). This process is discussed in detail below. So although the large organizations have much lower failure rates than other categories, they are not impervious to failure, and failure is a more common outcome than downsizing.

SYNTHESIZING DISTINCT LIFE CYCLE LITERATURES

Organizational life cycle analysis is appealing to scholars because it can be applied across a wide range of industries. As an example, scholars have analyzed industries as diverse as technology companies (Kazanjian, 1988), government agencies (Cosier, 1991), human service organizations (Hasenfeld and Schmid, 1989), airlines (Gudmundsson, 1998), and wineries (Beverland and Lockshin, 2001). The general applicability of a life cycle framework, however, should not detract from important differences in organizational processes that arise based upon the types of organizations studied and the markets in which they operate. We expect there to be important conceptual and empirical differences in life cycle stages across these industries.

Similarly, we expect organizational life cycles to vary based upon organizational form because of key differences in ownership structure, governance models, and capital constraints. The nonprofit sector and the social enterprise space have distinct characteristics that will impact how organizations grow and mature. As an example, Ben-Ner (1988) applied life cycle analysis to worker-owned firms in market economies. This required an adaptation of the traditional life cycle model since cooperatives have different capital and risk structures, but the life cycle model still offered insights into how these organizations grow and change. Following this initial step, several researchers applied different variations of life cycle theory to the nonprofit sector (Bailey and Grochau, 1993; Bess, 1998; Alexander, 2000; Jawahar and McLaughlin, 2001).

Although the life cycle framework is very flexible and can be applied with differing numbers of stages and definitions of when an organization enters a new stage, it is useful to consider how the life cycle may vary by sector: for-profits, nonprofits, and (various kinds of) social enterprise. Differences in organizational form across sectors will shape the life cycle process. Nonprofits cannot offer equity investments, for example, which can constrain efforts to scale up. This can be especially challenging in mixed-market industries where nonprofits compete directly with for-profits; witness that nonprofits have gradually lost market share to their for-profit counterparts in these circumstances (Salamon, 2015). Similarly, having a clear social mission can guide an organization, but it can also constrain its ability to adapt to opportunities within the marketplace as the organization tries to curtail mission drift. Small and agile for-profit forms like the LLC can operate with a small number of owners and a simple governance structure, whereas the nonprofit organizational form mandates a separation between management and governance, representing strategic complexity that can introduce challenges in scaling. Conversely, many nonprofit enterprises have missions with a local scope, and thus size is not considered important for impact. Thus, we might expect to see fewer nonprofits progressing through organizational stages to the point of large mature entities compared to for-profit vehicles that are built for scale.

For-profit firms often grow through product differentiation and the use of existing technologies to exploit new market niches. IBM started life as the Computing-Tabulating-Recording Company with expertise in manufacturing calculators and clocks. It eventually evolved into a leading computer and hard-disk manufacturer, and later exited commoditized markets by abandoning computers for business intelligence services and cloud computing. 3M started its organizational life manufacturing equipment for mining, but has evolved into the consumer and medical products company that we know today (think yellow Post-it notes). Although the decision to exit an existing industry and enter a new one is never easy, the corporate charter allows for this type of flexibility and adaptation since the primary duty of managers and the board is fiduciary responsibility. Many forms of social enterprise, on the other hand, have the organization's mission baked into the DNA of the company, whether this is simply part of the culture or has been formalized in corporate legal documents. As a result, increased financial viability is not a sufficient reason to evolve. Nonprofits and other social enterprise organizations do experience mission drift, which is a term with negative connotations in the social sector despite the fact that it is often driven by learning and survival. But how far social enterprises can drift from initial organizational purpose is assumedly more constrained than it is for their corporate counterparts.

There have been some initial steps towards formulating life cycle stages and needs for social enterprises specifically, though notably little from academia. The European Economic and Social Committee issued an opinion in 2011 explaining the need for such stages and briefly described the potential for hybrid finance types in helping organizations address the difficulties in scaling (Rodert, 2011). Consultants have offered guidance on unique management and finance techniques using life stages for social enterprise as well, though with little to differentiate the stages from the models of other sectors (Larson, 2012; ICS & Context, 2015). There are notable exceptions, however. One is a chapter by Jacokes and Pryce (2010), which applies a generic life stages model, but equips it with financing needs tailored to the unique social enterprise market. A second is a report published by Foresters Community Finance that draws on case studies of clients to construct organizational life stages (Burkett, 2010). A third is a toolkit developed by a triumvirate of three consulting agencies for UnLtd, a UK foundation for social entrepreneurs, which structures its recommendations along a matrix built on life cycle stages (HEFCE, Simpacta, and Red Ochre, 2012). Notably, practitioners have undertaken the majority of this work rather than academics, showing a demand for information from the field unmet by current research efforts.

CARING FOR ANIMALS AT EACH STAGE

Life cycle research has taught us general lessons about how organizations grow and change. Miller and Friesen (1984) highlight corporate strategies, organizational structure, and decision-making processes that drive the progression through each life stage. Gupta and Chin (1994) emphasize aspects of organizational culture that are important for progression through these stages, and are also protective of organizations during periods of decline. Phelps et al. (2007) demonstrate that transition through stages does not occur gradually, but rather through a tipping point or punctuated equilibrium process. The most actionable information that this research paradigm yields emerges from observations about proficiencies and deficiencies of organizations at each stage. What sorts of challenges should entrepreneurs or managers anticipate as they move from one stage to the next in the social enterprise zoo? What warning signs should they watch out for to prevent demise? In this final section, we combine groups that face similar challenges and consider three broad stages of life: formation or birth, growth and scaling, and maturity.

Nascent and Emerging Organizations

Newly formed organizations are frail because they represent a collection of untested hypotheses, many of which must be proven true if the
organization is to be born and survive (Andersson, 2015). For example,
organizations assume that there is actual demand for the product or
services that is being offered, and that they will be able to adequately
furnish that need at a planned rate for expected compensation from some
group (potentially separate from the service recipients). The process of
testing these assumptions and creating a stable business model is grueling.
Customer discovery can be daunting. Business models can change quickly.
Many entrepreneurs have multiple opportunities, and thus there is a high
opportunity cost associated with staying with a specific venture that does
not take off quickly. Most new companies are started by teams, so toxic
team dynamics can undermine success. New firms are often undercapital-
ized, so unexpected expenses can derail progress. New products or services
often lack legitimacy in markets, so significant investments are needed to
establish a brand; further, in social enterprise, the very concept of "social
enterprise" and potentially the chosen corporate form may also lack sufficient legitimacy due to their own newness. Collectively, these reasons contribute to organizational volatility for new ventures. Careful planning and
implementation can address some of these factors; research on appropriate
business models, adequate capital reserves, and rapid prototyping to iron
out program logic and team dynamics can all ease the launch. But these
strategies can only mitigate some of the risks, and often the best way to test
a business model is through creating the business, not excessive planning.

As an example, consider the case of Virgin Airlines started by Richard
Branson, an entrepreneur with no previous experience in aviation, after a
bad experience on a flight. In this case, the unfamiliar industry, the high
regulatory burden, and high capital costs of business formation created
significant challenges. Additionally, it was not clear if there was market
demand for a premium airline. The new venture represented an experiment
comprising many untested hypotheses about how customers would react
to a new product. Failure would result from any of Branson's assumptions
about customers and costs being wrong. In Branson's case, although he
was an experienced entrepreneur (he had already successfully built Virgin
Records), he took a risk by entering an unfamiliar marketplace. Although
these stories capture the public imagination because they are unique and
memorable, they are the exception and not the rule in the entrepreneurial
space. Most businesses are started by people with many years of professional experience in the industry they are entering (Shane, 2008). New ventures represent small variations of business models that the entrepreneurs

are familiar with; in this way they are able to minimize the number of assumptions they bring to the table. Similarly, a recent survey found that over half of nonprofits exist in some informal manifestation before they formalize as a registered organization. They operated an average of five years before incorporating (Van Slyke and Lecy, 2012), which provides plenty of time to iterate through program models, build a base of support, and test assumptions before making the entity official and becoming subject to scrutiny. Across organizational forms, a common way to mitigate risk is to utilize a familiar or tested business model.

Young, small, and informal organizations also face challenges stemming from inability to support an individual full time. Relying on volunteers for operations, governance, and administrative work can take its toll on key internal stakeholders quickly. Paperwork and taxes for any organization is complex, so the absence of paid staff puts the burden on the volunteers. The departure of core members of the volunteer team can take its toll, especially if institutional memory is lost and record-keeping thin. Organizations without staff battle volunteer fatigue until revenues can support staff who can shoulder the burden of the dry operational aspects of the organization that are necessary to pursue mission. Reaching a scale where the organization can support a full-time staff member (often simply allowing the founder to quit his or her job) creates the slack needed to begin building organizational capacity, the first step towards growth (Lecy and Searing, 2015). For example, the $160k milestone is important for nonprofits because it is roughly the threshold where they can support their first staff member, the point at which nonprofits can start formalizing organizational structures (Figure 6.6).[4]

When social entrepreneurs start mission-driven ventures, they will likely consider which organizational vehicles are best suited for their specific projects. Such considerations can include not only legal and financial advantages, but also the sector experience of the founding team, desires for autonomy, and public opinion on the form (Searing, 2014). In this book, Chapter 3 offers a useful glossary of corporate forms and their legal advantages, while Chapter 8 connects the type of good or service an organization provides with the type of finance best suited to it. It is also useful to consider differences in start-up dynamics across the sectors including start-up capital, organizational governance, and founding teams.

Although it is commonly assumed that new businesses fund their ventures through alternatives such as angel investments and bank loans, the vast majority of small business owners use their own personal capital and credit to fund their businesses, prominently including credit cards (Shane, 2008). Only 28 percent of nonprofit founders, on the other hand, contribute their own capital, and only 20 percent report taking on debt (Van Slyke

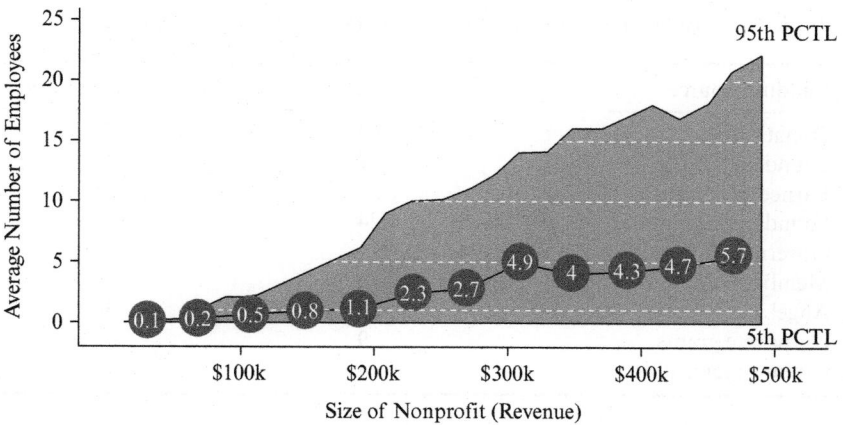

Figure 6.6   The relationship between nonprofit size and employment levels

and Lecy, 2012). The most important form of start-up capital for nonprofits is donations, with 69 percent reporting receiving them, and 37 percent reporting that donations are the most important source of early capital. Forty-nine percent of new nonprofits also report receiving grants from foundations, government, or corporations (Table 6.2). So not surprisingly, donative or philanthropic sources of capital are significant for nonprofits, which give nonprofits some advantages over other organizational forms. For-profit entities, on the other hand, can offer equity to outside investors. Although not a predominant form of capital for new for-profits, this can be a powerful source for those that have strong income-generating potential and desire to scale quickly.

In the past, start-ups were generally driven by a single entrepreneur who managed both daily operations and strategic vision (Scott, 1971; Adizes, 1979). Now, although one individual might be responsible for the vision and implementation, the Panel Study of Entrepreneurial Dynamics shows that between 40 and 50 percent of US businesses are started by teams (Ruef et al., 2003; Van Gelderen et al., 2005). Most entrepreneurial teams consist of friends and relatives from founders' existing relationships (Timmons, 1979; Neiswander et al., 1987). This is more prominent in the nonprofit sector with 93 percent of nonprofit start-ups reporting more than one founder, with a median team size of five (Van Slyke and Lecy, 2012). In addition, new nonprofits also include engaged board members. Thus team dynamics are especially important for small organizations; poor team dynamics and internal conflict can lead to dysfunction that can be destructive in the early stages (Searing, 2015).

Table 6.2   Reported sources of first-year funding by new nonprofits

Funding Source	Received (%)	Most Important (%)
Donations	69	37
Founders	28	14
Earned revenues	26	13
Foundation grants	24	12
Government grant	16	9
Member fees	16	6
Angel	13	3
Corporate grants	9	1
Parent organization	8	4

Source: Lecy and Van Slyke (2012).

Small and Growing Organizations

Organizational growth has been defined as the expansion of the product portfolio beyond the initial debut offering (Scott, 1971). Increased product or program complexity requires more complex institutional frameworks to manage operations (Downs, 1967). Growth can be dependent on the synergy between the life stage and the internal processes of an organization. For example, Kazanjian and Drazin (1990) found that decentralization and formalization of decision processes occurred as the organization passed through life cycle stages, and the degree to which the organization had these structures facilitated their success in each stage. Growing organizations face common problems surrounding cash flow, maintaining quality of production, and formalizing management processes (Dodge and Robbins, 1992).

Small organizations encounter a difficult paradox. Growth is hard – it forces an organization to stretch current capacity, mobilize resources, create liabilities, and experiment with new systems. The strain can be perilous; if investments do not pay off the organization can be thrust into a downward spiral that can lead to closure. Conversely, failure to grow poses its own challenges. It is easier to engage stakeholders in efforts to create something new or scale to increase impact, but it can be difficult to get support to simply maintain operations. Similarly, key employees can be lured to join an organization when they feel that they can make valuable contributions to shaping organizations as they grow. A big push can focus the efforts of the management team and the board through a sense of urgency and novelty, but energy can dissipate during periods of stagnation. As a result, small organizations can face challenges no matter what

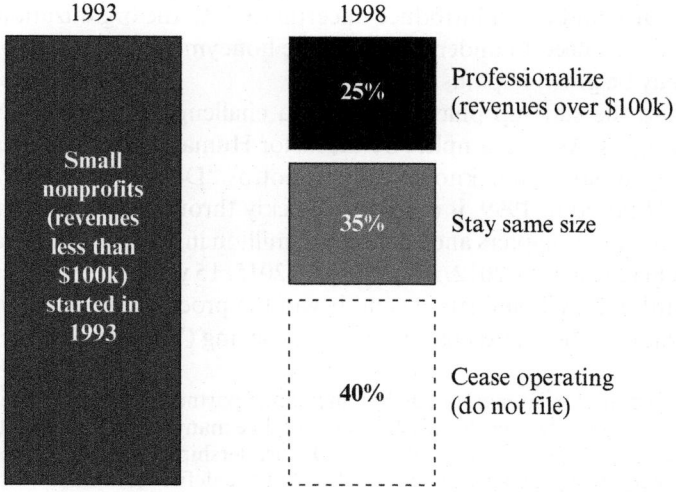

Figure 6.7   The fate of small nonprofits started in 1993 after five years

strategy they embrace – trying to maintain a modest operation, or trying to scale to something bigger.

Growth is the exception, not the rule. In many industries new organizations are more likely to close than they are to expand. As an example, a cross-section of nonprofit data shows that 40 percent of new, small nonprofits closed within five years, versus 35 percent that maintained their same size (revenues less than $100k), and 25 percent that began to professionalize (revenues over $100k) (see Figure 6.7).[5]

In the nonprofit realm, reaching between $100k and $150k in revenues (the point at which nonprofits start investing in professional overhead) and hiring the first staff member is a significant achievement for a small organization. Although there is now a better chance of avoiding volunteer fatigue, a small nonprofit still finds itself in a precarious situation. It needs to grow larger in order to achieve organizational sustainability, but it is also outgrowing its start-up identity. New organizations can benefit from passionate board members and committed donors that are generous with time and resources in order to breathe life into a new idea. The process of creating something from scratch can be quite exciting, so founding teams are animated by passion and enthusiasm. As the organization transitions out of this start-up phase it will often start to lose founding members, board members, and donors, some of which are burnt out from the big push to get the organization off the ground. The leadership may need to move from a start-up mentality to a more professional mindset. This transition can be hard, and it can introduce uncertainty into the organization. Small organizations need to understand that the honeymoon phase will pass and there may be growing pains.

Beyond the start-up phase, scaling is a challenging endeavor for small organizations. As an example, Architects for Humanity was a sophisticated and edgy organization known for its motto, "Design Like You Give a Damn." Started in 1999, it expanded quickly through an affiliate network of international chapters and achieved $6 million in revenue in 2011 and $12 million in revenues by 2012. In January of 2015, 15 years after it was started, the board declared bankruptcy and began the process of closing down the organization. The board chair is quoted as saying (Winston, 2015):

> Architecture for Humanity has had incredible partners and funders that made our work possible over the last 15 years but, like many charity organisations, we have had serious funding challenges. Our leadership worked to overcome the funding gaps to the best of their ability, but the deficit combined with budget overruns and an overall decrease in donations finally became an insurmountable situation.

Architecture for Humanity had a solid program model with strong supporters operating out of the international chapters. Its brand was well recognized – it had received the prestigious TED Prize and had inspired the Open Architecture Network. But operations were supported almost entirely by donations and grants, meaning it needed a sustained commitment from its base of support. The founders left the organization in 2013 to pursue other ventures, and the organization faltered shortly afterwards. Its story is fairly typical for an organization that is trying to transition from a new organization to a larger and more sustainable one.

The stages of scaling up, and slower, organic growth, are where we see the greatest differences between the for-profit and nonprofit sectors. The easier (though not necessarily "easy") access to capital for certain for-profit forms impacts the ability to scale quickly, since a large injection of funds is often needed. The transition to "professionalism" that nonprofits make with the hiring of their first paid employee also does not map perfectly to for-profits; though entrepreneurs in both sectors often don't draw salary and benefits at very early stages, many nonprofits will exist as voluntary organizations in perpetuity. Motives for growth may also differ, since very few (if any) for-profits want to remain voluntary, though some may want to remain small. This can likely be extrapolated to social enterprises across the two sectors, however, since all are (by definition) reliant on market income and should have a long-term goal of sustaining revenues.

Scaling is risky in a variety of ways. In order to grow organizations often take on debt and make a big push to build out programs and systems.

Donors are engaged to offer additional support during a period of scaling. These processes introduce stress into the finances of the organization and can lead to fatigue of founders, managers, staff, and donors. The process of expansion can lead to quality control problems that can damage the brand. Unless the organization can consolidate gains and achieve a sustainable base of customers or donors throughout the process they risk burnout. The exit of directors or staff will deplete organizational capacity, and the loss of engagement of key donors will result in financial shortfalls. Each of these risks can be damaging, if not fatal, to an organization that is trying to push from young adulthood to mature adulthood.

Mature Organizations

The final stage in a life cycle model is mature adult, the point at which an organization has achieved a scale at which it is sustainable. This stage does not imply that the organization will not continue to evolve or expand, but it will tend to have a core business model that can maintain it through the ups and downs of the business cycle, and provide some organizational slack as it evolves.[6] The challenges that mature organizations face are different from the challenges of younger organizations that are attempting to formalize operations and grow. They are challenges of sustaining operations and adapting to changing markets.

Mature organizations are characterized by longevity and the institutionalization of internal protocols. Leadership by a single person is uncommon and unhealthy (Kazanjian, 1988; Dodge and Robbins, 1992). Financial and managerial sophistication also increases with maturity. Miller and Friesen (1984) find that mature organizations view cost controls with much greater interest than younger, growing organizations; Kallunki and Silvola (2008) find that activity-based costing is also highly correlated with organizational maturity. For a small organization with $100k in revenues, a process that yields a 1 percent efficiency gain will only save $1k, a sum that is hardly worth the efforts to implement a new budgeting or managerial system. For an organization with $1 billion in revenues, 1 percent increase in efficiency yields $10 million in savings. As a result, large organizations have more incentive to adopt formal managerial controls.

The price of formalization is rigidity, which can ultimately result in poor performance and potential organizational demise (Walsh and Dewar, 1987). Organizational change must contend with existing organizational processes, power structures, and external stakeholders. As a result, although large organizations have more capacity for activities like research and development of new products or services, they also tend to be less flexible, which can make them unresponsive to changes in the environment and challenges from insurgent organizations. This process has been termed the liability of senescence (Hannan, 1998; Pérez et al., 2004), and is prominent in both for-profit and nonprofit industries.

Large organizations of any form can fail because of internal crisis. The most common form is financial fraud or embezzlement. The Association of Certified Fraud Examiners estimates that an average of 5 percent of revenues for businesses and nonprofits is lost to fraud each year (Boselovic, 2010). The most destructive forms are perpetrated by managers and staff within the firm, often through embezzlement made possible by inadequate checks and balances within the financial system (Greenlee et al., 2007). Similarly, ethical breaches by the director or managers can be extremely destructive. The poster boy for this type of behavior is William Aramony, president and CEO of United Way of America for 22 years. Aramony would reportedly reward female employees with financial benefits if they slept with him, used $450000 of company funds to woo his 17-year-old girlfriend, and siphoned $1.2 million to spin-off companies controlled by him and his friends. He was convicted of 25 felony accounts and went to prison for seven years (American Institute of Philanthropy, 2016). When the news story broke it created a crisis for United Way, which took many years to recover from it.

Another class of challenges that large organizations face stems from a loss of legitimacy that results from unscrupulous use of program funding, perceived or real. The Red Cross found itself in a firestorm over the reallocation of donations, following the 11 September 2001 terrorist attacks, to prepare for future disasters. It suffered heavy criticism and loss of revenues, but recovered (Associated Press, 2005). The grassroots advocacy organization, ACORN, was not so lucky. It became the target of undercover activists that visited ACORN offices and purportedly asked for assistance with illegal activities like sex trafficking. Video of interactions with staff was used by mass media to vilify the organization, and initiated a hearing in Congress to pull ACORN funding. Subsequent review of the videos found that they had been heavily edited and that ACORN staff were not complicit in any of the alleged activities. But the damage was done, and the public relations catastrophe toppled the organization (Memoli, 2010).

Large organizations, since they are visible and lucrative, must take special care to develop proper oversight and control from the board or executive members. It should be assumed that it is not a matter of whether fraud, ethical violations, or program scandals will occur, but when and how the organization will address them. In addition to these punctuated events, large organizations must also guard against pursuing new opportunities that may lead to mission drift. Each additional program area that a nonprofit develops will generate new organizational complexity and create new risks, so opportunities must be weighed carefully. Alternatively, a large organization cannot be resistant to change when markets and society are evolving. Many large for-profit organizations have notoriously imploded when new technologies have threatened their core business and they failed to adapt.

CONCLUSION

We have presented here several considerations regarding organizational life cycles. We contend that the basic life cycle model manifests itself in fairly consistent ways across all social enterprises. Each organization, whether for-profit or nonprofit, must survive the travails of start-up, must discover and refine its core business model, work to formalize organizational processes, then scale until it achieves sustainability and impact. These processes roughly coincide with life stages of birth, adolescence, and adulthood. Any organization that wishes to grow into a mature, large entity must pass through these stages. A low proportion of for-profits or nonprofits will reach the end stage, either because of choice to remain small or failure. Nonprofit data has been analyzed here to highlight these empirical patterns of organizational growth and transition between stages, although rates of transition and growth vary significantly by industry.

There are limitations to our broad approach. First, the literature on for-profit life stages is far larger and better developed than comparative nonprofit literature. By contrast, the availability of firm-level data, especially financial, is much more robust for nonprofit organizations than for closely held for-profit ones. Since many for-profit social enterprises are very young, this data limitation especially complicates the comparison between the sectors. However, this does lead to a very robust path for further research. Stronger firm-level comparisons will improve understanding of organizational health on the animal (organization) and species level. With the attention and scrutiny now being given to for-profit social enterprises and their accompanying funding innovations, this data looks like it may be on the horizon. Similarly, the academic literature and theoretical foundations for life cycle theory for social enterprises needs development, which should result from additional studies. Recent applications of life cycle theory to such "new" industries as open source software development are providing further empirical evidence and insights into such questions as the ability of enterprises to negotiate a more modern dynamic market than has been available to date (Wynn, 2003; Guimarães et al., 2013). Similarly, the application of life cycle theory to markets with social goals and fluid boundaries offers a fruitful line of research questions and empirical findings.

The particulars of the growth process will vary for each of the animals in the social enterprise zoo. Nonprofits are unique in that they can't raise capital through equity and the board structure generates complexity that organizational vehicles like LLCs do not have to address. As such, organizational capacity will look different across each organizational type, and the specific tasks at each stage may vary. Some businesses require large up-front start-up costs and others can be developed with a few thousand dollars in capital. Additionally, each specific industry will exert its own external forces on nonprofits. Some industries are crowded and competitive. Other industries change rapidly and force organizations to adapt. These characteristics are going to shape the specific challenges that an organization confronts at each stage of life. The cut points of $100k, $1 million, and $10 million in the nonprofit sector are simply rules of thumb to represent points where a business transitions from a side-pursuit or volunteer enterprise to a formal entity, from a small one-person shop to a professional organization, and from a small company to a large and sustainable company. These revenue mile markers will also vary by industry and organizational type.

The fundamental point is that life cycles matter for organizations, certainly those in the social enterprise zoo. Challenges are distinct, real, and often unique at each stage. Although not all organizations attempt to expand into large and mature entities, those that do will be expected to confront obstacles at each juncture. Having a sense of an organization changes over the life cycle can help managers and zoo-keepers prepare the animals, both individually and as species, for a long and healthy life in the zoo.

NOTES

1. The number of nonprofit life stages and the revenue cut points have been derived by looking at changes in the structure of nonprofit finances as they grow using IRS Statistics of Income (SOI) data, but transitions are not always crisp and alternative frameworks are possible. For details see Lecy and Searing (2013).
2. Death is observed by the absence of tax filings in the year 2010. Some measurement error is possible if the nonprofit has filed a 990 postcard or missed filing for the year.
3. Calculated from Foundation Center statistics that recorded 153 821 grants in 2012, totaling $22 350 012 897.
4. Analysis uses the National Center for Charitable Statistics (NCCS) 2010 Core Files with employment levels measured using the NUMEMPES variable.
5. Analysis uses the NCCS Core Trend data using organizations with a 1993 ruling date and revenues less than $100k in 1993.
6. In the nonprofit example, we find that finances stabilize around $10 million in revenues, but nonprofits can continue to expand to several billion in revenues. The adult stage has a wide range.

REFERENCES

Adizes, I. (1979), "Organizational passages – diagnosing and treating lifecycle problems of organizations," *Organizational dynamics*, **8** (1), 3–25.

Alexander, J. (2000), "Adaptive strategies of nonprofit human service organizations in an era of devolution and new public management," *Nonprofit Management and Leadership*, **10** (3), 287–303.

American Institute of Philanthropy (2016), "CharityWatch hall of shame," accessed 17 June 2016 at https://www.charitywatch.org/charitywatch-articles/charitywatch-hall-of-shame/63.

Andersson, F.O. (2015), "Nascent nonprofit entrepreneurship: exploring the formative stage of emerging nonprofit organizations," *Nonprofit and Voluntary Sector Quarterly*, 0899764015603203.

Associated Press (2005), "Despite huge Katrina relief, Red Cross criticized," *NBCNews*, 28 September, accessed 17 June 2016 at http://www.nbcnews.com/id/9518677/ns/us_news-katrina_the_long_road_back/t/despite-huge-katrina-relief-red-cross-criticized/#.Vp0PaFltVyU.

Bailey, D. and K.E. Grochau (1993), "Aligning leadership needs to the organizational stage of development: applying management theory to nonprofit organizations," *Administration in Social Work*, **17** (1), 23–45.

Ben-Ner, A. (1988), "The life cycle of worker-owned firms in market economies: a theoretical analysis," *Journal of Economic Behavior and Organization*, **10** (3), 287–313.

Bess, G. (1998), "A first stage organization life cycle study of six emerging nonprofit organizations in Los Angeles," *Administration in Social Work*, **22** (4), 35–52.

Beverland, M. and L.S. Lockshin (2001), "Organizational life cycles in small New Zealand wineries," *Journal of Small Business Management*, **39** (4), 354–62.

Boselovic, L. (2010), "Fraud is more common than you think," *Pittsburgh Post-Gazette*, 6 June, accessed 17 June 2016 at http://www.post-gazette.com/business/heard-off-the-street/2010/06/06/Fraud-is-more-common-than-you-think/stories/201006060181.

Burkett, I. (2010), *Financing Social Enterprise: Understanding Needs and Realities*, accessed 17 June 2016 at http://knode.com.au/wp-content/uploads/Knode_FinancingSocialEnterprise_E1LR_58p.pdf.

Carroll, G.R. (1984), "Organizational ecology," *Annual Review of Sociology*, **10** (1), 71–93.

Cosier, R.A. (1991), "Organizational life cycles: structural implications for OSD," *Public Administration Quarterly*, **15** (2), 224–38.

Cyert, R.M. and J.G. March (1963), *A Behavioral Theory of the Firm*, Englewood Cliffs, NJ: Prentice Hall.

Dibrell, C., J. Craig, and E. Hansen (2011), "Natural environment, market orientation, and firm innovativeness: an organizational life cycle perspective," *Journal of Small Business Management*, **49** (3), 467–89.

Dodge, H.R. and J.E. Robbins (1992), "An empirical investigation of the organizational life cycle model for small business development and survival," *Journal of Small Business Management*, **30** (1), 27–37.

Downs, A. (1967), "The life cycle of bureaus," in *Inside Bureaucracy*, San Francisco, CA: Little, Brown and Company, pp. 296–309.

Eggers, J.H., K.T. Leahy, and N.C. Churchill (1994), "Stages of small business growth revisited: insights into growth path and leadership/management skills in low- and high-growth companies," INSEAD Working Paper.

Eisenhardt, K.M. and C.B. Schoonhoven (1990), "Organizational growth: linking founding team, strategy, environment, and growth among US semiconductor ventures, 1978–1988," *Administrative Science Quarterly*, **35** (3), 504–29.

Gage, D. (2012), "The venture capital secret: 3 out of 4 start-ups fail," *Wall Street Journal*, 20 September.

Greenlee, J., M. Fischer, T. Gordon, and E. Keating (2007), "How to steal from a nonprofit: who does it and how to prevent it," *The Nonprofit Quarterly*, 21 December.

Gudmundsson, S.V. (1998), "New-entrant airlines' life cycle analysis: growth, decline and collapse," *Journal of Air Transport Management*, **4** (4), 217–28.

Guimarães, A.L., H.J. Korn, N. Shin, and A.B. Eisner (2013), "The life cycle of open source software development communities," *Journal of Electronic Commerce Research*, **14** (2), 167–82.

Gupta, Y.P. and D.C. Chin (1994), "Organizational life cycle: a review and proposed directions," *The Mid-Atlantic Journal of Business*, **30** (3), 269–94.

Hannan, M.T. (1998), "Rethinking age dependence in organizational mortality: logical formalizations 1," *American Journal of Sociology*, **104** (1), 126–64.

Hannan, M.T. and J. Freeman (1993), *Organizational Ecology*, Cambridge, MA: Harvard University Press.

Harrison, T.D. and C.A. Laincz (2008), "Entry and exit in the nonprofit sector," *The BE Journal of Economic Analysis and Policy*, **8** (1), 1–42.

Hasenfeld, Y. and H. Schmid (1989), "The life cycle of human service organizations: an administrative perspective," *Administration in Social Work*, **13** (3–4), 243–69.

HEFCE, Simpacta, and Red Ochre (2012), *A Comprehensive Guide to Developing Your Social Enterprise*, accessed 17 June 2016 at https://unltd.org.uk/wp-content/uploads/2012/12/full-toolkit1.pdf.

Hurst, E. and B.W. Pugsley (2011), "What do small businesses do?," *Brookings Papers on Economic Activity*, accessed 17 June 2016 at http://www.brookings.edu/~/media/Files/Programs/ES/BPEA/2011_fall_bpea_papers/2011_fall_bpea_conference_hurst.pdf.

ICS & Context (2015), "Supporting social enterprises from pre-start-up to scalability: challenging the status quo," paper presented at the Scaling Social Business in East Africa Symposium 2015, Kampala, Uganda, accessed 17 June 2016 at https://scalingsocialbusiness.com/wp-content/uploads/ICS_Context_paper_DEF.pdf.

Jacokes, J. and J. Pryce (2010), "The life cycle of social enterprise financing," in S.E. Alliance (ed.), *Succeeding at Social Enterprise. Hard-Won Lessons for Nonprofits and Social Entrepreneurs*, San Francisco, CA: Jossey-Bass.

Jawahar, I. and G.L. McLaughlin (2001), "Toward a descriptive stakeholder theory: an organizational life cycle approach," *Academy of Management Review*, **26** (3), 397–414.

Kallunki, J.-P. and H. Silvola (2008), "The effect of organizational life cycle stage on the use of activity-based costing," *Management Accounting Research*, **19** (1), 62–79.

Kazanjian, R.K. (1988), "Relation of dominant problems to stages of growth in technology-based new ventures," *Academy of Management Journal*, **31** (2), 257–79.

Kazanjian, R.K. and R. Drazin (1990), "A stage-contingent model of design and growth for technology based new ventures," *Journal of Business Venturing*, **5** (3), 137–50.

Kotter, J.P. (1995), "Leading change: why transformation efforts fail," *Harvard Business Review*, **73** (2), 59–67.

Larson, R. (2012), "Life cycle financing options," *Social Enterprise* [blog], accessed 17 June 2016 at http://managementhelp.org/blogs/social-enterprise/2012/03/07/life-cycle-financing-options/.

Lecy, J.D. and E.A.M. Searing (2013), "Growing up nonprofit: a coming of age story", paper presented at the Association for Research on Nonprofit Organizations and Voluntary Action Conference, Hartford, CT, 21–23 November.

Lecy, J.D. and E.A.M. Searing (2015), "Towards a theory of the nonprofit professionalization and growth process," paper presented at the Public Management Research Association Conference, Minneapolis, MN.

Levie, J. and M. Hay (1998), "Progress or just proliferation? A historical review of stages models of early corporate growth," unpublished manuscript, London Business School.

Lippitt, G.L. and W.H. Schmidt (1967), "Crises in a developing organization," *Harvard Business Review*, **45** (6), 102–11.

Memoli, M.A. (2010), "ACORN filing for Chapter 7 bankruptcy," *L.A. Times*, 2 November, accessed 17 June 2016 at http://articles.latimes.com/2010/nov/02/news/la-pn-acorn-bankruptcy-20101103.

Miller, D. and P.H. Friesen (1984), "A longitudinal study of the corporate life cycle," *Management Science*, **30** (10), 1161–83.

Morris, G. (2012), "Average venture capital deal sizes globally in 2012 – December 2012," *Prequin* [blog], 20 December, accessed 17 June 2016 at https://www.preqin.com/blog/101/6044/vc-deals-2012.

Neiswander, D.K., B.J. Bird, and P.L. Young (1987), *Entrepreneurial Hiring and Management of Early Stage Employees*, Cleveland, OH: Weatherhead School of Management, Case Western Reserve University.

Pérez, S.E., A.S. Llopis, and J.A.S. Llopis (2004), "The determinants of survival of Spanish manufacturing firms," *Review of Industrial Organization*, **25** (3), 251–73.

Phelps, R., R. Adams, and J. Bessant (2007), "Life cycles of growing organizations: a review with implications for knowledge and learning," *International Journal of Management Reviews*, **9** (1), 1–30.

Quinn, R.E. and K. Cameron (1983), "Organizational life cycles and shifting criteria of effectiveness: some preliminary evidence," *Management Science*, **29** (1), 33–51.

Rodert, A. (2011), "Social entrepreneurship and social enterprise. Exploratory opinion (INT/589)," Brussels: European Economic and Social Committee.

Ruef, M., H.E. Aldrich, and N.M. Carter (2003), "The structure of founding teams: homophily, strong ties, and isolation among US entrepreneurs," *American Sociological Review*, **68** (2), 195–222.

Salamon, L. (2015), *The Resilient Sector Revisited: The New Challenge to Nonprofit America*, Washington, DC: Brookings Institution Press.

Scott, B. (1971), *Stages of Corporate Development Part I, Case No*, Boston, MA: Harvard Business School Press.

Searing, E.A.M. (2014), "Judging a book by its cover: the role of corporate form in social enterprise start-ups," accessed 17 June 2016 at http://papers.ssrn.com/sol3/papers.cfm?abstract_id=2534782.

Searing, E.A.M. (2015), "Beyond liabilities: survival skills for the young, small, and not-for-profit," doctoral thesis, Georgia State University, Atlanta.

Shane, S.A. (2008), *The Illusions of Entrepreneurship: The Costly Myths that Entrepreneurs, Investors, and Policy Makers Live By*, New Haven, CT: Yale University Press.

Smith, K.G., T.R. Mitchell, and C.E. Summer (1985), "Top level management priorities in different stages of the organizational life cycle," *Academy of Management Journal*, **28** (4), 799–820.

Steinberg, R. (1986), "The revealed objective functions of nonprofit firms," *The RAND Journal of Economics*, **17** (4), 508–26.

The Foundation Center (2016), *Foundation Directory Online* [website], accessed 17 June 2016 at https://fdo.foundationcenter.org/.

Timmons, J.A. (1979), "Careful self-analysis and team assessment can aid entrepreneurs," *Harvard Business Review*, **57** (6), 198–206.

Van Gelderen, M., R. Thurik, and N. Bosma (2005), "Success and risk factors in the pre-start-up phase," *Small Business Economics*, **24** (4), 365–80.

Van Slyke, D.M. and J.D. Lecy (2012), "Profiles of nonprofit startups and nonprofit entrepreneurs," ARNOVA National Conference, 15–17 November, Indianapolis, Indiana, *Andrew Young School of Policy Studies Research Paper Series*, No. 12-28, accessed 20 June 2016 at http://papers.ssrn.com/sol3/papers.cfm?abstract_id=2175676.

Walsh, J.P. and R.D. Dewar (1987), "Formalization and the organizational life cycle [1]," *Journal of Management Studies*, **24** (3), 215–31.

Winston, A. (2015). "Architecture for Humanity board to file for bankruptcy," *Dezeen Magazine*, 23 January.

Wynn, D.E. (2003), "Organizational structure of open source projects: a life cycle approach," paper presented at the 7th Annual Conference of the Southern Association for Information Systems, Georgia.

PART III

Managing and governing the zoo

7. The role of social entrepreneurs in the social enterprise zoo*

Dennis R. Young and Jesse D. Lecy

INTRODUCTION

The purpose of this chapter is to understand why the social enterprise zoo supports a diverse ecology of animals and to analyze the particular nature of that diversity. Our unit of analysis is the animals (social enterprise ventures) in the zoo. The central character in our analysis is the (social) entrepreneur who as curator selects animals to be brought into the zoo. That is, social entrepreneurs are influential in the formative stages of a social enterprise, choosing to configure it in one form or another within the set of alternatives circumscribed by the boundaries of the social enterprise zoo (see Chapters 1 and 2) or possibly choosing to operate outside the zoo. Note, we use the term "entrepreneur" to connote the broader category of individuals (and teams; see below) who undertake new activities in the economy at large, and the term "social entrepreneur" for those likely to engage in social enterprise within the confines of organizations balancing profitmaking with social purpose as described in Chapter 3.

Several important implications flow from this analysis. First, we learn that social enterprise is not just about social innovation because development of the zoo depends both on innovators and imitators. The former break ground with new breeds while the latter support their dissemination, maintenance, and growth over time; hence the relative frequency of these two categories of social entrepreneur, as well as the variation of preferences within these categories, will help determine the overall character of the zoo. Of course, the degree to which the economic and policy environments differentially support these entrepreneurial variants (see Chapters 4 and 9, for example) will also influence the mix of animals in the zoo, the nature of the local ecologies in which they interact (see Chapter 5), and whether particular animals prosper or fail (see Chapter 11). The characteristics of the prospective animals in the zoo that entrepreneurs can consider include legal form, field of service, size and scale, and interfaces with business and government. Thus, our analysis suggests that designing the social enterprise zoo requires careful consideration of the set of choices potentially available to social entrepreneurs of various persuasions. While social entrepreneurs often come up with new ideas, these ideas are limited by context. Maximum diversity and possibility are achieved where external constraints are minimal and the resource and policy environment supports the freedom of social entrepreneurs to pursue their various goals.

Nonetheless, the role of the entrepreneur is central to the operation of the social enterprise zoo. Social entrepreneurs provide important curation activities related to the introduction and balancing of populations of organizations within the zoo through a matching process that is driven by their motivations, styles, and experiences on the one hand, and the choices of enterprise venture possibilities, on the other. Here we embrace a definition of entrepreneur that differs from commonly employed definitions in order to challenge some tautological aspects of popular perspectives. In particular, we rely on a distinction between 'conventional' entrepreneurs and 'Schumpeterian' entrepreneurs (Schumpeter, 1942) in order to develop a nuanced picture of motivation and behavior by the curators of the zoo. Additionally, we explore variations of entrepreneurial orientation within these categories. We then discuss how the two broad categories of social entrepreneurs work in tandem to shape the zoo through their complementary activities, and how variations within entrepreneurial categories further influence the population of animals in the zoo.

We expect conventional entrepreneurs and Schumpeterian entrepreneurs to approach the entrepreneurial process in distinct ways, and thus have different kinds of influences on the zoo. Schumpeterian entrepreneurs have impact through innovations that shape products, services, and market processes in ways that can transform industries. Conventional entrepreneurs have impact through the extension of existing technologies and business models. Thus, Schumpeterian social entrepreneurs shape the composition of the social enterprise zoo in new and interesting ways through reorganization of habitats, for example, creating new markets, seeking public policy changes, or introducing new animals and species – that is, organizations and industries offering new services or ways of doing business. Our analysis here focuses mostly on entrepreneurs' selection and nurturing of social enterprise animals. Conventional social entrepreneurs ensure that the animal populations are robust through appropriate health management, breeding and population control programs. In this way, both types of social entrepreneurs play vital roles in the birth, growth, and stability of populations, habitats, and ecosystems in the zoo. Entrepreneurial activity also reflects the fact that the social enterprise zoo is dynamic and that change may occur as part of a process of growth, adaptation, and demise over time.

The overall allocation of resources across species and habitats within the zoo will be driven by the way social entrepreneurs self-select into specific forms of social enterprise. If social entrepreneurs want to impact water quality in a specific village, they will have a choice. They can incorporate a nonprofit and support some or all of the activities through tax-exempt donations. They can incorporate a limited liability company (LLC) and try to drive change through ethical and strategic business practices, perhaps seeking to attract angel capital if there is a business proposition to be made. Or they can choose a for-profit social business form where the social mission is "baked into" the DNA of the organization so that investors are restrained from undermining the social mission in the name of profits. Such choices face both conventional and Schumpeterian social entrepreneurs and understanding them requires examination of the motivations extant in each of these entrepreneurial groups. Below, we consider how social entrepreneurs with alternative styles and motivations may gravitate towards selection of particular types of social enterprise. For example, if the motives include pursuit of personal wealth then the nonprofit form may be highly constraining and the social entrepreneur might opt for a different alternative. Enhancement of power, on the other hand, may not be so constrained in nonprofits or might be pursued through a variety of other organizational forms as well.

Entrepreneurs tend to act strategically, but there is no established decision manual for social entrepreneurs to help them choose a particular organizational form given a specific mission or motive. In many cases the choice represents a trade-off, not a hard constraint that favors one form over another. The decision will depend on a variety of factors in addition to intrinsic motivation, not the least of which is the feasibility of the proposed core business model. If market revenues cannot possibly sustain the organization while it is pursuing its mission then the nonprofit form is likely to be preferred as it can augment business activities with donations or grants, for example. Experience is also a powerful factor that will influence an entrepreneur's strategic behavior. Since risk is the entrepreneurs' ubiquitous and often fearsome companion when starting an organization, they are likely to operate through a familiar organizational vehicle and in a familiar industry in order to better manage risk, even if it is not the optimal strategy from an objective vantage point. The start-up costs associated with understanding a business model, an accounting system, and laws governing activities of a specific organizational form are significant and likely to influence behavior.

These factors – the mission of the nascent organization, the influence of experience on business strategy, the underlying motivations, and the willingness to innovate – will shape the choice of industry and organizational form in different ways for conventional versus Schumpeterian social entrepreneurs. Hence we expect alternative social entrepreneurial types to play different but commensurately important roles in the shaping of the zoo.

LITERATURE

The research literature on entrepreneurship covers a broad range of discussions about the nature of entrepreneurs, including the nature of entrepreneurial work, the degree to which entrepreneurs are oriented towards innovation, their demographic backgrounds, and their diverse motivations. All these are relevant to understanding the choices that social entrepreneurs make in selecting animals for the social enterprise zoo.

Characteristics of Entrepreneurs

Much of the literature emphasizes the innovative nature of entrepreneurs as it is this quality that is associated with successful companies and economic growth. We take a more skeptical view and acknowledge that innovation is important but also rare, even in the population of entrepreneurs. Although a highly desirable quality, we do not presuppose that the social enterprise zoo is dominated by innovative social entrepreneurs. Rather, we begin with a core set of characteristics common to entrepreneurs and then differentiate innovative from noninnovative types.

Despite Schumpeter's emphasis on innovation his basic definition of an entrepreneur can serve as the basis of a broader definition. Schumpeter saw entrepreneurs as individuals who implement "new combinations of the means of production" in five possible ways: introducing a new economic good; introducing a new method of production; opening a new market; conquest of a new source of raw materials of partially manufactured goods; and the reorganizing of an industry (Young, 2013). While the borderline between innovation and imitation is sometimes hard to discern, the essence of Schumpeter's definition is that the entrepreneur is an organizer and implementer of something new. This may be a new organization, a new program or service within an organization or a new way of offering an existing service. In this broader sense every entrepreneur creates something new, even if it is a replica of a service, program, project or organization in a new setting or market. Here we view the entrepreneur as the catalytic agent for getting something new in place, whether or not it is considered a true innovation in a deeper sense. In the context of social enterprise, this means that social entrepreneurs are the ones that establish new ventures and bring them into the social enterprise zoo. Some may consider themselves innovators and others not. Some may introduce exotic new animals and others more common breeds. But all social entrepreneurs are important for populating the zoo and establishing the character of the zoo animals.

There is of course a diverse, partially contradictory literature on what an entrepreneur actually does. It is fair to say, however, that entrepreneurs must make sure certain things do get done – whether by themselves alone or through delegation, contract, and working in teams. These tasks include establishing a vision for what is to be accomplished, and assuring that the requisite financial and human resources and structures are put in place to carry out that vision. While there is no necessary connection between entrepreneurship and risk taking or actually managing a venture, these are usually connected. An entrepreneur may put his or her own financial and time commitments on the line, be vulnerable to financial, reputational and career consequences of failure, and undertake to actually run the day-to-day operations once the venture is established. Alternatively, an entrepreneur may raise external capital, thus sharing financial risk with other parties, organize staff and governing boards and delegate responsibilities to them, and remain aloof from day-to-day operations. In all cases, however, the entrepreneur remains the "product champion" who, in the end, must make sure that all the pieces are in place and working in tandem so as to maximize conditions for success. In the social enterprise zoo, this puts social entrepreneurs in the position of choosing appropriate organizational forms, identifying and mobilizing resources to support those structures, and often leading organizations as their founding executives in the early years. But here too variants abound. Social enterprises may be initiated within existing organizations as well as outside them (e.g., commercial ventures within established nonprofit organizations), and entrepreneurs may choose only to get things started and move on to other things. (Serial entrepreneurs may go on to establish and spin-off multiple ventures over time.) Whatever the scenario, however, the social entrepreneur will shape the content and character of the social enterprise zoo with his or her choices and efforts to ensure venture viability.

The choices that social entrepreneurs make reflect a variety of motivations and circumstances. For our purposes here, we are interested in how social entrepreneurial motivations affect the content of the zoo, given the variety of legal forms and other strategic choices to be made for their ventures. This phenomenon is made more complex by the fact that entrepreneurs, social or otherwise, often work in teams. Nonetheless, there is a common perception that individuals start companies. We associate Ford with Henry Ford, Apple with Steve Jobs, and Facebook with Mark Zuckerberg. But in each of these cases the company was created by a founding team.[1] The confusion is understandable since there is often a spokesperson that acts as the face of the company, although this perception is misleading. The Panel Study of Entrepreneurial Dynamics (PSED) shows that between 40 and 50 percent of US businesses are started by teams (Ruef et al., 2003; Van Gelderen et al., 2005). A recent survey of US nonprofit start-ups found that 93 percent of nonprofits have more than one founding team member and the median start-up team has five members (Van Slyke and Lecy, 2012). The difference between for-profits and nonprofits may be the fact that for-profit ventures don't want to dilute ownership whereas nonprofits do not face that constraint. In either case we can assume that most social enterprises will be started by teams. It is also useful to note that the European (EMES International Research Network) perspective treats a group of citizens as the unit of analysis for social entrepreneurship, not the individual or team (Hoogendoorn et al., 2010). In the context of social cooperatives, we would also assume that these collectives are rarely founded by individuals. Although we will use the language of (solo) social entrepreneurs in shaping the social enterprise zoo, the reader should keep in mind that quite often it will be a founding team or group, not just a specific individual. The underlying assumption is that teams operate by consensus around common goals, motivations, and styles of operation.

Conventional versus Schumpeterian Entrepreneurs

Mark Zuckerberg's entrepreneurial pursuits were portrayed in an edgy and compelling fashion in the movie *The Social Network*. Mark Cuban entertains viewers as the over-confident yet likable billionaire entrepreneur on the US TV series *Shark Tank*. While not starting businesses, Richard Branson spends his fortune and free time trying to set world records or travel to space. It is easy to see why these fascinating individuals have captured the imagination of many and why they often serve as icons for the entrepreneurial world. However, their experiences are not the norm. Popular coverage of highly successful entrepreneurs leads to a skewed view of the aspirations and actions of many entrepreneurial actors.

In this chapter we offer a model for understanding how the motivations and behaviors of entrepreneurs shape the population of organizations in the social enterprise zoo. In order to develop the model, we need to first consider entrepreneurial motivations. In keeping with the broad social enterprise zoo framework we define an entrepreneur as anyone that has started a business, nonprofit, social cooperative or other form of economic venture, possibly within the context of an existing organization. Because media and scholarship often focus on the exceptional and interesting classes of entrepreneurs we need to be careful to differentiate "conventional" entrepreneurs from a special variety that we will refer to as "Schumpeterian" entrepreneurs.

The "conventional" entrepreneur is the representative case of an individual who has started an organization, new program or business venture in any sector. There are many theories about how entrepreneurs might differ from other individuals in orientations toward risk (Stewart and Roth, 2001) or distinctive abilities (Hartog et al., 2010). Studies have found that risk tolerance or tolerance of anxiety-invoking situations early in life predicts self-employment later in life (Burke et al., 2000; Uusitalo, 2001; Van Praag and Cramer, 2001). In general, though, conventional entrepreneurs are not very different from the general population. Specifically, Shane (2008) points out that the age and race of an individual tells you much more about entrepreneurial capacity than a battery of psychological characteristics. In contrast, Schumpeterian entrepreneurs are distinguished by an exceptional level of agency, a drive and capacity to achieve long-term goals, and a penchant for innovation. The term innovation is used broadly here to include a new technology or product, or a policy or initiative that stimulates social change.

The distinction is necessary because motivations vary between the two basic entrepreneurial types, and thus the ways in which each type shapes the social enterprise zoo. Relatively few entrepreneurs exhibit Schumpeterian tendencies, but they are the entrepreneurs often highlighted in the news and thus shape common perceptions of how entrepreneurs behave. Conversely, although they constitute a small subset of all entrepreneurs, Schumpeterians tend to have a disproportionate impact on industries and society, so they are an important class of actors. However, while conventional entrepreneurs have smaller effects individually, there are disproportionately more of them, so their considerable contributions are realized in the aggregate.

As noted, there is a common perception that entrepreneurs exhibit a higher capacity for innovation relative to the general public. The conventional entrepreneur, however, is not very innovative or strategic. Most businesses do not bring new products or services to markets, but rather they tend to enter very crowded markets with low financial returns and they do not deploy new technologies. Christensen (1997) differentiates between disruptive innovations (new products or services) and sustaining innovations (incremental changes to existing technologies or business models). Conventional entrepreneurs would be associated with sustaining innovations, whereas Schumpeterians would ignite disruptive innovations.

Demographics of Entrepreneurs

Despite popular perceptions of entrepreneurs as young whizz-kids dropping out of college and working in high-tech industries, the conventional entrepreneur is much more likely to be extra-ordinary rather than extraordinary. According to Shane (2008, p. 40):

> He is a white man in his forties. He is married with a working spouse. He attended college but might not have graduated. He was born in the United States and has lived here his whole life. He has spent much of his life in the town where he started his business. He is just trying to make a living, not trying to build a high-growth business. He worked previously in the industry in which he started his company, something like construction or insurance or retail. He has no special psychological characteristics.

These demographics offer a counterbalance to the popular biases about entrepreneurs stemming from media attention, and are useful for shaping a mental model of the typical entrepreneur operating within the zoo. These statistics are derived from large samples of individuals that start businesses (Reynolds et al., 2004), so they are useful in the sense that they are grounded in an empirical reality and highlight the quotidian character of conventional entrepreneurs. Schumpeterian entrepreneurs, however, are likely to be better educated, have strong technical skills sets, exhibit "grit" (Duckworth et al., 2007), and may differ on some important personality traits as well.

Although we know a great deal about characteristics of business entrepreneurs through large-scale studies, we know comparatively little about the demographic characteristics of social entrepreneurs (Hoogendoorn et al., 2010; Short, 2014). Some scholars have begun to develop databases of nascent social entrepreneurs (see Battiliana et al., 2012), but these studies tend to sample from specific programs like Echoing Green, which is likely not representative of the entire population of social entrepreneurs. Conversely, there are some efforts to use specific codes from the PSED II in order to identify nascent social entrepreneurs (Germak, 2013); subsamples using these codes might be more representative of the social entrepreneurial population but they still may not capture the full spectrum of social entrepreneurs. As a result, a definitive demographic profile of the social entrepreneur has yet to emerge. It is hard to tell if the average social entrepreneur varies from the average for-profit business founder in important ways other than motivation. Demographic profiles of nonprofit entrepreneurs differ slightly from their for-profit counterparts in that the former are older (the average age is 50 for nonprofit entrepreneurs and 45 for for-profit entrepreneurs) and have higher levels of education and income (Van Slyke and Lecy, 2012).

Motivation

Entrepreneurs commonly pursue multiple goals that include diverse personal objectives (Zahra et al., 2009). One might guess the most prominent would be wealth and power, but by and large the entrepreneur is motivated by other, more modest factors – primarily they seek autonomy, not success, and they often take a pay cut through self-employment in return for more independence (Hurst and Pugsley, 2011). Or to put it succinctly, "Most people start businesses simply because they just don't like working for someone else" (Shane, 2008, p. 43). Unemployment is also a strong motivator; more new businesses are started during periods of economic downturn than during stable periods because people are laid off from their jobs and have to find alternative means of employment (Koellinger and Thurik, 2012). Many people are pushed to entrepreneurship because they are marginalized from normal labor markets because of things like poor academic performance or criminal records (Fairlie, 2002).

Research also suggests that Schumpeterian entrepreneurs differ in motivation from conventional entrepreneurs. For example, Schumpeterians are characterized by stronger individual agency (McClelland, 1987), higher levels of education and greater technical skills (Crowe, 2015). They tend to be people for whom achieving recognition or meeting role expectations are important, they have greater confidence in themselves in social settings, a cognitive style that is focused on better approaches rather than novelty, and a stronger preference for individual work than the rest of the entrepreneurial population (Shane, 2008).

ANALYSIS

In an effort to understand entrepreneurs in the nonprofit sector, Young (1983 [2013]) introduced a multifaceted framework of entrepreneurial stereotypes that continues to be useful for scratching below the surface of the broad distinction between conventional and Schumpeterian entrepreneurs and for understanding how different types of social entrepreneurs may select alternative forms of enterprise for the social enterprise zoo. We reproduce this taxonomy in Table 7.1.

According to Young's original analysis, these stereotypes differ in their propensity to excel along four key dimensions: engendering trust, responding to extant market and societal demands, efficiency in the use of resources, and innovation. All but three types (independents, believers and conservers) were identified as having a propensity to innovate, but for different reasons. Professionals seek to innovate to achieve acclaim

Table 7.1   Entrepreneurial stereotype models

Type	Principal Source of Satisfaction
Artists	
Architect	Pride in building and workmanship
Poet	Creativity and implementation of ideas
Professional	Acclaim of disciplinary peers
Believer	Pursuit of a cause or mission
Searcher	Self-identity
Independent	Autonomy
Conserver	Preservation of a cherished organization
Power seekers	
Controller	Stimulation and security of feeling in control of people
Player	Acclaim, notoriety, and excitement of having power
Income seeker	Wealth

Source: Young (1983 [2013]).

in their disciplines; architects innovate by building new organizational structures; poets innovate to promote and implement creative new ideas; players innovate by making new deals, for example, partnerships, in the political and economic environments in which they operate; controllers innovate by offering new internal structures and processes to achieve better organizational performance; income seekers innovate by exploiting new opportunities for personal wealth enhancement; and searchers innovate by scanning the environment and finding new opportunities and identities for themselves. Given the preponderance of motivations and models that *may* lead to innovation, it may seem odd that Schumpeterian entrepreneurs overall are the rarer breed. However, note that with the possible exception of poets and professionals, all varieties of entrepreneur may follow the path of conventional entrepreneurs – choosing to engage in ventures that embrace no particularly innovative thrust. Thus Schumpetarian entrepreneurs represent a (possibly small) subset of architects, players, controllers, income seekers and searchers, while typical entrepreneurs would draw from all of these types as well as from independents, believers, and conservers.

Moreover, social entrepreneurs are more likely to draw on certain subtypes than others. For example, income seekers may be more likely to self-select into the conventional business sector, while controllers may be drawn more strongly into government, rather than engage in social enterprise.

Table 7.2   The distinction between conventional and Schumpeterian entrepreneurs

Conventional Entrepreneurs	Schumpeterian Entrepreneurs
Stay in the industry that matches professional experience	Willing to enter an unfamiliar industry
Low risk tolerance	Willing to take risks
Not profitable	Can be highly profitable
Redeploy existing technologies and services	Innovative
Self-employment or slow growth	Seek to scale

Behavioral Differences

The distinction between conventional and Schumpeterian entrepreneurs is not easy to observe. Both groups start new, market-based ventures. A conventional entrepreneur may end up with a very successful and lucrative venture despite no initial intentions to scale it up. A Schumpeterian entrepreneur might fail to disrupt an industry and end up with a very modest venture. There is a strong tendency in the entrepreneurship literature to categorize and sort by success, but we believe this is misguided since many entrepreneurs fail. Rather, in addition to motivations as considered above, we would look more closely at behavioral differences such as those shown in Table 7.2.

These behavioral differences can be important in the social enterprise zoo. Schumpeterian social entrepreneurs will select and nurture zoo animals that are different from their conventional counterparts. In particular, the former will be more experimental, introducing more dynamic high-risk forms while the latter are more likely to be more traditional in their choices. We parse this issue further below, examining the choices social entrepreneurs are likely to make among alternative business, nonprofit and hybrid forms.

Definition of Social Entrepreneurs

As previously noted, social entrepreneurs are individuals who pursue some mix of social goals and market success through the creation of a social enterprise. They are a subset of the general entrepreneurial population, and they are distinct from other community leaders in that they employ revenue-generating activities and work through markets to achieve social aims. They are different from other entrepreneurs in their explicit intention to achieve social impact (Mair and Marti, 2006), and they may also exhibit higher levels of ethical and prosocial behavior (Germak and Robinson, 2014).

The literature on social entrepreneurship has tended to characterize all social entrepreneurs as Schumpeterian. Consider some of the definitions of social entrepreneurs in the literature:

- "The change agents for society, seizing opportunities others miss, and improving systems, inventing new approaches, and creating sustainable solutions to change society for the better" (The Skoll Foundation, in Light, 2005, p. 5).
- A different kind of leader "who identifies and applies practical solutions to social problems by combining innovation, resourcefulness, and opportunities" (The Schwab Foundation, in Light, 2005, p. 5).
- Individuals with "the committed vision and inexhaustible determination to persist until they have transformed an entire system" and who "go beyond the immediate problem to fundamentally change communities, societies, and the world" (Ashoka Society in Light, 2005, p. 5).
- "The most prevalent use of the term social entrepreneurship focuses on the role of the risk-taking individual who, against all odds, creates social change" (Light, 2006, p. 47).

We concur with these proposed definitions only insofar as some social entrepreneurs do possess these characteristics and their impact is very important. However, these definitions tend to describe the Schumpeterian type and not the general case of social entrepreneur. Furthermore, definitions that include success as a criterion run the risk of becoming tautological. Admittedly, the academic literature is more measured (Zahra et al., 2009), but still tends to favor the Schumpeterian variety (Peredo and McLean, 2006). Given that we expect there to be a conventional class of social entrepreneurs who deploy sustaining versus disruptive innovations, and are more risk-averse than the Schumpeterians, our concept is broader and more representative than what we find in the mainstream literature.

Shaping the Zoo

In this section, we address the question of how social entrepreneurs shape the social enterprise zoo through the curation and replenishment of populations of their organizations and ventures. To answer this question, we must examine the process by which entrepreneurs select specific organizational vehicles to achieve their intended goals. Following Young (1983

[2013]) we postulate that entrepreneurs influence the population of the zoo through a sorting and selection process that matches an entrepreneur's motivation and style to a particular organizational form in any given field of service or industry.

Young's (1983 [2013]) original analysis described a two-stage process through which entrepreneurs were sorted first by industry and then by sector (public, nonprofit, business) within industries. In this chapter we will apply the model in a slightly different way – first asking how social entrepreneurs sort themselves by various organizational forms available to them for entry into the social enterprise zoo. Subsequently we apply this sorting analysis along other dimensions including field of service or industry, and organizational size. Implicitly we also assume that most entrepreneurs will select themselves out of the zoo because their interests do not fall within the quadrant of Figure 2.1 in Chapter 2 that requires both profitability and positive social impact. As described in Chapters 1, 2, and 3 in this volume, social enterprise may assume many different forms within the array of possible organizations that are both (potentially) profitable and have a positive social impact on society (Figure 2.1, Chapter 2). Broadly speaking, the choices are as follows:

- *Private nonprofit organizations* that must sustain themselves in the marketplace and that address a social mission while prohibiting the distribution of profits.
- *Social businesses* that may distribute profits to their owners but that also explicitly state their intent to address particular social goals.
- *Sustainable businesses* that are profit seeking but also promise to avoid social and environmental damage or contribute certain social benefits.
- *Social cooperatives* that may share financial surpluses among their members but also seek to address broad social goals. Context (habitat) is an important factor in the prominence of social cooperatives. In Europe or Quebec, for example, where the social economy concept prevails over a strictly sectoral perspective of separate nonprofit, for-profit and government sectors, social cooperatives, with their combination of social purpose and limited profit distribution may occupy a niche similar to that of US-style nonprofits.

As discussed in earlier chapters, there are numerous variations and combinations of these forms including so-called public sector nonprofits (Mook et al., 2015), which are nonprofit organizations established or authorized by government, public–private partnerships that engage businesses, government agencies and nonprofits in various combinations and arrangements, and several variants of social businesses as described in Chapter 3. However, these four will suffice here to consider how latent populations of social entrepreneurs sort themselves out so as to yield particular combinations of forms in the social enterprise zoo. We are especially interested in the question of whether certain forms of social enterprise are likely to be innovative by attracting Schumpeterians into the zoo. This is best approached by considering each of the entrepreneurial types with a possible innovative bent who are thus the source of Schumpeterians in the social enterprise zoo:

- *Professionals* seem more likely to employ the nonprofit form for their ventures, so as to emphasize the intrinsic merits of their innovations and the recognition they would receive from them, as compared with the material rewards. Social cooperatives may provide another alternative for professionals in certain contexts.
- *Architects* may find attractive the freedom and flexibility of private, for-profit forms of social enterprises – either sustainable businesses or social businesses – for indulging their propensities to make deals and build their organizations. Architects may also be drawn to these forms because of the availability of equity capital that can underwrite faster growth. However, barriers to entry for nonprofits also tend to be low in many fields; thus nonprofits may also offer a desirable alternative to architects who can exploit the multiple possible sources of funding that nonprofits offer – including philanthropic and governmental resources.
- *Poets* seem more likely to operate within the nonprofit sector, or through social cooperatives, where they can pursue their visions without heavy pressures towards profitability and where they can appeal to diverse philanthropic or member interests. Still, a visionary poet might also find a niche in a social business if private investors can be found who share the social entrepreneur's ideas.
- *Players* are likely to find more flexibility to wheel and deal in the for-profit sector – through social purpose or sustainable businesses, especially where they can find investors, and perhaps engage public and nonprofit sector partners, to work with.
- *Controllers* seem best suited for the nonprofit form where they can engage supportive but noninterfering governing boards, be selective in the kinds of funders they solicit, and avoid the conflicting pressures that might be imposed by external investors concerned about profits or favoring different strategic approaches to profitable social ventures. However, nonprofit boards and various types of funders can certainly be constraining or directive in their behaviors, so

controllers must be strategic in designing their governance arrangements and managing their enterprises to assure their authority.

- *Income seekers* are more likely to be attracted to sustainable businesses and some forms of social business that do not strongly inhibit
  the distribution of profits to shareholders. Alternatively, income
  seekers can sometimes find ways to assure lucrative compensation
  through nonprofits or other forms.
- *Searchers* are the most difficult kind of entrepreneur to discern.
  They are opportunity seekers who haven't quite figured out what it is
  they want to do or accomplish. All forms of social enterprise would
  receive their scrutiny and could engage their energies.

These sorting propensities suggest that innovative social enterprises
are likely to be brought into the zoo by Schumpeterian social entrepreneurs of multiple persuasions. Surely standard nonprofits offer opportunities for certain potentially innovative types including professionals,
poets, controllers, and searchers. In addition, business forms including
sustainable and social businesses may be preferred by players, income
seekers, and possibly architects and searchers, either for the flexibility
they offer or the opportunities for personal wealth enhancement that
they present.

A similar sorting process will face conventional social entrepreneurs, but
with a somewhat different mix. In particular, independents may prefer the
autonomy afforded by nonprofits with compliant governing boards and
dependable funding sources or perhaps more likely they may favor social
or sustainable businesses that are privately owned and not reliant on influential shareholders. Similarly, believers may prefer the option to engage
through nonprofits or social cooperatives that do not impose severe trade-
offs between pursuit of their goals and financial success. Additionally,
conservers will undertake their efforts within established organizations,
most likely nonprofits or cooperatives whose socially impactful work they
cherish, although conservers may also act to make sustainable businesses
to which they are loyal more socially responsible in order to preserve their
long-term viability.

For many conventional social entrepreneurs, the selection of forms
for the social enterprise zoo is likely to follow similar logics to those of
Schumpeterians with whom they share motives and values, as considered
above. The fact that conventional entrepreneurs also embrace types with
weaker propensities to innovate (independents, believers, conservers) may
shift their choices proportionally towards nonprofit and cooperative forms
compared to business forms of social enterprise.

Combining our analyses of Schumpeterian and conventional

entrepreneurs, we can expect the different forms of social enterprise to exhibit different propensities as to whether they are internally driven by entrepreneurial motives or responsive to external pressures and opportunities. In particular, the various entrepreneurial types can be clustered into two broad categories of responsiveness to their environments: (1) *opportunistic social entrepreneurs* including income seekers, searchers, architects, and players are most responsive to incentives and opportunities stemming from the market and external sources of funding; (2) in contrast, *internally-driven social entrepreneurs*, including poets, professionals, and believers, are more likely to follow their own muses with respect to ideas, causes and favored solutions. As discussed below, this dichotomy comes into play in analyzing the performance of social enterprises both in terms of the quality of services and their responsiveness to constituent needs.

Impact and Expectations

Schumpeter linked business cycles to economic growth through a theory of creative destruction. Innovative firms generate new products or services that lead to the development of new industries and markets, but these markets are constantly upended by new technologies. The VCR generated a robust market for home movies, and was then replaced by the superior DVD technology, which was replaced by Internet streaming of movies. In each case new industries emerged and markets were dominated by specific players. RCA popularized the VCR format and enjoyed a dominant position, but lost market power when DVDs replaced the VCR format. Blockbuster served as a dominant distributor of DVDs for home consumption until Netflix improved upon the delivery process through mail and Internet streaming options. A firm has incentive to innovate because it does not have to compete with incumbents on their own terms, but rather can shape new markets and enjoy leverage from early entry. Figure 7.1 illustrates the waves of destruction and innovation described by Schumpeter such as the video technology example above.

Industries follow a predictable life cycle. The emergence of a new industry attracts the attention of entrepreneurs and companies since there is an opportunity to gain a share of a growing market. Many firms enter the new market and failure rates are low because there is little competition and plenty of customers to go around. As the industry ages, though, competition intensifies as a result of the number and size of existing firms and markets become saturated. More firms begin to fail at higher rates and fewer new firms are created.

Schumpeterian and conventional entrepreneurs have different roles to

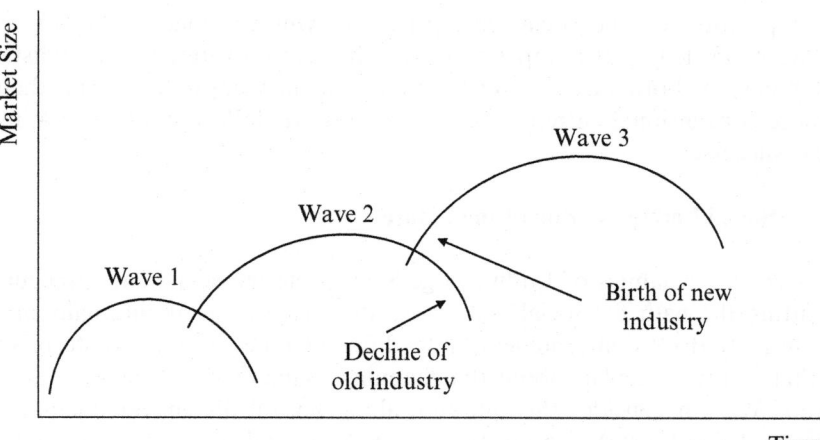

Figure 7.1   The process of creative destruction in industry through waves of innovation

play in generating impact. In this model the Schumpeterian entrepreneurs will be the ones that develop technologies and institutions that lead to the creation of new industries. In many cases this involves changing public policy or making huge infrastructure investments (often through public support) in order to make it possible for the industry to operate. They absorb many of the collective action costs associated with bringing a new business to the market, and thus create opportunities for subsequent waves of (conventional) entrepreneurs to enter a more stable market with lower entry costs (Thornton et al., 2012).

We argue here that the process of populating the social enterprise zoo is similar to the Schumpeterian process of industrial development and evolution. We expect that Schumpeterian social entrepreneurs, motivated by various factors that lead them to create innovative new ventures, will provide a leading edge to the zoo, which nonetheless will be largely populated by ventures led by conventional social entrepreneurs who keep the fires burning and adapt over time to the new ways established by their Schumpeterian colleagues when the latter's ventures succeed. To the extent that Schumpeterians make different choices of social enterprise forms to bring into the zoo than their conventional counterparts, we can expect to see the composition of the zoo change over time. If our theory is correct, this may signal a more prominent future role for social and sustainable businesses that are somewhat more favored by Schumpeterians, and an adaptive bent on the part of nonprofits and cooperatives to embrace social innovations. There seems little doubt therefore that the composition of the social enterprise zoo will continue to evolve, as enterprises led by Schumpeterians of various motivational and stylistic persuasions both succeed and fail with their new approaches, and their more conventional entrepreneurial counterparts follow suit by imitating the successes.

The Social Enterprise Zoo of the Future

Given the dynamics of leading edge Schumpeterian social entrepreneurs cutting the path for social enterprise, and the sorting of internally and externally driven entrepreneurs into different types of social enterprise, what can we speculate about the changing shape of the social enterprise zoo? We can consider this question along several dimensions including sectoral (legal form), composition (types of animals in the zoo), the relations with government and business that will alter the habitats of the zoo, the fields of service in which social enterprise will manifest itself, the scales of provision at which social enterprise will operate (big animals or small), and the emphases on quality and responsiveness of social enterprise services (performance of the animals and the zoo as a whole). To pursue this analysis, we will consider first the Schumpeterians of various persuasions and the conventional social entrepreneurs who will follow in their wake. Of course, this exercise is intended only to generate hypotheses that ultimately require empirical investigation.

Legal forms

As suggested above, Schumpeterian social entrepreneurs such as architects, players and income seekers are likely to exploit the new possibilities for social enterprise outside of the traditional nonprofit and cooperative sectors, especially the proliferation of new forms of social business as documented in Chapter 3. In contrast, players, controllers, and searchers are likely to innovate within the nonprofit and cooperative sectors. However, given the proclivities of architects, players, and income seekers to experiment and foster growth, the new business sector possibilities seem likely to expand disproportionally within the social enterprise zoo. Meanwhile, the more conventional independents, conservers, and believers are likely to maintain and exploit existing nonprofit and cooperative forms, so that overall the social enterprise zoo will maintain a relative balance of old and new forms. Schumpeterian-led "creative destruction" may lead to some competition among forms but no one form seems likely to dominate over time.

Fields of service

The availability of new legal forms opens up social enterprise beyond the human services, arts, and other fields conventionally addressed by the non-profit and cooperative sectors. We can thus imagine a much wider variety of animals in the social enterprise zoo than is currently the case, many in the form of new social businesses. Schumpeterian architects, professionals, poets, players, income seekers, and searchers will explore territory heretofore confined to commercial enterprise, such as expanding telecommunications (for low-income populations), starting small businesses (in low-income areas), offering new and more economical and accessible products to address health, nutrition, sanitation, transportation, and education needs (of remote or low-income populations), and so on. In other words, the social enterprise zoo of the future offers latent social entrepreneurs more fields of activity in which to operate. Schumpeterians will exploit this opportunity to address human needs in more creative ways than has heretofore been possible through traditional profit-maximizing business or conventional nonprofit and cooperative enterprises. Conventional social entrepreneurs, especially independents, will follow suit, imitating early successes of their Schumpeterian predecessors, to move into new fields of service and maintain social enterprises in these domains.

Relations with business and government

The social enterprise zoo offers the opportunity for Schumpeterian social entrepreneurs to continue to blur the boundaries between business, government, and social enterprise. Hybridity has become almost a mantra in recent years for efforts to address social problems in new ways (Billis, 2010). Schumpeterian architects, poets, players, and income seekers are likely to be more and more sector agnostic in their efforts to address their goals, hence encouraging partnership and other arrangements that bring business, government, and nonprofit forms together around social issues. While, government agencies and traditional businesses are unlikely animals in the zoo itself, social enterprises may be manifested in the form of bridging organizations, networks, and other arrangements that will populate and modify the habitats within the zoo. While, Schumpeterians lead the charge towards greater hybridity, some conventional social entrepreneurs, including believers, will join the party as the efficacy of hybrid arrangements is more firmly established.

The growth of hybridity has different implications for business and government. Government will continue to have more of a regulatory and supportive role, especially financial, while withdrawing further from direct service delivery. Business is more and more likely to enter the social enterprise zoo itself (in the form of sustainable or social businesses), or to link up with other animals in the zoo, as Schumpeterian social entrepreneurs within the business sector push their corporate hosts to become more economically and environmentally sustainable and more willing to evaluate the social impacts of their actions. This tendency may be driven by income seekers and players who see the handwriting on the wall, and embraced by the conventional social entrepreneur conservers who may fear for the future of their companies if they remain insensitive to social issues. In all, the social enterprise zoo, tended by social entrepreneurs of various persuasions, is fertile ground for continued hybridization and the proliferation of mixed forms of social enterprise at the expense of the purer contemporary types of today. In all, the biodiversity of the social enterprise zoo seems likely to increase over time.

Scale: big animals and small
Preferences on the size of organizations vary among the different types of social entrepreneurs. Among those with a Schumpeterian bent, professionals, architects, players, controllers, and income seekers benefit most from large organizations that can better accommodate their goals, while poets and searchers can satisfy their needs in smaller, more flexible and nimble organizations. Among conventional social entrepreneurs, independents and believers also favor smaller organizations while conservers seek to protect long-standing enterprises, large and small. Thus we expect organizations of varying size to be introduced into the zoo by Schumpeterians and to be nurtured by their conventional social entrepreneurial counterparts. Since conventional entrepreneurs are likely represented substantially in every variant of social entrepreneurial preference, we can expect the ecology of social enterprise in the zoo to continue to be well represented along a wide spectrum of organizational sizes, within the accommodations of the political and economic environment and life cycle constraints (see Chapter 6). As suggested below, however, the tendency to grow may vary by type of social enterprise as a result of the sorting of entrepreneurial motivations.

Quality and responsiveness
As noted, entrepreneurs of different persuasions will sort themselves out among alternative types of social enterprise. This in turn will have implications for the quality of services and the responsiveness to funding and market opportunities for different types of social enterprise. Table 7.3 summarizes what we may expect to develop along these lines as the choices of social enterprise vehicles become more salient.

As Table 7.3 suggests, profit-limited forms of social enterprise such as nonprofits and cooperatives can be expected to be largely internally driven, piecing together their resources to address self-conceived social goals and

Table 7.3   *The sorting process of types of social entrepreneurs and the types of enterprises they gravitate towards*

Type of Enterprise	Social Entrepreneurs	Quality and Responsiveness
Nonprofits	Believers, conservers, poets, professionals, independents, controllers, searchers Largely internally driven	Primary attention to quality as defined by entrepreneurial ideas, within constraints of donor and other funder preferences
Social cooperatives	Believers, poets, conservers, searchers Largely internally driven	Primary attention to quality as defined by entrepreneurial ideas, constrained by member and funder preferences
Social businesses	Independents, believers, income seekers, architects, players, searchers Largely externally driven	Primary attention to market opportunities and investor preferences, shaped by entrepreneurial ideas and social interests
Sustainable businesses	Income seekers, independents, architects, players, conservers Largely externally driven	Primary attention to market opportunities and pressures and investor preferences, shaped by entrepreneurial interests

solutions. By contrast, for-profit variations of social enterprise including social and sustainable businesses are likely to be more opportunistic and more responsive to social needs as defined by investors and consumers. Translating these tendencies into net social impact is complex. Profit-limited forms may face more severe resource limitations although their services may often be path-breaking and more sources (such as philanthropy and volunteering) may be open to them. For-profit forms will take advantage of a wider array of capital funding opportunities (despite limited access to certain sources such as philanthropy) and investor interests and while their offerings may be more mainstream and closer to market and investor preferences they may have greater opportunities for growth and large scale impact.

CONCLUSION

The social enterprise zoo as it manifests itself in various places around the world is likely still in an early stage of its evolution. Its future development will depend heavily on the energies of social entrepreneurs whose choices will help determine the variety and character of the animals in the zoo. Leading-edge Schumpeterian social entrepreneurs will continue to introduce new forms of enterprise, new ideas for addressing social problems, and new partnership arrangements and they will widen the field of services and industries in which social enterprises operate. Their conventional social entrepreneurial counterparts will imitate, tend and nurture the innovations that take root. Given a supportive economic and political environment, we can expect the biodiversity of the zoo to increase, with social enterprises large and small, profit and nonprofit, cross-sectoral partnerships, and hybrids all having a place in the zoo. The boundaries of the zoo may exclude enterprises indifferent to social good or market success, but otherwise they are likely to be wide open to problem-solving products, programs, and services of every variety previously confined either to markets, governments or traditional third sector organizations. New pharmaceuticals, transportation and communication technologies, educational products, nutritional and agricultural initiatives, and energy projects will take their place alongside more conventional healthcare, education, social service, environmental and cultural programming, to populate the social enterprise zoo of the future, at least if opportunistic and internally-driven social entrepreneurs have their way. Accommodative public policies governing the zoo (see Chapter 9), sufficient allocation of public and voluntary as well as market resources (see Chapter 8) and supportive social policies (see chapter 4) will be needed to assure that possibility.

NOTES

*   This chapter is based on ideas discussed in Young and Lecy (2014).
1.   Microsoft (2007), "If you are going to launch a start-up, how many friends would you need?," accessed 18 June 2016 at http://blogs.msdn.com/b/testing123/archive/2007/02/23/if-you-are-going-to-build-a-start-up-how-many-friends-should-you-start-up-with.aspx.

REFERENCES

Battiliana, J., M. Lee, J. Walker, and C. Dorsey (2012), "In search of the hybrid ideal," *Stanford Social Innovation Review*, **10** (3), 50–55.
Billis, D. (ed.) (2010), *Hybrid Organizations and the Third Sector*, Basingstoke, UK: Palgrave Macmillan.
Burke, A., F. Fitzroy, and M. Nolan (2000), "When less is more: distinguishing between entrepreneurial choice and performance," *Oxford Bulletin of Economics and Statistics*, **62** (5), 565–86.

Christensen, C.M. (1997), *The Innovator's Dilemma: When New Technologies Cause Great Firms to Fail*, Watertown, MA: Harvard Business Review Press.
Crowe (2015), "Here's what you need to study in college to become a billionaire," *Business Insider UK*, 26 March, accessed 18 June 2016 at http://www.businessinsider.com/heres-what-to-study-to-be-a-billionaire-2015-3.
Duckworth, A.L., C. Peterson, M.D. Matthews, and D.R. Kelly (2007), "Grit: perseverance and passion for long-term goals," *Journal of Personality and Social Psychology*, **92** (6), 1087–101.
Fairlie, R.W. (2002), "Drug dealing and legitimate self-employment," *Journal of Labor Economics*, **20** (3), 538–67.
Germak, A.J. (2013), "Social entrepreneurship motivation: a quantitative analysis of nascent social entrepreneurs," *EMES-SOCENT Conference Selected Papers*, No. LG13-69, accessed 18 June 2016 at http://www.emes.net/site/wp-content/uploads/Germak_ECSP-LG13-69.pdf.
Germak, A.J. and J.A. Robinson (2014), "Exploring the motivation of nascent social entrepreneurs," *Journal of Social Entrepreneurship*, **5** (1), 5–21.
Hartog, J., M. van Praag, and J. van der Sluis (2010), "If you are so smart, why aren't you an entrepreneur? Returns to cognitive and social ability: entrepreneurs versus employees," *Journal of Economics and Management Strategy*, **19** (4), 947–89.
Hoogendoorn, B., H.P.G. Pennings, and R. Thurik (2010), "What do we know about social entrepreneurship: an analysis of empirical research," *ERIM Report Series Research in Management*, No. ERS-2009-044-ORG.
Hurst, E. and B.W. Pugsley (2011), "What do small businesses do?," *NBER Working Papers*, No. 19041.
Koellinger, P.D. and R. Thurik (2012), "Entrepreneurship and the business cycle," *Review of Economics and Statistics*, **94** (4), 1143–56.
Light, P. (2005), "Searching for social entrepreneurs: who they might be, where they might be found, what they do," paper prepared for presentation at the annual meeting of the Association for Research on Nonprofit and Voluntary Association, 17–18 November.
Light, P. (2006), "Reshaping social entrepreneurship," *Stanford Social Innovation Review*, Fall.
Mair, J. and I. Marti (2006), "Social entrepreneurship research: a source of explanation, prediction, and delight," *Journal of World Business*, **41** (1), 36–44.
McClelland, D.C. (1987), "Characteristics of successful entrepreneurs," *The Journal of Creative Behavior*, **21** (3), 219–33.
Mook, L., J.R. Whitman, J. Quarter, and A. Armstrong (2015), *Understanding the Social Economy of the United States*, Toronto: University of Toronto Press.
Peredo, A.M. and M. McLean (2006), "Social entrepreneurship: a critical review of the concept," *Journal of World Business*, **41** (1), 56–65.
Reynolds, P.D., N.M. Carter, W.B. Gartner, and P.G. Greene (2004), "The prevalence of nascent entrepreneurs in the United States: evidence from the Panel Study of Entrepreneurial Dynamics," *Small Business Economics*, **23** (4), 263–84.
Ruef, M., H.E. Aldrich, and N.M. Carter (2003), "The structure of founding teams: homophily, strong ties, and isolation among US entrepreneurs," *American Sociological Review*, **68** (2), 195–222.
Schumpeter, J.A. (1942), *Capitalism, Socialism and Democracy*, London and New York: Routledge.

Shane, S.A. (2008), *The Illusions of Entrepreneurship*, New Haven, CT: Yale University Press.

Short, J. (ed.). (2014), *Social Entrepreneurship and Research Methods, Volume 9*, Bingley, UK: Emerald Group Publishing.

Stewart Jr., W.H. and P.L. Roth (2001), "Risk propensity differences between entrepreneurs and managers: a meta-analytic review," *Journal of Applied Psychology*, **86** (1), 145–53.

Thornton, J.P., J. Gonas, and F.T. Lohrke (2012), "The social entrepreneur as trailblazer: a non-normative role for social enterprise in a market economy," *SSRN Electronic Journal*, accessed 18 June 2016 at https://www.researchgate.net/publication/256039573_The_Social_Entrepreneur_as_Trailblazer_A_Non-Normative_Role_for_Social_Enterprise_in_a_Market_Economy.

Uusitalo, R. (2003), "Homo entreprenaurus?" *Applied Economics*, **33** (13), 1631–8.

Van Gelderen, M., R. Thurik, and N. Bosma (2005), "Success and risk factors in the pre-start-up phase," *Small Business Economics*, **24** (4), 365–80.

Van Praag, C. and J. Cramer (2001), "The roots of entrepreneurship and labour demand: individual ability and low risk aversion," *Economica*, **68** (269), 45–62.

Van Slyke, D.M. and J.D. Lecy (2012), "Profiles of nonprofit start-ups and nonprofit entrepreneurs," *Andrew Young School of Policy Studies Research Paper Series*, No. 12–28.

Young, D.R. (1983 [2013]), *If Not for Profit, for What?*, Digital Reissue, Georgia State University Library, accessed 18 June 2016 at http://scholarworks.gsu.edu/facbooks2013/1/.

Young, D.R. and J.D. Lecy (2014), "Defining the universe of social enterprise: competing metaphors," *Voluntas*, **25** (5), 1307–32.

Zahra, S.A., E. Gedajlovic, D.O. Neubaum, and J.M. Shulman (2009), "A typology of social entrepreneurs: motives, search processes and ethical challenges," *Journal of Business Venturing*, **24** (5), 519–32.

8. Feeding the animals

Elizabeth A.M. Searing and Dennis R. Young

INTRODUCTION

In order to prosper, every animal in the social enterprise zoo must be nourished by an appropriate diet of financial and material resources. Such diets may be substantially different from one enterprise to another, given the variety of missions, corporate forms, stages of organizational development (life cycle; see Chapter 6) and environments or habitats (Chapter 4) in which social enterprises operate within the zoo. Though many definitions of social enterprise presuppose earned income as the primary revenue source, it is not the only one or even the primary one in many instances. For example, aside from earned revenue, nonprofit enterprises traditionally rely on resources such as philanthropy, member fees, government support, debt, income-in-kind, and investment income. For-profit social businesses and cooperatives can also take advantage of many of the same resources, as well as sale of equity to attract investment capital. Thus, in this chapter we address the complex question of what to feed the different animals, both for financing capital needs and supporting day-to-day operations.

Understanding the role and place of each source of sustenance requires an overarching conceptual framework. For this purpose we look to benefits theory (Young, 2007), which links the public and private nature of the outputs of social enterprises to their potential sources of operating income and capital financing. This provides us not only with a snapshot of how different types of financial resources are currently employed, but also how financing methods could be fine-tuned to improve the health and performance of social enterprises over time. One insight from applying the benefits theory framework is that there is no fixed mix of sources or formula for the sustenance of social enterprise animals, even of a given legal form in a particular habitat. Variation can be expected because of the wide variety of social missions undertaken by social enterprises of a given type, which in turn leads to different mixes of benefits linked to alternative sources of support. Nonetheless, we do expect that, on average, the diets of social enterprise animals will be different across forms and habitats, leading us to conclude that social enterprise animals need to be studied at the subspecies level where differential missions can be taken into account.

This chapter describes the different financial resources that are available to for-profit, not-for-profit, cooperative and other (hybrid) social enterprises. We focus primarily on the US context but with an eye towards application elsewhere. Each type of financial instrument or method is described in some detail, including its traditional and potential applications. This includes the several new types of financial resources designed or adapted specifically for social enterprise, such as program-related investments (PRIs) and social impact bonds. We then apply benefits theory to assess where in the zoo, and to which types of social enterprise animals, these various kinds of financial sustenance are most likely to apply. We begin with a short description of benefits theory itself.

BENEFITS THEORY IN THE ZOO

Benefits theory was originally developed and empirically tested for formally incorporated nonprofit organizations in the United States, although its tenets are quite general in nature (Young, 2007; Wilsker and Young, 2010; Young et al., 2010; Fischer et al., 2011). Simply stated, nonprofits produce a variety of generic economic goods, each of which is linked to a natural source of finance. In particular:

- Some nonprofits produce public goods such as clean air or water projects, which are logically linked to governmental support because of the widespread public benefits produced, and to philanthropic support where goods affect particular populations that place high value on them.
- Some nonprofits produce group goods, such as research on particular genetic illnesses or community programs for the elderly, which may collectively affect limited populations that directly (or indirectly through sympathetic donors or specialized foundations) support the goods through gifts and grants.
- Some nonprofits produce private goods that accrue directly to individuals and are excludable and rival in character, thus amenable to financing through fee income in the marketplace – for example, private schooling or theatre performances.
- Some nonprofits produce redistributive goods that are basically private in nature but purposefully delivered to populations of individuals who have difficulty paying for them, such as meals or

subsidized medical care. Such goods are logically supported through a combination of low fees and government or philanthropic support.

- Some nonprofits produce trade or exchange goods that are essentially targeted exchanges of (essentially private) benefits between nonprofits and particular sponsors or support groups. For example, a corporation may trade financial or material support to a nonprofit for the publicity and additional market value of associating its credit card with a social mission, or docents may supply their in-kind labor in exchange for the chance to see orchestral performances or museum shows.
- Some nonprofits offer so-called associative goods (Bowman and Bingham, 2015) that provide benefits specifically to members, supported by a particular form of fee income called dues. Examples include health and social clubs.

Most nonprofit organizations, and we argue here, social enterprises of all types, offer various mixes of public, group, private, redistributive, trade and associative goods and services, underpinning the expectation that social enterprises in general can be supported and most efficiently financed by particular mixes of income sources corresponding to the mixes of their outputs. This is why James (1983) characterized nonprofits as "multi-product firms" that generate profits on some services (private goods) through fees in order to cross-subsidize other (public, mission-related) services that are especially important to them. The logical extension of this understanding of nonprofits is that nonprofit leaders pursue a variety of sources of support in order to sustain a preferred mix of public and private goods (Weisbrod, 1998). Similarly, recent work by Bowman and Bingham (2015) demonstrates that nonprofit associations vary in the mix of private and group goods they provide for their members and the group or public goods they produce for their collective or public beneficiaries. In particular, charitable associations such as research societies (e.g., Association for Research on Nonprofit Organizations and Voluntary Action – ARNOVA), which are focused both on supporting the individual scholarly needs of their members and expanding the body of knowledge for everyone, are less dependent on dues and more likely to obtain philanthropic funding than associations such as social clubs that exclusively serve their members and hence are primarily supported by dues. As Bowman and Bingham (2015) show, this pattern is intensified for associations that prefer to limit their memberships (so as not to degrade the quality of their group and private goods through congestion and lower standards) compared to associations that welcome all comers.

More generally, the complex missions of most nonprofits are likely to entail a mix of benefit types, by virtue of their intrinsic nature. Nonprofits devoted to education provide private benefits to their students in the form of better life and career prospects, to society by virtue of promoting a more productive or less marginalized citizenry, and to alumni proud to be associated with their alma maters. Free health clinics improve the welfare of their clients (a redistributive good), reduce contagion (a public good), offer learning opportunities for medical students (an exchange good with their schools), and bolster community morale (a group good). And so on.

Interestingly, these arguments are generic, and not associated with particular legal forms of social enterprise. Thus, social cooperatives also depend on a mix of dues, fees revenue and philanthropic or government support, the balance of which may reflect the associative versus public goods that they provide and the private goods that they may sell. For example, an organic foods cooperative is logically supported by member dues, product market sales, and general philanthropic or public funding because of the various ways that it benefits its members, customers, and communities. Similar arguments can be made for social businesses that may attract the capital of socially minded as well as conventional investors, and the patronage of consumers both interested in supporting a good cause and those looking for a bargain. The efficiency frontier diagram (Figure 2.1) in Chapter 2 suggests that different social enterprise forms tend to emphasize public versus private benefits in different proportions. But these are just tendencies: unless a social enterprise is perfectly efficient, it can increase both its private and public benefits without conflict (the notion of shared value) and hence look towards appropriate sources of finance for each. It is true, however, that alternative legal forms entail different constraints and incentives that are likely to influence the degree to which particular sources of income can be engaged. Strictly profit-minded investors are unlikely to invest in conventional nonprofits (which are prohibited from profit distribution) or in social businesses that prioritize social mission exclusively. Philanthropic donors are likely to be wary of social businesses that solicit gifts unless they can be otherwise assured that funds will be allocated to mission. Socially conscious consumers may be reluctant to patronize social businesses unless convinced of their sincerity and integrity. As a result, certain forms of finance work better for social enterprise animals of a particular legal variety. But we must scratch below this veneer in order to assess the actual potential of the various means of financial sustenance to feed social enterprises in various parts of the zoo. More specifically, we need to parse the broad categories of social enterprises (species) in order to assess the applicability and limits of different income sources to subspecies, as differentiated by mission, services, and beneficiary groups, in the social enterprise zoo. Below, we examine how this plays out in practice.

A SMORGASBORD OF RESOURCES

The potential resources available to social enterprises vary widely, and their utilization will depend on type of good or service (mission and benefits), as well as corporate form and several other organizational and environmental factors. The suitability of a resource is, therefore, a question of fit: which attributes of the resource best match the purposes and constraints of the organization.

Daily Care: Operating Funds

Earned income

Revenue generated in exchange for goods and services has long been a part of the nonprofit sector in addition to being the mainstay of the business sector. Earned income plays a special role in the field of social enterprise; indeed, many definitions of social enterprise consider the presence of market income as a prerequisite for inclusion in the category (Social Enterprise UK, 2012), though this is not necessarily the case. Additionally, earned income can be mission related or not, and it can result from activities as diverse as selling coffee in an art museum to renting part of a building to another organization. Even for nonprofits, earned revenues are normally the most flexible type of funding available because once earned (to pay for services delivered) it is not limited in terms of how it can be spent (Williams, 2003).

Benefits theory suggests why earned revenues are such a prevalent part of the social enterprise diet. Earned income here refers to revenue earned from both individual payers and those where the revenue originates from a third party; the important part is that money is exchanged for the enterprise's goods or services, not necessarily who the end payer is. This benefit is often both rival and excludable, meaning that the benefit can be withheld if payment is not made, and cannot be shared simultaneously by more than one consumer. But this does not limit earned revenues to private goods exchange directly between service provider and service recipient. There are also *redistributive* goods, which are private goods where part of the earnings are paid directly by the beneficiary and part by an outside party, for example, through a per unit reimbursement or insurance arrangement such as a health insurance plan. Redistributive goods may also be internally subsidized by profit generated from the sale of other private goods. The key factor is that earned revenue is generated in exchange for service, and this approach can be used by almost all social enterprise animals (corporate forms) as long as the appropriate benefits are provided.

Government contracts

Government contracts can apply to for-profits, nonprofits, and various other social enterprise animals; they are often awarded in a competitive application or bidding process. Unlike a grant or gift, for which a *quid pro quo* is not explicit, a contract implies a relationship where the contractor is expected to provide a "deliverable," that is, a specific good or service in exchange for the funding. The provision of this good is often meticulously documented, and compliance is generally high since the organization often wants to remain the contractor for that particular good or service in the future. This administrative burden can entail a significant investment of human resources since different government levels and agencies commonly have different, often intensive, requirements for the administration of their funds (Pettijohn et al., 2014). However, there does appear to be diminishing marginal costs once government work is successfully achieved: in Rhode Island in 2013, 19 percent of nonprofit organizations had contracts or grants with one government agency, but 42 percent had a contract or grant with four or more government agencies (ibid.).

Government contracts, which are often large, transfer services provision from the state to third parties. This is known as the "hollowing out" of the state (Milward, 1994; Bardach and Lesser, 1996; Milward and Provan, 2000). The resulting delegation of responsibilities for public welfare causes some concern, especially when contracts are awarded to for-profit agencies. For example, there was a general outcry when Lockheed Martin bid (unsuccessfully) on a public services contract in 1996 (Ryan, 2002). There is also concern about the impact of such funds on the contractor organizations themselves, especially if they are nonprofits. The fear is that nonprofits will isomorphically mimic aspects of the state (e.g., become more bureaucratic) (DiMaggio and Powell, 1991, p. 64; Ramanath, 2009), or that they may drift from their mission in order to maintain their government funding (Smith and Lipsky, 1995). Finally, there is concern as to whether the introduction of government money in a nonprofit's revenue mix "crowds out" other sources of funds (Seaman, 1980; Andreoni and Payne, 2003; Brooks, 2003).

Despite these issues, government contracting for public services is an important source of income, especially for nonprofit social enterprises. The benefits provided to recipients are often also rival and excludable, such as the provision of services to children with special needs; this ability to parcel the benefits lends itself to contractual or by-service arrangements, just like earned revenues from the private market. However, such services also normally contain a larger element of public good than ones bought on the private market; this partly public nature of the good is what warrants the government's involvement. Since it is public money, however, greater levels of public accountability are often required than with private revenues. The government will work with various corporate forms (though there can be preferences for particular types of service delivery), but the accountability requirements often mean that very small or very young organizations of any form are less likely to engage in government contracting.

Foundation grants

Foundation grants are monetary awards that are given by private or community foundations, which are tax-exempt entities that exist solely to support other organizations dedicated to social welfare (Internal Revenue Service, 2014). These grants are normally applied for and often granted on a highly competitive basis, and can vary in size and scope. Sometimes a grant will include money to cover indirect costs (or overhead); however, while this practice is gaining in popularity, it is by no means universal. Often, the application for and administration of grant funding can require a dedicated staff position within the social enterprise organization since these tasks are time-consuming and require special expertise.

Foundations support a wide variety of charitable causes. Though traditionally grants are made to charitable nonprofits, this is no longer exclusively the case. Grant programs targeting for-profit start-ups, university spin-offs, or social enterprises exist though they are currently uncommon. (Recent initiatives by funders such as Google or Mark Zuckerberg to establish philanthropies in other forms such as limited liability companies [LLCs] or business corporations testify in part to the limits of what foundations can and do fund.) Further, foundations interested in supporting the activities of a for-profit business will often opt for the program-related investment financial instrument rather than a straightforward grant (see below). Often foundation grants are made for start-up purposes or to support new initiatives rather than to fund ongoing operations.

The merits and drawbacks to social enterprises of foundation grants are similar to those for government contracts. Mission capture or drift is a risk since the same incentive exists to pitch programs to fit the mission or orientation of the foundation, especially for sizable and renewable grants. However, many foundation grants are one-time awards rather than renewable, though the chance of getting another grant increases after an organization has gained legitimacy through previous grant experience (Faulk et al., 2012). The time involved in grant applications can be substantial, including search for opportunities in addition to writing sometimes extensive grant applications. The paperwork required in administration of the grants can also be significant (though usually not as onerous as for government grants). Often, private consultants are brought in to perform these tasks; nonetheless, these requirements may serve as a barrier to many enterprises attempting to successfully apply. Finally, private foundation grants do not always include provisions for the overhead expenses of administering the grant or running the organization, which has contributed to the loss of capacity in nonprofit organizations (Lecy and Searing, 2014).

In general, foundation grants apply to social enterprises seeking to support services with a group, redistributive or public goods character, and they are highly dependent on the particular mission of a foundation or the interests of its donors. Moreover, some foundations seek to limit themselves to capital gifts (see below) and may not be responsive to requests for operating support, though this too is changing. Legal constraints tend to limit foundation grants to nonprofit organizations although there are strategies such as program-related investments (see below) that can circumvent this limitation.

Federated gifts and grants
Some charities serve as conduits for funds to other organizations. A federated gift is one that has been given to a larger central organization that is then distributed to other affiliated nonprofits. For example, a local or regional United Way campaigns for funds and then distributes these dollars to other local charities. The Combined Federal Campaign receives donations from federal workers, deducted directly from their paychecks; recipient nonprofits that meet particular qualifications apply to receive a portion of these funds. These grantees may provide many different types of goods (public, group, redistributive, or private). Individuals with various charitable interests choose to donate to such campaigns because of the convenient information they provide and the mark of legitimacy for charities included in the campaign. Usually, donors have the choice of designating their gifts for particular qualifying charities, while some simply give undesignated funds to the campaign. The funds are then distributed by a committee within the fund itself and/or guided by the choices of those who designated funds, depending on the mechanism of the campaign (Bowman, 2003). Donors therefore minimize search costs looking for the "right" charity while still being able to contribute to worthy causes. However, with the increasing availability of information on charities to the general public, gifts to federated campaigns are declining relative to gifts made directly to the operating enterprises themselves (McCambridge, 2013).

Resources from affiliates
Many social enterprises begin life as either a subsidiary or partner of an existing organization. There are several benefits to this: legitimacy by extension from the established partner, a pre-established extended network

of clients and human capital, and an alternate source of revenue should one organization or the other fall on difficult times.

There are several kinds of possible affiliated relationships. First, a social enterprise may be founded as a subsidiary activity of a parent organization. This is commonly done with the LLC form, since it allows pass-through taxation. In this case, the enterprise is often a revenue provider for the parent organization. Sometimes the social enterprise is set up in a "sibling" relationship with other organizations. The fact that social enterprises are generally considered distinctive because they are market-centered means that commercial revenue is often the central reason for an entity's founding as part of a portfolio of subsidiary organizations. Indeed, partnerships among peer organizations more generally, especially those between for-profits and nonprofits, may have been the first "hybrid" organizations before the speciation of special legal forms of for-profit social enterprises. Such relationships can also be "nested," such as a nonprofit running a work entry program that is affiliated with a restaurant where its clients are trained to enter the workforce. Here, the nonprofit portion is able to attract independent sources of revenue through grants and donations, but also can receive money from the business side of the organization once the costs of the restaurant are covered. This is often the case if there are large capital requirements, such as buildings: the for-profit will have lined up the equity, while a nonprofit performs service provision from within the building and provides rental income. Though these relationships are often highly symbiotic and generally flexible according to the types of benefits that they support, they are not common enough to be considered a steady resource for most enterprises. In any case, the funding through affiliate relationships reflects the mixed public and private benefits that these social enterprise combinations provide.

Individual contributions (large/few)
Whether large contributions from individuals serve as operating income or sources of capital depends on the stage and type of the enterprise. Initially, almost all organizations start out self-funded through their founders or individuals within the founders' network – at this stage, these resources serve as both revenue and potential long-term capital. Following this phase, angel philanthropists or angel investors may become involved. These are individuals who may provide substantial funding and, often, entrepreneurial acumen (Van Slyke and Newman, 2006). In exchange, depending on legal form, the recipient enterprises may provide ownership stakes and/or a seat on the governing board. Later in the process, additional venture capital or venture philanthropy may be engaged, often when the organization is ready to expand. For most for-profit enterprises,

earned revenues begin to assume a larger share of the revenue portfolio at this stage, as injected cash is expended and owners assume their equity stakes (assuming initial capital investments are convertible). The dynamics are slightly different among corporate forms. For example, closely held for-profit corporations can attract outside capital, but the lack of initial public offering (IPO) potential makes them slightly less attractive to outside investors. LLCs may also attract individual investors outside of the founders' circle, but this often involves making the funder a partner in the enterprise. On one hand, this can be desirable for an investor since the flow-through, positive or negative, can be set against personal taxes; however, it involves more investment of time and energy, and the original founding team may have reservations. In any case, these investments can serve as operating cash in the early stages of the company. For nonprofits, large individual contributions can provide a revenue source on a continuing basis, as large gifts or bequests may be used to form endowments.

The form of large initial and second-stage contributions to a new social enterprise, that is, whether they take the form of investments or charitable gifts, depends on the ultimate character of the enterprise's mission and the mix of private and public benefits it ultimately provides. Private investors will be more focused on social enterprises that produce earned income streams based on private goods provision, while philanthropists will focus on public, group, and redistributive benefits.

Individual contributions (small/many)

Unlike large investors, whose funding can be applied to a wide variety of social enterprise animals (especially in their initial stages), small contributors play a potentially significant role mostly in nonprofits and, to a limited degree, cooperatives. The donative nonprofit is emblematic of the sector, partly because the tax code incentivizes giving: any gift to a 501(c)(3) (tax-exempt) registered charity in the USA can be deducted from the personal taxable income of the donor. This applies to both cash and other goods that can be monetized, except for volunteering of one's time. This tax benefit supplements the tax exemption benefits realized by non-profits themselves, which can include exemption from property taxes and taxes on surplus revenues (profits) that are related to their missions.

The importance of a social enterprise (nonprofit) having multiple small versus a few big givers is actively debated. From an organizational standpoint, the marginal value of a dollar spent on wooing a potential large donor may be higher than one spent on trying to attract a crowd of lesser givers. However, concentrating donations and, thus, the potential influence in the hands of a few, poses risks for organizational governance and potentially for society at large (Rooney, 2007). The same issue affects cooperatives, which, depending on the jurisdiction (state), can also register as nonprofits. However, most cooperatives (at least in the USA) do not operate on a very large scale, suggesting that their contributions function more as "memberships" and less as "donations." So-called social cooperatives (common in some countries such as Italy; Bassi, 2011) have created additional regulatory distinctions to separate those organizations that only provide associative goods from those that also provide public goods. Even among social cooperatives, however, we would expect to find a blend of both private, group, and public benefit goods since the election of a cooperative form rather than a charity implies some level of non–public benefits.

In general, contributions support social enterprises that provide a significant level of public and group benefits, although contributions to cooperatives entail a significant component of private member or associative benefits while nonprofits may offer various private benefit incentives to encourage small gifts. For example, nonprofits offer a wide variety of discounts, logo-emblazoned items, individual recognitions and other private goods as inducements and acknowledgments for contributions.

Memberships
Dues are payments that members (individuals or organizations) make in order to belong to an organization; in exchange members may receive specific services, access to facilities, and a role in organizational governance. Some of these benefits are described as associative goods since they may depend on the access to, and characteristics of, other members (such as networking and status benefits) (Bowman and Bingham, 2015). Dues income does not comprise a large fraction of overall income in the nonprofit sector of the USA. The activity subcategory where it is most prevalent, recreation and sports, only brings in approximately 11 percent of its revenues from memberships, which is proportionally more than twice as much dues income as any other category (Steinberg, 2007). Dues income does, however, comprise a larger part of the revenues of cooperatives and professional and trade associations such as 501(c)(6) (politically active tax-exempt) entities in the USA.

In summary, dues revenues reflect the degree to which a social enterprise serves its members in the form of associative goods. They can be distinguished conceptually from membership fees that reflect the clustering of private goods for the purpose of package pricing. For example, a YMCA will offer memberships to users of its services rather than charge separately for the various health, recreation, and social programming activities that it offers, simply as a matter of efficiency and convenience. Nor should dues revenue be conflated with memberships in a museum or orchestra that are basically acknowledgements of charitable gifts. Neither of these cases involves governance rights or substantial benefits resulting from the proximity of other members.

Endowment/investment income
Building an endowment can be a daunting challenge. However, according to Bowman et al. (2007), there are three major reasons for nonprofit social enterprises to develop one. First, even if the assets themselves have restricted use, the revenue generated from those assets may be unrestricted. Second, having an endowment provides a hedge against a financial shock or adverse funding climate. Finally, donors may prefer to give gifts that last in perpetuity rather than simply have a one-time mission impact. However, some scholars suggest that allowing nonprofits to stockpile assets leads to agency problems (Core et al., 2006). In terms of benefit theory, the investment revenue generated as return on endowment loosens the connection between an enterprise's benefits and beneficiaries and its income. While endowments may be built from contributed income or profits from sales, such beneficiaries cannot always hold the enterprise accountable for the use of returns on those endowments. However, for this same reason, endowment income may provide an enterprise with greater expenditure flexibility than other income streams more directly tied to benefits.

There is also empirical evidence that an endowment is less flexible than other forms of value storage. For example, endowments are not generally liquid and their values will fluctuate; both of these features generally limit endowments from providing assistance during a financial shock (Ramirez, 2011). Bowman (2007) insists that a nonprofit with fixed assets should routinely establish an endowment sufficient to provide for maintenance of those assets. However, Calabrese (2013) found empirically that the presence of an endowment decreases the amount of operating surplus held and that there is an inverse relationship between fixed assets and endowments.

Endowments can be used to finance a wide variety of benefit types; however, since the source of endowments is likely be large donations, public, group or redistributive benefits generally underwrite the rationale for their development. Nonetheless they also often entail an element of private benefit in the form of recognition to the donors. For example, "naming rights" are frequently associated with endowments designated for building construction and maintenance, scholarships and professional positions such as professorships, curatorial chairs, or scholarships.

Long-term Health: Capital Financing

Grants

Foundation grants as a form of capital financing generally apply to nonprofit enterprises, although grants are sometimes made for start-ups of social businesses, spin-offs from university research, or other special projects. Competition is steep for capital grants, but many grants specifically targeting capacity building and infrastructure are available and some foundations actually specialize in grants for capital projects. This is because nonprofit organizations, given their prohibition from distributing profits or selling ownership shares, are disadvantaged in accessing capital for infrastructure projects. This is particularly pronounced for organizations dependent on government contracts and foundation or government grants, which may not adequately cover overhead costs or pay for expenses on a timely basis. Such enterprises are therefore limited in their ability to accumulate capital funds for maintenance, renovations and new projects. Therefore, although social enterprises may deliver a variety of benefits, those nonprofits that provide public or redistributive goods have more urgent needs for capital grants.

Internal sources

Several different types of financing can originate within an enterprise rather than tap outside sources. The first is "sweat equity," which refers to the combined resources of the organization that are not strictly monetary. In start-ups, this is often the unpaid time that individuals give to the organization. In nonprofits, volunteer labor of founders is often considered "sweat equity."

Another type of internal financing is retained earnings. Retained earnings are the gradual accrual of operating surpluses over time. In for-profits, this can be quite small because the profits are sometimes paid out to shareholders or members; however, many firms accumulate "war chests" to be used either in expansion or in cases of emergency. In nonprofits, the accumulation of retained earnings may be restrained by normative pressures (e.g., constituent expectations to spend maximally on mission-related services) or because contracts or grants limit reimbursement to narrow coverage of marginal or "out-of-pocket" costs.

A third type of internal financing is referred to as "patient capital." This originates from founding investors at an early stage of the enterprise. Patient capital is designed to pay off over time, and often at a lower expected rate of return than other types of finance. So-called "angels" can be sources of patient capital since their financial support often comes with a deeper and more active role in the company than would characterize a conventional venture capitalist or philanthropist. Thus, patient capital often comes with governance rights and a degree of control and sometimes with an ownership share in the organization.

Sweat equity and patient capital reflect a mix of underlying public and private benefits. Volunteers may be purely motivated by the social enterprise's public mission or may be investing in future returns from the sale of private goods. Patient capital investors usually want a return from the provision of ultimately profitable sales of private goods as well as satisfaction deriving from support of the enterprise's public mission. Retained earnings are premised on the sale of private goods since it is generally difficult to retain surplus funds from gifts and grants, or government contracts.

Equity
Sale of equity is generally restricted to for-profit or cooperative enterprises since it is premised on ownership of a piece of the enterprise; the degree of equity also depends on both the type of organization and its projected path. For those organizations seeking to scale up significantly in the provision of private or potentially redistributive benefits, several "rounds" of funding are possible, and the likelihood of getting a later round of funding improves once money is secured in an earlier round. Different types of investors are also attracted to different rounds: angel investors often like to get in during the seed round in order to have a greater say in the development of the organization, while conventional venture capital often comes in later (pre-IPO) rounds (Flach, 2012).

Many organizations, however, eschew this path in favor of other means; even among corporations that do not declare a social purpose, only 2 percent of them involve any kind of formal venture capital (Bartlett, 1995, p. 7). For social enterprises, even those not intending to scale up, equity is still an option for capital funding. This can take the form of stock (public or closely held), partnership, or membership, depending on the corporate form (e.g., corporation, limited liability company, cooperative). The exchange of cash for ownership of a piece of the enterprise, however, is the unifying concept. And this in turn reflects the expectation of an income stream from the provision of benefits based on the sale of private goods.

Equity-equivalent or quasi-equity
Quasi-equity describes instruments that have elements of both debt and equity, for example a loan that is convertible to equity at a certain time or under certain circumstances. This type of financing can be very attractive in the initial stages of a social enterprise, where an angel or venture capitalist may convert the loan into an ownership stake if the value of the ownership exceeds the value of the loan. Because it entails ownership of the

enterprise at some stage, this is generally only applicable to for-profit forms that accommodate outside ownership: a sole proprietorship with no plans of formalizing would be unattractive, and nonprofit forms do not technically have owners and must abide by a nondistribution of profit constraint that precludes return on equity. There have been some attempts to create equity-equivalent instruments for nonprofits such as the equity-equivalent investments (EQ2s) for community development financial institutions (CDFIs) established by National Community Capital (Lipson, 2002), but these are uncommon. In general, capital financing through the sale of equity assumes an earned income stream from the provision of private benefits through the marketplace.

Debt

Debt allows capital costs of a social enterprise to be spread over a period of time commensurate with the expected service life of the asset (Yan et al., 2009). There are several types of debt, each suited to different recipients and to accomplish different purposes. Lending from commercial banks is widespread, but can be difficult to achieve for start-ups or if the enterprise has an asset lock that would prevent liquidation; this is somewhat less true for mortgages, since a building can serve as collateral for the loan. There are also loan providers that will target specific audiences in order to provide group benefits and better serve a select constituency. For example, CDFIs specifically target banking and credit needs in underprivileged communities (CDFI Coalition, 2012); they often have available a mix of instruments for both operating and capital financing, in addition to micro-loans (Benjamin et al., 2004). Nonprofits are also capable of essentially issuing their own debt through state and local governmental institutions; for example, the Dormitory Authority of the State of New York issues tax-exempt bonds for nonprofits. Tax-exempt bond financing is generally limited to larger nonprofit institutions such as universities and hospitals because these bond issues are large in scale and require substantial institutional administrative capacity.

More generally, the use and type of debt also depends on firm type and size. Empirical studies suggest that nonprofits prefer internal sources of finance to debt, potentially because funders expect them to be more risk averse than for-profit enterprises (Fama and Jensen, 1983; Calabrese, 2011). Small to medium-sized for-profit enterprises (SMEs) also show a pecking-order preference for internal equity over debt, especially enterprises that are closely held (Watson and Wilson, 2002). This is not to say that such organizations do not use debt, however. The type of debt seen most often in nonprofits is a line of credit from a bank. Tapping into this source allows nonprofits to smooth out their expenses over time, which is often necessary due to the cyclical or fickle nature of funding. However, much like consumer credit cards, it is the constant dipping into borrowed money that often deepens long-term financial problems (Hager and Searing, 2015).

Overall, debt financing depends on having commensurate assets as collateral or predictable streams of earned income. While all social enterprises can use debt to some extent, those that provide private benefits supported by earned income and those that have accumulated physical or financial assets (such as endowments) find it easier to borrow.

The Special Needs of Start-ups

Start-up social enterprises, regardless of sector, often have special financial needs. First, there are start-up costs such as various licensures, wages, and materials. For example, if an organization seeks to attract donations, then fees for filing for tax-exempt status will be required. In addition, expenditures such as advertising and fundraising are needed to build initial capacity and legitimacy, the latter a primary factor in whether the organization will be able to survive (Singh et al., 1986).

Second, the types of revenue and financing will sometimes vary drastically at start-up compared to other stages in an organization's life cycle. For example, for-profit social enterprise start-ups often rely on grants in their early stages, a resource traditionally associated with the nonprofit sector (Wuttunee et al., 2008). Different corporate forms often compete for the same spaces in social incubators, which then influences their access to financial and human capital. Once an organization seeks to expand, however, there are substantial differences: for-profit institutions can look to private investors to purchase equity stakes in hopes of making a profit, but nonprofits cannot provide the same incentive. Thus, scaling up for nonprofits can be difficult. At maturity, for-profit organizations almost universally rely heavily on earned income, while there is a much wider diversity of revenue options for nonprofits. Finally, most unincorporated social enterprises will choose to incorporate if the venture becomes successful enough to permit scaling up. Viewed through the lens of benefits theory, start-up enterprises usually promise to provide public benefits, no matter what their ultimate form. Virtually all babies in the zoo are cute and promising, and can be nurtured in a similar manner. Once they begin to grow, however, the nature of the particular benefits they offer begins to matter, and their sources of capital financing and operating support become differentiated accordingly.

New Additions to the Menu

Crowdsourcing
Though crowdsourcing arose shortly after the turn of the twenty-first
century in response to economic conditions and exploding technological capability (Baumgardner et al., 2015), it still retains a great deal of
its edginess and popularity. Crowdsourcing entails the gathering of
resources through large numbers of small pledges from people outside
the social enterprise's traditional circle; this often means gathering of
monetary resources (otherwise known as "crowdfunding"), but can also
apply to volunteer hours and other contributed goods. The most well-
known gateways from which to crowdfund are online platforms such
as Indiegogo, GoFundMe, Kickstarter, and several others. Some sites
specialize in a particular sector, such as www.petridish.org for science
research or www.donorschoose.org for teachers, while others are more
general. These gateways allow donors or small investors to choose the
type of (public, private or redistributive) benefits they prefer to support.
Payments can underwrite for-profit invention prototypes, technology for
a particular classroom at a public school, or assistance with a personal
medical crisis; online gateways or platforms allow donors/investors a
wide choice among ventures usually entailing a significant component
of public or redistributive benefits, though this includes projects with
prospective profitmaking potential as well. Further, many of these
sites encourage gifts by offering private benefits or incentives, such as
first access to a prototype or dinner with a celebrity board member.
Crowdfunding emphasizes the ease of information and access for donors,
in addition to personal giver choice.

   Though important legislation has recently been passed regarding crowdfunding, there are several areas of the law that remain ambiguous. For
example, the 2012 US Jumpstart Our Business Startups (JOBS) Act
included an exemption for crowdfunding from being regulated like a
security (Cohn, 2012); since many sites offer incentives such as prototypes
and small shares of equity, the exchange of such for cash would have been
considered a security and would need to be registered with the Securities
Exchange Commission. This would have caused additional paperwork and
headaches, the absence of which is one of the attractive elements of crowdfunding (ibid.). Those organizations that do not offer equity, however,
are an even larger concern: should they be required to register with the
state charitable solicitation office like any other organization seeking
donations would (Searing, 2012)? Such registries were created in order to
prevent donors from being swindled by unscrupulous people masquerad-
ing as solicitors for good causes; since crowdfunding allows a great deal

of freedom and anonymity, registration may be worthwhile to protect the donor.

In summary, crowdfunding can support various mixes of public, private, and redistributive benefits; as such this is a hybrid sort of food for social enterprise animals, neither exclusively donations to support public, group or redistributive goods nor exclusively equity investments or payment in exchange for private benefits. Hence, this source is especially appealing for start-ups for which the benefit mix and legal forms are not yet fully differentiated.

Loan guarantees

Rather than providing funding, guarantees such as credit guarantees or bond backing can help encourage lending by mitigating part of the risk through a third party institution (Bill and Melinda Gates Foundation, 2012). The US Small Business Administration (SBA) has been offering loan guarantees for quite some time. Loans from the SBA are actually given through traditional lenders, but they are guaranteed at 90 percent of the loan (Markiewicz, 2011).

An example of this is the social impact bond package offered by New York City, Goldman Sachs, and Bloomberg Philanthropies (Chen, 2012). Though most of the press focused on the social impact bond itself, the reason that Goldman Sachs entered the contract was that Bloomberg Philanthropies guaranteed the performance of the program. Therefore, if the program performed well, Goldman Sachs would receive a profit on their original loan and reimbursement of the cost by government. However, since the program did not perform sufficiently well, rather than lose money (which is what would have happened in a traditional PRI), Bloomberg Philanthropies offset part of the cost. This mitigation of risk made the deal more attractive to Goldman Sachs. In theory, however, such guarantees should also make access to capital easier for social enterprises that do not have the revenue history or the stability to provide a service entailing large barriers to entry or deployment costs. In general, loan guarantees are meant to encourage banks or private investors to lend to social enterprises that offer to provide substantial public or redistributive benefits but present a substantial risk of financial or program failure.

Pooling (cross-collateralization)

Pooling involves the collection of debt from several different institutions and bundling it together. Though this concept lost some favor during the 2007–09 financial crisis, it has continued as a way to manage risk and increase the uptake of debt by organizations that would likely not have access to it. After bundling, debt is re-sliced into tranches based on risk. Investors then buy into the tranches rather than buy the issued debt of any particular enterprise. In theory, the bunched and re-sliced debt is less risky than the debt from one organization alone, and investors are able to select the tranche level they are comfortable with (Bugg-Levine et al., 2012). The mortgage crisis in the United States, however, showed that the risk of loss and even total system calamity cannot be eliminated entirely and indeed irresponsible debt pooling can increase risk. Pooling is still rare for social enterprises. Nonetheless, pooling does allow nonprofit and other social enterprises of small size or limited credit worthiness to access debt financing.

Overall, pooling of debt is conceptually appropriate and potentially attractive to social enterprises offering widely different benefit mixes, consistent with their capacities and needs to take on debt to support capital requirements and short term or cyclical operating expenses.

Program-related investments (PRIs)

PRIs were developed by Congress in 1969 as a way to expand the abilities of charitable foundations to provide resources to socially worthy enterprises consistent with their philanthropic missions (Tyler, 2010). In particular, PRIs allow foundations to invest in ventures from which they may be able to profit (Searing, 2012). They can take the form of equity, debt, or loan guarantees, and they can be offered to for-profit, low-profit, or nonprofit entities. A PRI to a nonprofit often takes the form of a loan, where the foundation receives some interest (normally at a below-market rate) as well as repayment of the loan principle. This allows the foundation to "recycle" its funding over time among alternative social investments. PRIs also count toward the mandatory annual 5 percent distribution required of private foundations (GPS Capital Partners, 2009).

Investing PRIs in for-profit social enterprise entities is slightly more complicated than investing them in nonprofits. First, the gains must be reasonable in order to avoid the appearance that the goal of the investment is profit-seeking rather than furtherance of a social mission. Since the success of an investment is not fully known beforehand, this accounts for much of the hesitation of foundations to engage in PRIs. Foundations must also ensure that the money invested by them is, in fact, used by the recipient enterprise for its stated goal. If the IRS were to decide that either of these conditions was violated, the fines for a foundation would be steep, and would be added to unrelated business income tax on the net proceeds of the PRI itself. However, these potential drawbacks are offset by the opportunity to both realize a return and avoid capital gains taxation on the proceeds (Tyler, 2010). As of this writing, there is some hope that the hesitation behind foundations' use of PRIs will diminish if the IRS provides additional clarification about the circumstances involving excessive profit, though this advice does not appear to be forthcoming soon.

In general, PRIs are a potential source of income or capital funding for social enterprises that produce various forms of earned income that can be used to repay the granting foundation. In general, this points to social enterprises that can produce private goods at a profit while generating public, group or redistributive benefits as well.

Social impact bonds

Social impact bonds are designed to bring resources of the private sector into public service provision. With traditional bonds, the investor receives a fixed return on investment; with social impact bonds, the investor receives returns only if the program is judged a success according to standards set in the contract (Humphries, 2014). The first social impact bond was issued in the UK at HM Prison Peterborough, where the government and Social Finance Ltd. partnered to address recidivism (*The Economist*, 2012). Social Finance paid for the initial deployment of the program; if the program is successful, then the government reimburses Social Finance. If the program is not successful, then Social Finance will have expended the money without compensation.

The verdict on the first social impact bond is mixed. The evaluation showed an 8.4 percent decrease in recidivism rates, which is laudable, but not the 10 percent that was required to prompt payment to investors (Birkwood, 2014). The project has until 2016 to achieve the net repayment threshold of 7.5 percent. Though the third phase of the project has been cancelled, optimism remains regarding whether the current success will hold and ultimately be sufficient to trigger repayment. Additionally, the social impact bond at Peterborough could be considered a success on the public relations level; according to the Rockefeller Foundation (Ganguly, 2014), as of August 2014 there were 26 active social impact bonds and more than 100 proposals around the globe. Thus, although they are not common enough to be considered a dependable food source for any of the social enterprise zoo animals, their growing prominence should yield interesting insights over the next few years as to whether public goods and private money marry well in a financial instrument.

The Importance of a Varied Diet

It is often important for animals and organizations to have balanced diets because this reduces the risk of nutrient deficiencies and insulates from potential shortfalls in any particular source of sustenance. Think of the plight of the panda, who only consumes bamboo, compared to the omnivorous black bear; the loss of habitat has a greater impact on the panda since it requires a special food whose supply is also shrinking. In finance, this notion is reflected in portfolio theory, which stipulates that the risks of dependency on a particular revenue source can be mitigated by relying on several different types of resources that are not tightly correlated with one another. (In the social enterprise zoo, even birds should avoid putting all their eggs in one basket!) This reduces the chance of financial vulnerability and calamity if any given revenue source is diminished or disappears (Tuckman and Chang, 1991; Hager, 2001; Bowman, 2011).

Though often discussed in the context of the varied revenues common to nonprofits, similar thinking applies to for-profits and other forms of social enterprise. Rarely should all revenue stem from the same client, product, or even market. In addition to risk mitigation, having a diverse product portfolio opens the possibility of cross-subsidization. This means that an activity with an important mission component that may not be self-sufficient can receive support from a profitable activity that is less tied to mission (James, 1983). For example, museum gift shops generate sales revenue that subsidizes the primary mission of the museum. Nor is this an uncommon case. James's original paper theorizing cross-subsidization in nonprofit organizations characterized the latter as "multiproduct firms" (ibid.). Indeed, it is the rare case that a nonprofit organization offers just one type of good or service, and hence just one type of benefit. According to benefits theory this underwrites the potential for a diversified income portfolio. Similar arguments apply to other social enterprise animals though their prospects for a varied diet may be more limited by legal constraints, eligibility for government funding, and donor preferences.

TOWARDS A THEORY OF SOCIAL ENTERPRISE FINANCE

Benefits theory, developed specifically for nonprofit organizations, can provide the basis for understanding the operating and capital resource bases of other animals in the social enterprise zoo as well. Especially in the start-up phase, social enterprise pups promise a variety of types of benefits – services or goods for the public in general, redistributive services for disadvantaged populations, and personal benefits to purchasers and private investors. Thus young social enterprise animals may seek philanthropic and crowd-sourced gifts and grants, as well as private investors, almost without regard to their ultimate choice of corporate form. In fact, at this early stage of life social enterprise animals may prospectively have a wider selection of foods than more mature animals because the benefits they promise are not yet clearly differentiated into public and private. To the contrary, however, new social enterprises may not have the administrative capacity or sophistication to manage multiple different sources of income; moreover, they may not qualify for sources of funds better suited to larger, sophisticated organizations – such as substantial government contracts or tax-exempt bonds.

The advisability and potential for varied diets is clearly established in the literature for nonprofits. To see the application of benefits theory to the differentiation of food sources for other forms of social enterprise, one needs only consider the fact that other forms are also rarely confined to provision of singular products and services or a narrow band of public or private benefits. For example, social businesses naturally rely on earned income but they may also attract socially minded investors, government grants, and contracts, PRIs from foundations, and indeed socially minded consumers willing to pay more than market value for a product that promotes a social good. Indeed, fair-trade social enterprises are based on this latter idea. Similarly, social cooperatives, designed fundamentally to serve their members and support themselves through dues and membership fees, may also be eligible for government contracts and grants and even private individual donations and foundation grants because of the social benefits they offer.

The application of benefits theory to the sustenance of the various animals in the social enterprise zoo goes further than portfolio theory in guiding zookeepers about how to sustain various animals through alternative sources of finance. As noted here, portfolio theory addresses the amelioration of risk and argues for optimal diversification for a given level of desired social impact and financial gain (desired location on the efficiency frontier diagram of Chapter 2). In contrast, benefits theory does not anticipate formulaic diet diversification per se, but rather diversification according to the relative proportions of public and private benefits provided by a social enterprise with a particular mission. Unlike the risks and uncertainty addressed in portfolio theory, the choice of benefit mix is to a greater extent under the control of the social enterprise itself. Choice of mission implies a certain mix of public- and private-type benefits and consequent choices of income support. Capacity to sell private goods and services underlies the ability of a social enterprise to cross-subsidize profits from one activity to pay for another. This is the zookeeper's task – to design the diets of each of the animals in the zoo so as to ensure their financial health and desired levels and types of social impact.

REFERENCES

Andreoni, J. and A.A. Payne (2003), "Do government grants to private charities crowd out giving or fund-raising?," *The American Economic Review*, **93** (3), 792–812.

Bardach, E. and C. Lesser (1996), "Accountability in human services collaboratives – for what? And to whom?," *Journal of Public Administration Research and Theory*, **6** (2), 197–224.

Bartlett, J.W. (1995), *Equity Finance: Venture Capital, Buyouts, Restructurings, and Reorganizations, Volume 1*, New York: Aspen Publishers Online.

Bassi, A. (2011), "Interview with Stefano Zamagni: the Italian third sector," *Nonprofit Policy Forum*, **2** (2).

Baumgardner, T., C. Neufeld, and P.C.-T. Huang et al. (2015), "Crowdfunding as a fast-expanding market for the creation of capital and shared value," *Thunderbird International Business Review*, doi: 10.1002/tie.21766.

Benjamin, L., J.S. Rubin, and S. Zielenbach (2004), "Community development financial institutions: current issues and future prospects," *Journal of Urban Affairs*, **26** (2), 177–95.

Bill and Melinda Gates Foundation (2012), "Program-related investments: leveraging our resources to catalyze broader support for our mission," accessed 19 June 2016 at https://www.missioninvestors.org/tools/bill-melinda-gates-foundation-program-related-investments-leveraging-our-resources-to-catalyze.

Birkwood, S. (2014), "Peterborough prison social impact bond pilot fails to hit target to trigger repayments," *Third Sector*, 7 August, accessed 19 June 2016 at http://www.thirdsector.co.uk/peterborough-prison-social-impact-bond-pilot-fails-hit-target-trigger-repayments/finance/article/1307031.

Bowman, W. (2003), "Workplace giving: a case study of the Combined Federal Campaign," *New Directions for Philanthropic Fundraising*, **2003** (41), 27–37.

Bowman, W. (2007), "Managing endowment and other assets," in D. Young (ed.), *Financing Nonprofits: Putting Theory into Practice*, Lanham, MD: AltaMira, pp. 271–90.

Bowman, W. (2011), "Financial capacity and sustainability of ordinary nonprofits," *Nonprofit Management and Leadership*, **22** (1), 37–51.

Bowman, W. and B. Bingham (2015), "Toward a theory of membership association finance", paper presented at the Association for Research on Nonprofit Organizations and Voluntary Action Conference, Chicago, IL, November.

Bowman, W., E. Keating, and M. Hager (2007), "Investment income," in D. Young (ed.), *Financing Nonprofits: Putting Theory into Practice*, Lanham, MD: AltaMira Press, pp. 157–82.

Brooks, A.C. (2003), "Do government subsidies to nonprofits crowd out donations or donors?," *Public Finance Review*, **31** (2), 166–79.

Bugg-Levine, A., B. Kogut, and N. Kulatilaka (2012), "A new approach to funding social enterprises," *Harvard Business Review*, **90** (1/2), 118–23.

Calabrese, T.D. (2011), "Testing competing capital structure theories of nonprofit organizations," *Public Budgeting and Finance*, **31** (3), 119–43.

Calabrese, T.D. (2013), "Running on empty: the operating reserves of US nonprofit organizations," *Nonprofit Management and Leadership*, **23** (3), 281–302.

CDFI Coalition (2012), "What are CDFIs?," accessed 19 June 2016 at http://www.cdfi.org/about-cdfis/what-are-cdfis/.

Chen, D.W. (2012), "Goldman to invest in city jail program, profiting if recidivism falls sharply," *The New York Times*, 2 August, accessed 19 June 2016 at http://www.nytimes.com/2012/08/02/nyregion/goldman-to-invest-in-new-york-city-jail-program.html?_r=0.

Cohn, S. (2012), "The new crowdfunding registration exemption: good idea, bad execution," *Florida Law Review*, **64** (1), 1433–46.

Core, J.E., W.R. Guay, and R.S. Verdi (2006), "Agency problems of excess endowment holdings in not-for-profit firms," *Journal of Accounting and Economics*, **41** (3), 307–33.

DiMaggio, P.J. and W.W. Powell (1991), *The New Institutionalism in Organizational Analysis*, Chicago, IL: University of Chicago Press.

Fama, E.F. and M.C. Jensen (1983), "Separation of ownership and control," *Journal of Law and Economics*, **26** (2), 301–25.

Faulk, L., J. Lecy, and J. McGinnis (2012), "Nonprofit competitive advantage in grant markets: implications of network embeddedness," *Andrew Young School of Policy Studies Research Paper Series*, No. 13-07.

Fischer, R.L., A. Wilsker, and D.R. Young (2011), "Exploring the revenue mix of nonprofit organizations: does it relate to publicness?," *Nonprofit and Voluntary Sector Quarterly*, **40** (4), 662–81.

Flach, M. (2012), "Phases of company growth and financing" [diagram], accessed 24 June 2016 at http://www.nanowerk.com/nanotechnology/investing/funding_nanotechnology_companies_1.php.

Ganguly, B. (2014), "The success of the Peterborough social impact bond," accessed 19 June 2016 at http://www.rockefellerfoundation.org/blog/success-peterborough-social-impact.

GPS Capital Partners, LLC (2009), "Program-related investment: flexible tool in focus," paper presented at the Investing with Impact Conference, San Francisco.

Hager, M.A. (2001), "Financial vulnerability among arts organizations: a test of the Tuckman-Chang measures," *Nonprofit and Voluntary Sector Quarterly*, **30** (2), 376–92.

Hager, M. and E.A.M. Searing (2015), "The top ten ways to kill your nonprofit," *Nonprofit Quarterly*, 6 January.

Humphries, K.W. (2014), "Not your older brother's bonds: the use and regulation of social-impact bonds in the United States," *Law and Contemporary Problems*, **76** (3), 433–52.

Internal Revenue Service (2014), "Private foundations," accessed 19 June 2016 at http://www.irs.gov/Charities-and-Non-Profits/Charitable-Organizations/Private-Foundations.

James, E. (1983), "How nonprofits grow: a model," *Journal of Policy Analysis and Management*, **2** (3), 350–65.

Lecy, J.D. and E.A.M. Searing (2014), "Anatomy of the nonprofit starvation cycle: an analysis of falling overhead ratios in the nonprofit sector," *Nonprofit and Voluntary Sector Quarterly*, **44** (3), 539–63.

Lipson, B. (2002), "EQ2: equity equivalent investments," *Federal Reserve Bank of San Francisco, Community Development*, 4 March, accessed 19 June 2016 at http://www.frbsf.org/community-development/initiatives/community-development-finance/investment-vehicles/equity-equivalent-investments/.

Markiewicz, D. (2011), "Small business loans soar under Jobs Act SBA loan program extension," *Atlanta Journal-Constitution*, 24 January, accessed 19 June 2016 at http://www.ajc.com/news/business/small-business-loans-soar-under-jobs-act-sba-loan-/nQpPw/.

McCambridge, R. (2013), "Philanthropy – not even the same stream once," *Nonprofit Quarterly*, 15 August, accessed 19 June 2016 at https://nonprofitquarterly.org/2013/08/15/philanthropy-not-even-the-same-stream-once/.

Milward, H.B. (1994), "Nonprofit contracting and the hollow state," *Public Administration Reviews*, **54** (1), 73–7.

Milward, H.B. and K.G. Provan (2000), "Governing the hollow state," *Journal of Public Administration Research and Theory*, **10** (2), 359–80.

Pettijohn, S.L., E.T. Boris, and M.R. Farrell (2014), *National Study of Nonprofit-Government Contracts and Grants 2013: State Profiles*, accessed 19 June 2016 at http://www.urban.org/sites/default/files/alfresco/publication-pdfs/412949%20-%20National-Study-of-Nonprofit-Government-Contracts-and-Grants-State-Profiles.pdf.

Ramanath, R. (2009), "Limits to institutional isomorphism: examining internal processes in NGO–government interactions," *Nonprofit and Voluntary Sector Quarterly*, **38** (1), 51–76, doi: 10.1177/0899764008315181.

Ramirez, A. (2011), "Nonprofit cash holdings: determinants and implications," *Public Finance Review*, **39** (5), 653–81.

Rooney, P. (2007), "Individual giving," in D. Young (ed.), *Financing Nonprofits*, Lanham, MD: AltaMira Press, pp. 23–44.

Ryan, W.P. (2002), "The new landscape for nonprofits," in V. Futter, J.A. Cion, and G.W. Overton (eds), *Nonprofit Governance and Management*, Chicago, IL: American Bar Association, pp. 13–28.

Seaman, B.A. (ed.) (1980), *Economic Models and Support for the Arts*, Cambridge, MA: ABT Associates.

Searing, E.A.M. (2012), "Feeding the zoo: a survey of social enterprise finance," *EMES-SOCENT Conference Selected Papers*, No. LG13-48.

Singh, J.V., D.J. Tucker, and R.J. House (1986), "Organizational legitimacy and the liability of newness," *Administrative Science Quarterly*, **31** (2), 171–93.

Smith, S.R. and M. Lipsky (1995), *Nonprofits for Hire: The Welfare State in the Age of Contracting*, Cambridge, MA: Harvard University Press.

Social Enterprise UK (2012), "About social enterprise," accessed 19 June 2016 at http://www.socialenterprise.org.uk/about/about-social-enterprise#what%20are%20ses.

Steinberg, R. (2007), "Membership income," in D. Young (ed.), *Financing Nonprofits: Putting Theory into Practice*, Lanham, MD: AltaMira Press, pp. 121–56.

The Economist (2012), "Being good pays," 18 August, accessed 19 June 2016 at http://www.economist.com/node/21560561.

Tuckman, H.P. and C.F. Chang (1991), "A methodology for measuring the financial vulnerability of charitable nonprofit organizations," *Nonprofit and Voluntary Sector Quarterly*, **20** (4), 445–60.

Tyler, J. (2010), "Negating the legal problem of having two masters: a framework for L3C fiduciary duties and accountability," *Vermont Law Review*, **35** (1), 117–61.

Van Slyke, D.M. and H.K. Newman (2006), "Venture philanthropy and social entrepreneurship in community redevelopment," *Nonprofit Management and Leadership*, **16** (3), 345–68.

Watson, R. and N. Wilson (2002), "Small and medium size enterprise financing: a note on some of the empirical implications of a pecking order," *Journal of Business Finance and Accounting*, **29** (3–4), 557–78.

Weisbrod, B.A. (1998), "Modeling the nonprofit organization as a multiproduct firm: a framework for choice," in *To Profit or Not to Profit: The Commercial Transformation of the Nonprofit Sector*, New York: Cambridge University Press, pp. 47–64.

Williams, C. (2003), "New trends in financing the non-profit sector in the United States," in Organisation for Economic Co-operation and Development (ed.), *The Non-profit Sector in a Changing Economy*, Paris: OECD.

Wilsker, A.L. and D.R. Young (2010), "How does program composition affect the revenues of nonprofit organizations? Investigating a benefits theory of nonprofit finance," *Public Finance Review*, **38** (2), 193–216.

Wuttunee, W.A., M.M. Chicilo, R. Ruthney, and L. Gray (2008), "Financing social enterprise: an enterprise perspective," Working Paper, University of Saskatchewan, Centre for the Study of Co-operatives.

Yan, W., D.V. Denison, and J. Butler (2009), "Revenue structure and nonprofit borrowing," *Public Finance Review*, **37** (1), 47–67.

Young, D.R. (2007), "Toward a normative theory of nonprofit finance," in *Financing Nonprofits: Putting Theory into Practice*, Lanham, MD: AltaMira Press, pp. 339–72.

Young, D.R., A.L. Wilsker, and M.C. Grinsfelder (2010), "Understanding the determinants of nonprofit income portfolios," *Voluntary Sector Review*, **1** (2), 161–3.

9. Governing the zoo

Francesca Calò and Simon Teasdale

INTRODUCTION

In many countries, government, through public policy and alternative social welfare regimes, plays a critical role in overseeing the social enterprise zoo, a point that is neglected in much of the social enterprise literature. In part this neglect stems from federal government in the United States (where much of the academic literature derives) adopting a laissez-faire approach to social enterprise. Even so, government policy has considerably shaped the social enterprise zoo in the USA. Much of the move towards commercial revenue by US nonprofits was a consequence of the contracting out of publicly funded services in the 1970s and 1980s (Salamon, 1987), while the positioning of the Office for Social Innovation and Civic Participation in the White House has attracted much attention. However, the role of this Office for Social Innovation (OSI) is largely symbolic. Nominally created to support the development of civil society initiatives to tackle social problems, OSI's budget is dwarfed by the millions of dollars ploughed into social enterprise development by foundations such as Ashoka, and venture-philanthropy groups such as Roberts Enterprise Development Fund. Non-financial advice to social entrepreneurs looking to develop social enterprises emanates from similar foundations and from an array of incubators and accelerators often created by business schools (Cooney, 2015). The new legal forms for social enterprise (see Chapter 3) have been developed by private and civil society actors rather than by government (Reiser, 2013).

However, in other countries government has played a much more proactive role in creating the social enterprise zoo, and regulating which species might inhabit different enclosures. In this chapter we adopt a historical lens in order to outline approaches to governing the zoo in Italy and in England – two countries with long traditions of state support for social enterprise. Italy is widely credited with developing the concept of social enterprise, and was one of the first countries in the world to develop a specific legal form for social enterprise through the social cooperative legislation of 1991

(Defourny and Nyssens, 2008; Galera and Borzaga, 2009),[1] while England has been portrayed as having the most developed state support apparatus for social enterprise of any country (Nicholls, 2010a). As such these two cases open a window to a world where government plays the role of zoo-keeper and oversees the social enterprise habitat. Our analysis shows how different policy approaches are used to achieve different public and political objectives, and demonstrates how the role of the (governmental) zookeeper has a significant impact on the evolution of different types of social enterprise. The historical approach we adopt also suggests that, despite different political starting points, and different approaches to governing the zoo, both Italy and England appear to be converging towards a governance model whereby organizational form is downplayed in favor of more instrumental approaches in which political support is provided to any organization or activity that can contribute towards policy goals.

SOCIAL ENTERPRISE IN ITALY

To understand how government has shaped and governed social enterprise in Italy, two introductory considerations are necessary. First, Italy has a decentralized system of government (Putnam et al., 1993; Ferrera et al., 2012) whereby regional governments have responsibility for public service delivery at the local level. Moreover, the nonprofit sector has traditionally taken a major role in addressing societal needs, often in partnership with regional government (Ascoli et al., 2003; Ranci et al., 2005). Second, and relatedly, central government terms of office in Italy are often unstable and short term in nature – since 1991 there have been 14 prime ministers (as compared to five in the United Kingdom). This makes it difficult for government to develop long-term legislative programs.

In Italy, social enterprises have historically been considered as one part of the wider non-profit sector. In this section we consider the role of government in their evolution through three phases of development: the birth of the social cooperative (1979–97); the "golden age" of the non-profit sector (1997–2001); and the expansion of the social enterprise legal form (2001–13). Finally, we reflect upon recent developments whereby Italian government has begun to mimic policies developed as part of the Big Society policy agenda in England.

1978–97: The Birth of Social Cooperatives

The late 1970s and 1980s saw a period of rapid social, cultural, and political change in Italy. New social movements based on trade unions and student protest emerged as the oil crises of the 1970s created economic and political turbulence (Ferrera et al., 2012). Perhaps reflecting a general dissatisfaction with weak central governments over the period, a new form of nonprofit organization – the social cooperative – which combined a political campaigning role with the direct provision of services to marginalized groups (Ranci and Montagnini, 2010) – emerged from these social movements and from the Catholic Church (Barbetta, 1997). These social cooperatives became involved in the provision of social care and health services at the local level, providing services that were funded by government and/or private citizens (Borzaga and Defourny, 2001; Galera and Borzaga, 2009).

In 1991, central government formally created a new law governing social cooperatives (Dlgs 381/1991). Social cooperatives were categorized in two types. Type A participated in caring activities (particularly social and healthcare). Type B focused on social inclusion through the employment of marginalized people (at least 30 percent) in their workforce (Thomas, 2004). Mutualistic aims, democratic governance, an asset lock and limited profit distribution were, and still are, the main legally defining characteristics of social cooperatives.

1997–2001: The Golden Age of the Nonprofit Sector

Between 1997 and 2001 Social Democratic coalition governments presided over what has been termed the "golden age" for social cooperatives and the wider nonprofit sector (Ranci et al., 2005). Traditional divisions between those close to the church and certain left-wing elements within the nonprofit sector were temporarily put to one side, in part due to a benign funding environment that permitted sufficient resources for all. In 1997 a representative committee (*Forum del terzo settore*) was created to represent the whole nonprofit sector in its relationships with government. This was the first time that all nonprofits were represented by a cohesive entity and served to further increase government interest in social enterprise.

During this "golden age," nonprofit committees were created within the Italian Parliament, a capacity fund was established to support social cooperatives, and a public agency (*Agenzia per il terzo settore*) was established and given formal responsibility for the development of the nonprofit sector. The most important legislation of this period in the context of this chapter (Dlgs 328/2000) saw social cooperatives becoming formally recognized as a partner in the planning of social policies and in the delivery of public services. The new law, although interpreted differently by each region, aimed to create clear rules and processes in evaluating quality and in controlling service provision (Ascoli et al., 2003). As part of the legislation, regional government was permitted to reserve small-scale public service contracts for Type B social cooperatives, while medium-sized contracts were permitted to contain social clauses favoring organizations employing marginalized people. Interestingly this does not seem to have had any significant impact on the growth of social cooperatives. In 1996 there were 3857 social cooperatives, while by 2002 there were apparently somewhere between 4000 and 5000 (Gosling, 2002).[2]

2001–13: Expansion of the Social Enterprise Legal Form

In 2001 a Berlusconi-led right-wing coalition government was elected. This initiated what has been labeled as a "retrenchment period" for the non-profit sector (Ranci and Montagnini, 2010). Central government adopted a more "clientistic" relation with nonprofits, seeing them as service deliver-ers rather than partners (Ranci et al., 2005). Symbolic of this period was the closure of the *Agenzia per il terzo settore* in 2013.

However, during this period, two new social enterprise laws were intro-duced (Dlgs 118/2005; Dlgs 155/2006) that recognized social enterprise as a wider legal category than just social cooperatives. Any trading organiza-tion with a social goal could register as a social enterprise. Additionally, any organization (whatever its legal form) whose workforce comprised at least 30 percent marginalized people (such as people with disabilities or addictions, and ex-offenders) could formally register as a social enterprise (although there were no fiscal advantages to doing so) so long as it did not distribute dividends to shareholders and maintained an asset lock. In 2008 supplementary legislation added that only organizations that derived at least 70 percent of revenues through trading, and that produced a social impact report, could register as social enterprises. Nonetheless, by 2014 only 1200 social enterprises had formally registered, out of some 95000 that were eligible to do so (Venturi and Zandonai, 2015). This has been attributed to the legislation failing to provide clear guidance as to what would happen to assets following dissolution of the social enterprise, and more pertinently, a complete lack of fiscal incentive for organizations to register as social enterprises (Fiorentini and Calò, 2013).

To some extent these developments were reflective of a more market-driven governmental agenda that saw organizational form (and demo-cratic governance) as subservient to meeting social (or government) goals. Relatedly, towards the end of this period a broad coalition of politicians, financial intermediaries and consultants, inspired by social finance models developed in the UK and United States, gathered together around a theme of "social impact." For this group social impact could best be achieved by redesigning markets to serve public goals, for example through social impact bonds and other forms of social investment. The underlying idea was that by making social impact profitable, millions of euros might be attracted to tackling social problems.

2014: From Zoo to Circus?

In 2014, the latest coalition government launched a consultation to discuss proposed changes to social enterprise laws. The documentation displays three interrelated areas of debate that may affect the Italian social enterprise habitat. First, Italian social enterprises (and particularly social cooperatives) have hitherto been legally defined with reference to their social aims and activities. However, under the proposed legislation social enterprises would become legally defined by reference to their "measurable" social impact. Given the problems in defining, let alone measuring social impact (see Chapter 12), some commentators argue that this opens up the Italian social enterprise zoo to more predatory for-profit animals.

Second, the creation of a new public–private fund (based on the UK's Big Society Capital – see below) to invest in the equity of (the new) social enterprises was announced at the end of 2014. This necessitates the removal of constraints on dividend distribution, and any asset lock that had always been seen as a means to guarantee social purpose. It has been claimed that the restructuring of financial instruments can guarantee profits for organizations meeting specified social objectives, and thus foster social innovation while making organizational form irrelevant (Giorio, 2015).

Finally, the proposed legislation also allows, for the first time, representatives of public and private corporations to become involved in owning and managing social enterprises. Opponents see this as closing off the open and democratic government structures inherent in social cooperatives.

While it is still not clear how these debates will play out in the legislative process, the Italian case does demonstrate a movement away from a model whereby the Italian government tightly specified the social cooperative legal form and clearly distinguished between different types of social cooperatives. The social enterprise laws of 2005–06 and supplementary legislation of 2008 can be seen as a relaxing of these criteria, thus opening the zoo to a wider variety of species. Moreover, at the end of 2015 a legal form mutated from US benefit corporation (*Società Benefit*) has been created. However, no specific financial inducements were offered to encourage other organizational animals into the zoo. Over the last few years it has been possible to identify a movement, culminating in legal recognition through proposed legislation, which would open the zoo to any organization that can demonstrate social impact. This would be achieved through the reshaping of markets in order that private profit and social impact can be effectively combined. With reference to our zoo metaphor, and from a Western European perspective, this appears as a move away from a tightly controlled zoo housing the two types of social cooperative (in the 1990s) and towards a safari park (in the 2000s) whereby different species of social enterprise might roam freely outside of the cages reserved for social cooperatives. The proposed legislation currently passing through Parliament suggests a further move towards a circus more akin to the model adopted in England whereby the organizational form and characteristics of the social enterprise animals become subservient to the "tricks" they might perform for financial incentives.

SOCIAL ENTERPRISE IN ENGLAND

Unlike Italy, England has a tradition of strong and centralized government. It is often characterized as a liberal welfare regime (Esping-Andersen, 2002) although a tradition of publicly owned services and strong trade unions means that in some respects England has historically been a closer fit with a social-democratic model. In the 1980s the marketization and privatization of public services began under Thatcher's Conservative government, and later continued under Blair's New Labour government of 1997–2010. It was within this context that social enterprise first entered the policy mainstream. Initial policy interest was focused on the ability of social enterprise to achieve the political objective of regenerating deprived communities (Teasdale, 2012). While policy objectives have shifted considerably since 1997, government has maintained considerable influence over the social enterprise zoo, through financial incentives and policy rhetoric, in order to achieve those objectives.

1997–2001: The Birth of Social Enterprise

The social enterprise concept was brought into popular use by Social Enterprise London (SEL), which was established in 1997 by cooperative practitioners aiming to modernize the cooperative movement and capture public and political interest in the work of cooperative development agencies (Ridley-Duff and Bull, 2011; Teasdale, 2012):

> Among the company objectives were "to promote cooperative solutions for economic and community development" and "to promote social enterprises, in particular cooperatives and common ownerships, social firms, and other organisations and businesses which put into practice the principles of participative democracy, equal opportunities and social justice." (Teasdale, 2012, p. 109)

A network of interested and influential people connected to the New Labour government soon built around SEL. SEL also quickly built links with other organizations sharing similar democratic values. Community enterprises such as Development Trusts were assimilated into the social enterprise movement (Bland, 2010). While sharing commitments to democratic governance with the worker coops that dominated SEL, community enterprises tended to have a broader membership, and relied less on trading income.

This period was a time of rapid policy change. A New Labour government had been elected in 1997 with a strong commitment to social and economic reform. Their "Third Way" stance marked a dramatic shift from "Old Labour," particularly as regards its acceptance of the market and rejection of state ownership (Newman, 2007). This had opened up a policy space that SEL and its political allies were quick to exploit by positioning social enterprises as able to respond to regeneration in areas characterized by market failure, thus persuading the New Labour government to facilitate social enterprise development (Ridley-Duff and Bull, 2011).

In 1999 the Treasury's Neighbourhood Renewal Unit report *Enterprise and Social Exclusion* (HM Treasury, 1999) borrowed heavily from SEL's own material in describing social enterprises (Brown, 2003). However, the range of organizational types highlighted in the report was wider than that provided by SEL. Examples included "large insurance mutual and retail cooperatives, smaller cooperatives, employee owned businesses, intermediate labour market projects, social firms (e.g. for production by people with disabilities), or social housing" (HM Treasury, 1999, p. 105). A policy commitment was made to grow the social enterprise sector, and to commit government resources to assessing its impact (Teasdale, 2012).

2001–05: Institutionalizing Social Enterprise

Following the creation of the Social Enterprise Unit within the Department for Trade and Industry in 2001 it would appear that policymakers were constructing a big tent that included all groups claiming to be social enterprises (Bland, 2010). The Social Enterprise Unit deliberately created a loose policy definition of social enterprise to permit the inclusion of a wide range of organizational forms (Department for Trade and Industry, 2002, p. 8): "A social enterprise is a business with primarily social objectives, whose surpluses are principally reinvested for that purpose in the business or in the community, rather than being driven by the need to maximize profit for shareholders and owners." The report highlighted that social enterprises adopt a wide range of legal forms including private and for-profit "companies limited by share" (ibid., p. 7). A characteristic exhibited by "successful" social enterprises according to *Social Enterprise: A Strategy for Success* was to be "financially viable, gaining their income from selling goods and services" (ibid., p. 16). This implied that social enterprises relied primarily on trading for their income, and reflected the growing influence of a discourse that social and economic objectives were not mutually exclusive. It should be noted that the UK social enterprise definition has never been a legal definition. Unlike in Italy, government has avoided creating a legal category of social enterprise. No tax advantages are available to organizations self-identifying as social enterprises. However, many also take a charitable (nonprofit) legal form that does offer certain tax advantages.

Government's approach to developing the social enterprise sector in the UK (prior to 2005) focused primarily on funding advice and support through the Social Enterprise Coalition and Regional Development Agencies. Towards the end of New Labour's second period of office policy interest in social enterprise became more focused as a way to reform state services that had (supposedly) been stifled by bureaucracy and a lack of innovation:

> The Government believes social enterprises have the potential to play a far greater role in the delivery and reform of public services. . . Entrepreneurial behaviour combined with a continuing commitment to delivering public benefit, can lead to local innovation, greater choice, and higher quality of service for users. (Ibid., p. 24)

There was resistance to this new agenda, which was seen by those in the cooperative movement as diluting the (democratic and radical) ethos of social enterprise (Teasdale, 2012). A move away from the notion of social enterprise as democratically controlled was evident in the creation of a new legal form for social enterprises in 2005, the community interest company (CIC). Unlike existing industrial and provident society legal forms, CICs had no requirement for democratic control and ownership (Smith and Teasdale, 2012). CICs did allow the limited payment of dividends to external investors, and can be seen as equating in some ways to L3Cs (low-profit limited liability companies) and B Corps (corporations meeting the requirements of the nonprofit standards-setting organization B Lab; see Chapter 3) in the USA.

2005–10: The Expansion of Social Enterprise

The Office of the Third Sector (OTS) was created in 2006 following a period of lobbying by strategic alliances of voluntary organization representatives

(Alcock, 2010), and saw responsibility for social enterprise moving to the Cabinet Office. This led to the policy emphasis that: "social enterprises are part of the 'third sector,' which encompasses all organisations which are nongovernmental, principally reinvest surpluses in the community or organisation and seek to deliver social or environmental benefits" (Office of the Third Sector, 2006, p. 10). An underlying assumption was that voluntary organizations and social enterprises could potentially deliver public services more cost effectively than the public sector. However, infrastructure bodies such as the National Council for Voluntary Organisations (NCVO) and the Social Enterprise Coalition (now SEUK) argued that an injection of resources from the state was necessary to enable organizations to scale up and adapt to a new policy environment. Continuing the policy of funding social enterprise through investment in infrastructure, considerable resources were subsequently invested in third sector infrastructure to enable third sector organizations to bid for and deliver public services (Di Domenico et al., 2009; Nicholls, 2010a). A second strand of financial support to social enterprises developed as central and local government increasingly commissioned social enterprises to deliver publicly funded services. In particular, the National Health Service encouraged social enterprises to bid to deliver health services. In addition, Right to Request legislation encouraging public sector spin-outs (supported by state-financed funds such as the Social Enterprise Investment Fund in the Department of Health) was introduced, which expanded the concept of social enterprise to also include "public sector mutuals" (Roy et al., 2013).

A third strand of policy support to social enterprise has focused on social investment. Started in 2000 by the Social Investment Task Force – a group of financiers and social investment activists who aimed to lobby the New Labour government – social investment developed under New Labour as a way for individuals and organizations to invest in community redevelopment through the Community Investment Tax Relief (CITR) scheme (Nicholls, 2010b). This gradually shifted under New Labour towards direct grant and loan investment into social enterprises via government-funded intermediaries. In 2008 legislation paved the way for capitalization of a new wholesale social investment bank funded through unclaimed bank assets (ibid.). In 2010 one of the final acts of the New Labour government was to introduce the world's first social impact bond. Social impact bonds are based upon the concept of social investment whereby investors finance government's social policy initiatives delivered by social enterprises, charities, or private companies and are paid an agreed rate of return if the initiative is successful (McHugh et al., 2013, p. 248; see also Chapter 8). Although the organizations involved in delivery of this "Peterborough"[3] initiative would usually be considered social enterprises, social impact bonds do not necessarily rely on any particular type of organization to deliver programs. The basic premise is that organizational form is subservient to societal impact.

New Labour's final term of office marked a shift of policy emphasis away from the discourses of social business and cooperative/community enterprise that were prevalent in the early years of social enterprise. However, rather than suggesting the meaning of social enterprise had changed, it is more accurate to say that the meaning had further expanded to include voluntary organizations delivering public services. This shift was driven in part by the changing policy environment where the main policy driver was reforming public service delivery (particularly to reduce the overall cost) (Teasdale, 2012). The reform of public service delivery became an increasingly important theme following the financial crisis that began in 2008, and which was framed by opposition parties as a consequence of high public spending. The Conservative-led coalition government, which came to power in 2010, made cutting public spending a primary policy goal, and one that social enterprise was to play a key role in tackling.

2010–15: A Radical New Direction?

Following the election of a Conservative-led coalition government in 2010, one of its first acts was to "ban" the use of the term "third sector" and rename OTS the Office for Civil Society (OCS) (Alcock, 2012). This was closely followed by a decision to dramatically cut infrastructure support to the sector. The representative body, Social Enterprise UK, previously funded primarily by government, had to "downsize" significantly. However, rhetorical support for social enterprise appears to have been maintained, and policy support has continued, albeit through a seemingly radical new direction.

Although the Conservative Party had demonstrated some support for social enterprise while in opposition – David Cameron was the keynote speaker at Social Enterprise UK's national conference in 2009 – many Conservative politicians were seemingly unaware of the concept. Cameron had outlined his governing philosophy that positioned the Big Society as a counterbalance to the overbearing Big State (ibid.). One aspect of this idea was an enhanced role for voluntary and community organizations and social enterprises in the delivery of public services (Cabinet Office, 2010).

A newly elected Conservative MP – Chris White – introduced what was then called the Public Services (Social Enterprises and Social Value) Bill. The framing of this bill was radical in that it indelibly associated social enterprise with social value creation, and suggested that social enterprises should be favored by commissioners and procurers of public services due to the added social value they create:

> The Bill attempts to strengthen the social enterprise business sector and make the concept of "social value" more relevant and important in the placement and provision of public services. New duties will be placed upon central and local government authorities to publish explicit strategies for supporting these values and the public procurement process will need to reflect and measure them. (Edmonds et al., 2010)

The original bill contained three significant clauses: to publish a national social enterprise strategy; to amend the 2000 Local Government Act such that every local authority should include proposals for promoting engagement with social enterprise in their area; and for local authorities to consider how contracts might improve the economic, social or environmental well-being of the UK (ibid.). Social enterprise was to be (loosely) defined as: "being a business, the activities of which are being carried on primarily for a purpose that promotes or improves the social or environmental well-being of the United Kingdom" (Parliament, 2012). Although considerable resources had been given to organizations (and particularly infrastructure bodies) claiming to be social enterprises over the past decade, the third clause was particularly radical as it potentially offered social enterprises favorable treatment by public services commissioners. This led to huge debate within Parliament as to what was (and was not) a social enterprise, and, in particular, what was meant by social value and which organizations created it.[4] To briefly summarize the debate here, one wing of the Labour Party emphasized the need for democratic ownership and accountability within social enterprise; a "Big Society" group of Conservative MPs emphasized the non-profit distribution constraint as an essential criterion; while a third group of market-liberal Conservative MPs emphasized that for-profit companies create social value and that the social enterprise label should not be limited to third sector organizations. Within this third group there was considerable differences of opinion as to whether only small (local) businesses should be treated as social enterprises, or whether larger organizations such as Tesco should also be seen as social enterprises due to the jobs they create in local communities and the money they put back into the community (Teasdale et al., 2012).

Rather than address this definitional complexity, the government dropped the first and second clauses from the bill, and considerably watered down the third clause such that commissioners of some public services need only "consider" whether to incorporate wider social value when commissioning public services. Social value was left undefined, leaving commissioners responsible for deciding whether it was intrinsic to social enterprises, or whether multinational corporations might also create social value; commissioners were also left responsible for determining how to measure social value.

Under the Coalition government social enterprises became central to key agendas of radical reform in policy areas including: health services (Cabinet Office, 2011) and welfare and work (Shutes and Taylor, 2014). The New Labour policy emphasis on social investment was accentuated. The social impact bond program was extended; and the Social Investment Wholesale Bank was renamed "Big Society Capital." In his speech marking the launch of the Big Society philosophy, Prime Minister David Cameron outlined the developing emphasis on outcomes as opposed to organizational form: "We believe in paying public service providers by results. It encourages value for money and innovation at the same time" (Cameron, 2010).

In many ways the government treatment of social enterprise in England parallels developments in Italy. Emerging from the cooperative movement the concept has expanded as policymakers have enthusiastically embraced it, although notably at no time has government created a legal definition of social enterprise. Policy support has been partly rhetorical, but considerable financial resources have also been targeted at social enterprises that address government objectives, and more widely, the aim of creating a social enterprise sector. Since the election of the Conservative-led coalition government in 2010 the label social enterprise has been used less as market-liberal politicians try out alternative concepts such as "social venture," perhaps because these are less laden with left-of-center notions of social democracy, and more with a new way of thinking that sees social value creation compatible with the accumulation of private profit. Like Italy, the English social enterprise zoo has expanded to include a wider variety of organizational forms. Similarly, we also see over time a move away from the protection and nurturing of particular forms, and towards an emphasis upon what the animals can do, as opposed to what they look like.

CONCLUSIONS

Italy can initially be seen as having a tightly controlled approach to governing the zoo. The types of animal permitted in the zoo were heavily regulated, with only thoroughbred species conforming to the social cooperative (and later) social enterprise models allowed. Public policy has provided a sheltered environment within which Italian social enterprises can grow safe from competition from public and private predators. However, concerns have recently been raised that this tightly controlled approach to governing the zoo prevents innovation and the development of new species.

The English policy environment has involved a more permissive approach to governing the social enterprise zoo, with no strict legal definition. Over time the concept has also evolved to include a wider variety of animals. The change of government in 2010 marked a change in approach to social enterprise policy. Under New Labour the role of the zookeeper was to increase the supply of social enterprises through measures such as funding regional development agencies to support fledgling social enterprises, and developing new legal forms such as the community interest company (see Smith and Teasdale, 2012). The subsequent (center–right) coalition government sought to increase demand for goods and services produced by social enterprises, in particular through public policy approaches such as the Public Services (Social Value) Bill, and the creation of public sector mutuals, both of which aim to increase the role of social enterprises in public service delivery. A related evolution in policy under the Coalition government was a move towards a more Hayekian approach to letting the market decide which social enterprises were worth protecting, at the expense of direct support to social enterprise support bodies.

Our two social enterprise zoos (Italy and England) both look very different in 2015 compared to when they were established in the 1990s. In both countries the zoos emerged from a cooperative tradition and were supported by social-democratic policymakers who saw a fit between cooperative and mutual values and political ideologies of the time. However, policymakers in both countries also had instrumental reasons: in Italy social enterprises were seen as a way to provide social care services, and to enable the reintegration of disadvantaged people into the labor force, while in the UK policymakers initially saw social enterprise as an economic tool to regenerate deprived communities.

The two countries adopted rather different approaches to managing their social enterprise zoos. In Italy the types of animals permitted in the zoo were tightly controlled through social cooperative and later social enterprise laws. Social enterprises were nurtured in protected public sector markets, and were subsidized. In England no legal definition of social enterprise has ever been produced, although a new community interest company legal form was devised for some social enterprise organizations. Social enterprises were nurtured, initially through money channeled through support organizations, and later through social investment policies, and compensation for delivering public services.

Initially the social enterprise zoos in each country reflected particular historical, political, and cultural factors (Kerlin, 2013). However, despite different approaches to managing the zoos in both countries, there appears to have been recent convergence towards a (neo) liberal model of zoo keeping whereby the organizational form of the social enterprise is seen as secondary to the policy goals that social enterprises can achieve. In turn, resources in both countries are distributed only to those social enterprises that are seen as able to contribute towards particular policy goals. Thus social enterprises have to compete with private for-profit providers for social investment or to deliver public services. Unlike in Italy, the introduction of new species to the zoo in England has led to dramatic expansion of the different forms within the zoo and in the overall size of the zoo (Teasdale et al., 2013). This is likely related to the indirect and direct financial support offered to social enterprise in England. Going forward, in both countries we observe a tendency towards a policy approach that opens up the zoo to any organization that can contribute towards policy goals through the restructuring of markets to encourage private investment and payment by results to any organization. To some extent this approximates the US model discussed elsewhere in this book (in particular, see Chapters 3, 4, and 8). However, a notable distinction between European and US zoos (or even circuses) is that in Europe government will retain the zookeeper role.

NOTES

1. Although as this chapter shows the social cooperative is just one form of social enterprise recognized in Italian law.
2. As of January 2015 there are 12 570 social cooperatives, supporting an estimated 5 million beneficiaries, employing 500 000 people and turning over 10 billion euros of revenues (Venturi and Zandonai, 2015).
3. The first social impact bond was issued in the UK at HM Prison Peterborough, where the government and Social Finance Ltd. partnered to address recidivism (see Chapter 8 and The Economist, 2012).
4. This debate is analyzed in Teasdale et al.'s (2012) paper.

REFERENCES

Alcock, P. (2010), "A strategic unity: defining the third sector in the UK," *Voluntary Sector Review*, **1** (1), 5–24.

Alcock, P. (2012), "The Big Society: a new policy environment for the third sector?" *Third Sector Research Centre, Working Papers*, No. 82, accessed 19 June 2016 at http://www.birmingham.ac.uk/generic/tsrc/documents/tsrc/working-papers/work ing-paper-82.pdf.

Ascoli, U., E. Pavolini, and C. Ranci (2003), "La nuova partnership: i mutamenti nel rapporto fra stato e organizzazioni del terzo settore in Italia" [The new partnership: the changes in the relationship between state and third sector organization in Italy], in U. Ascoli (ed.), *Il Welfare Mix in Europa*, Rome: Carocci Editore.

Barbetta, G.P. (1997), *The Nonprofit Sector in Italy*, Manchester, UK: Manchester University Press.

Bland, J. (2010), *Social Enterprise Solutions for 21st Century Challenges: The UK Model of Social Enterprise and Experience*, Helsinki: Publications of the Ministry of Employment and the Economy.

Borzaga, C. and J. Defourny (2001), *The Emergence of Social Enterprise*, London and New York: Routledge.

Brown, J. (2003), "Defining social enterprise," paper presented at the Small Business and Entrepreneurship Development Conference, Surrey University, accessed 19 June 2016 athttp://www.huckfield.com/wp-content/uploads/2014/05/02-Brown-Defining-Social-Enterprise.pdf.

Cabinet Office (2010), *Modernising Commissioning: Increasing the Role of Charities, Social Enterprise, Mutuals and Cooperatives in Public Service Delivery*, London: The Cabinet Office.

Cabinet Office (2011), *Business Support for Social Enterprises*, London: The Cabinet Office.

Cameron, D. (2010), "Speech on the Big Society," 19 July, Liverpool, accessed 19 June 2016 at http://www.britishpoliticalspeech.org/speech-archive.htm?speech=321.

Cooney, K. (2015), "Social enterprise in the United States: WISEs and other worker-focused models," *ICSEM Working* Papers, No. 9.

Defourny, J. and M. Nyssens (2008), "Social enterprise in Europe: recent trends and developments," *Social Enterprise Journal*, **4** (3), 202–28.

Department for Trade and Industry (DTI) (2002), *Social Enterprise: A Strategy for Success*, London: DTI, accessed 19 June 2016 at http://webarchive.national archives.gov.uk/20070108124358/http:/cabinetoffice.gov.uk/third_sector/docu ments/social_enterprise/se_strategy_2002.pdf.

Di Domenico, M., P. Tracey, and H. Haugh (2009), "Social economy involvement in public service delivery: community engagement and accountability," *Regional Studies*, **43** (7), 981–92.

Edmonds, T., K. Parry, D. Webb, and J. Woodhouse (2010), "Public Services (Social Enterprise and Social Value) Bill, Bill No. 6 of 2010/11," *Commons Library Research Paper*, No. 10/73, accessed 19 June 2016 at http://researchbrief ings.parliament.uk/ResearchBriefing/Summary/RP10-73.

Esping-Andersen G. (ed.) (2002), *Why We Need a New Welfare State*, Oxford: Oxford University Press.

Ferrera, M., V. Fargion, and M. Jessoula (2012), *Alle radici del welfare all'italiana. Origini e futuro di un modello sociale squilibrato* [At the Root of all Italian Welfare. Origins and Future of an Unbalanced Social Model], Venice: Marsilio Editori.

Fiorentini, G. and F. Calò (2013), *Impresa sociale and innovazione sociale. Imprenditorialità and entrepreneurship nel terzo settore e nell'economia sociale* [Social Enterprise and Social Innovation. Entrepreneurship in the Third Sector and in Social Economy], Rome and Milan: Franco Angeli Editore.

Galera, G. and C. Borzaga (2009), "Social enterprise: an international overview of its conceptual evolution and legal implementation," *Social Enterprise Journal*, **5** (3), 210–28.

Giorio, A.C. (2015), "Il selfie del terzo settore e dei suoi stakeholder: proposte della società civile per la riforma del terzo settore" [A selfie of the third sector and its stakeholders: proposals of civil society for third sector reform], *Impresa Sociale*, 4, 6 December, accessed 19 June 2016 at http://www.rivistaimpresasociale.it/ rivista/item/97-il-selfie-del-terzo-settore-e-dei-suoi-stakeholder-proposte-della-societ%C3%A0-civile-per-la-riforma-del-terzo-settore.html.

Gosling, P. (2002), *Social Cooperatives in Italy: Lessons for the UK*, London: Social Enterprise London.

HM Treasury (1999), *Enterprise and Social Exclusion*, London: HM Treasury National Strategy for Neighbourhood Renewal: Policy Action Team 3.

Kerlin, J. (2013), "Defining social enterprise across different contexts: a conceptual framework based on institutional factors," *Nonprofit and Voluntary Sector Quarterly*, **42** (1), 84–108.

McHugh, N., S. Sinclair, and M. Roy et al. (2013), "Social impact bonds: a wolf in sheep's clothing?," *Journal of Poverty and Social Justice*, **21** (3), 247–57.

Newman, J. (2007), "Rethinking 'the public' in troubled times: unsettling state, nation, and the liberal public sphere," *Public Policy and Administration*, **22** (1), 27–47.

Nicholls, A. (2010a), "Institutionalizing social entrepreneurship in regulatory space: reporting and disclosure by community interest companies," *Accounting, Organizations and Society*, **35** (4), 394–415.

Nicholls, A. (2010b), "The institutionalization of social investment: the interplay of investment logics and investor rationalities," *Journal of Social Entrepreneurship*, **1** (1), 70–100.

Office of the Third Sector (OTS) (2006), *Social Enterprise Action Plan: Scaling New Heights*, London: Cabinet Office of the Third Sector.

Parliament (2012), *Public Services (Social Value) Bill 2012*, accessed 19 June 2016 at http://services.parliament.uk/bills/2010-11/publicservicessocialvalue.html.

Putnam, R., R. Leonardi, and R. Nanetti (1993), *Making Democracy Work: Civic Traditions in Modern Italy*, Princeton, NJ: Princeton University Press.

Ranci, C. and E. Montagnini (2010), "The impact of the commodification of social care on the role and identity of the third sector in Italy," in A. Evers and A. Zimmer (eds), *Third Sector Organizations Facing Turbulent Environments*, Baden-Baden: Nomos Verlagsgesellschaft, pp. 107–23.

Ranci, C., M. Pellegrino, and E. Pavolini (2005), "The third sector and the policy process in Italy: between mutual accommodation and new forms of partnership," accessed 21 June 2016 at http://eprints.lse.ac.uk/29011/.

Reiser, D.B. (2013), "Theorizing forms for social enterprise," *Emory Law Journal*, **62** (4), 681–738.

Ridley-Duff, R. and M. Bull (2011), *Understanding Social Enterprise: Theory and Practice*, Thousand Oaks, CA and London: SAGE.

Roy, M.J., C. Donaldson, R. Baker, and A. Kay (2013), "Social enterprise: new pathways to health and well-being," *Journal of Public Health Policy*, **34** (1), 55–68.

Salamon, L. (1987), "Of market failure, voluntary failure, and third-party government: toward a theory of government–nonprofit relations in the modern welfare state," *Nonprofit and Voluntary Sector Quarterly*, **16** (1–2), 29–49.

Shutes, I. and R. Taylor (2014), "Conditionality and the financing of welfare services: implications for the social divisions of work and welfare," *Social Policy and Administration*, **48** (2), 204–20.

Smith, G. and S. Teasdale (2012), "Associative democracy and the social economy: exploring the regulatory challenge," *Economy and Society*, **41** (2), 151–76.

Teasdale, S. (2012), "What's in a name? Making sense of social enterprise discourses," *Public Policy and Administration*, **27** (2), 99–119.

Teasdale, S., P. Alcock, and G. Smith (2012), "Legislating for the big society? The case of the Public Services (Social Value) Bill," *Public Money and Management*, **32** (3), 201–8.

Teasdale, D., F. Lyon, and R. Baldock (2013), "Playing with numbers: a methodological critique of the social enterprise growth myth," *Journal of Social Entrepreneurship*, **4** (2), 113–31.

The Economist (2012), "Being good pays," 18 August, accessed 19 June 2016 at http://www.economist.com/node/21560561.

Thomas, A. (2004), "The rise of social cooperatives in Italy," *Voluntas*, **15** (3), 243–63.

Venturi, P. and F. Zandonai (2015), *L'impresa sociale in Italia: identità e sviluppo in un quadro di riforma* [The Social Enterprise in Italy: Identity and Development in a Framework of Reform], Iris Network Report.

PART IV

Performance of the zoo

10. Social innovation in the zoo

Thema Monroe-White and Jesse D. Lecy

OVERVIEW

Social innovation plays an important role in the social enterprise zoo. As led by Schumpeterian social entrepreneurs (see Chapter 7) innovation reflects the *means* (or tools) used to disrupt the status quo in pursuit of a social *end*. Various types of innovation are employed by social entrepreneurs and their associates to achieve social impact. In this chapter we develop a taxonomy of social innovation that distinguishes among social ventures through both their theory of change, and the type of innovation that they employ. The taxonomy is applied to a prominent database of social entrepreneurs to help us understand what types of innovations are common among social enterprises. This taxonomy is one way of describing the clusters of animals found in the social enterprise zoo.

Narrow definitions of the term limit innovation to the adoption or generation of new or novel behavior. However, these definitions do not adequately account for the solution-focused organizations found in the social enterprise zoo, often emerging under environmental conditions (i.e., low human capital, lack of resources, cultural factors) that prohibit entirely new and novel adaptations aimed at addressing social problems. Thus, there may be a wide array of potential social innovations, from incremental (those addressing particular market failures, in which the product or service itself remains relatively unaltered, for example, "base of the pyramid" activities), to disruptive (those targeting an entire system, through the implementation of an entirely new incentive model, for example, climate change initiatives) (see Nicholls and Murdock, 2012 and Monroe-White, 2014 for more examples).

One important aspect of the innovation process is the social entrepreneur's theory of change. A theory of change is a mental model that an entrepreneur holds that informs his or her idea of how the specific social venture will create impact. Each social entrepreneur will have an explicit or implicit theory of change. It is useful to understand that theory because the mechanisms of each mental model will operate differently,

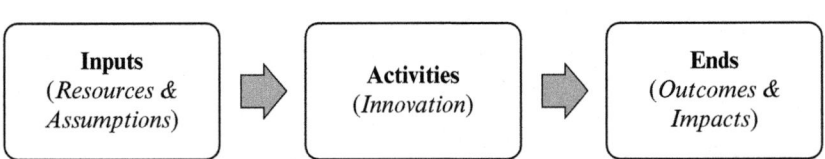

Figure 10.1   Generalized theory of social change

and understanding the mechanisms can help improve the enterprising process. It is often presented as a statement about the activities of the organization and the ultimate outcomes that are achieved, but it can be parsimoniously represented as a chain of events using arrows to show the event sequence. We define seven broad types of these mental models below. Figure 10.1 represents how a theory of social change may be conceptualized generically.

In this chapter, we use the combination of theory of change and type of innovation to develop a taxonomy of social innovation. This taxonomy organizes social enterprises along two dimensions while still allowing for wide variation in their areas of impact (e.g., health, environment, education, income inequality, etc.) and legal form. Below, we describe the theory of change model in detail, and define the different generic types of innovation, with examples of each. One aim in this chapter is to help develop a language that can be used by social innovators to describe their models of social change, or applied by outsider observers to better understand how a social venture seeks social change.

METHODS AND ANALYSIS

In order to develop and refine a typology of social innovation we have employed an iterative and grounded approach using examples of ventures that have been identified as social enterprises. We use a convenience sample of the most recent 200 enterprises supported through the Echoing Green fellowship. This is a useful and appropriate source because the entrepreneurs have self-identified with social enterprises by submitting applications to the fellowship, and they received external validation of their status through judges that selected awardees. The Echoing Green Fellows Program provides an archival database of awardees that is readily accessible online (http://www.echoinggreen.org/fellows) and includes mission statements, biographies, and links to external sources. Data on key organizational characteristics were harvested from the site and placed into a database for review and analysis.

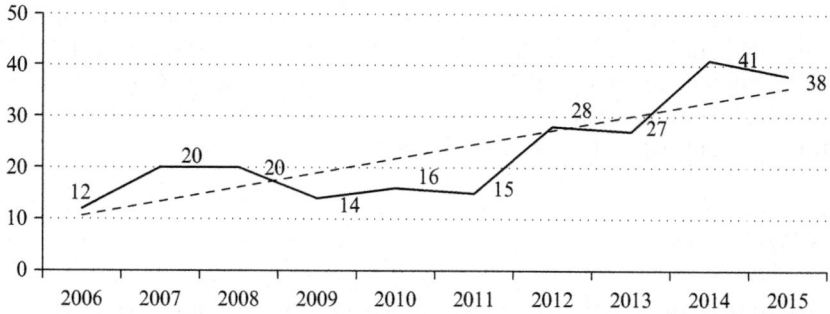

Figure 10.2   Number of Echoing Green organizations awarded per year (2006–15)

Although the number of fellowships awarded has fluctuated over the years, there has been a clear and drastic up-tick in the average number of applications received (reportedly "thousands" per year) and individual fellowships awarded over the past ten years (52 in 2015 up from 12 in 2005; Figure 10.2). Similarly, the number of social enterprise organizations has tripled during that same time frame. Given the prominent status of the Echoing Green organization and the small number of fellowships relative to the applications received, the sample should be treated as a convenience sample rather than one that is representative of all social enterprises. The database is primarily useful as an archive that contains both for-profit and nonprofit businesses that are clearly part of the social enterprise zoo. It is also not necessary to have a representative sample for the purposes of developing a taxonomy as long as all potential instances of social innovation and theories of social change are represented in the cases that have been evaluated.

DATA COLLECTION: THE ECHOING GREEN DATABASE

Admittedly, the Echoing Green roster is a preferential list of social entrepreneurs and their corresponding enterprises. Fellows include the founders of some of the most well-known organizations in the world including: Teach for America, Code2040, City Year, College Summit and SKS Microfinance. Award decisions are based on Echoing Green's review criteria; as such, awardees are not necessarily representative of the broader social enterprise landscape. Although we are not apprised of the Echoing Green review criteria used for selecting entrepreneurs and/or their organizations, the Echoing Green website provides access to organizational details on each Fellow's social enterprise, appropriate for descriptive analysis. We identified 203 social enterprises from the Echoing Green website beginning with 2014 awardees (the most recent data available at the time of analysis) and back through 2005.

ANALYSIS

Qualitative analysis based on grounded theory techniques (Glaser and Strauss, 2009) was used to generate the social innovation taxonomy. The organization summary text from each social enterprise was entered into a database and pattern coded using thick descriptions (Miles and Huberman, 1994). The textual data describing each enterprise's programs and intended impact were obtained from each enterprise's "Bold Idea" and/or "Organization" summary statement provided on the Echoing Green website. Sample text from each organization summary is reproduced (either in whole or in part) beneath each theory of change and innovation example below. Initial categories within the taxonomy were developed after reviewing "chunks" of data (phrases, sentences or paragraphs) that conveyed a meaningful idea or set of ideas (Guest and MacQueen, 2007; Krippendorf, 2013). These data were used to categorize each enterprise into one primary theory of change category and one social innovation category. In many cases the enterprises employed elements of more than one theory of change or innovation, so we selected what appeared to be the most prominent approach for each observation. Assignment was done in an iterative fashion with additional categories developed when specific enterprise models did not fit into existing groups. Additional theory of change and innovation categories were developed until the point of saturation, when additional analysis no longer contributed to the discovery of new categories (Strauss, 1987). The full sample of 203 organizations was then coded, yielding the final taxonomy as presented below.

THEORY OF CHANGE

In its simplest form the theory of change is a causal statement that describes the social entrepreneur's understanding of how the actions of an organization impact community members. It can be characterized as "the product of a series of critical-thinking exercises that provides a comprehensive picture of the early- and intermediate-term changes in a given community that are needed to reach a long-term goal articulated by the

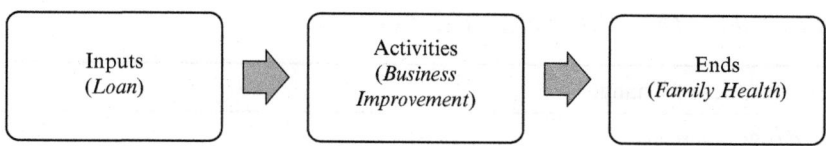

Figure 10.3   Microfranchise theory of social change

community" (Anderson, 2005, p. 1). For example, a microfinance franchise might say: "We provide loans for women, who then start or expand a business, generating income, which is then used to feed, house, and educate children of the borrowers. We expect to see improvements in income, nutrition, and education outcomes."

Note that each theory of change has many embedded assumptions similar to each business model for a new venture (Osterwalder and Pigneur, 2010). In this example we assume that if women receive loans they will invest in growing businesses. We assume that the women can be successful enough at their business ventures to increase income. And we assume that the income will be used to care for the family (men are often assumed to spend the money in a less judicious manner, which is why microfinance tends to focus on female entrepreneurs). This results in the theory of change found in Figure 10.3.

The theory of change can be helpful in a variety of ways. It assists in identifying untested assumptions that can be probed before trying to scale an idea. It is a helpful communication mechanism for outside stakeholders. And it also highlights the core activity of the social venture. Each core activity will have a set of protocols and risks that might be mitigated through experience and knowledge.

The exercise of coding Echoing Green cases is instructive because it helps group projects into categories that share similar theories of change. Each organization attempts to create social change through a variety of business models and program activities, but we see some distinct strategies emerge in the aggregate. Organizations that share the same theory of change will be working on similar problems and employ similar organizational structures, so there may be lessons that can be shared within a group. Across categories though, strategies and business models diverge significantly. If one wants to advise or nurture social enterprises, the theory of change may be the best way to group organizations in order to target mentorship and create learning opportunities across organizations.

The six broad theories of change that were identified within the Echoing Green sample are described in Table 10.1. Examples of mission statements

Table 10.1   Theory of change categories

Six Theories of Change	
1. *Business development*	
Business development/incubation	14
Financing	5
Franchise	3
Business processes/inputs/supply chains	12
2. *Education and training*	38
3. *Building networks*	
Advocacy	39
Knowledge/innovation	7
Negotiation and leverage	6
Social support	34
4. *Health systems*	6
5. *Environmental protection*	
Behavioral change	4
New technology/business model	13
6. *Product innovation*	22
Total	203

of the social enterprises presented on their Echoing Green profile pages are included to offer concrete examples of each category.

Business Development

This theory of change focuses on actions that help create new businesses and grow existing organizations. The social enterprises in this group concentrate on developing business ideas and skills, often nurturing young enterprises through incubators or scaling through franchise models. This category also contains enterprises that focus on building financial tools for small businesses or enhancing the business environment through better production inputs and market information. The theory of change emphasizes business development as a means to create jobs and employment in communities, summarized in Figure 10.4.

Examples

- "Project Equity builds economic resiliency in low-income communities by increasing worker ownership. [Project Equity] incubate[s] and grow[s] scalable cooperative businesses, and catalyze[s] change-makers across business, nonprofit, government and education sectors

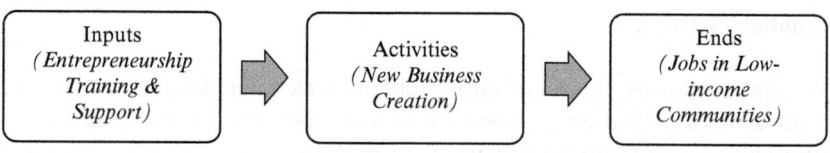

Figure 10.4 Business development theory of social change

to integrate worker ownership into local ecosystems for economic development."

- "Qorax partners with local educational institutions to create renewable energy business incubators. The incubators use a collaborative process to define the most critical local energy issues and train entrepreneurs to create businesses that scale the adoption of high-impact, clean domestic energy technologies."

Education and Training

This theory of change focuses on developing skills and knowledge that prepare individuals for professional or vocational work. This may be done through starting new schools, developing new curriculums, employing novel educational pedagogy or technology, creating access to educational resources such as libraries or tutorials, creating learning cohorts, and investing in the professionalization of teachers and schools. The work often targets underserved or vulnerable populations.

Examples

- "Fundi Bots uses robotics training inside and outside African schools to create and inspire a new generation of students and innovators who are better prepared for careers in the technology sector and who can become change-makers in their communities."
- "Eneza Education is looking to make kids in rural Africa smarter by offering a virtual tutor and teacher's assistant that works on a simple low-cost mobile phone."
- "Anew provides unprecedented academic and socio-emotional training to African-American boys who have been labeled "at-risk." It transforms the bottom 5 percent of students in Tennessee into the top 25 percent in the state after five years through a seamless middle-to-high school."
- "3.2.1 [Education Foundation]'s vision is to create India's first high-quality charter-like school network that will create a new standard of excellence for educating children from marginalized communities."

Building Networks

In some instances, the social entrepreneurs seek to achieve impact by creating new organizations for economic development or enhancing opportunities for education and training so that individuals can be employed within organizations. They primarily use the organization as the vehicle for change. In other circumstances the social problem is not well served by the boundaries of an organization or its formality. In many cases social change is achieved through collective action endeavors that involve connecting diverse groups of people or spanning organizations in order to facilitate the transfer of knowledge and coordination of action. In these cases, networks are preferred vehicles for social change as they may have advantages over other organizational forms, including efficient information exchange through informal ties and low transaction costs (Powell, 1990; Jones et al., 1997).

In each case within this category the social entrepreneurs build networks to achieve a goal, but the goals can be flexible. We identified four distinct cases in the Echoing Green sample: advocacy, support, innovation, and leverage. The advocacy case is unique in that the goal is outward-facing policy or cultural change. A network of individuals or organizations is assembled for the purpose of influencing actors outside of the network. The social support case is an inward-focused network. The individuals participate because they share a common set of experiences or challenges, so each member can benefit from the knowledge, experience, and support of other members. Innovation networks (also called epistemic communities) are problem-solving networks. Members are typically working on similar problems, and they participate to facilitate the exchange of information, ideas, and collaborations. Leverage networks are created for collective bargaining. Members participate because they have more power in numbers, whether in negotiating prices or as a party in a labor conflict. This theory is summarized in Figure 10.5.

Examples: advocacy networks

- "JustLeadershipUSA is a national nonpartisan membership advocacy organization with an audacious goal: to reduce crime and cut the US prison population in half by 2030. [It] will accomplish this goal by empowering people and communities most impacted by crime and incarceration to drive, amplify, and sustain policy reform."
- "The Accountability Lab empowers and educates citizens to find their voices and works to make sure those voices are heard and acted upon by governments. The Lab provides training, mentorship,

Figure 10.5   Building networks theory of social change

networks, management support, and seed funding for the development of low-cost, high-impact anti-corruption tools."

Examples: social support networks

- "Village of Wisdom (VOW) empowers parents to enhance the resilience of their Black boys, promoting greater academic performance. Even great parents need extra support to assist their sons in navigating the unique challenges Black boys face. Led by elder parents, VOW parents form learning communities where they examine proven strategies, surface collective knowledge, and develop personal approaches for supporting their children's self-worth and positive identity development."
- "iFoster aggregates the thousands of organizations and millions of caregivers in child welfare into a single online community to share resources, leverage their collective power and amplify their common voice to ensure that this country's most vulnerable children are put on the path to becoming independent successful adults."

Examples: research and development networks

- With the "Bold Idea" of pioneering a "big-picture, systems-based approach that will rapidly translate advances in biomedical research into meaningful knowledge and effective treatments for patients with overlooked cancers. . .the Chordoma Foundation [is] a nonprofit organization that initiates, facilitates, and funds research to develop treatments, and eventually a cure for chordoma – a bone cancer of the skull and spine."
- Hello Housing was founded by Mardie Oaks who had the "Bold Idea" of housing "Californians in need by bringing together real estate financing tools with innovative design options to create cutting-edge housing solutions."

Examples: leverage in networks

- "BlocPower aggregates groups of consumers – like Groupon – to negotiate energy savings, pricing discounts, and community hiring quotas with renewable and energy efficiency firms."
- "As much as twenty-nine percent of Los Angeles County's workforce is estimated to be employed by an underground economy of contractors and subcontractors that perennially ignore the judgments for unpaid wages, unjustly keeping these wages as their profit. The Wage Justice Center works to provide a systematic solution to protect the basic economic rights of workers and enforce the collection of the approximately $50 million in unpaid wages by these employers."

Health Systems

Social enterprises in this category spend their efforts building sustainable local health networks to fill a void left by nonexistent or ineffective public health programs. These networks often utilize new information technologies for diagnostics, records, and coordination. The technologies themselves are not sufficient to catalyze change, however. The social enterprises work to create a network of volunteers, health workers or clinics that can labor collectively to address serious health problems.

Many of the health services are delivered through networks, but we found these to be distinct from the network category above because the "network" often consists of multiple locations of a single organization (Clínicas del Azúcar), or consists of a group of people that receive information and act in a structured way similar to a hierarchical organization (SaveLIFE Foundation). We found the term "health system" to be more fitting to the nature of the task of coordinating care within health networks as opposed to the organic information exchange, support, learning, and advocacy that happens in other networks. This theory of change is described in Figure 10.6.

Figure 10.6   Health systems theory of social change

Examples

- "India suffers the highest number of road accident deaths in the world. In countless cases victims perish because emergency care fails to reach them. SaveLIFE Foundation (SLF) is a nonprofit organization established to fill this severe gap in India's medical services by enabling community-driven emergency medical responses for road accident victims."
- "Diabetes in Mexico is called 'the disease of the rich,' because current care alternatives are expensive, inconvenient, and out of reach for ninety percent of the population. By developing innovative evidence-based algorithms for diagnosis and disease management, and by creating a chain of low-cost diabetes clinics, Clínicas del Azúcar is revolutionizing the way diabetes care is delivered in developing countries and for the 14 million patients with diabetes in Mexico."
- "[Medic Mobile] empower[s] health workers in poor countries to communicate, coordinate patient care, and provide diagnostics using low-cost mobile technology."

Environmental Protection

This theory of change focuses on activities that lead to better environmental practices, either through technologies or systems that can spur behavioral changes that protect the environment, or through new technologies and business practices that are better for the environment. They focus on creating alternatives for current practices or behaviors, and use creative programming or incentives to facilitate adoption of these alternatives. The theory is summarized in Figure 10.7.

Figure 10.7   Environmental protection theory of social change

Examples

- "WattTime empowers homeowners, building managers, and organizations to know where their electricity comes from, and to choose sources they support. [Their] innovative 'environmental demand response' software platform combines open data and cutting-edge analytics to inform and engage consumers, as well as to enable smart devices to automatically prioritize cleaner power sources in real time."
- Green Power aims to "realize sustainable, decentralized micro-hydro energy and distribution systems to provide electricity to rural Kenya."
- Green Coast Enterprises is a "sustainable development corporation that builds environmentally sound and affordable structures in the Gulf Coast."

Product Innovation – Improving Lives

This theory of change identifies a problem that can be solved through the use of a new product or technology, by creating an innovative solution and building a sustainable way to distribute the solution in low-income communities. The new technology is often related to health – for example, water quality, sanitation, or diagnosis of disease. The product can often have a big impact on a household, but it is not always affordable or easy to obtain. Therefore, the social entrepreneurs find ways to broadly distribute the new technology to households in need and to subsidize it when necessary, either through grants to reduce the cost of purchasing the product or through cross-subsidy, using net revenues from high-income communities to sell the product in low-income communities at a reduced price. These organizations are more likely to be for-profit businesses that can commodify the product and develop sustainable and potentially profitable revenue streams. The theory is represented in Figure 10.8.

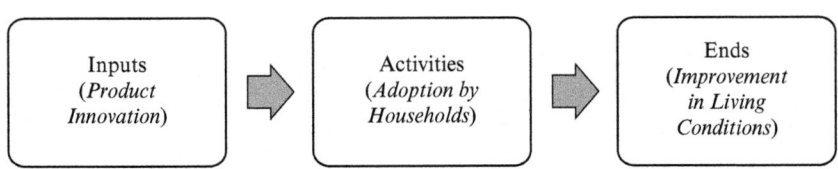

Figure 10.8   Theory of social change through innovative products

Examples

- "EarthEnable's mission is to improve the health and housing of low-income communities, by providing affordable and sanitary floors to the 80 percent of Rwandans and billions of people globally who live and sleep on dirt floors."
- "Bempu is a life-saving baby temperature monitoring wristband designed to drastically reduce rates of hypothermia and temperature-related illnesses in resource-poor settings, like those in India. If a newborn's body temperature falls outside the safe 37°C range, the band intuitively alerts the mother to take action well before any life-threat[en]ing issues occur."
- "A Single Drop for Safe Water (ASDSW) combines low-cost technology with local community ownership to bring effective water systems to villages across the country. The BioSand Filter, one of ASDSW's many technologies, is a household water treatment that removes ninety-five to 100 percent of disease-causing organisms, which helps families take responsibility to improve their own health."

LEVELS OF ACTION FOR EACH THEORY OF CHANGE

The six theories of change target communities in different ways. Some focus on the individual or household, some focus on the organization, and some focus on collections of individuals or organizations – the network (Figure 10.9). This observation is helpful for grouping social enterprises

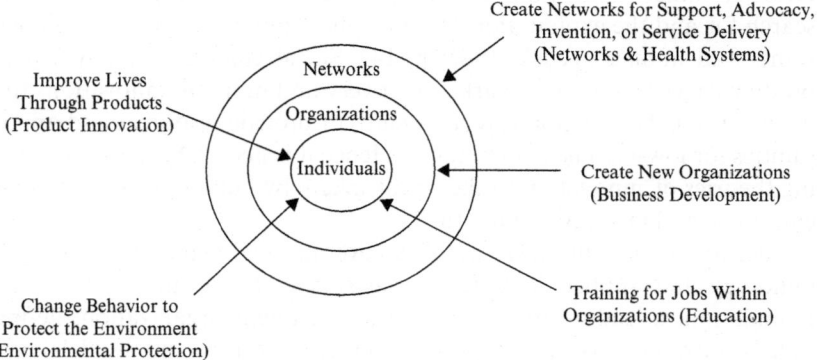

Figure 10.9   Levels of action for each theory of change

by their primary theory of change. Is the target of the organization an individual or household? Is the entrepreneur building an organization or a network? The skills needed for endeavors at each level are quite distinct. Knowledge of behavioral change at the individual level is useful when working with people to commit to rigorous education programs, adapt a new technology, or change a consumption behavior. General management skills are important for creating new businesses. And skills related to community organizing, social media, and running campaigns would benefit a social entrepreneur trying to build a network. An organization like Echoing Green could use these insights to match fellows with mentors and create meaningful peer groups for effective learning.

INNOVATION

The entrepreneurship literature recognizes the importance of innovation as it drives the process of creative destruction that animates economic markets, but the relationship between innovation and social change is less understood in social systems. Assuredly, social innovations are instrumental in upending the status quo, but the mechanisms have not received the attention that product and technological innovation have. For example, there is no agreed upon definition of social innovation (Mulgan et al., 2007; Lettice and Parekh, 2010; Murray et al., 2010) as the concept of innovation alone is not well understood by social enterprise scholars (Nicholls and Murdock, 2012). Furthermore, theories of innovation have traditionally focused on the innovative practices and products of profit-driven enterprises, for example emphasizing innovation as the element that separates business owners from entrepreneurs (Schumpeter, 1934; Utterback, 1996). Drucker linked innovation directly to opportunity recognition as "the search for and the exploitation of new opportunities for satisfying human wants and human needs" (1985, p. 14). Social change may rely less on products, technology, and market discovery and more on innovations that upend entrenched economic relationships or provide resources and opportunities for low-income communities. Hence it is necessary to extend existing theories of innovation to the social sphere by building upon the social enterprise and innovation literatures.

Recently, social enterprise authors have adopted some innovation terminology and applied it to the social sphere. For example, The Skoll Foundation, a leading social enterprise investment organization, defines social innovation as: "new ideas (products, services and models) that simultaneously meet social needs and create new social relationships or collaborations. . .innovations that are both good for society and enhance society's capacity to act" (Murray et al., 2010, p. 3). Nicholls and Murdock (2012) present yet another definition of social innovation: "social innovation is defined. . .as varying levels of deliberative change that aim to address suboptimal issues in the production, availability, and consumption of public goods defined as that which is broadly of societal benefit within a particular normative and culturally contingent context" (p. 7). However, many authors define social innovation more broadly as new ideas aimed at addressing unmet needs (Cahill, 2010), while others choose a narrower definition restricting it to its systemic impact (Westley and Antadze, 2010). Specifically, Phills et al. (2008) explain: "unlike the terms social entrepreneurship and social enterprise, social innovation transcends sectors, levels of analysis, and methods to discover the processes – the strategies, tactics, and theories of change – that produce lasting impact" (p. 37).

These definitions of innovation emphasize the benefits to society and/or the creation of lasting social change by meeting the individual and/or social needs (i.e., needs of users, consumers, and/or other beneficiaries). By coupling our theory of change models with the innovation categories outlined below, we stay true to this unifying aspect of the social innovation literature, and expand on it by systematically exploring its applicability to a large number of social enterprise organizations.

Below we draw on the conventional innovation literature to guide the creation of a taxonomy of social innovation (see Phills et al., 2008). In particular, we build on the well-established *Oslo Manual* definition of innovation to frame our initial thinking behind our innovation categories (Tanaka et al., 2005). The *Oslo Manual* is widely recognized as the world's leading source on the collection and use of innovation data.[1] The *Oslo Manual* definition of innovation reads as follows: "an innovation is the implementation of a new or significantly improved product (good or service), or process, a new marketing method, or a new organizational method in business practices, workplace organization or external relations" (p. 46). This definition accounts for four types of *firm-level* innovations: product, process, marketing, and organizational. It does not, however, account for industry-wide, or economy-wide changes (e.g., the reorganization of an industry, the emergence of a new market etc.), that is, it does not account for systemic change. Therefore, in our review of the Echoing Green 2014 Fellows, we identified two additional types of innovation, not explicitly discussed in the *Oslo Manual*: institutional and ecological. Both are aimed at addressing system-level changes within or across other organizations or networks of organizations.

As considered in earlier chapters, there are numerous factors capable of shaping the types of innovations an organization is able or willing to employ. Factors span the micro-, meso- and macro-levels. Micro-level factors that influence innovation include the value orientation and risk perception of the founder(s) or primary decision-makers (McDonald, 2007; Kirkman, 2012). Meso-level factors include organizational structure (size, and age), sources of revenue (earned-income vs grant-based), system of accountability (stakeholders vs shareholders), employee characteristics (volunteer vs paid) and ownership structure (nonprofit or for-profit legal status) of the enterprise (Damanpour, 1991; Alter, 2007). At the macro-level, factors include national and/or international institutions (history, culture, economic status, international aid, etc.) (Kerlin, 2009, 2013). While we recognize the importance of these enabling conditions of innovation, we are not focused on any particular opportunity or constraint here. Instead, we use the innovation types to demonstrate the variation in the means by which social entrepreneurs choose to enact their theory of change models.

Successful entrepreneurial innovations have historically been characterized by profit-generating firms (Schumpeter, 1927) with a technological focus (Lundvall, 1992). This means that the systems developed to cultivate profit-seeking entrepreneurs may not apply to social entrepreneurs. Focusing on social innovation highlights the key mechanisms by which social entrepreneurs carry out their theories of change. It is also important to note that social innovations (like conventional ones) are not mutually exclusive and may be combined, either sequentially or in tandem (e.g., process and marketing). The examples provided below are used to illustrate a particular type of innovation; however, each example may also contain other innovations that are not explicitly discussed. In all, the six types of innovation represent the *how* behind the *why* (e.g., theory of change) of social enterprise. The distribution of innovations among the five broad innovation categories identified within the Echoing Green sample is described in Table 10.2.

Table 10.2   Innovation categories

Five Categories of Innovation	
1. *Product*	114
Service	73
Product	41
2. *Process*	51
3. *Marketing*	29
4. *Institutional*	8
5. *Ecological*	1
Total	203

Product Innovation

Product innovation is the introduction of a good or service that is new or significantly improved with respect to its characteristics or intended uses. This includes significant improvements in technical specifications, components, and materials, user friendliness or new combinations of existing knowledge or technologies. Examples include the development of new products or services, and the improvement of existing products, services or technologies with the goal of increased efficiency or performance.

Examples

- *Product good*: "Kriyate. . .has built a Braille Smartphone for the visually impaired which allows users to read mobile content using only their fingertips, and has also released a gesture-based accessibility app."
- *Product service*: "Farm Builders "reduce[s] poverty and transform[s] Liberia's rural communities by providing smallholder tree crop farmers with management services and access to long-term investment capital."

Process Innovation

Process innovation is the implementation of a new or significantly improved production or delivery method. This includes significant changes in techniques, equipment and/or software. Examples include the development of new distribution networks that change the way products or services are delivered within specific markets or communities.

Examples

- "Boond creates a sustainable ecosystem for clean energy access through sales of solar systems financed by rural banks and microfinance institutions and serviced by trained local technicians. The Boond model eliminates the initial cost barrier that hinders the penetration of renewable energy products in remote poor areas and ensures that the systems last for the requisite life through reliable after sales service."
- "As opposed to sending cash, Regalii allows Latinos in the U.S. to send gift cards (via SMS). Family members in LAC [Latin American and Caribbean countries] can redeem their Regalii in local stores and supermarkets where remittance recipients already shop."

Marketing Innovation

Marketing innovations are aimed at better addressing customer needs, opening up new markets, or newly positioning a firm's product on the market. Most importantly, the function or user characteristics of the product or service are not altered with marketing innovations. Examples include base-of-the-pyramid efforts, which take existing products and/or services and introduce them to low-income populations who would otherwise not have access to them.

Examples

- "Hot Bread Kitchen captures lost human capital by bringing women's traditional bread recipes to market, which builds recognition of the contribution of immigrant communities. Paid training in baking, access to a diverse professional and social network, and a flexible schedule allow women to develop careers that work for them."
- "Stockbox Grocers believes that every community should have access to good food, to promote healthful living, social equity, and economic vibrancy. [They] improve this access by placing small-format neighborhood grocery stores throughout urban communities, to offer fresh produce, meal solutions, and grocery staples."

Organization Innovation

Organization innovation is the adaptation of new governance or management structures within an organization in order to enact change by giving employees opportunities, resources and choices. Examples include social enterprises aimed at changing the managerial strategies, workplace dynamics or nature of the work itself (e.g., employee-run, participatory management practices). It differs from process innovation in that it is inward facing, attempting to achieve impact by improving the lives of people working in the firm, versus changing management processes to improve productivity or quality in the firm.

Example
"Project Equity builds economic resiliency in low-income communities by increasing worker ownership. [It] incubate[s] and grow[s] scalable cooperative businesses, and. . .catalyze[s] change-makers across business, nonprofit, government, and education sectors to integrate worker ownership into local ecosystems for economic development."

Institutional or Policy Innovation

Institutional or policy innovation is outward facing: the implementation of new methods of affecting policies, norms or laws within pre-existing organizations and frameworks. Examples include advocacy groups seeking to alter the way decisions are made within current legal systems, particularly those affecting marginalized groups including women and people of color.

Example

"SAAJHA builds leadership capacity of School Management Committee (SMC), a body consisting of parents and teachers, to ensure accountability for children's learning in primary public schools of India. SAAJHA supports SMCs to create forums for parent teacher interaction. It also wants to facilitate a coalition of SMCs to create national demand for good governance in schools. SAAJHA is a Hindustani word that means collaboration, the organization's core value. SAAJHA aims to impact 100 000 schools by 2025."

Ecological (or Business Model) Innovation

Ecological innovation is the emergence of new organizational forms (e.g., cooperatives, low-profit limited liability companies [L3Cs]) creating or adapting new forms of organizations (mostly cooperatives, social franchises, etc.) in order to pursue a particular outcome (in the social context usually access or leverage to resources or influence).

Example

"B Lab is fueling a global movement to redefine 'success' in business, so that all companies compete not only to be the best in the world, but the best for the world. B Lab is challenging the status quo by building a new sector, legal structure, and standards; empowering a community of certified B Corporations;[2] and advancing public policies that enable companies to create financial, social, and environmental value for both its shareholders and for society. With 20 states having passed Benefit Corporation legislation, nearly 1,000 B Corporations certified, and 16,000 companies using its tools, B Lab is focused on accelerating the global adoption of this new model."

INNOVATION IN THE ZOO

Taxonomies help biologists identify, understand, and compare animals to one another. This chapter offers a taxonomy to examine social innovation in its various forms. Although innovation is intrinsic to the social enterprise zoo, the for-profit literature has a strong emphasis on products, technology, and marketing that do not translate easily to the broader social context. The taxonomies presented here have been created to support research endeavors that aspire to operationalize social innovation in this particular context to better understand the distinct role of social innovation in social enterprise development. As such, innovation provides one way of understanding the composition of the social enterprise zoo.

Innovation in organizations drives efficiency, market share, and survival. However, for social enterprises, the innovative process is often undertaken in order to enable or amplify impact more so than to gain competitive advantage and market share. In order to seek a systematic understanding of innovation in social enterprise we have adapted a taxonomy of innovation developed through the *Oslo Manual* for the social context. In doing this we have expanded on the *Oslo Manual*'s classifications to include two additional types of innovation: institutional and ecological. These additions were necessary to capture all of the tools, techniques, and strategies used by the enterprises in our sample. Social innovations are expressed here as the *how* within the *why* (theory of change) of a social enterprise; as such, innovations are dynamic and evolutionary in nature. As animals in the zoo, social enterprises employ innovation strategies, approaches, and tactics to ensure their survival. As needs change, animals will evolve to meet present and future environmental needs. The social innovation taxonomy presented here suggests the variety of tactics social enterprise animals will take to achieve their goals.

Social enterprises are distinct from their conventional business sector counterparts in that they are motivated at least in part by social impact. This underlies the link between social entrepreneurs and a theory of change. Innovation extends beyond products and processes into other strategies for creating social impact. Innovation in this context is best understood in the context of a theory of change that includes an end goal and assumptions about how organizational activities can impact the outcome. The Echoing Green database has been used to identify the various theories of change that are manifested within existing social enterprises.

Table 10.3 presents a cross-tabulation of the six theories of change and five innovations with the 203 social enterprises in our sample. In the theories of change category, the creation of networks for advocacy, support, leverage, and invention are the most prevalent strategy for enacting change (42 percent). Among the innovation categories, products, particularly product services are the most prominent undertaking (36 percent). With the exception of the theory of change category that aims to improve lives through products, it is interesting to note that there is not a high

Table 10.3 Theory of change by innovation

Theories of Change	Innovation (%)				Product		Grand Total
	Ecological	Institutional	Marketing	Process	Good	Service	
Business development	0.5		3.0	4.4	2.5	6.4	16.7
Environment		0.5	0.5	2.5	3.4	1.5	8.4
Health				1.0	0.5	1.5	3.0
Education			3.4	4.4	4.4	6.4	18.7
Networks		3.4	6.4	11.3	2.5	18.7	42.4
Product			1.0	1.5	7.0	1.5	10.8
Grand total	0.5	3.9	14.3	25.1	20.2	36.0	100 (n = 203)

correlation between any particular theory of change and any particular innovation strategy. We believe this shows that most social entrepreneurs are industrious and pragmatic problem-solvers that use a variety of tools to achieve goals. These data demonstrate that enterprises working in the same space such as education are approaching similar problems from broad perspectives and using a variety of innovations to enact change. This diversity is the strength of a social sector that can support a plurality of activities to generate the experimentation necessary for progress in the social enterprise zoo.

CONCLUSION

As discussed in Chapter 7, innovation is a tool used by Schumpeterian entrepreneurs to disrupt current markets and industries, or in the social context, social systems or institutions. Because innovation can be powerful in this regard it is important to have an understanding of the forms that it may take. The taxonomy presented in this chapter frames innovation as a means of achieving a social end as defined by a theory of change. In this context, no one theory of change is wedded to a particular innovation strategy. Innovation in and of itself is seen as necessary but not sufficient to achieve impact, that is, it is a means to achieving a social end. The two dimensions of the social innovation taxonomy can each be adjusted to meet new or existing environmental needs, allowing for the organizational flexibility and adaptability required for long-term organizational survival and impact.

NOTES

1. See Oslo Manual at http://www.oecd.org/innovation/innovationinsciencetechnologyand industry/oslomanualguidelinesforcollectingandinterpretinginnovationdata3rdedition. htm, accessed 22 June 2016.
2. For-profit companies certified by the nonprofit B Lab to meet rigorous standards of social and environmental performance, accountability, and transparency.

REFERENCES

Alter, K. (2007), "Social enterprise typology," *Virtue Ventures, LLC,* accessed 22 June 2016 at http://www.4lenses.org/setypology.

Anderson, A.A. (2005), "An introduction to theory of change," *The Evaluation Exchange,* **XI** (2), Summer, accessed 22 June 2016 at http://www.hfrp.org/evaluation/the-evaluation-exchange/issue-archive/evaluation-methodology/an-introduction-to-theory-of-change.

Cahill, G. (2010), "Primer on social innovation: a compendium of definitions developed by organizations around the world," *The Philanthropist,* **23** (3).

Damanpour, F. (1991), "Organizational innovation – a meta-analysis of effects of determinants and moderators," *Academy of Management Journal,* **34** (3), 555–90.

Drucker, P.F. (1985), *Innovation and Entrepreneurship: Practice and Principles,* New York: Harper & Row.

Glaser, B.G. and A.L. Strauss (2009), *The Discovery of Grounded Theory: Strategies for Qualitative Research,* New Brunswick, NJ: Transaction Publishers.

Guest, G. and K.M. MacQueen (eds) (2007), *Handbook for Team-based Qualitative Research,* Lanham, MD: Rowman AltaMira.

Jones, C., W.S. Hesterly, and S.P. Borgatti (1997), "A general theory of network governance: exchange conditions and social mechanisms," *Academy of Management Review,* **22** (4), 911–45.

Kerlin, J. (ed.) (2009), *Social Enterprise: A Global Comparison,* Lebanon, NH: Tufts University Press.

Kerlin, J. (2013), "Defining social enterprise across different contexts: a conceptual framework based on institutional factors," *Nonprofit and Voluntary Sector Quarterly,* **42** (1), 84–108.

Kirkman, D. (2012), "Social enterprises: a multi-level framework of the innovation adoption process," *Innovation Management, Policy and Practice,* **14** (1), 143–55.

Krippendorff, K. (2013), *Content Analysis: An Introduction to its Methodology,* Thousand Oaks, CA: SAGE.

Lettice, F. and M. Parekh (2010), "The social innovation process: themes, challenges and implications for practice," *International Journal of Technology Management,* **51** (1), 139–58.

Lundvall, B.-A. (ed.) (1992), *National Systems of Innovation: Towards a Theory of Innovation and Interactive Learning,* London: Pinter Publishers.

McDonald, R.E. (2007), "An investigation of innovation in nonprofit organizations: the role of organizational mission," *Nonprofit and Voluntary Sector Quarterly,* **36** (2), 256–81.

Miles, M.B. and A.M. Huberman (1994), *Qualitative Data Analysis: An Expanded Sourcebook*, Thousand Oaks, CA: SAGE.

Monroe-White, T. (2014), "Creating public value: an examination of technological social enterprise," in L. Pate and C. Wankel (eds), *Emerging Research Directions in Social Entrepreneurship*, Dordrecht: Springer, pp. 85–109.

Mulgan, G., S. Tucker, R. Ali, and B. Sanders (2007), "Social innovation: what it is, why it matters and how it can be accelerated," *The Young Foundation*, March, accessed 22 June 2016 at http://youngfoundation.org/publications/social-innovation-what-it-is-why-it-matters-how-it-can-be-accelerated/.

Murray, R., J. Caulier-Grice, and G. Mulgan (2010), *The Open Book of Social Innovation*, London: National Endowment for Science, Technology and the Arts.

Nicholls, A. and A. Murdock (2012), "The nature of social innovation," in A. Nicholls and A. Murdock (eds), *Social Innovation: Blurring Boundaries to Reconfigure Markets*, London: Palgrave Macmillan.

Osterwalder, A. and Y. Pigneur (2010), *Business Model Generation: A Handbook for Visionaries, Game Changers, and Challengers*, Hoboken, NJ: John Wiley and Sons.

Phills, J.A., K. Deiglmeier, and D.T. Miller (2008), "Rediscovering social innovation," *Stanford Social Innovation Review*, **6** (4), 34–43.

Powell, W.W. (1990), "Neither market nor hierarchy," in B.M. Staw and L.L. Cummins (eds), *Research in Organizational Behavior, Volume 12*, Greenwich, CT: JAI Press, pp. 295–336.

Schumpeter, J. (1927), "Explanation of the business cycle," *Economica*, **21**, 286–311.

Schumpeter, J.A. (1934 [2008]), *The Theory of Economic Development: An Inquiry into Profits, Capital, Credit, Interest, and the Business Cycle, Volume 55*, New Brunswick, NJ and London: Transaction Publishers.

Strauss, A.L. (1987), *Qualitative Analysis for Social Scientists*, New York: Cambridge University Press.

Tanaka, N., M. Glaude, and F. Gault (2005), *Oslo Manual: Guidelines for Collecting and Interpreting Innovation Data, Volume 3*, Paris, France: OECD and Eurostat.

Utterback, J. (1996), *Mastering the Dynamics of Innovation: How Companies Can Seize Opportunities in the Face of Technological Change*, Boston, MA: Harvard Business School Press.

Westley, F. and N. Antadze (2010), "Making a difference: strategies for scaling social innovation for greater impact," *The Innovation Journal*, **15** (2), 1–19.

11. Resiliency and stability of the zoo animals

Jung-In Soh, Elizabeth A.M. Searing, and Dennis R. Young

INTRODUCTION

As earlier chapters have made clear, the social enterprise zoo potentially embraces a very wide variety of animals operating in different kinds of habitats. Not all animals will do well in the zoo, and unless the zoo is properly designed and operated some that could do well may not. Alternatively, some animals may be quite hearty and able to survive and thrive under diverse conditions. Indeed, over a long enough time period, some social enterprise animals may evolve or transform themselves into variants better adapted to their circumstances. In any case, the more the zookeepers and curators know about the capacities and propensities of social enterprise animals to survive and adapt to their circumstances, and the nature of the circumstances under which they do well or poorly, or change, the better they will be able to design and manage the zoo, or indeed select the animals that belong in the zoo in the first place.

For actual zoos, the African forest elephant is a case in point. On the one hand, protecting these elephants in zoos can serve the long-term goal of maintaining biodiversity and the survival of this intelligent species of animal. In the wild, depending on their location in Africa, the distribution of these animals can be uncomfortably crowded or dangerously sparse; indeed, they are confronted with loss of habitat, isolation from other elephant groups, death by poachers, and tense encounters with humans (Redford et al., 2011). On the other hand, elephants often do not do well in zoos, where they could face crowding or isolation. Understanding the conditions under which elephants do well is prerequisite to deciding whether to include them in the zoo, how to design their accommodations, and manage their needs as individual animals and as a species.

The fact that the environment of zoos themselves is dynamic makes the problem of animal management even more complex. How are various animals affected by severe weather events or by strains in the economic or political environment that threaten the resources and even the physical security that zoos require? Events like the great recession of 2008–09 or Hurricane Katrina put great, even catastrophic strains on zoological institutions (Fertel, 2006; Strahl, 2010). The same may be said of social enterprises. Indeed, in the United States nonprofit organizations are still straining under the weight of lost resources and increased demands stemming from the traumatic circumstances of the great recession (Nonprofit Finance Fund, 2015).

In this chapter, we examine the tendencies towards stability, transformation or demise of animals in the social enterprise zoo, and their adaptability, resistance to, or inability to cope with environmental change. We pursue this analysis by employing resiliency theory, a construct originally developed to understand the dynamics of environmental systems, but also recently applied to the dynamics of organizations and other social phenomenon. As described below, resiliency theory employs the concept of *thresholds* to examine when organisms or systems remain stable or undergo transformational change of one kind or another. The crossing of thresholds is in turn dependent on particular characteristics and environmental conditions of the organisms or organizations under scrutiny (Walker et al., 2004). Our strategy in this chapter is to conceptualize how resiliency theory applies to animals in the social enterprise zoo, including what parameters influence their threshold-related behaviors, and then to apply resiliency analysis to a particular sample of social enterprises at an especially ominous point in time. Specifically, we empirically explore the reactions of nonprofit enterprises in the Atlanta housing subsector to the federal budget sequester of 2013 in order to gauge the resiliency of such nonprofits in a volatile funding environment. Subsequently, we take insights drawn from this analysis to ask how we may begin to understand the resiliency of other forms of social enterprise in alternative circumstances.

LITERATURE AND CONTEXT

Defining Resilience

Holling (1973) introduced the concept of resiliency to help explain how ecological systems could achieve (or fail to achieve) a stable equilibrium while subject to a host of pressures and tendencies. This analysis expanded the notion of system equilibrium from a singular equilibrium focus to include "multiple stability domains" and "multiple basins of attraction" (Folke, 2006, p. 254). In other words, systems could change in multiple directions and settle in alternate stable states including demise. Resiliency theory has since been developed as a way to understand the mechanics underlying shifts in social-ecological systems more broadly (Walker and Meyers, 2004). According to resiliency theory, changes in systems can vary in source and magnitude, and the result of such changes may be innovation, adaptation or fundamental shifts in character (Holling, 1996; Scheffer and Carpenter, 2003; Folke, 2006). Recently the theory has been extended specifically to organizations and segments of the economy, with the idea of a "resilient" organization or sector becoming increasingly compelling, especially in disaster planning (Berke and Campanella, 2006; Kapucu, 2006; Gotham and Campanella, 2011) and for nonprofits (Salamon, 2003, 2012; Bowman, 2011b).

Salamon chose to use the word "resilient" to describe the nonprofit sector in its entirety in his landmark book series (2003, 2012). Often, however, the resiliency framework is applied on an organization level. Bowman (2011a, 2011b) describes resiliency as the short-term goal of a nonprofit; an organization should have sufficient operating reserves to stave off resource shocks. Young and Kim (2015) apply the four resiliency criteria from Walker et al. (2004) to the concept of social enterprise, suggesting that there is a basic tension between market forces and mission achievement in social enterprise that can fundamentally alter the character of a social enterprise over time. This chapter builds on Young and Kim (2015) to ask what factors allow social enterprise to be resilient, or alternatively, subject to instability in the environment of the social enterprise zoo.

Internal and environmental tensions are intrinsic to social enterprise. First, the tension between mission and market goals has been widely acknowledged (Sanders, 2013; Ebrahim et al., 2014; Ramus and Vaccaro, 2014). This tension can influence major functions such as governance and programming, as well as particular decisions such as pricing and conflict resolution (Young et al., 2010; Mason and Doherty, 2015). Further, as the scope of for-profit social enterprise expands and the tax exemption status of nonprofits receives further scrutiny, increasing levels of tension result from competition or perceived competition for resources (Young, 2001). Though it has been occurring in subfields such as hospitals and daycare for quite some time, this tension also shapes numerous niches for social enterprise through market forces, norms, or regulatory actions (Hirth, 1997; *Federal Trade Commission* v. *Phoebe Putney Health System, Inc.*, 2013). The motivation to survive and achieve mission in a competitive and dynamic landscape, as well as internal contradictions built into various forms of social enterprise, drive our analysis of organizational resilience in the social enterprise zoo.

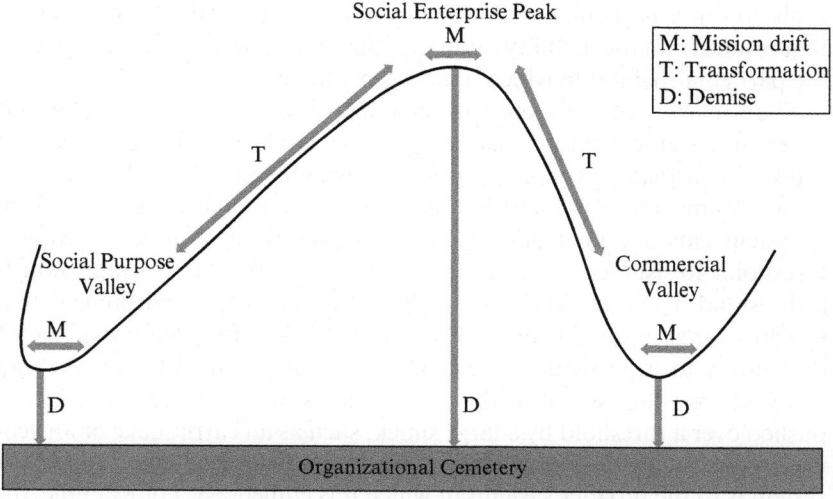

Figure 11.1   Movement types within the resiliency landscape

The Basics of Resiliency Theory

Resiliency theory posits that a system can exist in various states of stable equilibria, unstable equilibria or can spiral towards dissolution or demise. Within the system are thresholds, which, once crossed, signify the change into a different state. The theory asks what factors might lead a system to cross a threshold and destabilize from its current state into another one. Social businesses are constrained by two types of thresholds: mission and market. Crossing a threshold implies that a social business trying to balance a social mission with financial success has shifted toward a more exclusive focus on one or the other (Young et al., 2012; Young and Kim, 2015). What elements of the organization or environment might cause such a threshold to be crossed? Further, what factors would influence whether the organization would actually go bankrupt and achieve neither? Figure 11.1 illustrates the movement types within resiliency theory.

In a home, crossing a threshold marks the transition from the outdoors to the indoors, or from one room to the next. In resiliency theory, thresholds are reflections of fundamental changes in the character of an organization that push it from one equilibrium to another. For animals in the social enterprise zoo, thresholds may apply to both long- and short-term transitions – for example, from fundamental change in goals (for instance, from social purpose to profit-making) that result from a long-term evolution in a particular environment, to a shorter-term financial failure that results from the inability of an organization to successfully compete in the particular habitat in which it has been situated.

The resiliency of a system has been described in the literature by four different parameters that characterize the level of risk of crossing a threshold: *latitude, resistance, precariousness*, and *panarchy* (Walker et al., 2004; Young and Kim, 2015). Latitude describes the degree to which a system can deviate from its current equilibrium without crossing a threshold. Resistance describes the degree of friction in moving towards a threshold resulting from countervailing forces in the environment that inhibit change once it begins. Precariousness describes the proximity of the system to a particular threshold; this is important because even an extremely resistant system with wide latitude and strong resistance can be pushed over a threshold by a large shock, such as an earthquake or an economic recession. Finally, panarchy describes how susceptible a particular system is to the broader systems in which it is embedded. For example, the social enterprise zoo exists within local economies and political systems whose disruption may severely affect the ability of the animals or the zoo as a whole to remain stable or sustainable.

For organizations, and social enterprises in particular, there are several factors thought to determine the above parameters that characterize the risk of crossing a threshold. Young and Kim (2015) summarize these as *governance, financial structure, organizational slack*, and *leadership*. Governance refers to the nature of the governing board, and whether the organization is a sovereign (incorporated) firm, a project or subdivision of a parent organization, or a partnership of two or more independent organizations. Financial structure refers to the reward system implicit in an organization's legal form and the economic environment in which the organization operates. Organizational slack refers to how efficiently an organization performs and how stringent an economic environment it operates within, hence how much leeway it has to cushion external shocks with internal resources. Leadership refers to the capacities and vision of current leaders and executives and whether the visions and culture of founders and other key leaders are institutionalized so that they become viable when those leaders are no longer in charge. To these four forces influencing the value of threshold parameters we would add "embeddedness" in networks and supportive institutions and hence the degree to which an organization has its own safety net should it come on hard times (Hager et al., 2004).

APPLYING RESILIENCY THEORY TO SOCIAL ENTERPRISE ANIMALS AND THE ZOO

As events unfold in the context of the social enterprise zoo, organizations have a variety of ways to respond depending on their own special circumstances, resources, and internal character. These factors will determine how closely they come to crossing critical thresholds, as illustrated in Figure 11.1.

There are four types of movement that can disturb the equilibrium of a social enterprise ensconced in a particular state or local equilibrium as represented by the hilltop and valleys of Figure 11.1. These movements are: *inertia, drift, transformation*, and *demise*. If a social enterprise has been operating under a particular premise or source of funding for a long time, it is likely to continue to do so despite even substantial changes in its environment. This inertia is often determining for organizations that continue to be led by their founders for many years (Block and Rosenberg, 2002). The founders' external networks, vision, and familiarity can provide stability (English and Peters, 2011; Carman and Nesbit, 2013), though possibly at the expense of longer-term instability if the organization fails to renew itself or adapt over time. This can be envisioned in Figure 11.1 as a stationary organization in a changing landscape (illustrating panarchy). If the landscape changes sufficiently the organization may cross a threshold and be displaced from its equilibrium.

Drift is the slow progression away from a particular equilibrium state; in the case of social enterprises, it most often refers to incremental movement away from the original mission of the organization. This can happen for a multitude of reasons. One is a realignment of strategic priorities to favor financial success at the expense of mission gain (Weisbrod, 1997). For example, enterprises may feel compelled to set aside funds for future operations of the organization at the expense of current mission priorities. Some degree of net asset accumulation (see organizational slack below) is necessary for good financial health and risk management, even for nonprofits (Calabrese, 2012); however, there may also be a temptation to accumulate beyond that marker or even engage in anti-competitive practices, either for personal gain or an increased share of funding or market share for a presumably worthy cause (Searing, 2014). Second, there may be a shift in mission in response to client needs; Minkoff and Powell (2006, p. 592) refer to mission as a "compass" since it provides guidance through a shifting and potentially powerful storm of institutional and environmental factors. For example, the March of Dimes (founded as the National Foundation for Infantile Paralysis) began a series of mission changes in the late 1950s as polio was eradicated and mission scope was widened to include birth defects, and later maternal and neonatal health (Baghdady and Maddock, 2008). But this begs the question: how much drift can occur before an enterprise is transformed into an entirely different state?

Transformation is a third type of movement, which may begin with drift or a shock. If there are increasing tensions associated with the mission and these are causing gradual movement, then this "drift" may or may not result in a change in the equilibrium state; if it does, then a transformation has occurred. This may manifest itself as a change in corporate form (Goddeeris and Weisbrod, 1998), though not necessarily so. It can be argued that the actual change in formal documents for the March of Dimes would constitute the shift from "drift" to "transformation." Such transformations can also be inspired by major changes in the conditions for funding. When the Helms Amendment required recipients of funds from the National Endowment for the Arts to sign a pledge to abstain from displays of an obscene nature, many organizations chose to forgo federal funding (O'Neil, 1991). Other organizations accepted the new limitations and changed their own programming to match those preferences dictated by the grant. Formally or not, transformation occurred in the latter cases in response to an external shock in order to save the life of the organization.

Demise is a fourth, albeit dramatic, type of organizational movement from a state of equilibrium. Organizations can die of their own internal management or governance failures, and organizations that cannot find a way to adapt to changes in their environments may also die or go dormant, whether via bankruptcy, merger, or a prolonged period of inactivity. This does not necessarily reflect a "survival of the fittest" process, since social enterprises may conceivably determine that their social mission is unachievable and that strict survival is not worthwhile (or alternatively that their mission has been achieved or no longer relevant). In 1999, Hager described eight different reasons that contributed to the closure of a non-profit organization. These varied from organizational characteristics such as youth to degrees of embeddedness in networks, to failure to achieve mission (Hager, 1999). Moreover, one reason alone was rarely responsible.

In summary, social enterprise organizations may cross thresholds from their current states of equilibrium to other states in a number of different ways, for a variety of reasons, and provoked or inhibited by various internal and external factors. Thus, organizations may drift but never cross a threshold into another state, they may undergo a major transformation or they may die. The likelihood of crossing thresholds will be influenced by their governance, financial context, degree of organizational slack, leadership, and embeddedness in networks. Changes may be imminent as signaled by their proximity to thresholds and may be provoked by internal developments such as management or governance failures and changes in mission-related or financial goals, or by external factors such as changes in the funding environment, consumer or clients needs or tastes, and governmental policy priorities. Moreover, changes may develop gradually or be precipitated by a shock such as an economic recession or new legislation. In the remainder of this chapter, applying resiliency theory, we study the changes in social enterprises in one particular context, the housing sector in Atlanta, during a period of financial stress stemming from the sequester of federal funding. The intent is to illuminate how the various factors underlying the likelihood of crossing a threshold affect the resiliency of social enterprises in this subsector and their risks of financial failure and radical mission change.

METHODOLOGY

The impact of the sequester of federal funding on nonprofit housing organizations in Atlanta is a case study of panarchy where the system in which these social enterprises are embedded experienced a major disruption, threatening their stability. On 2 August 2011, the Budget Control Act was signed, which called for federal spending cuts; these cuts had not been assigned to specific line items, but rather became across-the-board reductions on 1 March 2013 (Congressional Budget Office, 2011). Thus began "sequestration," continuing until 10 December 2013, with a period of 16 days where the government was shut down entirely. Though the periods of time for both the sequester and the shutdown were brief, they were long enough to interfere with existing service delivery through third-party providers (United States Government Accountability Office, 2014). Further, the impact that such shutdowns have on the funding climate appears to be long-lasting.

Data: The Atlanta Nonprofit Housing Sector

The authors conducted interviews with nonprofit organizations in the Atlanta housing subsector[1] in order to understand the resiliency of both the individual organizations and the subsector as a whole. As seen in Figure 11.2, the revenue portfolios of the Atlanta nonprofit housing subsector are diverse, with the majority of the funding stemming from earned program revenues originating with the government or clients.

In-depth case studies of four nonprofits were constructed from interviews conducted with selected organizational leaders. The leaders were drawn from nonprofits that responded to a survey on financial conditions during the government shutdown and indicated that they were

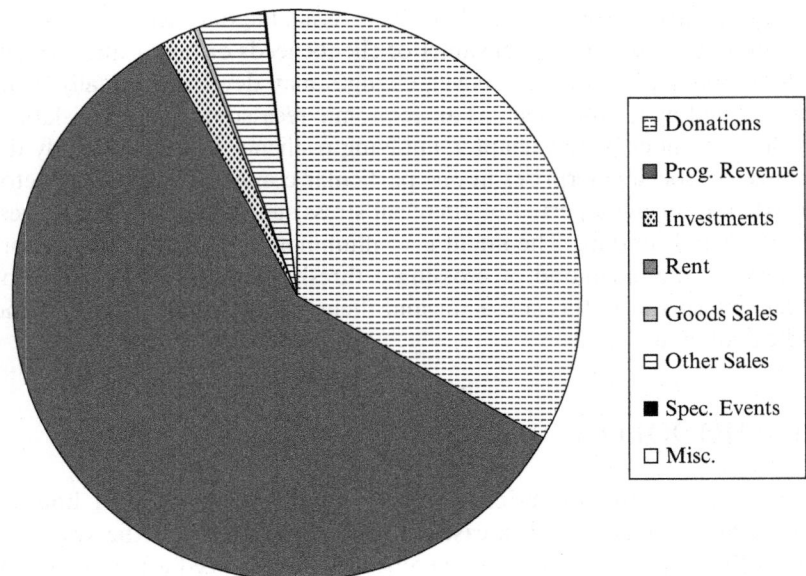

*Figure 11.2   Revenue composition by Form 990 category for the Atlanta
            nonprofit housing sector*

available for interviews. Two organizations from the Housing Development,
Construction and Management subsector (NTEE code L20) and two
organizations from Homeless Shelters (NTEE code L41) were selected.[2]
These organizations described their mission and financial conditions, as
well as contextual and operational information, during 90-minute semi-
structured interviews.

Case Study 1: Metro Community Development

Metro Community Development (MCD) is an L20 housing development, construction, and management organization that was formed in
the late 1980s. MCD's mission is to improve metro-Atlanta communities
by providing a variety of housing services and other community building
programs. Originally created to meet the housing needs of the neighborhood in which it is located, MCD later expanded its scope of services to
metropolitan Atlanta in response to increasing development costs in its
founding neighborhood and greater opportunities for program provision in other areas. After expansion, MCD changed its name, but not its
mission, to reflect its broader focus from a single neighborhood to four
different counties in metropolitan Atlanta.

Case Study 2: South Atlanta Development Corporation

South Atlanta Development Corporation (SADC) is another L20 housing development, construction, and management nonprofit organization. Formed in 1989 by community activists and leaders, SADC's mission is to revitalize the south Atlanta neighborhood that was negatively impacted by the construction of the Atlanta Braves (Turner Field) baseball field and expanding freeways. In comparison to MCD, SADC engages a greater variety of government, for-profit, and nonprofit partnerships in order to undertake construction projects and offer homeownership education.

Case Study 3: Atlanta Homeless Housing

Located near the downtown area, Atlanta Homeless Housing (AHH) provides housing and supportive services for homeless males. Originating from a church feeding program in 1981, AHH gradually expanded its program offerings and became a registered L41 homeless shelter in 1988. AHH's services have changed since its founding. For instance, the operation of the soup kitchen was turned back to the church and a new permanent housing program for veteran males was added to its roster of transitional housing and social services in 2013. Overall, however, the mission of the AHH has remained constant over time: to meet the needs of homeless men.

Case Study 4: Housing for Women and Children

In 2004, business and community leaders of a North Fulton County community created an L41 nonprofit homeless shelter, Housing for Women and Children (HWC), recognizing a need for transitional housing for homeless women and children. HWC opened in 2006 and provides emergency shelter and a gradually increasing range of social services. As its program offerings have changed, so has HWC's mission. At first, the mission was to provide emergency housing in the North Fulton area, but beginning in 2008, HWC broadened its mission to include social services to better assist families to permanently move out of transitional housing.

ANALYSIS

From the interviews and publicly available information, we analyzed the four case studies in three steps. First, we identified the ways in which each of the five factors affecting the risks of crossing a threshold – governance, financial structure, organizational slack, leadership and embeddedness – manifested themselves in the nonprofit's organization and environment. Here we consider the mission change and financial impacts of these factors separately for clarity and ease of presentation. Second, we evaluated the degree to which each of these factors propelled the organization towards a threshold. Finally, we rated the organization's overall potential to cross a mission or financial threshold. These judgments were coded into one of three levels – low, moderate, and high – based on a (albeit subjective) consensus of the authors. The summary of this analysis is displayed in Table 11.1 and explicated more fully below.

Case Study 1: Metro Community Development

Financial insolvency
In terms of governance, MCD is an affiliate of a congressionally chartered and federally funded organization. MCD received a significant proportion of funding from this organization until the 2013 sequester budget cuts reduced this revenue source by 80 percent, pushing MCD towards financial insolvency. However, MCD board members had real estate experience that helped MCD to navigate periods of financial downturn. Still, MCD's financial structure relies heavily on government funding and the real estate market, so when these sources simultaneously declined, MCD experienced a revenue shock, pushing it towards insolvency. To buffer these financial pressures, MCD, as a nonprofit, was able to draw on tax-deductible charitable donations to offset some of the losses. It also drew on organizational slack by selling some of its real estate assets.

MCD's executive and governing leadership have changed over the years, resulting in diverse revenue policies rather than a coherent strategy, possibly contributing to a weak financial foundation for the organization. For instance, MCD switched from holding a large annual fundraising event to profitable quarterly fundraising events in 2012, but after the Development Director (DD) left, MCD did not host any fundraising events at all and lost this source of funding. The Executive Director (ED) and succeeding DD planned a new annual fundraising event in 2014, though its impact is yet unclear. Finally, MCD's grounding in only a single neighborhood led it to expand its housing efforts into additional locations during the downturn. This initial lack of embeddedness in a wider network put MCD at risk. Together, these five forces appear to have created a high threat of financial insolvency.

Radical mission change
For MCD, governance is a buffer against mission change since the board of directors (BOD) turns over slowly. However, MCD's financial structure

Table 11.1 Threshold parameters of Atlanta nonprofit housing sector cases

	Case 1 (Metro Community Dev.)		Case 2 (South Atlanta Dev. Corp.)	
	Risk of financial insolvency	Risk of radical mission change	Risk of financial insolvency	Risk of radical mission change
Governance	*Moderate* Affiliate reduces funding Board of directors' real estate background helps navigate market	*Low* Stable board of directors (BOD) maintains mission	*Low* For-profit partner provides additional income stream	*Low* Community representation on 11-member BOD
Financial structure	*High* 2013 government budget cuts; weak real estate market Charitable donations	*Moderate* Service area expansion Mission and programs show consistency despite financial distress	*High* Impending loss of major revenue source; volatile revenue Charitable donations and earned income	*Moderate* Some lost funding is tied to certain programming; service area is expanding
Organizational slack	*Moderate* Sells assets to maintain solvency	*Moderate* Mission and programs show consistency despite financial distress	*Moderate* Maintains operating reserves to smooth volatility	*Low* Investment income
Leadership	*Moderate* Executive Director (ED), other leadership may change revenue strategies	*Moderate* Leadership changes can change mission Longstanding ED maintains mission	*Low* Stable leadership	*Low* Current ED strongly affiliated with founding ED

Table 11.1 (continued)

	Case 1 (Metro Community Dev.)		Case 2 (South Atlanta Dev. Corp.)	
	Risk of financial insolvency	Risk of radical mission change	Risk of financial insolvency	Risk of radical mission change
Embeddedness	*Moderate* Weak real estate market pushes housing development. efforts into more neighborhoods	*Moderate* Weak real estate market pushes programs into more neighborhoods	*Moderate* Area and scope expanding Strong community ties	*Moderate* New communities or existing clients may have new needs or approaches
Threat level	*High*	*Moderate*	*Moderate*	*Low*

	Case 3 (Atlanta Homeless Housing)		Case 4 (Housing for Women and Children)	
	Risk of financial insolvency	Risk of radical mission change	Risk of financial insolvency	Risk of radical mission change
Governance	*Low* 20-member BOD's financial and banking background helps navigate economy	*Low* Nonprofit, religious, and community representation on BOD	*Low* 20-member BOD has banking and other for-profit experience	*Moderate* Active board identifies new program needs
Financial structure	*Moderate* Charitable donations during economic downturn; possible social enterprise	*Low* New programs Targeting subgroups rather than new clients	*Moderate* Dwindling government funding; volatility Charitable donations and earned income	*Moderate* Multiple strong commercial revenue projects may impact mission

Organizational slack	*High* Dwindling cash reserves	*Low* Cash reserves	*Low* Maintains surplus; volunteer based	*Moderate* Increasing reliance on commercial revenue
Leadership	*Moderate* Multiple ED changes over time Recent ED stability	*Moderate* New leaders bring new ideas	*Low* Current ED involved with organization since founding; BOD instills culture of fiscal conservatism	*Moderate* Leaders support new initiatives Stable leadership
Embeddedness	*Low* Involvement in housing network and organizational history provide new revenue opportunities	*Moderate* Network, history, and location provide new program opportunities	*Low* Connection with local businesses provides commercial revenue opportunities	*Moderate* Multitude of programs respond to client and community needs
Threat level	*Moderate*	*Low*	*Low*	*Moderate*

and reliance on government and real estate ultimately led MCD to expand its service area, creating pressure to consider mission change in the future, at least in terms of geographic scope. Some degree of organizational slack in the form of disposable real estate assets also reduced pressure for considering mission change. By contrast, MCD's executive director (ED) and deputy director (DD) leadership changes heightened the risk of radical mission change. From MCD's founding in 1989 until 2010, MCD was led by the same ED. Although core service functions and the original mission to improve the local community and develop housing were institutionalized during this time, the new ED has discretion to substantially alter program offerings. Finally, MCD's embeddedness in Atlanta and in the housing subsector has created specialized knowledge of housing programs, enabling MCD to broaden its activity and funding base without drastically altering its core mission. Taken together, MCD appears to face only a moderate threat of radical mission change.

Case Study 2: South Atlanta Development Corporation

Financial insolvency

Unlike MDC, SADC did not suffer from the 2013 government sequester and shutdown, but it has experienced major revenue volatility in the past. In terms of its governance, interpreted broadly to encompass organizational structure, SADC was one of the founders of a for-profit organization that acquires foreclosed properties, which may have contributed to its stability during housing market and government funding downturns by offering SADC an additional revenue source. However, SADC's overall financial structure risks insolvency, since government revenue is project specific and tenuous from year to year. In 2017, SADC will also lose 20 percent of its revenue when stadium-parking revenue from a local sports team ends, heightening the threat of financial insolvency. Whether SADC crosses this threshold may depend on its ability to generate charitable donations and earned revenue. Compensating factors helping SADC to maintain equilibrium include organizational slack, in the form of operating reserves, and stable leadership. In particular, executive leadership has remained within the family of the founder, favoring financial stability so long as competence and flexibility are also maintained. Strong community ties provide a further hedge against insolvency, but past program service expansions have undermined these ties and weakened SADC's embeddedness in the community. Taken together, these factors suggest a moderate risk of SADC's crossing the threshold of financial insolvency.

Radical mission change
Since SADC's board of directors is a mix of industry and community representatives, its governance discourages radical departure from its neighborhood focus. However, the financial structure of SADC encourages program service area expansion to additional neighborhoods and the project-oriented nature of SADC's government funding can pull SADC into the provision of different types of services. That said, SADC's organizational slack buffers it from crossing a threshold. In particular, although variable over time, investment revenue has been as high as 90 percent of total revenue. The ability to draw on this source of revenue during times of financial distress allows SADC to avoid taking on housing projects outside of its mission. The longstanding tenure of executive and board leadership at SADC suggests institutionalization of the organization's mission and is a stabilizing factor. Indeed, the mission of SADC has not been altered drastically since its founding, although its geographic service area is somewhat broader than the South Atlanta neighborhood SADC originally served. The changing needs of the residents and the neighborhoods in its community may push SADC towards some modifications of its mission in the future. Overall, however, SADC appears to be at little risk of crossing a threshold of transformative radical mission change.

Case Study 3: Atlanta Homeless Housing

Financial insolvency
In terms of governance, AHH's board has financial experience that can help it navigate economic downturns. Moreover, its financial structure has been a stabilizing factor. Consistent with its history of partnerships with local churches and organizations, AHH's most important revenue source is charitable contributions, which has enabled the organization to survive economic downturns without excessive trauma. A special event in 2009 raised enough revenue to provide a degree of organizational slack when AHH lost government funding in 2012 and operated in deficit. However, reserves are dwindling and financial insolvency looms if current and additional revenue sources are not further cultivated. The recent financial setbacks may be attributed in part to leadership volatility, as AHH has had four EDs in the past ten years, although the current ED was involved with AHH for several years before becoming ED. AHH's embeddedness in the community as a homeless shelter and its longstanding relationship with government have been stabilizing factors, enabling the organization to offer a new government program and regain funding in 2013, avoiding financial insolvency. Moreover, the area in which AHH is located in downtown Atlanta is undergoing revitalization, which could open new, commercial

sources of revenue to hedge against financial failure. Cumulatively, AHH thus appears to face only a moderate threat of financial insolvency.

Radical mission change

AHH is governed by a diverse board of for-profit and community leaders that helps ensure that no single interest will significantly alter AHH's current mission. AHH's financial structure also suggests stability. Thus far, any new programs offered by AHH have been within its mission, engaging new subgroups of clients rather than creating a new focus or financial arrangements. However, a recent reduction in organizational slack in the form of diminished financial reserves could push AHH towards mission change in the future if it changes programming in order to chase funding opportunities. However, since AHH still maintains some reserves, this remains a low threat at present. AHH's leadership and embeddedness may also be forces for transformation. With executive changes come new ideas and openness to new initiatives, as evidenced by AHH's various program additions and closures over time, initiated by different EDs. AHH's embeddedness in a revitalizing downtown neighborhood provides a potential force for transformation as well, since neighborhood renewal will bring in new demographics and changing client needs. Taken as a cluster, these factors suggest a low overall risk of radical mission change.

Case Study 4: Housing for Women and Children

Financial insolvency

Among the four case studies, HWC is the youngest and most rapidly growing organization, nonetheless featuring several characteristics favoring maintenance of its current equilibrium. A large board of directors with financial and business experience governs HWC. HWC's financial structure, on the other hand, pushes the organization both towards and away from financial failure. Although there have been fluctuations in government support and other revenues, reliance on charitable donations and earned income enables HWC to hedge against insolvency. HWC has operated at a surplus for all but two years of operation, creating some organizational slack against future financial difficulty. HWC also employs almost 800 volunteers each year to provide services, with only ten paid staff members. This allows HWC to keep organizational expenses low and to reduce the threat of operating deficits by managing a flexible work force. The character of HWC's leadership also encourages stability. In particular, the ED and board members have a long history with HWC, favoring continuity in its particular cultivated revenue sources and overall fiscal conservatism. Embeddedness in North Fulton County has also allowed HWC to create a network with local businesses and exploit prospective earned income opportunities. Overall, therefore, HWC appears to face a low risk of financial insolvency.

Radical mission change

HWC's governance appears to be a moderate force for mission change as members of its robust board work to identify new program areas to better serve clients. However, the opening of two successful resale stores may alter the mission in the future if these earned income initiatives overtake the traditional focus of the organization and substantially modify its financial structure. HWC's growing reliance on this source of earned income, in the context of a competitive local economy, also suggests that HWC may have limited organizational slack with which to anchor its mission. Leadership and embeddedness are additional forces for change. HWC's leaders do initiate new programs but the stability of this leadership over time helps to maintain the organization's basic mission focus. HWC's embedding in the North Fulton neighborhood makes it responsive to changing client and community needs. This is reflected in the organization's addition of teen and children programs to better serve HWC's clients and broadening of its mission's scope over time to include emergency housing and social services such as counseling and career counseling to homeless clients. All told, the five factors that influence risk of crossing a threshold suggest a moderate likelihood of radical mission change for HWC in the immediate future.

IMPLICATIONS AND CONCLUSIONS

The cases studied here are clearly limited in terms of their generalizability and represent only a small sample within their particular subfield. Though they could be considered representative examples of the Atlanta nonprofit housing community or, to a lesser degree, the nonprofit housing sector at large, further and more targeted research needs to be conducted on other nonprofit subsectors.

Nonetheless, while Atlanta nonprofit housing organizations occupy only a small corner of the social enterprise zoo, their experiences in the face of systemic disruption manifested by the federal sequester of funds and government shutdown of 2011–13 provide some preliminary insights into the factors that allow animals in the zoo to maintain their equilibrium in terms of social mission and financial sustainability. In this chapter, resiliency theory provides the conceptual framework through which that stability can be analyzed. Resiliency theory asks whether individual or groups of enterprises are in danger of crossing thresholds that could destroy them or seriously alter their pursuit of goals and social mission. The theory suggests five factors influencing this risk – governance, financial structure, organizational slack, leadership, and embeddedness – all reflecting ways in which an organization's or population's viability can be steadied or undermined. In the zoo one can think of physical animals in small enclosures, with weak barriers protecting them from incursions or inadvertent excursions, located in proximity of steep cliffs or other kinds of dangerous terrain, and subject to major disruptions stemming from structural threats to the zoo itself such as weather events or economic collapse of the communities in which they are embedded. Careful management of each animal, each species, and their environments are necessary to promote the resiliency and stability of the system.

Our analysis of Atlanta housing nonprofits here reveals a number of factors determining the magnitudes and reactions to the threshold parameters. Prominent in the findings here are financial strategies that allow organizations to manage risk, particularly diversification of sources of income. Also notable are the benefits of embeddedness in host communities and in service systems that provide safety nets to help ensure that organizations don't go into free fall when catastrophic events occur or chronic conditions worsen to the point of crisis. Similarly, those organizations large or slack enough to have significant resources that can serve as insurance against disruption are also more likely to be resilient. The factors of leadership and governance can also be key protections against instability.

How do these findings apply to other forms of social enterprise? One clear observation is that the nonprofit form offers the advantage of income diversification with its mixed reliance on charitable sources, government funding and earned income. Not all forms of social enterprise have this advantage. For example, social businesses rely primarily on earned income, though they diversify customers and services within this category and can seek government project funding as well as capital support from philanthropic sources. Similarly, social cooperatives, while reliant on member support, can also seek external public or private funding for contracted projects and services.

Nonprofits also enjoy advantages of embeddedness in external supporting systems that other forms may not enjoy to the same extent. The Atlanta housing organizations are rooted in community and plugged directly into a variety of government agency sources; as evidenced in the cases, this can have positive and negative consequences. It is yet to be determined whether for-profit forms of social enterprise in the United States can be similarly embedded. Finally, it is unclear whether nonprofits enjoy any advantage with respect to building organizational slack. While pressures for efficiency may be muted relative to what for-profits may experience in an unfettered market, nonprofits also face different expectations. They are often criticized for running surpluses (indeed, our case study organizations were often in deficit) or for accumulating rainy day funds that critics argue should be used to address immediate program needs. For-profit forms of social enterprise would seem more immune to these normative pressures to stay slim and hungry although competitive market forces or influence from other providers or investors may indeed play this role in many cases.

In summary, by examining the threshold factors at play in various parts of the social enterprise zoo, policymakers (zookeepers), curators (entrepreneurs), and managers may be able to make better choices of social enterprise animals that can survive and thrive under extant conditions and to design zoo habitats and policies, such as legal regimes and funding opportunities, to ensure stability and effectiveness of their enterprises.

NOTES

1. These are organizations included in the National Taxonomy of Exempt Entities (NTEE) code "L."
2. The names of the nonprofits have been changed to protect confidentiality.

REFERENCES

Baghdady, G. and J. Maddock (2008), "Marching to a different mission," *Stanford Social Innovation Review*, Spring.

Berke, P.R. and T.J. Campanella (2006), "Planning for postdisaster resiliency," *The ANNALS of the American Academy of Political and Social Science*, **604** (1), 192–207.

Block, S.R. and S. Rosenberg (2002), "Toward an understanding of founder's syndrome: an assessment of power and privilege among founders of nonprofit organizations," *Nonprofit Management and Leadership*, **12** (4), 353–68.

Bowman, W. (2011a), *Finance Fundamentals for Nonprofits: Building Capacity and Sustainability, Volume 2*, Hoboken, NJ: Wiley.

Bowman, W. (2011b), "Financial capacity and sustainability of ordinary nonprofits," *Nonprofit Management and Leadership*, **22** (1), 37–51.

Calabrese, T.D. (2012), "The accumulation of nonprofit profits: a dynamic analysis," *Nonprofit and Voluntary Sector Quarterly*, **41** (2), 300–324.

Carman, J.G. and R. Nesbit (2013), "Founding new nonprofit organizations syndrome or symptom?," *Nonprofit and Voluntary Sector Quarterly*, **42** (3), 603–21.

Congressional Budget Office (2011), *Estimated Impact of Automatic Budget Enforcement Procedures Specified in the Budget Control Act*, accessed 22 June 2016 at http://www.cbo.gov/sites/default/files/09-12-BudgetControlAct_0.pdf.

Ebrahim, A., J. Battilana, and J. Mair (2014), "The governance of social enterprises:

mission drift and accountability challenges in hybrid organizations," *Research in Organizational Behavior*, **34**, 81–100.

English, L. and N. Peters (2011), "Founders' syndrome in women's nonprofit organizations: implications for practice and organizational life," *Nonprofit Management and Leadership*, **22** (2), 159–71.

Federal Trade Commission v. *Phoebe Putney Health System, Inc.*, 568 (Supreme Court 2013).

Fertel, R. (2006), "Katrina five ways," *Kenyon Review*, accessed 22 June 2016 at http://www.kenyonreview.org/journal/summer-2006/selections/katrina-five-ways/.

Folke, C. (2006), "Resilience: the emergence of a perspective for social-ecological systems analyses," *Global Environmental Change*, **16** (3), 253–67.

Goddeeris, J.H. and B.A. Weisbrod (1998), "Conversion from nonprofit to for-profit legal status: why does it happen and should anyone care?," *Journal of Policy Analysis and Management*, **17** (2), 215–33.

Gotham, K. and R. Campanella (2011), "Coupled vulnerability and resilience: the dynamics of cross-scale interactions in post-Katrina New Orleans," *Ecology and Society*, **16** (3), 12.

Hager, M.A. (1999), "Explaining demise among nonprofit organizations," doctoral dissertation, University of Minnesota.

Hager, M.A., J. Galaskiewicz, and J.A. Larson (2004), "Structural embeddedness and the liability of newness among nonprofit organizations," *Public Management Review*, **6** (2), 159–88.

Hirth, R.A. (1997), "Competition between for-profit and nonprofit health care providers: can it help achieve social goals?," *Medical Care Research and Review*, **54** (4), 414–38.

Holling, C.S. (1973), "Resilience and stability of ecological systems," *Annual Review of Ecology and Systematics*, **4** (1), 1–23.

Holling, C.S. (1996), "Cross-scale morphology, geometry, and dynamics of ecosystems," in F.B. Samson and F.L. Knopf (eds), *Ecosystem Management*, Dordrecht: Springer, pp. 351–423.

Kapucu, N. (2006), "Public–nonprofit partnerships for collective action in dynamic contexts of emergencies," *Public Administration*, **84** (1), 205–20.

Mason, C. and B. Doherty (2015), "A fair trade-off? Paradoxes in the governance of fair-trade social enterprises," *Journal of Business Ethics*, 1–19, doi: 10.1007/s10551-014-2511-2.

Minkoff, D.C. and W.W. Powell (2006), "Nonprofit mission: constancy, responsiveness, or deflection?," in W.W. Powell and R. Steinberg (eds), *The Nonprofit Sector: A Research Handbook*, 2nd edition, New Haven, CT: Yale University Press.

Nonprofit Finance Fund (201), *2015 State of the Nonprofit Sector*, accessed 22 June 2016 at http://survey.nonprofitfinancefund.org/?mode=print.

O'Neil, R.M. (1991), "Artists, grants and rights: the NEA controversy revisited," *New York Law School Journal of Human Rights*, **85** (1991–1992).

Ramus, T. and A. Vaccaro (2014), "Stakeholders matter: how social enterprises address mission drift," *Journal of Business Ethics*, 1–16, accessed 23 June 2016 at http://link.springer.com/article/10.1007%2Fs10551-014-2353-y.

Redford, K.H., G. Amato, and J. Baillie et al. (2011), "What does it mean to successfully conserve a (vertebrate) species?," *BioScience*, **61** (1), 39–48.

Salamon, L.M. (2003), *The Resilient Sector: The State of Nonprofit America*, Washington, DC: Brookings Institution Press.

Salamon, L.M. (2012), "The resilient sector: the future of nonprofit America," in *The State of Nonprofit America*, 2nd edition, Washington, DC: Brookings Institution Press.

Sanders, M.L. (2013), "Being nonprofit-like in a market economy: understanding the mission-market tension in nonprofit organizing," *Nonprofit and Voluntary Sector Quarterly*, 0899764013508606.

Scheffer, M. and S.R. Carpenter (2003), "Catastrophic regime shifts in ecosystems: linking theory to observation," *Trends in Ecology and Evolution*, **18** (12), 648–56.

Searing, E.A.M. (2014), "Charitable (anti)trust: the role of antitrust regulation in the nonprofit sector," *Nonprofit Policy Forum*, **5** (2), 261–88.

Strahl, S.D. (2010), "Telling our stories – animals, conservation, AND economic impact," *Association of Zoos & Aquariums*, accessed 22 June 2016 at https://www.aza.org/Membership/detail.aspx?id=12277.

United States Government Accountability Office (2014), *2013 SEQUESTRATION: Selected Federal Agencies Reduced Some Services and Investments, While Taking Short-Term Actions to Mitigate Effects*, accessed 22 June 2016 at http://www.gao.gov/products/GAO-14-452.

Walker, B. and J.A. Meyers (2004), "Thresholds in ecological and social-ecological systems: a developing database," *Ecology and Society*, **9** (2), 3.

Walker, B., C.S. Holling, S.R. Carpenter, and A. Kinzig (2004), "Resilience, adaptability and transformability in social-ecological systems," *Ecology and Society*, **9** (2), 5.

Weisbrod, B.A. (1997), "The future of the nonprofit sector: its entwining with private enterprise and government," *Journal of Policy Analysis and Management*, **16** (4), 541–55.

Young, D.R. (2001), "Organizational identity in nonprofit organizations: strategic and structural implications," *Nonprofit Management and Leadership*, **12** (2), 139–57.

Young, D.R. and C. Kim (2015), "Can social enterprises remain sustainable and mission-focused? Applying resiliency theory," *Social Enterprise Journal*, **11** (3), 233–59.

Young, D.R., T. Jung and R. Aranson (2010), "Mission – market tensions and nonprofit pricing," *The American Review of Public Administration*, **40** (2), 153–69.

Young, D., J. Kerlin, and S. Teasdale et al. (2012), "The dynamics and long term stability of social enterprise," in S. Bacq and J. Kickul (eds) (2012), *Patterns in Social Entrepreneurship Research*, Cheltenham, UK and Northampton, MA, USA: Edward Elgar Publishing, pp. 217–42.

12. Social impact of the social enterprise zoo

John E. Tyler III*

INTRODUCTION

Extraordinary volumes of good have been accomplished for humankind, quality of life, and standards of living by harnessing incentive structures and opportunities of "traditional" business and philanthropy. At the same time, that good is not universally enjoyed nor have benefits extended as broadly or as deeply as they might. The generation of that good also has left a wake of scars and challenges. Stated differently, for all the good accomplished by traditional approaches, their potential has not been reached nor have their achievements been without costs and consequences, some perhaps avoidable.

Increasingly traditional approaches seem to be adopting characteristics of social enterprise (SE). Generalizations about traditional business universally neglecting social/environmental good in favor of profitability are not supported by experience. Business has embraced corporate social responsibility programs, actively engaged social programs, and increasingly considers and has historically considered "social"[1] interests in decision-making (Collins and Porras, 2000; Kay, 2010). At a minimum, any traditional business responds to employees, consumers, policymakers, and others who are attuned to those interests. Even so, business remains most often driven by (or at least tempered by) impact based on such things as market penetration and profitability, nearly all of which are quantifiable and comparable, with perhaps secondary or tertiary consideration of "social" interests and measures.

Like business, traditional philanthropy can quantify a variety of outputs and even outcomes as indicators of impact (Mook, 2013).[2] There is a rising swell that equates such metrics – including measures reflecting revenue, expenses, and surpluses – with success. But philanthropy is almost never able to fully quantify its impact. One patron of the arts, one person fed, one research breakthrough are certainly important and relevant metrics, but such numbers fail to capture the substantive effect on the person's life, thinking, emotions, intellect, and so on, or the ripple effects on family, community, and beyond. Such are the ultimate impact objectives of philanthropy, and they remain elusive despite the efforts of social accounting (Mook, 2013; Mook et al., 2015), social return on investment (Moody et al., 2015), and other assessment tools and theories.

Perhaps that is where opportunities emerge for SE: striving to find new ways to balance otherwise competing interests and purposes in order to accomplish more and in a better way; and trying to generate value that is additive to, yet distinct from, traditional approaches without their respective downsides or at least having meaningfully mitigated them. Inherent in that challenge is the need to not just produce such value but also to demonstrate it. Failure to do both – either independently from or as enhancements to traditional approaches – risks SE merely allowing people to feel better about themselves and their efforts.

Feeling positive, hopeful, and motivated about intentions and efforts is wonderful in context, but proponents of SE seem to expect more. Moreover, extrapolating from good intentions to declarations about impact without knowing actual impact – good and otherwise – or honesty about what is known and knowable risks deception that is likely to undermine interest, attention, availability of resources, and even hope!

To say that exploring the impact of SE is complicated is a gross understatement. The complications only begin with the difficulty of assessing the essential things that cannot be measured easily or well,[3] notwithstanding efforts to break through that barrier (Mook, 2013). Difficulty continues in how SE simultaneously operates on numerous levels: individual, organizational, communal, societal, and within its own movement. SE's impact also extends to its intersection with regulation, including whether SE negates or enhances accountability and enables or inhibits fraud and abuse.

Of course, being complicated or challenging or even presently unprovable is no excuse for not trying, as quixotic as it may seem. After all, many advances in human welfare began with a concept that evolved into an idea that became a hypothesis that was tested, assessed, adjusted, and the process repeated until usefulness was demonstrated, opportunity pursued, and eventually impact understood and quantified. Idealistic or not, much has been and can be gained from degrees of living ideally in a practical world.

It is in that spirit that this chapter approaches assessing the impact of SE, its potential, and its distinguishing character.[4] First, there is the impact of the zoo itself, considered in the next section; that is, SE in a macro sense. Second, there are more concentrated impacts on specific habitats (e.g., industries, geographies) and animals (i.e., discrete enterprises), addressed in the subsequent section, for which metrics, measures, and standards might be more accessible but for which accurate cross-purpose benchmarking is still a challenge. Third, there are the broader contexts of traditional business, philanthropy, and regulatory/"zookeeper" oversight within which the SE zoo exists with reciprocal effects – particularly with regard to the very essence of SE: its priorities among various purposes and its accountability to those goals.

We cannot accurately quantify the true and complete impact of the SE zoo...yet. But we know more than we used to, and we are expanding our understanding in ways that will improve how we identify and pursue opportunities, recognize efficiencies and waste, allocate resources, establish enabling policies, and make a variety of decisions. Much of that understanding is and will be derived from what we can discern about those impacts that we can identify even if we cannot quantify them.

IMPACT OF "THE ZOO"

SE's dual nature (or tripartite if environment is considered distinct) requires that both financial performance and social benefits be assessed and found meaningful. Of course, belying that statement are presumptions about "meaning" and the presence of standard(s) against which to ascertain it. Therein lie the challenges.

There are many ways to conceive of such standard(s) and conclusions. One could compare the zoo's performance relative to traditional approaches; that is, the financial returns and social impact of business and the social impact of philanthropy. Another would be to have benchmark(s) based on conditions at a given moment in time (such as a community's economic, health or environmental conditions or some index or composite of a variety of factors) and compare changes, especially social changes, relative to the benchmark(s). A third way of considering the zoo's impact might be in purely qualitative terms based on awareness and incorporation of SE principles into societal norms.

A Comparator Approach

Given SE's origination in either frustration with traditional approaches or seeing opportunities in their gaps, a natural comparator for assessing SE's impact are the two traditional approaches of business and philanthropy. This comparator approach requires three steps: (1) conceptualizing standards on which to make comparisons; (2) identifying and collecting consistent, reliable information from respective approaches about foci on return of financial capital, growth of that capital, and social impact; and (3)

Table 12.1 Assessing the SE zoo's comparative impact

		Return of Financial Capital	Growth/Distribution of Capital	Social Outcomes
1	Traditional business	3	3	1
2	Traditional philanthropy	0	0	3
3	Utopian ideal	(= Bus) 3	(= Bus) 3	(>/= Phil) 3
4	Modified business	(= Bus) 3	(= Bus) 3	(> Bus) 2
5	Kinder, gentler business	(Phil <) 2 (< Bus)	(Phil <) 2 (< Bus)	(> Bus) 2
6	More aggressive Philanthropy	(Phil <) 1 (< Bus)	(Phil <) 1 (< Bus)	(>/= Phil) 3
7	No interest loan	(= Bus) 3	(= Phil) 0	(>/= Phil) 3

Note: Numerals in the table are for illustrative purposes only and should not be construed as presenting absolute or relative judgments. Moreover, they are not intended to suggest that assessments can or will be quantified, quantifiable or even objective.

drawing conclusions from the analysis about the extent to which effects are beneficial, harmful, or neutral – in other words "meaning" or "impact."

Conceptualizing standards for comparison

Table 12.1 presents conceptions of ways to consider the two traditional approaches and various SE approaches on three key priorities: return of capital, distributable growth of that capital, and social outcomes. In the chart, a "3" in any given cell signifies intentional focus and legal accountability while a "0" indicates a presumptively "prohibited" focus. Traditional business might be assigned 3s for both return of capital and its distributable growth and a 1 for permitted and/or incidental social outcomes; after all, businesses' social gains are not zero! Traditional philanthropy gets a 3 for focus on social outcomes but 0s for capital return and growth because philanthropy can have no owners to receive returned capital or realize its growth. Approaches to SE then get illustrative numerals depending on the foci.

One SE approach might aspire to results that equal or exceed those of both traditional business and philanthropy; that is, capital returns and realizable growth at least comparable to business along with social benefits that equal or exceed philanthropy. This utopian ideal has 3s in all columns of the third row – "utopian" because, in reality, compromises must be made, and traditional approaches surely would already be exploiting such pursuits if they were possible. Instead, traditional approaches have long provided the dichotomy, standards, and legal accountability for making those choices, which is why there is even a zoo to discuss.

A more realistic conception of SE might be as presented in row four: return and growth of capital similar to traditional business (3s) with social impact that is better (or "not as bad as") and more intentional than that of traditional business, thus a 2 in that column. This "modified business" approach is becoming more common and, arguably, has provided a foundation upon which the zoo has been built or vice versa.

Two approaches incorporate willingness to compromise owner value while targeting social impact; that is, greater risk of losing some or all of the principal and likely less growth (if any) than from traditional investment, but in both cases greater potential for return and growth of capital than is available from traditional philanthropy. Hence, the 2s assigned to the owner value cells in rows five and six.

These approaches differ in their focus on social impact. One strives to do better than traditional business, perhaps a "kinder, gentler" approach to business (with a 2 in that column in row five). The other pursues social impact that equals or exceeds what might be expected of philanthropy, perhaps a more "aggressive" form of philanthropy (with a 3 in that column in row six).

A variation might compromise growth of financial capital but not necessarily its return. In other words, a loan's principal is repaid but without interest. The social impact comparator presumably would be to equal or exceed that of philanthropy; otherwise, why intentionally sacrifice reasonably expected financial growth (or the charitable deduction) for the same social outcomes available without the sacrifice? Row seven has a 3 priority on return of capital, 0 for its growth, and 3 for social impact.

Data/information for comparing financial and social impact

A primary challenge for Table 12.1's usefulness is the ability to populate it with meaningful data and information, especially with regard to social benefits or harms (Organisation for Economic Co-operation and Development, 2015). There has been progress regarding data on SE's financial performance for return of capital and its realizable growth.

One 2015 study by Cambridge Associates and the Global Impact Investing Network (GIIN) compared performance of conventional funds with that of 51 private investment funds begun between 1998 and 2010 with the intent of generating social or environmental impact (GIIN and Cambridge Associates, 2015). For the entire sample, the study found only a 15 percent difference in performance with conventional funds returning 8.1 percent versus 6.9 percent for the "impact" investors. But for funds of less than $100 million, "impact" funds more than doubled the return of conventional funds: 9.5 percent versus only 4.5 percent. Comparing "impact" investments in emerging markets, where 70 percent of the deals occurred (JPMorgan and GIIN, 2014), those in developed markets showed a similar difference with returns of 9.1 percent from emerging "impact" investments compared to 4.8 percent from those in developed markets (GIIN and Cambridge Associates, 2015).

Morgan Stanley released a similar study in 2015 in which it sought to assess whether "sustainable" companies underperformed or experienced greater risk of loss than traditional companies (Morgan Stanley, 2015b). This study defined "sustainable" as being focused on both present and future well-being. Morgan Stanley found that returns from investment in sustainable companies either met or exceeded absolute and risk-adjusted returns. It found that sustainable mutual funds equaled or exceeded median returns of traditional approaches and equaled or exceeded volatility for 64 percent of the traditional companies. It found a positive correlation between sustainable activity and stock price. It also found that a social investment mutual fund begun in 1990 had outperformed the S&P 500 by 45 basis points (ibid.).

Thus, the Cambridge/GIIN and Morgan Stanley 2015 studies begin filling in the financial capital side of Table 12.1, including whether returns can be comparable, the extent and areas in which they are not, and to what degrees financial compromise might be expected or not. However, neither study purported to separately assess social impact.

For the above framework to be truly useful, there must be means by which to gather information, analyze it, draw conclusions, and make comparisons in the context of the complete SE zoo – especially its elusive social impact. Because that information is not comprehensively available, the comparative framework seems at best aspirational.

Benchmarking

Another way to assess the zoo's impact might be to evaluate whether (and which of) SE's efforts provide social benefits, cause social harm, or are neutral relative to a given benchmark of existing conditions. In other words, did social conditions change and, if so, were the changes for the better or worse?

Traditional business and markets have many indicators of their status and performance. Interest rates, firm formations, market exchanges, employment, underemployment, durable goods orders, and others contribute to the analysis. Even these have various subparts, such as the multiple sources for interest rates (i.e., LIBOR, Fed funds rate, *Wall Street Journal*, Treasuries, etc.) and exchanges (i.e., Dow Jones, S&P 500,

Russell, mercantile exchanges, etc.) from which to choose. More narrowly, any number of purported indices of entrepreneurial activity in countries, states, and communities have emerged in recent years to facilitate assessing public policy as related to entrepreneurship (Ortmans, 2015).

Perhaps the SE zoo's impact might be approached similarly; that is, with a variety of competing but complementary indicators, indices, or composites that focus on social returns.[5] In doing so, however, their likely significant limitations must be top of mind and their utilization undertaken carefully (ibid.). As with other indices, a social impact index or set of indices might provide a productive starting point for understanding strengths, gaps, and opportunities, provided that care is taken to guard against exaggeration and misapplication.

From that perspective, the general impact of SE might be gauged by (1) combining meaningful information from a variety of relevant sources; (2) assigning weights that objectify relative importance; (3) creating a benchmark(s) using current or historical information, including possibly from the traditional approaches as a "control group" of sorts; (4) collecting the information on a regular basis; and then (5) tracking trends and movement.

This is in part where the framework proposed above can help distinguish among information that is interesting and that which more meaningfully presents impact. For instance, there will be information that might serve as a proxy for expressed intent to do well and not cause harm at a given moment in time, although expressions of intent should not be confused with actual results, outcomes, or impact. While interesting and relevant in a different context, indications of intent alone cannot be meaningfully inserted into the framework presented above and compared against social outcomes generated by traditional approaches.

With that filter in mind, at least five types of objective information might be collected and analyzed to generally assess the zoo most broadly and possibly contribute to relevant indexes and composites. If limitations can be addressed – including the dearth of useful quantifiable information – these and other types of information might eventually give rise to benchmarks against which to assess performance of the SE zoo broadly.

One component might be the number of states that have formalized business structures that enable focus on SE, which have grown from zero in 2007 to more than 30 in 2015 (see Chapter 3). Related could be the number of entities that have adopted formal hybrid structures.[6] A comprehensive indicator also might account for other entities that satisfy a clear definition of being "SE" but through traditional structures, such as numbers of certified "B Corps"[7] provided they are not double counted. This information could be supplemented by numbers of enterprises that have specifically incorporated aspects of third party standards into their operations, such as those of IRIS[8] or B Analytics.[9]

Although not indicative of actual social impact, these activities evidence interest in SE reinforced by decisions followed by tangible actions to execute on that interest. Moreover, there is some degree of third-party recognition of those intentions and actions, though not necessarily validation or affirmation of legitimacy.

Other components might be borrowed from traditional business, provided their inherent limits are accounted for as indicators (much less full measures) of social impact. Among these might be aggregated information about sales volume, revenue or profits earned, number of transactions, customers, products, and/or employees at social enterprises. Although these might suggest degrees of activity or perhaps attention, they do not differentiate from traditional business (Toniic Institute, 2012) nor do they necessarily present reliable or even presumptively useful information about the impact of SE.

For instance, sales volume, revenue, and profitability might indicate commitment to or awareness of social impact, or they might reflect a quality marketing campaign and have no relationship to social outcomes and whether social purposes were served. Low revenue or profitability might be because of bad luck, bad decisions, or willingness to sacrifice financial returns to desired social objectives. Number of employees and/ or wage levels may be similarly deceptive as employees may be retained or wages inflated to serve social purposes despite resulting inefficiencies or other problems.

Finding reliable, unqualified criteria for assessing the SE zoo's broad impact is challenging. Adding to the challenge is the zoo's explicit concern about limiting or mitigating harms caused.

Consistency and avoiding hypocrisy may require accounting for more than SE's good or beneficial outcomes. It may require also factoring in reasonably knowable "negative" consequences – intended, assumed, unintended, and incidental. After all, certain SE criticisms of traditional business approaches are grounded in their "negative" impacts on environment, employment, standards of quality, and so on. This will likely lead to arguments about what is "negative" for SE, but principled consistency dictates that consequences of all types be understood. SE is not immune to "negative" impacts merely because its intentions are good, whether at the level of zoo or among its diverse species and animals.

Perhaps it might be argued that such harms are tolerable when intentions target social benefits, but the ultimate effects do not change because of good intentions. Such tolerance becomes even more suspect when processed in a context of purportedly comparing outcomes with traditional business in which case the social benefits and harms of each should be factored fairly, objectively, and consistently. Therefore, any scale based on comparisons must permit a possibility that traditional business performs better.

Even with their limitations, and provided social impact is not exaggerated, attempts to generate indices and composites, and discussion of them in context, might help place SE performance and progress "in the public eye" (Ortmans, 2015). That awareness could enhance understanding and development of more appropriate policies, objectives, and activities among policymakers, entrepreneurs, investors, employees, researchers, and others interested in the zoo and its distinctive pursuit of not just intending to do well but also actually doing it!

Intentionality-based Influence and Awareness

Quantification of actual outcomes or results is not the only way to consider SE's impact nor is it the only (or even best) way to determine whether the impact is meaningful. Of course, deviating from direct assessments risks expanding gaps among intent, efforts/action, outputs/outcomes, and ultimately impact. As gaps grow, so too do problems establishing causation. That does not mean that intentions and effort are not relevant or that they should not be assessed to the extent possible. After all, intent and effort shape behavior that others observe and form awareness sufficient to influence their intentions and effort, which in turn might shape their behavior. Ultimately, a critical mass of meaningful, measurable, socially beneficial impacts might arise.

Which leads to a third way to assess the zoo's impact – an area in which the zoo has had unquestionable impact; that is, generating awareness of alternative ways to consider and approach purposes, priorities, decision-making, and accountability. Regarding general awareness, Morgan Stanley reports that media mentions of sustainable investment doubled from 2010 to 2014 (Morgan Stanley, 2015a), certainly a strong indicator of attention and mindshare penetration. Similar indications might be derived from mainstream and/or social media references to SE more broadly or to its specifically identified forms or principles. That information might be aggregated with the numbers of academic courses, articles and/or journals that prioritize the topic, and/or trade associations or other organizations dedicated to the topic (including chapters and membership). Also relevant might be references to SE in public company annual reports and/or Securities and Exchange Commission or exchange filings, in traditional and non-traditional advertising, in popular entertainment media, and/or on floors of legislatures and or in executive office addresses. Such data, in context, might contribute to an index or composite of some sort.

More than mere awareness, one important aspect of SE is its effort to attract new financial resources, attention, and approaches to solving or mitigating specific social problems otherwise neglected by traditional approaches. Even though more cannot alone definitively equate to better, information about investment activity and interest can say a great deal about intent to generate social or environmental impact (GIIN and Cambridge Associates, 2015) and trends in whether that intent is growing, contracting, or infiltrating.

Those trends might be increasingly relevant as women and Millennials expand their influence in investment decisions. Morgan Stanley reports that women are more than twice as likely as men to consider both financial returns and social impact and that Millennials are twice as likely to target specific social or environmental outcomes (Morgan Stanley, 2015a).

Data about the growth of SE investment dollars and funds and the financial returns on such investments show a level of commitment to the field. Morgan Stanley has reported that impact investment assets under management in the United States grew from one-ninth of such assets in 2012 (about 11 percent) to one-sixth in 2014 (about 17 percent) (Morgan Stanley, 2015a, 2015b). A 2014 report from JPMorgan and GIIN found a 20 percent increase in SE deals and a 10 percent increase of SE assets under management globally from 2012 to 2013, which represents only about 0.02 percent of the $210 trillion then held in global capital markets (US National Advisory Board, 2014).

Related indicators might be the growth in impact investment fund vehicles worldwide to more than 350 or the almost ten-fold membership increase GIIN experienced in growing from 25 to more than 220 in 2015 (Bouri, 2015).

Perhaps such data might even inform a benchmark from which to identify trends that reflect interest, awareness, or even cultural immersion. Care should be taken, however, to protect against conflating interest, activity alone, or awareness with actually improved or worsened conditions. After all, year-to-year increases in an awareness or activity benchmark would not alone support concluding or even inferring that anything meaningful had changed, except perhaps in the hope that improvement is possible and being actively pursued.

THE IMPACT OF "ANIMALS" WITHIN THE SE ZOO

Other indicators of awareness that might inform a benchmark or contribute to an index of the SE zoo's impact might be the efforts and attention given to deriving standards and criteria for assessing the impact of specific "animals" or any given "animal" in the zoo. Whether substantively indicative of impact or not, these standards, their applications, and lessons learned from them reflect commitment to understanding more about new approaches to business and philanthropy and the possible impact of more specific micro-efforts. There has been a proliferation of such attempts. According to McKinsey, the Foundation Center makes available 150 "tools and resources for assessing social impact."[10] Greico and her colleagues (2015) analyzed "a wide but not complete set of" 76 social impact assessment models. As with investment activity discussed above, more does not necessarily mean better overall, but it may mean something, possibly even actual impact at a micro-level.

Perhaps an inductive approach to the impact of the SE zoo from its component animals or any one of them might be more productive than generalizations. With time and experience in designing, using, and critiquing such tools, reliable indicators of the zoo's social impact overall might emerge.

The Zoo's "Animals" Generally

Homing in on narrower aspects of the SE zoo – its resident animals – evokes new questions about and challenges to assessing the zoo's impact:

- What are the specific subject areas to which social impact applies?
- Is it enough that doing well in any one area qualifies as positive without regard to harm caused in other areas?
- Are all areas equal or are there "firsts among equals" or areas of greater or lesser importance?

There are multiple approaches to and definitions of subject matter areas. Some overlap but others' elements are distinctive, and they generally seem to embrace their compartmentalization without necessarily addressing the latter two questions above.

As Monroe-White and Lecy explore in Chapter 10, one approach is that taken by Echoing Green, which uses theories of change from which to derive six categories with more specific subparts: business development, education, networks and advocacy, health systems, environmental protection, and product innovation. Various GIIN studies identify subject areas: agriculture, energy, aquaculture, tourism, consumer goods, urban development (e.g., housing, water, sanitation), and basic services (e.g., healthcare, education, water/sanitation, energy access, and financial services) (GIIN and Open Capital Advisors, 2015). Another study targets jobs at portfolio companies, clients within a target demographic, financial services specifically to the disadvantaged, jobs in an area of need, improved economic conditions and standards of living (e.g., basic infrastructure), and sustainability (e.g., healthy and environmentally friendly products and services, sustainable farming, improved education outcomes or expanded access) (GIIN and Cambridge Associates, 2015). Other reports disaggregate urban development, basic services, infrastructure, or other catchall categories into certain component parts (Toniic Institute, 2012; JPMorgan and GIIN, 2014; GIIN, 2015), or they might have different terminology or definitions that represent the same elemental aspirations or objectives.

Some differentiate microfinance from other financial services (JPMorgan and GIIN, 2014); others combine the two or are less clear about whether "financial services" is narrowly defined (Toniic Institute, 2012; GIIN, 2015; GIIN and Open Capital Advisors, 2015). At least four focus specifically on microfinance and financing efforts and activities within underserved markets (FIELD at the Aspen Institute,[11] Microfinance Information Exchange [aka MIXMarket],[12] Aeris,[13] and the Community Development Investment Fund). However, neither individually nor in the aggregate do they seem to present a coherent assessment of the social impact of microfinance. Traditional economic indicators, like standards of living, quality of life, or mobility out of poverty,[14] might be a necessary complement to demonstrating correlational connections to impact in a given community.

Certain "animals" may have less to do with subject matter areas and more with impacting particular geographies or demographics within an area. Aggregated information by geography might more readily evidence improvement and impact. GIIN has a number of studies that present economic and demographic information about conditions and activities in various geographic areas (GIIN and Open Capital Advisors, 2015).[15]

A geographic approach might usefully capture and present activity in an area. It might even present information about impact. But there will be challenges in determining causal or even correlational connections with SE, particularly its distinctive contributions relative to those of traditional approaches or government. It may be that a particular area's character is such that all efforts in or for it qualify as part of the zoo, in which case the distinctions may not be relevant.

Notwithstanding their limits, which should not be neglected, both approaches to "animals" can help identify baselines, progress, gaps and opportunities in resource allocations, opportunities for improvement, and more specific conditions or circumstances that might be changeable (JPMorgan and GIIN, 2014; GIIN and Open Capital Advisors, 2015). They might inspire shared infrastructure, information, "deal flow," personnel, and best practices in operations, definitions, and standards. They might inform other decisions and actions across a variety of decision-makers: policymakers, private association membership, community organizers, enterprise or entity owners and operators, and individuals for themselves. All of which might contribute to the zoo's impact, which may or may not be measurable or distinguishable but will be impactful nonetheless!

The Impact of Individual "Animals"

Efforts to understand and even quantify social impact get increasingly more manageable and easier – but still not simple – moving from the general zoo through its animals generally to each specific animal. These efforts enable enterprises to generate their own baselines against which to assess their unique social impact performance, track trends, and project trajectories. From these baselines, entities might develop meaningful assessments grounded in a reality applicable to their discrete circumstances.

If enough organizations share their information and enough others are consistent in adopting the similar baselines and definitions, a set of useable standards and external benchmarks might arise against which aggregated information might be developed. That information might contribute to better and more actionable understandings of the zoo's impact, which might inform decisions about policy and allocation of resources.

Several sources exist for individual animals to begin assessing their specific impact. Among the most prevalent of these is GIIN's Impact Reporting and Investments Standards,[16] which presents some 450 points of reference for which information might be collected to assess an enterprise's social, environmental, and financial performance. GIIN has understandably incorporated elements of IRIS into a number of its studies, including a 2014 spotlight conducted by JPMorgan (JPMorgan and GIIN, 2014) and GIIN's 2015 ImpactBase (GIIN, 2015). External validation of the effort to develop IRIS might be inferred from adoption of aspects of it into the B Impact Assessment,[17] MIXMarket (which uses 11 of the 450 points), G4 Sustainability Reporting Guidelines from 2013 (GRI, 2013), Land Conservation Impact Metrics (Manta Consulting, 2013), the National Community Investment Fund Social Performance Metrics,[18] and Toniic Institute (2012). Among other sources of criteria, data, and/or tools by which enterprises might gauge their social impact in particular are the Global Impact Investment Rating System (GIIRS),[19] Aeris, and PULSE App.X.[20]

The field of social accounting and its emphasis on engaging and reporting to stakeholders provides alternative accounting models and a means by which individual animals might assess their social impact, including through expanded value statements, social return on investment, the natural step framework, and variations derived from these methodologies (Mook et al., 2015).

There also are a number of existing aggregated sources against which to benchmark or compare key financial, social and environmental indicators. Mook presents two such tools: Bottomline (a software tool developed at the University of Sydney) and the Social Audit Network Limited methodology from the UK for a single entity or a system as a whole (Mook, 2013).

Not surprisingly given the relative ease with which financial information can be ascertained, investors have a variety of resources from which to garner "best practices" data, and tools for their impact investing initiatives. Among these are Cambridge Associates, JPMorgan, Morgan Stanley, Rockefeller Brothers, and McKinsey (Social Venture Technology Group, 2008; Toniic Institute, 2012; European Venture Philanthropy Association, 2013; GRI, 2013; Social Impact Investment Taskforce of the G8, 2014; GIIN, 2015; GIIN and Cambridge Associates, 2015; Morgan Stanley, 2015a, 2015b).

Unfortunately, most of these focus on balancing "intention" to consider both financial and social returns and/or they seek to compare the market returns of such investments so as to encourage (or at least not discourage) deployment of capital into the social realm. Given that one of the goals of SE is to attract capital resources to otherwise neglected social causes, reports that demystify zero-sum and presumptive whole loss thinking make sense.

There is expanding awareness of and interest in using capital for other than its own growth. More than mere aspirational awareness, such deployment is actually happening, and trajectories suggest that behavior and motivations for it are increasing and will continue to do so, involving sums in the range of US$400 billion to US$1 trillion (Monitor Institute, 2009; JPMorgan, the Rockefeller Foundation, and GIIN, 2010; Calvert Foundation, 2012), particularly as evidence grows favorably comparing performance for investments that intend social impact relative to conventional investment activity (GIIN and Cambridge Associates, 2015; Morgan Stanley, 2015b).

However, information about actual social impact – as distinct from intentions or aspirations – of impact investing remains elusive. A 2015 JPMorgan study of 29 impact investors epitomized the challenges with assessing social impact, as "few" of those studied had systems in place to aggregate the impact of their portfolio beyond the number of lives touched and jobs supported (JPMorgan Chase, 2015); however, this should not be undervalued even though at least one study questions whether such information is relevant because it does not differentiate SE enough from traditional business (Toniic Institute, 2012).

Such elusiveness should not be a surprise nor is it a criticism given that data about social impact similarly eludes others in the zoo, government, academia, and philanthropy. Such data is not only hard to obtain reliably, but data that is available is particularly difficult to extrapolate to causation or other conclusions. That challenge is most clearly manifest in caveats that accompany information from data providers.

For instance, on a variety of its pages regarding its IRIS standard, GIIN appropriately cautions: "Stand alone numbers cannot by themselves indicate positive or negative performance, or necessarily be compared across companies or products." Among these pages are those for the B impact assessment, small and growing business, prism, community banking, healthcare delivery, early-stage enterprises, social performance for microfinance, impact employments, international financial institution private sector, and smallholder agricultural finance.[21]

GIIN's 2014 *Spotlight* report with JPMorgan, a survey of 125 impact investors, suggests that using its report for direct comparisons of year-to-year performance "may not be valid" (JPMorgan and GIIN, 2014). They further (and rightly) ground their warning in differences in respondent samples from the prior year, thus also exemplifying challenges with any year-to-year comparisons. Certainly, output metrics reported "regularly over time" can provide "rich, useful data" that might suggest a connection to positive social change (Toniic Institute, 2012), but consistency and exactness in criteria, methodology, definitions, standards, and other aspects of surveys and reports are essential before inferring too much from any given assessment(s).

GIIN's 2015 ImpactBase highlights problems with self-reported information. It specifically disclaims responsibility for the accuracy of its report because the information is self-reported (GIIN, 2015). A 2012 Toniic Institute report similarly recognized limits of self-reported data by encouraging impact investors to corroborate such information with field visits, meetings, and other inputs from customers, vendors, and competitors (Toniic Institute, 2012). Even so, self-provided data may be the best available information. Depending on how it is used and whether incentives to distort can be mitigated, until more reliable indicators can be developed, collecting and using self-reported information remains indispensable as long as temptations to misuse are tempered by appropriate warnings about basing exaggerated conclusions or less than careful action on uncorroborated, self-reported information.

These cautions reflect the realities and difficulties of accurately measuring or even estimating the social impact of SE, particularly regarding causation. At one extreme, those wanting to use the information might neglect the warnings or ignore them as "legal" niceties in favor of promulgating grandiloquent (but distorted), conclusory declarations. On the other, those who see no value in the underlying data might take the warnings out of context to the point of disregarding the studies to which they are attached and missing important lessons.

As with most things, the best opportunities and most useful applications are with healthy doses of both reality and hope appropriate to the circumstances. It would be incongruous if something like SE could not strike this balance.

IMPACT OF PRIORITIES AND ACCOUNTABILITY OF AND ON THE ZOO

The SE zoo does not exist in isolation. As noted earlier, it functions relative to both business and philanthropy. It also operates in, is subject to, and impacts the regulatory environment.

If increased voluntary focus on social impact and other than distributable profits presents business and market opportunities, attracts investment and sales, motivates employees, and/or facilitates innovation, business likely welcomes modifications proffered by the zoo and will maximize their advantages. However, if modifications are broadly mandated by law or cause confusion about duties, decision-making responsibilities and process, and/or legal accountability, then the reception is not likely to be as hospitable – not just within business but also among regulators, economists, policymakers, and others who see benefit in orienting toward owner value. There is evidence of such confusion and therefore reason for attention to SE's impact on business, particularly its approaches to priorities of purpose and accountability (Tyler et al., 2015).

Within philanthropy, some embrace chances for the zoo to attract new money, energy, ideas, ingenuity, discipline, personnel, collaborations, and other resources to address some of the problems on which the sector focuses. Others are concerned about the threat that SE presents to the work of philanthropy because of potential for diverting resources from its own efforts and/or damaging its credibility because of fraud and misuse, misguided points of view, or misunderstandings. The extreme pros and cons both suggest the "zoo's" impact on philanthropy, particularly about the need for definitional and operational clarity of priorities and accountability.

The rapid expansion of states providing new organizational forms within which to structure social enterprises suggests that state legislators and governors generally share enthusiasm for new approaches, potential for new resources, and alternative conceptions of opportunity. State attorneys general, on the other hand, seem more understandably focused on the confusion and concerns introduced because of the zoo, particularly about the extent of clarity, complexity, or ambiguity about priorities and accountability (Grant, 2013; Manny, 2013; Spenard, 2013; Tyler, 2013; Wexler, 2013; Brakman Reiser, 2014).

Thus, one clear impact of the zoo is to have introduced (or perhaps exacerbated) new ways of thinking about priorities and accountability, and that new thinking has generated complexity and lack of clarity not just for the zoo but also more broadly.

Priorities: Owner Value, Charitable Purpose, Social Good, Flexibility?

For business, it is generally accepted that legal priority is to maximize owner value whether defined by law as return and growth of capital or by agreement of the owners as whatever they agree to. At worst, those duties are ambiguous enough that most directors and officers trend away from risking personal liability for breaching those duties as so conceived without some meaningful protections in place (Tyler et al., 2015).

For philanthropy, federal and state laws prioritize charitable purposes to the exclusion of owner value or even impermissible private benefit (IRC § 501(c)(3)). In that context, "charitable" purposes are not as broad as social good or public benefit writ large. Instead, the former is a subset of the latter such that "charitable" will also be a social good and of public benefit but social good and public benefit will not necessarily also be "charitable."

As Brewer discusses in Chapter 3, the L3C hybrid form prioritizes furthering charitability over other purposes, including owner value, which is not only secondary but is explicitly deprioritized. Unlike philanthropy, though, the L3C permits owners to receive distributable profits and realize capital gains.

Other hybrid forms are less clear about priority of owner value relative to social purposes, including those that might be charitable. Instead, the other forms generally require or permit consideration of owner value along with a variety of social purposes with no specific ordering or weighting (Tyler et al., 2015). Thus, the other existing hybrid forms primarily prioritize decision-maker flexibility in choosing what to prioritize and when to prioritize it in any given context. As such, these forms are always subject to the ability of the then current owners to change their minds with impunity and without regard to their own prior understandings of priorities or that of prior owners.

Thus, current structures permit priority among three purposes: owner value, charitable purpose, and flexibility. What is missing, then, is the unencumbered, continuing ability to prioritize social good over and at the expense of owner value, flexibility, or even charitable purposes. Stated more strongly, what is missing is legal accountability for ensuring persistent and enduring priority of social good, which is frequently touted as the distinguishing feature of the zoo. In some ways, then, one impact of the zoo is the introduction of flexible decision-making as a legitimate business purpose.[22] Another is to have introduced confusion about whether social good is or can be a business's primary purpose for which there is accountability.

Accountability

There is an interesting symbiotic relationship between the zoo and the traditional environment regarding accountability. Each influences the other, particularly in asking and answering questions about "accountability for what": actual outcomes/impact or informed decision-making and good faith efforts toward desired outcomes/impact.

For instance, traditional notions of legal accountability in business inspired the zoo's formal hybrid forms and their intentional (rather than incidental or accidental), simultaneous adoption of multiple approaches to accountability: primary dependence (as in traditional business) on the owners who appoint and remove directors and managers and secondary dependence on public reporting to inform and permit potential mobilization of public opinion. The essence of such accountability is two-fold: (1) unpredictability in whether the object of accountability is outcomes/impact or effort and (2) flexibility in moving between such objects.

By de-emphasizing (or even debilitating) legal accountability through causes of action and remedies grounded in fiduciary duty or contract, a reciprocal impact of traditional approaches to legal accountability on the zoo may be in exposing a critical paradox: a lack of meaningful legal accountability to social good as a clearly distinctive priority. Given that void, of course there is no way to determine whether legal accountability is to actual results or their good faith pursuit.

Practical/Owner Accountability

As a practical matter, a certain segment of the ownership interests (usually a majority) of any business enterprise – traditional or hybrid – elects and removes directors and managers. That reality is arguably more directly relevant and immediately useful than any other aspect of accountability. It permits a subset of coalesced owners to effectuate change depending on how they conceive the relative importance or level of outcomes/results or effort at that given time and regardless of positions held by prior owners and/or prior boards at prior times.

The question for the zoo is how much reliance can or should be vested in a requisite subset of owners for pursuing impact and balancing owner-ship interests and social good. Certainly there is, has been, and should be a meaningful role for such reliance, but should that reliance be as extensive as the hybrid forms in particular depend on? And what about the views of the minority owners, especially those that might have a higher tolerance for and commitment to social good over distributable profits? Should there be a form less dependent on persuading a critical mass of fellow owners (Tyler et al., 2015)?

Accountability to Public Opinion

Business, philanthropy, and government are all subject to stakeholder ability to mobilize critical mass to persuade decision-makers to prefer certain options and disfavor others. The SE zoo is not immune to such mobilizations. In fact, the corporate species of SE in the United States specifically embrace and depend on this accountability to public opinion. Not content to rely on the haphazard availability of relevant information, the corporate hybrid enabling statutes mandate certain types of reporting and disclosures to inform shareholders and the public of social objectives as a condition of their status. Despite the enhanced availability of infor-mation, there is still dependence on the existence of an interested relevant critical mass.

How that critical mass emerges in the zoo parallels traditional approaches. It might be based on the desire to achieve expected outcomes (whether financial, social or otherwise) or the failure to have done so. Mobilization also might be derived from personality, politics, misinformation, rumor and innuendo, or nothing in particular. Such mobilizations can impact sales, employees or volunteers, productivity, culture, supply chains, con-tract relationships, investors or donors, creditors, appointments, elections, and so on. Impact of such mobilizations can change behavior and policies. Broadly, SE has excelled at marshaling this form of accountability. By expanding social awareness in decision-making, SE has impacted the broader business environment and contributed to the revitalization of corporate social responsibility, the shaping of priorities and relationships, and otherwise. When global dissemination of an idea, notion, or opinion occurs at the click of a button, the power of public opinion is more vibrant than ever, and it is not likely to dissipate as social media tools and interest proliferate. However, the realistic effectiveness of accountability to public opinion still depends on grabbing and holding the attention of a critical mass, uniting it in purpose, motivating it to act, and sustaining the efforts and attention over time, which still may or may not change behavior. Thus, accountability to public opinion in practice is an uncertain approach for ensuring priority of social good in decision-making much less for socially beneficial outcomes.

Legal Accountability

Legal accountability is substantially more nuanced and complex in that it involves distinctive areas of fiduciary duty, contract, and regulatory oversight and their respective causes of action and available remedies. Despite meaningful influence in this area, the zoo's impact is not as extensive or clear as is sometimes attributed to it. Substantive gaps remain in legal accountability for pursuing distinctive social good as a priority over other purposes (Tyler et al., 2015). Even so, accountability to public opinion and practical accountability to owners remain and, given degradation of legal accountability, assume greater significance, which may or may not be well placed under given circumstances.

Fiduciary duty
At the risk of oversimplification, the law imposes certain duties of loyalty and care on business directors, officers, and managers, and it allows owners to hold them legally liable for breaching those duties, including failing to adhere to processes and standards dedicated to maximizing owner value. Remedies might include disgorging monetary gains derived from breaches and possible punitive damages not available otherwise (Kairis, 2011).

Within the zoo, one impact of the hybrid forms in the United States is to have redefined fiduciary duties and accountability thereto. The corporate species require consideration or balancing of various stakeholders and interests as imposed by statute and/or adopted by the enterprise. In every case, however, enabling statutes require or at least permit consideration of or even giving priority to the impact of decisions on owners. But none of the corporate hybrid statutes impose priorities, and Minnesota even prohibits them unless expressly declared in the articles of incorporation (see Del. Code Ann. tit. 8, § 362; Minn. Stat. Ann. § 304A.201).

Therefore, one impact of the zoo has been to legally protect flexibility for prioritizing various social goods over owner value – a level of protection that does not exist elsewhere. There are no causes of action or remedies if directors duly consider the impact of decisions on the requisite stakeholders and interests. Even then, if due consideration is not given, what are the remedies? Return to the boardroom to consider impact on affected stakeholder/interest? To what end? The directors are still free to decide against the "victorious" stakeholders/interests even after due consideration? That freedom and flexibility make it challenging to know what position to return litigants to other than the one in which they find themselves anyway. This defeats their efforts to assess damages; hence, the nature of remediation and its purposes in furtherance of accountability remain unresolved. Flexibility can be and has been useful and is an important option as long as those involved understand and accept its limitations, including policymakers who make the organizational forms available and entrepreneurs and investors who adopt and execute on the forms' promises.

Although there is disagreement about whether the L3C actually changes fiduciary duties to create an enforceable priority of charitable purposes over owner value (Tyler, 2010; Brakman Reiser, 2013; Manny, 2013; Tyler et al., 2015), there is at least the potential that the L3C has done so in ways that could force those who breach to disgorge profits, be subjected to personal liability, and/or be exposed to punitive damages.

Regulatory Oversight

Another impact of the hybrid species on the broader environment includes disruptions of already complicated areas of general regulatory oversight, securities laws, and taxation (Tyler et al., 2015). Among the new questions are the following:

- What is the role of regulators for enforcement, especially with regard to application of charitable trust laws and principles and charity registration requirements, especially for L3Cs but also for benefit or social purpose corporations that adopt charitable purposes?
- How does a regulator know if an enterprise has exceeded its statutory bounded reasons for being; can they know?
- Should the principle and remedies of *ultra vires* acts be revived?
- How do regulators protect the integrity of the charitable sector from confusion intentionally or accidentally abetted?
- Are ownership interests in these forms "securities" under federal and state laws? Should they be and to what extent, especially if "social returns" are a bargained-for expectation not dissimilar to the bargained for expectation of financial returns (Heminway, 2013; Tyler et al., 2015)?
- Should these forms receive special tax designations or treatment because of their form as distinct from their behavior (Wexler, 2009; Mayer and Ganahl, 2014; Tahk, 2014; Tyler et al., 2015)?

These and other questions are beyond the scope of this chapter other than to note that the zoo's impact has elevated these topics to consciousness in the regulatory sphere. In reality, these and similar questions and concerns have (or should have) existed since the dawn of SE when pursued informally and via contract. The lack of attention to them has previously created problems with consistency and predictability, two critically necessary functions of law.

Contract

One impact of the US hybrid forms species has been to call attention to the strengths and weaknesses of contracting to prioritize social good. Some exhort that SE by contract suffices and that other approaches, such as the hybrid forms, are unnecessary to prioritize social purposes and provide for accountability thereto. While the contracting species has been, is, and will be useful and perhaps even dominant, its applications only go so far because enforcement is unreliable and remedies for breach are inadequate.

SE by contract is unreliable because nothing prevents contracting parties or their successors from changing their minds about prioritizing social good, which change need not be formal (e.g., in writing) but can happen informally by simply not enforcing underlying provisions or not pursuing their breach. This flexibility can be important and should be preserved, but it should also not be overstated or overly relied upon.

SE by contract is inadequate because of difficulty establishing elements required for a breach of contract claim, particularly relating to damages and causation. Damages in a contract claim are normally economic, financial, and assessed in light of such harms to the non-breaching party or perhaps third party beneficiaries with enforcement rights. Given SE's inherent economic risks and presumptions about likelihood of financial losses (or at least lack of monetary gains), proving that the breach, instead of the enterprise's underlying nature, caused economic losses will be problematic.

Moreover, what economic damages does a court award if a nominally social enterprise has been profitable by neglecting its social mission? If none, then legal accountability by contract fails. Even if damages might be ascertained, remedies are designed to put parties into the position they were in if the breach had not occurred. At best, then, the party claiming breach might get their investment back or perhaps the value of their underlying interest in the enterprise – a forced buyout. But that does not ensure priority of social good over owner value; it only protects the owner's economic interests.

Another limitation of SE by contract is that the person trying to enforce priority of social good cannot recover attorneys' fees and other costs. Therefore, he or she must have both the resources to dedicate to the case and the will to devote them knowing that they will be lost, even if they eventually "win."

In some (even many or most) cases, principled commitment to prioritizing social good will be enough, which is why SE by contract remains relevant, but its value owes more to the persistence of owners' goodwill than to legal accountability.

CONCLUSION

The impact of the SE zoo is nuanced. At the macro-level, there is no good, objective way to know its broad impact, despite evidence of extensive qualitative impact in how business decision-making has increasingly incorporated social considerations, how expectations and awareness of social intent or impact have expanded, and how many efforts are underway to meaningfully assess that impact. For individual animals, there are numerous ways for enterprises to begin understanding social impact in a particular microcosm, but there is nothing yet systematic even among species. Nor is there yet a quantifiable way to assess opportunity costs – financial or social – for choosing SE versus a traditional approach or vice versa, although there is data in the impact investment space to suggest comparable returns with some approaches.

The most significant and clearest impact of the SE zoo may be in its elevation of purposes pursued (including introducing flexibility as a legitimate purpose), their priorities (if any), and accountability thereto through whichever means and to whatever degree. While presenting opportunities for impact, the zoo in this regard has also exposed gaps that – until addressed through statutes, regulation, or judicial precedent – may inhibit the levels of success and in achieving the promise of exponential social change that many envision through the zoo, even as change happens in ways that count though cannot be counted!

NOTES

*   This work should not be construed as representing positions of the Ewing Marion Kauffman Foundation, with whom the author is affiliated. The author is grateful to Dennis Young and Cass Brewer for the invitation to contribute this chapter. He owes much to a number of people who have helped shape his thinking and analysis on this topic, including but not limited to Evan Absher, Cass Brewer, Marion Fremont-Smith, Jay Coen Gilbert, Kate Garman, Chloe Holderness, Bob Lang, Tony Luppino, Jill Manny, Lloyd Hitoshi Mayer, Chris Miller, Jonathan Ng, Marc Owens, Dana Brakman Reiser, Carl Schramm, Rick Sevcik, David Spenard, Dane Stangler, Rob Wexler, the editors of publications that have hosted his work, and others – not all of whom agree/d with his thinking, analysis or conclusions.

1.   Throughout this chapter, references to "social" interests, good, benefits, etc. are intended to include environmental interests, benefits, etc.
2.   The Kellogg Foundation has developed definitions, logic models, and a framework for

assessing inputs, activities, outcomes, and impact. See www.smartgivers.org/uploads/logicmodelguidepdf.pdf, accessed 23 June 2016.

3. Albert Einstein believed: "Not everything that counts can be counted, and not everything that can be counted counts." Nietsche said: "Would it not be rather probable that. . .precisely the most superficial and external aspect of existence – what is most apparent, its skin and sensualization – would be grasped first – and might even be the only thing that allowed itself to be grasped?" (Vedia, 1995, p. 157).

4. Because my practical experiences and scholarly activities have focused on the development and evolution of SE in the United States, this chapter is necessarily US-centric. Even so, the concepts, thoughts, and principles are not necessarily geographically limited in their application.

5. Something like the Dow Jones Sustainability Index would not likely qualify alone given that it is premised on companies "with a strong focus on long-term shareholder value."

6. Among the sites that track formations are the following: http://www.intersectorl3c.com/l3c_tally.html (low-profit limited liability companies: L3Cs); http://benefitcorp.net/businesses/find-a-benefit-corp (benefit corporations); http://socentlawtracker.org/#/map (benefit corps formed in Oregon); https://www.bcorporation.net/community/find-a-b-corp (certified B corps), all accessed 23 June 2016.

7. Corporations meeting the requirements of the nonprofit standards-setting organization B Lab; see Chapter 3.

8. "IRIS metrics are designed to measure the social, environmental, and financial performance of an investment" (https://iris.thegiin.org, accessed 23 June 2016).

9. See http://b-analytics.net/.

10. See McKinsey & Company, McKinsey on Society (undated), "What is social impact assessment?", accessed 15 December 2015 at http://mckinseyonsociety.com/social-impact-assessment/what-is-social-impact-assessment/ (referencing http://trasi.foundationcenter.org/).

11. See http://fieldus.org/index.html, accessed 23 June 2016.

12. See http://www.mixmarket.org/, accessed 23 June 2016.

13. See http://www.aerisinsight.com/, accessed 23 June 2016.

14. See Grameen Foundation USA, "Progress Out of Poverty Index," accessed 12 May 2015 at http://www.progressoutofpoverty.org/.

15. See http://www.thegiin.org/knowledge-center/, accessed 23 June 2016.

16. See https://iris.thegiin.org/, accessed 23 June 2016.

17. See http://bimpactassessment.net/, accessed 23 June 2016.

18. See http://www.ncif.org/inform/social-performance-metrics, accessed 23 June 2016.

19. See http://impactinvesting.marsdd.com/simt/global-impact-investing-rating-system-giirs, accessed 23 June 2016.

20. See http://www.app-x.com/products/pulse/, accessed 23 June 2016.

21. See https://iris.thegiin.org/, accessed 23 June 2016.

22. To some degree, constituency statutes contemplate flexibility because the statutes themselves are permissive rather than mandatory, but they usually only apply in discrete, limited circumstances rather than as a part of an enterprise's gene code (Tyler, 2010).

REFERENCES

Bouri, A. (2015), "A coming of age for impact investing," *Stanford Social Innovation Review*, 3 August, accessed 23 June 2016 at http://ssir.org/up_for_debate/article/a_coming_of_age_for_impact_investing.

Brakman Reiser, D. (2013), "Theorizing forms for social enterprise," *Emory Law Journal*, **62**, 681.

Brakman Reiser, D. (2014), "Regulating social enterprise," *University of California, Davis Business Law Journal*, **14**, 231.

Calvert Foundation (2012), *Gateways to Impact: Industry Survey of Financial Advisors on Sustainable and Impact Investing*, accessed 23 June 2016 at http://www.calvertfoundation.org/storage/documents/Gateways-to-Impact.pdf.

Collins, J. and J.I. Porras (2000), *Built to Last: Successful Habits of Visionary Companies*, London: Random House Business Books.

Del. Code Ann. tit. 8, § 362 (2015, current through 79 Del. Laws, Ch. 443).

European Venture Philanthropy Association (2013), *A Practical Guide to Measuring and Managing Impact*, April, accessed 23 June 2016 at http://evpa.eu.com/login/?redirect_to=%2Fdownloads%2F%3Fpdf%3D2015%2F06%2FIM-Guide-English.pdf&pub=2015%2F06%2FFIM-Guide-English.pdf.

GIIN (2015), *ImpactBase Snapshot: An Analysis of 300+ Impact Investing Funds*, April, accessed 23 June 2016 at http://www.thegiin.org/assets/documents/pub/ImpactBaseSnapshot.pdf.

GIIN and Cambridge Associates (2015), "Introducing the Impact Investing Benchmark," *Global Impact Investing Network*, 25 July, accessed 23 June 2016 at http://www.thegiin.org/knowledge/publication/introducing-the-impact-investing-benchmark.

GIIN and Open Capital Advisors (2015), *The Landscape for Impact Investing in East Africa*, 29 July, accessed 23 June 2016 at http://www.thegiin.org/knowledge/publication/the-landscape-for-impact-investing-in-east-africa.

Grant, E.M. (2013), "Hybrid enterprises and the application of state charitable regulatory principles as a guide toward an effective regulatory framework," presentation at the 2013 Charities Regulation and Oversight Project Policy Conference (Columbia University Academic Commons), accessed 23 June 2016 at http://academiccommons.columbia.edu/catalog?f%5Bseries_facet%5D%5B%5D=2013+Charities+Regulation+and+Oversight+Project+Policy+Conference.

Greico, C., L. Michelini, and G. Iasevoli (2015), "Measuring value creation in social enterprises: a cluster analysis of social assessment models," *Nonprofit and Voluntary Sector Quarterly*, **44** (6), 1173–93.

GRI (2013), *G4 Sustainability Reporting Guidelines*, accessed 23 June 2016 at https://www.globalreporting.org/standards/g4/Pages/default.aspx.

Heminway, J.M. (2013), "To be or not to be (a security): funding for-profit social enterprises," *Regent University Law Review*, **25**, 299.

JPMorgan Chase & Co. (2015), *Impact Investment Assessment In Practice*, 4 May, accessed 23 June 2016 at https://www.jpmorgan.com/cm/BlobServer/impact_assessment_may2015.pdf?blobkey=id&blobwhere=1320674289368&blobheader=application/pdf&blobheadername1=Cache-Control&blobheadervalue1=private&blobcol=urldata&blobtable=MungoBlobs.

JPMorgan Chase & Co. and GIIN (2014), *Spotlight on the Market: The Impact Investor Survey*, 2 May, accessed 23 June 2016 at http://www.thegiin.org/assets/documents/pub/2014MarketSpotlight.PDF.

JPMorgan Chase, Rockefeller Foundation, and GIIN (2010), *Impact Investments: An Emerging Asset Class*, accessed 23 June 2016 at https://thegiin.org/assets/documents/Impact%20Investments%20an%20Emerging%20Asset%20Class2.pdf.

Kairis, J.C. (2011), "Disgorgement of compensation paid to directors during the time they were grossly negligent: an available but seldom used remedy," *Delaware Law Review*, **13** [iii] (2011–2012).

Kay, J. (2010), *Obliquity: Why Our Goals are Best Achieved Indirectly*, New York: Penguin Book.

Manny, J. (2013), "Much ado about nothing: a comment on Tyler's paper on regulating charitable hybrids," *NYU Journal of Law and Business*, **9**, 587.

Manta Consulting (2013), "Land Conservation Impact Metrics," 1 June, accessed 23 June 2016 at http://www.mantaconsultinginc.com/wp-content/uploads/Land-Conservation-Metrics.pdf.

Mayer, L.H. and J.R. Ganahl (2014), "Taxing social enterprise," *Stanford Law Review*, **66** (2), 387.

Minn. Stat. Ann. § 304A.201 sub. 3, sub. 9 (West, Westlaw through 2014 Reg. Sess.).

Monitor Institute (2009), *Investing for Social and Environmental Impact*, accessed 23 June 2016 at http://monitorinstitute.com/downloads/what-we-think/impact-investing/Impact_Investing.pdf.

Moody, M., L. Littlepage, and N. Paydar (2015), "Measuring social return on investment: lessons from organizational implementation of SROI in the Netherlands and the United States," *NonProfit Management & Leadership*, **26** (1), 19–37.

Mook, L. (ed.) (2013), *Accounting for Social Value*, Toronto: University of Toronto Press.

Mook, L., J.R. Whitman, J. Quarter, and A. Armstrong (2015), (2015a), *Sustainable Signals: The Individual Investor Perspective*, February, accessed 23 June 2016 at https://www.morganstanley.com/sustainableinvesting/pdf/Sustainable_Signals.pdf.

Morgan Stanley Institute for Sustainable Investing (2015b), *Sustainable Reality: Understanding the Performance of Sustainable Investment Strategies*, March, accessed 23 June 2016 at https://www.morganstanley.com/sustainableinvesting/pdf/sustainable-reality.pdf.

Organisation for Economic Co-operation and Development (2015), *Social Impact Investment: Building the Evidence Base*, accessed 23 June 2016 at http://www.oecd.org/sti/ind/social-impact-investment.pdf.

Ortmans, J. (2015), "Indexes: challenges and opportunities for policymakers and researchers," *Policy Dialogue on Entrepreneurship. Ewing Marion Kauffman Foundation*, 31 August, accessed 23 June 2016 at http://www.kauffman.org/blogs/policy-dialogue/2015/august/indexes-challenges-and-opportunities-for-policymakers-and-researchers.

Social Impact Investment Taskforce of the G8 (2014), "Measuring impact: subject paper of the Impact Measurement Working Group," September, accessed 23 June 2016 at http://www.socialimpactinvestment.org/reports/Measuring%20Impact%20WG%20paper%20FINAL.pdf.

Social Venture Technology Group (2008), *Catalog of Approaches to Impact Measurement: Assessing Social Impact in Private Ventures (Version 1.1)*, May, accessed 23 June 2016 at http://svtgroup.net/wp-content/uploads/2011/09/SROI_approaches.pdf.

Spenard, D.E. (2013), "Crashing the party: a state regulator's observations and suggestions regarding the near-term supervision of the simultaneous pursuit of margin and mission through social enterprise, philanthrocapitalism, and mixed-purpose entities or hybrids," presentation at the 2013 Charities Regulation and Oversight Project Policy Conference (Columbia University Academic Commons, accessed 23 June 2016 at http://academiccommons.columbia.edu/

catalog?f%5Bseries_facet%5D%5B%5D=2013+Charities+Regulation+and+Ov
ersight+Project+Policy+Conference.
Tahk, S.C. (2014), "Crossing the tax code's for-profit/nonprofit border," *Penn State Law Review*, **118**, 489.
Toniic Institute (2012), *Toniic E-Guide to Impact Measurement*, accessed 23 June 2016 at http://www.toniic.com/wp-content/uploads/2011/12/Toniic-E-Guide-to-Impact-Measurement.pdf.
Tyler, J. (2010), "Negating the legal problem of having 'two masters': a framework for L3C fiduciary duties and accountability," *Vermont Law Review*, **35** (1), 117–61.
Tyler, J. (2013), "Analyzing effects and implications of regulating charitable hybrid forms as charitable trusts: round peg and a square hole?," *NYU Journal of Law and Business*, **9**, 535.
Tyler, J., E. Absher, K. Garman, and A. Luppino (2015), "Producing better mileage: advancing the design and usefulness of hybrid vehicle for social business ventures," *Quinnipiac Law Review*, **33** (2).
US National Advisory Board for Impact Investing (2014), *Private Capital, Public Good: How Smart Federal Policy Can Galvanize Impact Investing – and Why It's Urgent*, June, accessed 23 June 2016 at http://static1.squarespace.com/static/539e71d9e4b0ccf778116f69/t/53aa1681e4b04a6c515fac31/140365580948 9/Private_Capital_Public_Good.pdf.
Vedia, C.M.Y. (1995), *Philosophical Writings: Friedrich Nietzsche*, New York: Continuum International Publishing Group, Inc.
Wexler, R.A. (2009), "Effective social enterprise – a menu of legal structures," *The Exempt Organization Tax Review*, **63** (6), 565–76.
Wexler, R.A. (2013), "Attorney General regulation of hybrid entities as charitable trusts," accessed 23 June 2016 at the 2013 Charities Regulation and Oversight Project Policy Conference (Columbia University Academic Commons), accessed 23 June 2016 at http://academiccommons.columbia.edu/catalog?f%5Bseries_fac et%5D%5B%5D=2013+Charities+Regulation+and+Oversight+Project+Policy +Conference.

PART V

Conclusion

13. Implications for research, policy, and practice

Dennis R. Young, Elizabeth A.M. Searing, and Cassady V. Brewer

SUMMARY AND PERSPECTIVE

This book represents a collective effort by the authors to comprehend the concept and character of social enterprise from multiple perspectives that can be drawn together in a coherent way that respects the complexity, diversity, and dynamism that we observe in the world of social policy and practice today. As an overall phenomenon, social enterprise is a kind of pragmatic movement to break the boundaries of traditional approaches to social problem solving and bring new energy to the solution of confounding and seemingly intractable issues such as poverty and inequality, unemployment and homelessness, crime and rehabilitation, public health, educational achievement, environmental degradation, and economic development. Rather than restricting the address of these problems to government or the nonprofit sector per se, social enterprises seek to engage the market place, the energy of entrepreneurs, volunteers and social investors, and a variety of legal, financial, and policy tools, in specific and customized ways. We adopted the metaphor and paradigm of the zoo because it has provided us with a satisfying middle way between singular notions of social enterprise that fail to capture important aspects of its character and variety, and an unfettered, anything goes approach that fails to realize that policy and social choices do indeed influence the nature of social enterprise from one context to another. This is what is special about the zoo idea – it has an element of design while accommodating organic development within a loosely controlled context.

One contribution of the zoo metaphor is that it allows us to flesh out the nature of social enterprise diversity itself. In this volume we have examined social enterprise along several dimensions exhibiting diversity. The animals in the zoo can represent the different legal forms in which social enterprise is manifested, including generic categories (species) such as social

287

businesses, nonprofits or cooperatives, and specific varieties within these categories. The habitats in the zoo point us to the various political and economic environments in which social enterprises may operate, with consequences for the animals each type of habitat may support. The diversity of governance structures that prevail within the different habitats in the zoo allow us to consider structural parameters and policies that influence the viability and robustness of different social enterprise animals in those habitats, and perhaps more importantly, as Chapter 9 suggests, the mobilization of social enterprise for different social purposes and policy goals. Moreover, alternative habitats support different sources of economic sustenance (modes of finance) for social enterprises and different ecological systems that characterize the interactions among social enterprise animals and their sources of finance. Indeed, the zoo metaphor suggests the possibility of herbivores, carnivores, and omnivores – each type of enterprise dependent to a different degree on the flora (financial sources) in their habitats and on the fauna (one another).

Digging deeper, the zoo metaphor has led us to appreciate that social enterprise can be studied along other, less obvious manifestations of diversity. For example, animals in the zoo could be thought of as representing different approaches to innovation (e.g., entirely new breeds versus replication or minor modifications of existing ones), or different theories of social change. For example, some social enterprises (so-called WISEs – Work Integration Social Enterprises) are based on the idea that integrating marginal populations into the workforce will improve their social and economic welfare. Other social enterprises take a different approach, for example by emphasizing early childhood education or prenatal care. Alternatively, the zoo metaphor leads us to study the diversity of social enterprises in terms of the life cycles of these animals, and the implications for sustaining social enterprises at different stages of their development.

At the meta-level, zoos as a whole exhibit great diversity among themselves and can be designed and maintained in different ways. As noted in Chapter 2, zoos can be organized by animal types or habitats, for example, with consequent alternative ecologies within different parts of the zoo. The diversity of zoos at the international level, or within national political jurisdictions (states or provinces) offers a window on what designs and combinations of animals, sources of sustenance and regulatory or management regimes may work best. Moreover, just as the zoo metaphor raises anxiety about problems of actual zoos such as animal cruelty and disturbance of the natural environment when animals are taken into captivity, it also reminds us that there are good zoos and bad ones – zoos that serve positive purposes in promoting animal well-being and environmental conservation as well as entertainment and education, and zoos that may simply exploit animals and the natural environment for private economic gain. The metaphor compels us to explore design issues for regimes of social enterprise to ensure that the social enterprise zoo is a construct for social good.

The efficiency frontier diagram (Figure 2.1) introduced in Chapter 2 helps to illustrate both the diversity of social enterprises and the possibilities for improving their contributions to society. The diagram suggests that social enterprises belong in the northeast quadrant where economic and social impacts are both positive. Perhaps social enterprise does not embrace that entire quadrant, depending on one's point of view, but the boundaries of that quadrant rule out enterprises such as large corporations that embrace programs of corporate social responsibility but are found to cause net environmental or social damage when all of its activities are taken into account. This perspective asks us to examine very closely the so-called socially responsible businesses of the world in order to evaluate their claims as social enterprises. Nonetheless, we are reminded in Chapter 12 how very complex such evaluation is, not just for socially impactful businesses but for the entire range of social enterprises, especially where new legal forms leave ambiguous the relative importance of social impact versus profitability and management flexibility in determining preferred combinations of public and private gain.

In addition, the diagram illustrates the importance of social entrepreneurs and competent managers and leaders for every species of social enterprise. As noted in Chapter 7, both Schumpeterian and conventional entrepreneurs have a role to play. The former in adopting best practices to ensure that they guide their animals towards operation on the efficiency frontier, and the latter to push the frontier outward by introducing innovations of function and form that achieve greater economic and social performance with a given level of available resources.

Finally, the diagram makes clear that social enterprise is a matter of choice in terms of the balance between social impact and financial reward, and that various combinations of the two are legitimate occupants of the social enterprise zoo. This construct rejects the notion that social impact must be the primary objective of a social enterprise. A profitmaking business that primarily rewards its owners or a cooperative that primarily rewards its members, are legitimate candidates for the social enterprise zoo so long as they also contribute a significant social benefit. This understanding of the zoo in turn helps reframe the contemporary debate over social enterprises – that the issue isn't about forms of enterprise per se but rather about social purpose. Indeed, the merits of different forms can be considered side by side along the scale of social benefit, notwithstanding the ancillary private benefits that each form may entail. This view, in turn, brings us to refocus on social entrepreneurs and what they are trying to accomplish through their ventures. These curators of the social enterprise zoo are pragmatic actors with both selfish and selfless motives who will select whatever forms of enterprise best allow them to address both their personal goals and the particular social problems and missions with which they are engaged.

The chapters in this book not only describe and examine the variety and character of social enterprise but also probe its purposes. We have asked ourselves the question – why have a social enterprise zoo at all? Why not just a public sector to address social issues and problems? Why not a laissez-faire regime that leaves the address (or neglect) of social problems completely to private initiative? Why this delicate and complex combination of public and private, intentional design and organic development and evolution? And in the end, how can the social impact of the zoo and its inhabitants be meaningfully measured, monitored and assessed?

These questions bid us to reference the classical theories of market and government failure that have led economists to explain the emergence of the nonprofit sector – an integral part of the social enterprise zoo in our view. In its earliest form, the theory of market failure reasoned that demand for public goods and the generation of positive and negative externalities required the participation of government to achieve greater social efficiency. Government could coerce the support of public goods, and modify the levels of externalities, through direct provision of services, and taxation, expenditure, and regulatory policies. So to tell the economists' story in biblical terms, in the beginning there was a market and then government – just these two animals in the zoo. Economists subsequently added to this story by asking how and why private, voluntary effort and nonprofit organizations could further enhance social efficiency. Olson (1965) reasoned that some collective, voluntary effort would supplement the market because some "privileged donors" would derive a sufficient fraction of the benefits of public goods to provide for them voluntarily. (For example, the Rockefellers purchased the Palisades along the New Jersey side of the Hudson River to preserve the view from their estate and preclude its commercial development.) Weisbrod (1975) later reasoned that government provision of public goods would leave many individuals unsatisfied, opening a niche for voluntary, nonprofit provision of public goods by sufficiently motivated citizens, and Hansmann (1980) determined that asymmetric information between purchasers and providers would lead to an undersupply of certain private goods that require a high degree of trust between those parties. Thus, trust goods were undertaken by nonprofit organizations whose incentive to exploit consumer ignorance is less cogent. Other theoretical strands subsequently added so-called associative and club goods to the mix of collective and private goods that could be expected to develop in a market economy, through mutual and cooperative organizations, in order to increase social welfare (Hansmann, 1996).

In this volume we have found the social enterprise zoo to be a construct that allows the extension of market failure theory to the realm of social enterprise. Even with all of the classical forms of organization in place, the zoo has substantial room in it for other constructs that further contribute to social efficiency. For example, traditional nonprofit organizations appear to need greater access to financial capital in order to address extant social needs. New forms of social business provide access to equity capital that can be applied to social mission achievement. Alternatively, traditional businesses require public engagement in order to be more successful in commerce. So-called sustainable businesses offer that option while contributing to social good. Members of cooperatives have aspirations to improve their communities in addition to serving their own individual purposes. Social cooperatives provide them with that opportunity.

In essence, the social enterprise zoo defines a space in which enterprises find new forms and niches within which to address the remaining social inefficiencies left by traditional forms. In this way, the social enterprise zoo extends market failure theory to an all-encompassing frame of reference that not only accounts for contemporary innovations but also predicts their continuing discovery and development. In particular, it puts social scientists on the lookout for these new ways of organizing as they develop over time in response to evolving social problems and technologies for addressing them. Furthermore, the zoo emphasizes that all forms of social enterprise may be needed to achieve a high level of social efficiency, and that these various forms interact within the ecologies of the zoo. Just as there would be no lions without antelopes, there would be no community interest companies or benefit corporations without government or business.

While the zoo metaphor helps explain why social enterprise evolves within a market context, it begs the question of how much of a zoo is necessary. What type and level of explicit design is desirable and to what degree should policy just allow the political economy to evolve on its own? The chapters in this book call for greater scrutiny of this question, continued social experimentation among political jurisdictions within and among countries around the world, and exploration of diverse approaches to the assessment of social impacts. Too much constraint and regulation of the content of the zoo could result in suppression of innovative solutions to social problems while laissez-faire policies might waste valuable resources and fail to protect fragile species of social enterprise that make important social contributions. Design will affect whether some current varieties of social enterprise (for example, L3Cs in the United States) will survive. And survival or demise of various types of social enterprises, as considered in

Chapter 11, may or may not be a good thing depending on whether other animals in the zoo are more or less effective. The natural experiments that are now taking place among alternative zoos, in different countries around the world and among states and provinces in the United States and other nations, should be exploited for their research potential. The key questions include: How can social efficiency be improved by altering the mixes of animals in the zoo and the ways in which each species or subspecies are nurtured and protected? Where should the fences be placed to separate the social enterprise animals from others, and what rules, regulations, and incentives should constitute these fences? And indeed, to what extent can zookeepers actually control what happens in the zoo? That is, what might be the unintended consequences of policies designed to alter the zoo, or exert control over it, in the various ways suggested? This of course leads us to suggest that the work begun in this book be continued. In particular, how can we develop better theory and methodology to explain the emergence, character, and evolution of the zoo, gain greater insights into what goes on within the zoo, and gauge how its social impacts can be better assessed?

The poet Ogden Nash wrote short poems about many animals in nature's zoo, including fleas and flies, eels, jellyfish and shrimp, ostriches and eagles, praying mantises and centipedes, chipmunks and porcupines, camels and lions, cows and dogs, whales, turtles and ducks, hippopotami and of course-a-rus, the rhinoceros (Nash and Finamore, 1987). Perhaps there are not so many animals as these in the social enterprise zoo, but each is of interest in its own right as well as in context of all the others. Many are strange to us now, but as Nash wrote about the hippo, it all depends on one's perspective:

> Behold the hippopotamus!
> We laugh at how he looks to us,
> And yet in moments dank and grim,
> I wonder how we look to him.
>
> Peace, peace, thou hippopotamus!
> We really look all right to us,
> As you no doubt delight the eye
> Of other hippopotami.

The various perspectives of policymakers, social entrepreneurs, scholars, leaders and the general public, as the zoo's keepers, curators, managers and constituents, must determine what works in the social enterprise zoo – not just particular animals or species, but the different ecologies and habitats within the zoo – and how society at large, inside and outside the zoo, is affected.

REFERENCES

Hansmann, H.B. (1980), "The role of nonprofit enterprise," *Yale Law Journal,* **89** (5), 835–901.

Hansmann, H.B. (1996), *The Ownership of Enterprise,* Cambridge, MA: Harvard University Press.

Nash, O. and R. Finamore (1987), *Ogden Nash's Zoo,* New York: Stewart, Tabori and Chang Publishers.

Olson, M. (1965), *The Logic of Collective Action,* Cambridge, MA: Harvard University Press.

Weisbrod, B.A. (1975), "Toward a theory of the voluntary sector in a three sector economy," in E. Phelps (ed.), *Altruism, Morality and Economic Theory,* New York: Russell Sage, pp. 171–95.

Index

allocation of resources 5, 134, 145, 260, 270
  efficient 5
  externalities influencing 4–5
  inefficient 5
  voter preferences influencing 5
angel investments 128, 145, 175, 179–80
  see also income
anti-trust policies, encouraging competition 5
Argentina
  social enterprise model 71, 78
Atlanta nonprofit housing 243–4, 254
  see also resilience
  Atlanta Homeless Housing 245
    financial insolvency risk 251–2
    governance 251
    mission change risk 232
  Housing for Women and Children 245
    financial insolvency risk 252–3
    governance 253
    mission change risk 253
  Metro Community Development 244
    financial insolvency risk 246
    governance 246
    mission change risk 246, 250
  revenue composition 244
  sequester of government funding and 243
  South Atlanta Development Corporation 245
    financial insolvency risk 250
    governance 250, 251
    mission change risk 251
  threshold parameters of 247–9

benefit corporations
  hybrid legal form, as 50
  Italy, in 54–5

triple bottom line 51
US, in 8, 19, 25, 51–2, 120, 231
  –B Corps differentiation 56
  criticism of 52
  for-profit, being 51
  public benefit mandate 51
benefits theory 167, 168–70, 187–8
  see also income
  associative goods 169
  diversified income, potential for 187
  earned income 167, 171
  group goods 168, 169
  /portfolio theory distinction 188
  private goods 168, 169
  public goods 168, 172–3
  redistributive goods 168–9, 171
  start-ups and 182, 187–8
  trade/exchange goods 169
B Corps certification 55–6, 121, 200, 231, 264

chaordic nature 9–12, 34
charter schools 19, 115
civil society models 69, 71
  deferred democratization 65, 70, 71, 72, 78
  liberal 70, 71, 73, 80, 198
  social-democratic 70, 71, 73, 81, 198
  traditional 70, 71, 72, 77
  welfare partnership/state 70, 71, 72, 79, 81–2
  liberal 198
collective interest cooperative societies 47
  see also cooperatives
commercial nonprofit organizations *see* nonprofit organizations
community contribution company (CCC) (Canada) 54
community interest companies (CICs) 25–6, 48, 200, 205

295